Bring the War Home

The White Power Movement and Paramilitary America

Kathleen Belew

Harvard University Press   Cambridge, Massachusetts, and London, England | 2018

First Printing

Library of Congress Cataloging-in-Publication Data

Names: Belew, Kathleen, 1981– author.
Title: Bring the war home : the white power movement and paramilitary
    America / Kathleen Belew.
Description: Cambridge, Massachusetts : Harvard University Press, 2018. |
    Includes bibliographical references and index.
Identifiers: LCCN 2017041043 | ISBN 9780674286078
    (hardcover : alk. paper)
Subjects: LCSH: White supremacy movements—United States—History. |
    Paramilitary forces—United States—History. | Vietnam War,
    1961–1975—Veterans—United States. | United States—Race relations.
Classification: LCC HS2325 .B45 2018 | DDC 320.56/909073—dc23
    LC record available at https://lccn.loc.gov/2017041043

Bring the War Home

For G. and O., with all my best hopes

Contents

Note to Readers

LET ME BEGIN WITH a brief note about terminology and about my approach to writing about living people involved in the movement I describe. I use "white power" to refer to the social movement that brought together members of the Klan, militias, radical tax resisters, white separatists, neo-Nazis, and proponents of white theologies such as Christian Identity, Odinism, and Dualism between 1975 and 1995. Some have described this group of people with the terms "white nationalist," "white separatist," the "racist right," or "white supremacist." None of these terms is appropriate for describing the larger movement. Not all proponents of white power advocated white nationalism or white separatism, and white nationalism presumes a different outcome—one inherently less violent—than that envisioned by a vocal segment of the white power movement. The term "racist right" presumes a political continuum that does not properly describe this activism, which at times shared more with the revolutionary left than with the conservative mainstream. Therefore, the encompassing term "white power," which was also a slogan commonly used by those in the movement, is the most precise and historically accurate term.

Some people within the movement considered "Nazi" or "neo-Nazi" pejorative terms but nevertheless identified as National Socialist or adopted uniforms or symbols of the Third Reich. For purposes of simplicity, I refer to them as "neo-Nazi" because they shared a political ideology commonly understood as such. Similarly, although nonracist members of a music-driven counterculture have also adopted the term "skinhead," this book discusses only racist skinheads and does not make assertions about the broader skinhead scene.

I use the words "revolutionary" and "activist" to convey a specific type of political action and the people involved in that cause. A white power activist in these pages was not only a proponent of white power ideology but also used that ideology to attempt to bring about change. "Revolutionary violence" here refers to violence directed at the overthrow of the state (or components of the state); I use the phrase to distinguish white power violence from earlier vigilante violence, which usually worked to reinforce state power. My use of the terms "activist" and "revolutionary" is not meant to cast a positive light upon white power actors or the actions they undertook.

Because many people involved in this story are still living, I preserve privacy for people whose names are not already part of the public record and for children. For this reason, some notes based on documentation such as marriage and birth certificates omit names. In one well-documented case, Ruby Ridge, children's names are included for clarity and only because they have already been widely reported.

The white power movement generated rich archives of images and illustrations. Because the copyright to most of this work is still held by white power groups and activists, and because purchasing permissions to these images might constitute a financial contribution to their cause, this book does not reprint any material from these archives.

Bring the War Home

A federal agent arrests a white power activist attempting to deliver weapons to the Weaver family at Ruby Ridge, Idaho, 1992. The arresting officer and the activist both wear camouflage uniforms. *(Mason Marsh, Associated Press Photo)*

"WE NEED EVERY ONE OF YOU," proclaimed an anonymous 1985 article in a major white power newspaper. "We need every branch of fighting, militant whites. We are too few right now to excommunicate each other. . . . Whatever will save our race is what we will do!"[1] The article spoke of emergency and government treachery. It foretold imminent apocalyptic race war. It called to believers in white supremacist congregations, to Klansmen and southern separatists, and to neo-Nazis. The white power movement united a wide array of groups and activists previously at odds, thrown together by tectonic shifts in the cultural and political landscape. Narratives of betrayal and crisis cemented their alliances.

Though often described by others as "white nationalist" and by its members as patriotic, this movement did not seek to defend the American nation, even when it celebrated some elements of U.S. history and identity. Instead white power activists increasingly saw the state as their enemy. Many pursued the idea of an all-white, racial nation, one that transcended national borders to unite white people from the United States, Canada, Europe, Australia, South Africa, and beyond. The militant rallying cry "white power," which echoed in all corners of the movement, was its most accurate self-descriptor.

At the end of the tumultuous 1970s, in the wake of the Vietnam War and in the midst of economic turmoil and widespread distrust of public institutions, the white power movement consolidated and expanded. In these turbulent years, many Americans lost faith in the state that they had trusted to take care of them.[2] Loss in Vietnam and the Watergate scandal undermined their confidence in elected officials and besmirched the presidency itself.[3] As legislation dramatically increased immigration, many worried that the arrival of immigrants would change the very meaning of American identity.[4] They saw the rights movements of the 1960s redefine race and gender relations at home and at work. They noted with alarm the government's failure to help those who lost their farms to the banks or their factories to faraway places.[5] As the mainstream right and left took up these concerns in a variety of ways, so did this troubled social and political context incubate white power activism.

People from all regions of the country answered the white power movement's call to action, bridging the divide between rural and urban. They were men, women, and children. They were high school dropouts and holders of advanced degrees; rich and poor; farmers and industrial workers. They were felons and religious leaders. They were civilians, veterans, and active-duty military personnel. From its formal unification in 1979 through its 1983 turn to revolutionary war on the government and its militia phase in the early 1990s, the white power movement mobilized adherents using a cohesive social network based on commonly held beliefs. These activists operated with discipline and clarity, training in paramilitary camps and undertaking assassinations, mercenary soldiering, armed robbery, counterfeiting, and weapons trafficking. White power violence reached a climax in the 1995 bombing of the Alfred P. Murrah Federal Building in Oklahoma City.

A holistic study of the white power movement reveals a startling and un-expected origin: the aftermath of the Vietnam War. The story activists told about Vietnam and the response to the war on the right were major forces in uniting disparate strands of American white supremacism and in sus-taining that unity. As narrated by white power proponents, the Vietnam War was a story of constant danger, gore, and horror. It was also a story of soldiers' betrayal by military and political leaders and of the trivialization of their sacrifice. This narrative facilitated intergroup alliances and increased paramilitarism within the movement, escalating violence. In his speeches, newsletters, and influential 1983 collection *Essays of a Klansman,* movement leader Louis Beam urged activists to continue fighting the Vietnam War on American soil. When he exhorted readers to "bring it on home," he meant a literal extension of military-style combat into civilian space. He referred to two wars: the one he had fought in Vietnam and the white revolution he hoped to wage in the United States.[6]

White power activists would also engage in other wars. Some would be-come mercenaries in military interventions ranging from Latin America to southern Africa. Others would fight in the Gulf War. Although they comprised only a small number of the combatants in these conflicts, their mercenary and active-duty soldiering assimilated them into the broader militarization and paramilitary culture that was more prominent in American society. Their ventures set the stage for later encounters, such as the sieges of separatist compounds at Ruby Ridge and Waco by militarized police forces, which would, in turn, spur the movement to its largest mass casualty.

The white power movement that emerged from the Vietnam era shared some common attributes with earlier racist movements in the United States, but it was no mere echo. Unlike previous iterations of the Ku Klux Klan and white supremacist vigilantism, the white power movement did not claim to serve the state. Instead, white power made the state its target, declaring war against the federal government in 1983.[7] This call for revolution arrived during Ronald Reagan's presidency, which many historians have considered the triumph of the mainstream New Right.[8] Antistatism in general, and hos-tility toward the federal government in particular, had motivated and shaped earlier conservative and reactionary mobilizations as well as the New Right itself, but white power capitalized on a larger current of discontent among conservatives.[9] By 1984, *Time* magazine had noticed a "thunder on the right": a growing dissatisfaction, especially among evangelicals, with

the distance between Reagan's campaign promises and his policies, particularly concerning social issues that galvanized voters, such as abortion.[10]
White power activists responded to Reagan's first term with calls for a more
extreme course of action. Reagan's moderation, as activists saw it, revealed
conventional politics as unsalvageable and signaled a state of emergency
that could not be resolved through political action alone.[11] Their paramilitary infrastructure stood ready; the war could not wait.

After declaring war, activists plotted to overthrow the government through
attacks on infrastructure, assassinations, and counterfeiting to undermine
public confidence in currency. They armed themselves with weapons and matériel stolen from military installations. They matched this revolutionary
work with the publication and circulation of printed material, recruitment
drives aimed at mainstream conservatives, political campaigns, talk show
appearances, and radio programs. These activities both disseminated a
common set of beliefs, goals, and messages to the movement faithful and
worked to recruit new members. In the late 1980s, many activists reorganized into militias. Although some militias disclaimed white supremacy in
public, many shared funds, weapons, and personnel with white power
organizations.[12]

While white power was certainly a fringe movement, it surpassed earlier
mobilizations such as the anticommunist John Birch Society. Membership
alone is a poor measure of white power activity, with records often hidden,
distorted, or destroyed, but nevertheless illuminates the movement's relative
size. Scholars and watchdog groups who have attempted to calculate the
numbers of people in the movement's varied branches—including, for instance, Klansmen and neo-Nazis, who are often counted separately—estimate
that there were about 25,000 "hard-core members" in the 1980s. An additional
150,000–175,000 people bought white power literature, sent contributions to
groups, or attended rallies or other events, signifying a larger, although less
formal, level of membership. Another 450,000 did not themselves participate or purchase materials but read the literature.[13] The John Birch
Society, in contrast, reached only 100,000 members at its 1965 peak.[14]

With the 1983 turn to revolution, the movement adopted a new strategy,
"leaderless resistance." Following this strategy, independent cells and activists would act without direct contact with movement leadership. The aim
was to prevent the infiltration of groups, and the prosecution of organizations
and individuals, by formally dissociating activists from each other and by

eliminating official orders. Popularized throughout the underground, leaderless resistance changed recruitment goals, emphasizing the importance of enlisting a small number of fully committed activists rather than large groups of the less committed.[15] This is another reason membership counts alone could not accurately convey the movement's impact, activity, or capacity for violence.

Yet to the degree that there is power in numbers, the movement reached a new peak during its militia phase. At the height of its mainstream appeal in the mid-1990s, the militia movement counted some five million members and sympathizers, according to one watchdog analyst. That number certainly represents the upper bound of possibility, and it is likely that the white-power-identified cohort of militia members and sympathizers was significantly smaller. However, five million places the militia movement in line with the largest surge of the Ku Klux Klan, whose membership peaked in 1924 at four million.[16]

While white power activists held worldviews that aligned or overlapped with those of mainstream conservatism—including opposition to immigration, welfare, abortion, feminism, and gay and lesbian rights—the movement was not dedicated to political conservatism aimed at preserving an existing way of life, or even to the reestablishment of bygone racial or gender hierarchies. Instead, it emphasized a radical future that could be achieved only through revolution. While some white power activists might have longed for the reinstatement of Jim Crow laws, white-minority rule as in Rhodesia and South Africa, or slavery, most agreed that such systems could not be resurrected through electoral politics alone but would have to be achieved by more drastic measures. This abandonment of the political process reflects a profound shift in the American electorate wrought by the Voting Rights Act of 1965, which barred disenfranchisement on the basis of race. Reactionary politics, conservatism, and American nationalism had characterized the Klan in the early part of the twentieth century. The white power movement sought revolution and separation—the founding of a racial utopian nation.

Many activists connected ideas of a radical political future with belief in imminent apocalypse. The theologies espoused by white power activists in this period differed significantly from the Protestantism of the reactionary second-era Klan that peaked in the 1920s.[17] White power religious radicalism emerged in part from Cold War understandings of communism as a threat to Christianity. At the same time, a large contingent of white power activists in the post-Vietnam moment believed in white supremacy as a component of religious faith. Christian Identity congregations heard their pastors explain that whites were the true lost tribe of Israel and that nonwhites and Jews were descended from Satan or from animals. Other racist churches adopted similar theologies that lauded whiteness as holy and sought to preserve the white race. Activists also adopted Odinism and other forms of neo-Pagan white supremacy that posited a shared, pan-European white cultural heritage.[18]

The movement's religious extremism was integral to its broader revolutionary character.[19] While increasingly politicized evangelical congregations espoused belief in the rapture—a foretold moment when the faithful would be peacefully transported from the world as the apocalyptic end times began—Christian Identity and other white theologies offered believers no such guarantees of safety.[20] Instead, they held that the faithful would be tasked with ridding the world of the unfaithful, the world's nonwhite and Jewish population, before the return of Christ.[21] At the very least, the faithful would have to outlast the great tribulation, a period of bloodshed and strife. Many movement followers prepared by becoming survivalists: stocking food and learning to administer medical care. Other proponents of white cosmologies saw it as their personal responsibility to amass arms and train themselves to take part in a coming end-times battle that would take the shape of race war.[22]

A war of this scale and urgency demanded that partisans set aside their differences. The movement therefore was flexible in its adoption of racist symbols and beliefs. A Klansman in the South might participate in burning crosses, wear the white robe and hood, and embrace the Confederate battle flag alongside a Lost Cause narrative of the Civil War. A neo-Nazi in the North might march under the banner of the swastika and don an SS uniform. But the once-disparate approaches to white supremacy represented by these symbols and ideas were drawn together in the white power movement. A suburban California skinhead might bear Klan tattoos, read Nazi tracts, and attend meetings of a local Klan chapter, a National Socialist political party, the militant White Aryan Resistance—or all three. At the Aryan Nations compound in northern Idaho, Klansmen and neo-Nazis ignited both crosses and swastikas as they heard Christian Identity sermons and speakers from an array of white power groups. Activists circulated among groups and

belief systems, each of which might include theological, political, and pseudoscientific varieties of racism, antisemitism, and antifeminism.[23]

Amid this multiplicity of symbolic presentations and beliefs, most white
power activists found common ground. They believed in white supremacy
and the need for a white homeland. They feared that the government would
eradicate the white population through interference with the birth of white
children—through interracial marriage, rape, birth control, abortion, and
immigration. The antisemitism long espoused by the Klan was reinforced by
neo-Nazis. And the movement adopted a strict set of gender and familial
roles, particularly regarding the sexual and supportive behavior of white
women and their protection by white men.

Another unifying feature of the movement was its strident anticommunism, which at first aligned with mainstream Cold War conservatism and
then transformed into an apocalyptic, anti-internationalist, antisemitic set
of beliefs and conspiracy theories about what activists called the Zionist Occupational Government (ZOG) and, later, the New World Order. Increasingly, white power activists believed that the Jewish-led ZOG controlled the
United Nations, the U.S. federal government, and the banks, and that ZOG
used people of color, communists, liberals, journalists, academics, and other
enemies of the movement as puppets in a conspiracy to eradicate the white
race and its economic, social, and cultural accomplishments.[24]

To confront this grave threat, activists organized as a paramilitary army
and adopted masculine cultural forms. The article that levied the plea
"We Need Every One of You" was titled "White Soldier Boy" for a reason.
It targeted young white men, not women, for recruitment into the pre-
sumptively male world of camouflage fatigues, military-style camps and
drills, and military-grade weapons. It also spoke directly to combat veterans
and active-duty military personnel.

In this respect, white power can be understood as an especially extreme
and violent manifestation of larger social forces that wed masculinity with
militancy, in the form of paintball, war movies, gun shows, and magazines
such as *Soldier of Fortune* that were aimed at armchair and weekend warriors. This is not to suggest that such cultural forms were coequal with white
power, or with conservatism more broadly. But it is not by coincidence that
white power gathered steam amid the wider post-Vietnam "remasculinization of America." In the wake of military failure in Southeast Asia, masculinity provided an ideological frame for the New Right, challenged antiwar

sentiment, and idealized bygone and invented familial and gender orders throughout American society.[25] The white power movement capitalized on this wave of broader cultural paramilitarism for its own, violent ends.

However, the white power movement departed from mainstream paramilitary culture in carving out an important place for women, relied on as symbols of the cause and as activists in their own right. As bearers of white children, women were essential to the realization of white power's mission: to save the race from annihilation. More concretely, their supporting roles, auxiliary organizations, and recruiting skills sustained white power as a social movement.[26] They brokered social relationships that cemented intergroup alliances and shaped the movement from within.[27]

In all these ways—its unity, revolutionary commitments, organizing strategy, anticommunist focus, and Vietnam War inheritance— white power was something new. Yet it has often been misunderstood as a simple resurgence of earlier Klan activity. Historians divide the Klan into "eras," with the first following the Civil War, the second in the 1920s, and the third dedicated to opposing the civil rights movement. To understand white power as a Klan resurgence rests upon an artificial distinction between nonviolent and violent activism, in which the so-called fourth era refers to nonviolent, public-sphere activities, such as rallies and political campaigns, and the fifth era to the criminal activity of a secret, violent underground. This terminology arose from the white power movement itself and evokes previous surges in Klan membership that occurred one after another with lulls between.[28] But the supposed fourth and fifth eras occurred simultaneously. This terminology therefore hinders an understanding of the activism it attempts to describe. White power should be recognized as something broader than the Klan, encompassing a wider range of ideologies and operating simultaneously in public and underground. Such an understanding is vital lest we erroneously equate white power with covert violence and thereby ignore its significant inroads into mainstream society, which hardly came under cover of night. Activists such as David Duke mounted political campaigns that influenced local and national elections.[29] They produced a vibrant print culture with crossover appeal that reached more mainstream readers. They traveled from church to church, linking religious belief with white power ideology. They created a series of computer message boards to further their cause. They pursued social ties between groups, cementing their political affinities with one another through marriages and other intimate bonds.

These political activists were often the same people who trained in paramilitary camps, plotted race war, and carried out criminal and terrorist acts. The death toll included journalists, state and federal employees, political opponents, and white power activists themselves. The Oklahoma City bombing, undertaken by movement activists, killed 168 people, making it the largest deliberate mass casualty on American soil between the bombing of Pearl Harbor and the terrorist attacks of September 11, 2001.

But the body count alone cannot fully account for the effects of white power violence. That number ignores the lives disrupted by the movement's rage. The dead left behind grieving, struggling families. And while many were physically attacked, many others were threatened. It would be impossible to tally those who were harassed and wounded emotionally, left too afraid to speak or work. But these wounds, too, bear out the long and broad ramifications of the movement's violence.[30]

Although the movement's militancy, and therefore its violence, owes much to the right-wing framing of the Vietnam War, other elements of the 1970s also infused the movement. White power also responded to the changing meaning of the state, sovereignty, and liberal institutions in and after that decade. The dramatic, hard-won gains of feminism, civil rights, secularism, and gay liberation left the 1970s ripe for conservative backlash.[31]

Another factor was emerging economic threat. The post–World War II welfare state had promised jobs, education, and health, but, beginning in 1973, a series of economic shocks displaced the expectation of continued growth and prosperity.[32] An oil crisis brought about the realization that natural resources would not always be cheap and plentiful.[33] Wealth inequality grew and unemployment rose. For the first time since the late 1940s, the promise of prosperity stalled.[34]

Dwindling economic prospects became bound up with cultural backlash. Volition and need alike drove more women into the workforce, threatening both men's exclusive access to certain jobs and the Cold War–era vision of the suburban, white nuclear family with a wife who stayed at home.[35] The successful civil rights mobilizations of the 1960s gave way to white resistance as news coverage turned to black radicalism, urban riots, and integration.[36]

Forced busing of children to integrated public schools became a heated issue, and whites fought back both through school privatization and in heated public protest.

In this context, defense of the family intertwined with defense of free-market ideology. As the stark limitations of New Deal liberalism became clearer—and as civil rights laws made it more difficult to deny opportunities and benefits to nonwhites just as an economic downturn set in—the state could be recast as a menace to morality and prosperity.[37] For many Americans, the state became the enemy. White power activists, driven by their narrative of the Vietnam War, took this sentiment to the extreme in calling for revolution.

Some have argued that white power did not properly constitute a social movement. This claim typically turns on a supposed disconnect between white power and the militia wave, or on a narrow definition of social movements that rests on centralized leadership and harmony among members.[38] But social-movement theorists attuned to the grassroots mobilizations of the mid- to late twentieth century make the case for a more encompassing definition.[39] While white power featured a diversity of views and an array of competing leaders, all corners of the movement were inspired by feelings of defeat, emasculation, and betrayal after the Vietnam War and by social and economic changes that seemed to threaten and victimize white men. White power also qualifies as a social movement through its central features: the contiguous activity of an inner circle of key figures over two decades, frequent public displays, and development of a wide-reaching social network.[40]

White power activists used a shared repertoire of actions to assert collectivity.[41] They rallied openly, formed associations and coalitions, and gave statements to the press.[42] Public displays of uniformed activists chanting slogans and marching in formation aimed to demonstrate worthiness, unity, numbers, and commitment to both members and observers.[43] Activists encouraged dress codes and rules about comportment and featured the presence of mothers with children, Vietnam veterans, and active-duty military personnel. Members showed unity by donning uniforms and by marching and chanting in formation. They made claims about their numbers. They underscored their commitment with pledges to die rather than abandon the fight; preparing to risk their lives for white power; and undertaking acts that put them at legal and physical risk. A regular circulation of people, weapons, funds, images, and rhetoric—as well as intermarriages and other social relationships—bound activists together. These actions produced common "ideas and culture," what social movement theorists have called "frames," that served to "legitimate and motivate collective action."[44]

The primacy of the Vietnam War among these frames is clear in the cultural artifacts that inspired and coordinated the movement. These included uniforms, language, strategies, and matériel derived from the war itself. Activists adopted terminology, such as "gooks," associated with U.S. soldiers in Vietnam; camouflage fatigues; civilian versions of the era's military weapons, as well as the genuine articles, sometimes illegally obtained; and training and combat methods modeled on soldiers' experience and U.S. Army manuals. Also essential in binding the movement together was the 1974 white utopian novel *The Turner Diaries*, which channeled and responded to the nascent white power narrative of the Vietnam War.[45] The novel provided a blueprint for action, tracing the structure of leaderless resistance and modeling, in fiction, the guerrilla tactics of assassination and bombing that activists would embrace for the next two decades. Activists distributed and quoted from the book frequently. It was more than a guide, though. The popularity of *The Turner Diaries* made it a touchstone, a point of connection among movement members and sympathizers that brought them together in common cause.

Writing the history of a subversive movement presents archival challenges. White power activists routinely attempted to hide their activity, even when it was legal. Documentary resources are scattered and fragmentary. This is especially true of the period after 1983, when white power activists worked particularly hard to avoid being depicted as a coherent movement. They used old Klan strategies such as maintaining secret membership rolls, as well as new ideas such as cell-style organizing. Such strategies foiled government informants and forestalled public awareness of violence, obscuring the scale and intentions of the movement and limiting opposition. Activists understated or denied their involvement to protect themselves and their allies. But when they felt it useful, they also overstated their influence and membership in order to boost their apparent strength.

This deliberate obfuscation has clouded many journalistic and scholarly accounts. Press coverage too often portrayed organized white power violence as the work of lone gunmen driven by grievance and mental illness. Sensational true-crime and undercover reporting in pulp magazines and one-source interviews in small-town newspapers kept activists safely ensconced within their cells and depicted every case of violence as uniquely senseless. Thus groups went undetected, and the motivations underlying violence were rarely taken seriously. Accounts after the Oklahoma City bombing concluded that if white power had ever constituted a social movement, it had become so riddled by inter- and intragroup conflicts and personal vendettas that it no longer deserved the designation.[46] Yet infighting had been a constant feature of white power formation and activity. White power organizing did change in the late 1990s, but this resulted from large-scale historical shifts such as increased pressure and expanding online activity, not internecine feuds.

Not all journalistic accounts of white power were so flawed. Veteran reporters from the *Christian Science Monitor,* the *Oregonian,* and the *Houston Chronicle,* among others, spent years covering white power on their beats and began to connect local episodes to activity elsewhere. And even the one-off accounts can be useful to the historian because white power activists sometimes spoke to undercover reporters directly and contemporaneously about their motivations.[47]

The Federal Bureau of Investigation (FBI), Bureau of Alcohol, Tobacco, and Firearms (ATF), U.S. Marshal Service, and Department of Justice monitored the white power movement during this period, generating another source of archival materials. Authors of these records range from undercover agents who had deep familiarity with white power groups to clerical staff at the tail end of a long game of telephone, who sometimes misunderstood crucial details. The motivations of federal agents—some prevented crimes and mounted major prosecutions; others declined to report, prevent, or prosecute such groups; yet others unleashed their own violence upon separatist compounds—shaped these records as well, affecting their reliability. Government documents also vary widely in their level of redaction. Many such sources are accessible only through Freedom of Information Act requests, which means that not everything the government collected is available to researchers. Even full access would provide but a partial glimpse of white power activity, filtered through state interests and the perspectives of individual state actors.

When it comes to the flourishing of white power activism in prisons, sources are especially limited. Groups such as the prison gang the Aryan Brotherhood are largely absent from the archive. We can detect some effects of their mobilizations, such as monetary contributions sent beyond prison walls. Members who joined the movement while incarcerated and continued their activism after release also have greater presence in available sources. But much less is known about white power mobilizations within prison walls.

Legal documents, too, provide less information than we might hope, particularly because the white power movement flourished between the end of excellent paper recordkeeping and the beginning of effective digitization of documents. While several acts of white power violence and harassment have resulted in civil and criminal prosecutions, many resources from those trials have been lost or destroyed, in whole or in part. Some of what remains can be obtained only at prohibitive expense. And what is available comes with the same complications as any trial record. Some people who testified about their roles in the movement, especially women, may have done so under the threat of separation from their families. Several activists made plea deals in return for testifying against the movement. Legal documents, especially testimonies, must be read with such motivations in mind.

An important source of information about the movement is the opposition. Watchdog groups such as the Southern Poverty Law Center, the Anti-Defamation League, and the Center for Democratic Renewal collected material on white power activists as part of their mission to combat intolerance. Some compiled extensive databases including biographical information, photographs, news clippings, and legal records. They also obtained photographs, transcriptions of conversations from undercover informants, journalists' notes, and other items outside the published record. Although these files are rich with information, they, too, must be treated cautiously. Watchdog groups can have motives that reach beyond simple documentation: they exist through fundraising, and donations may increase when there is a sense of urgency. Watchdog groups may have sometimes overestimated the movement's influence and level of organization.

A final, essential resource is the archive created by the white power movement itself. This includes correspondence, ephemera, illustrations, autobiographies, books, printed periodicals, and "zines." Some printed material circulated widely and had a transnational readership. Activists self-published their writings on presses, mimeograph and Xerox machines, and the Internet.

Large collections of these published materials are housed at three university libraries in the United States.[48] Although these collections are fundamentally different—one assembled by a journalist writing on an episode of movement violence, one by an archivist who asked political extremists from across the spectrum for contributions, and one by collectors who obtained literature at meetings of extremist groups—the materials in these three archives are remarkably similar. They offer, therefore, a fairly complete picture of the movement's printed output.

At the same time, one must be mindful of what an archival study of white power cannot reveal. Military service records, for instance, are not publicly available, nor are the membership rolls of each white power group. In their absence, one cannot make a quantitative study of the levels of veteran and active-duty-military participation in the movement. The archive offers very little information on the childhood and early life of most activists. Information on marriages and divorces—particularly involving those who, as part of their antistatist activism, refused to register unions—cannot always be corroborated by official documents. Nor can an archival study stray from the stated beliefs and concrete actions of white power actors in an effort to attempt a psychological assessment. In most cases, the historian has neither the training nor the access to enter this discussion. However, one can grapple with the record of speech and action to offer an approximation of a historical actor's motives and actions.

Given these limitations, I have assumed that each document might reflect a particular agenda and have taken certain precautions as a result. When possible, I use multiple sources to corroborate information. If, say, a fact appears in a redacted FBI file, an undercover reporter's interview with a white power activist, and a mainstream press report, it probably can be relied upon. I present unverifiable statements as such and identify those that are demonstrably false. When relevant, I include information about sources, their biases, and possible alternative interpretations of the material in question.

That the archive is imperfect should disturb neither historians nor readers. Indeed, it is precisely the work of the historian to assemble an account based upon the information available, even if it is scattered, incomplete, and sometimes contradictory. In many ways, this approach enables a better understanding of how historical actors experienced their own moment, without the veneer of hindsight that clouds other kinds of accounts, such as interviews and memoirs produced years after the fact.

A sizable literature, both academic and journalistic, has engaged with portions of the white power archive, but this book is the first work to attempt a comprehensive approach. Unlike studies focused on one segment of white power—particular activists, events, locations, symbols, ideological discourses, or disputes—this one captures the entire movement as it formed and changed over time. I find in the archival sources the story of the emergence, rise, and fall of a unique, cohesive effort to build a new nation on the ashes of a state accused of having abandoned its own. To understand the impact of this effort on American society, politics, and culture, and to take stock of its relationship with mainstream conservatism, requires engaging it synthetically, not piece by piece.

Bring the War Home follows the formation of the white power movement, its war on the state, and its apocalyptic confrontation with militarized state power. Part I documents the role of violence in motivating and constituting the movement.[49] Chapter 1 traces the creation of a Vietnam War narrative that united the movement and inspired its paramilitary culture and infrastructure. Chapter 2 shows how paramilitary training camps worked to form white power groups and augmented their capacity for violence. In Chapter 3, I discuss the formal unification of the movement through a common experience of violence: the 1979 mass shooting of communist protestors in Greensboro, North Carolina. Chapter 4 documents the intersections between white power and other forms of paramilitarism by focusing on transnational antidemocratic paramilitary combat by mercenary soldiers, some with movement ties.

Part II turns to the white power revolution declared in 1983. At this point, the movement definitively distinguished itself from previous vigilante mobilizations, such as the earlier Ku Klux Klan, whose perpetrators claimed to act for the good of the state or to uphold its laws. In Chapters 5 through 7, I examine the movement's declaration of war, use of early computer networks, and deployment of cell-style organizing. Critical to these efforts were attempts, some successful, to obtain stolen military-grade weapons and matériel from the state. I also recount the acquittal of thirteen movement activists on federal charges including seditious conspiracy. Their defense, based on a purported need to protect white women, demonstrates that even though white power broke away from earlier white supremacist movements, it maintained a degree of ideological and rhetorical continuity with them—even as it turned to newly violent antistatism in its revolutionary actions.

Part III describes the crescendo and climax of white power revolution in which groups both confronted and participated in events characterized by apocalyptic, world-destroying violence. Although many were killed and others were harmed, the effort never achieved the biblical scale activists had anticipated. The movement was inflamed by encounters with state power, such as the standoff between federal agents and a white separatist family at Ruby Ridge, Idaho, and the siege of the Branch Davidians in Waco, Texas. Cataclysmic, militarized state violence helped to inspire the growth of militias, leading to the Oklahoma City bombing. That act stands as the culmination of two decades of white power organizing and is the most significant single event in the movement's history.

The bombing destroyed an edifice, lives, and families, but not only those. It also shattered meaning, wiping out a public understanding of the white power movement by cementing its violence, in public memory, as the act of a few men. Despite its many attempts to disappear, and despite its obscurity even at the height of its strength during the militia phase, the movement left lasting marks on mainstream American politics and popular culture. It has continued to instigate and shape violence years after the Oklahoma City bombing.

The story of white power as a social movement exposes something broader about the enduring impact of state violence in America. It reveals one catastrophic ricochet of the Vietnam War, in the form of its paramilitary aftermath. It also reveals something important about war itself. War is not neatly contained in the space and time legitimated by the state. It reverberates in other terrains and lasts long past armistice. It comes home in ways bloody and unexpected.

PART I   **FORMATION**

1   The Vietnam War Story

Forever trapped in the rice paddies . . . of Vietnam.
—Louis Beam, 1989

Louis Beam ignites a boat painted "*U.S.S. Viet Cong*" at a Klan rally in Santa Fe, Texas, 1981. *(Ed Kolenovsky, Associated Press Photo)*

LOUIS BEAM SPENT eighteen months in Vietnam. He served an extended tour as a gunner on a UH-1 Huey helicopter in the U.S. Army's 25th Aviation Battalion. He logged more than a thousand hours shooting at the enemy and transporting his fellow soldiers, including the injured and fallen, to and from the front. By his own account, he killed between twelve and fifty-one "communists" before returning home to Texas, decorated, in 1968.[1] But he never stopped fighting. Beam would use his Vietnam War story to militarize a resurgent Ku Klux Klan and to wage a white power revolution.

He brought many things home with him: his uniforms, virulent anticommunism, and hatred of the Viet Cong. He brought home the memory of death and mutilation sealed in heavy-duty body bags. He brought home racism, military training, weapons proficiency, and a readiness to continue fighting. His was a story about government betrayal, soldiers left behind, and a nation that spat upon his service and would never appreciate his sacrifice. Indeed, he brought home the war as he fought it, and dedicated his life to urging others to "bring it on home."[2]

On both the right and left of the political spectrum, the war worked to radicalize and arm paramilitary groups in the post–Vietnam War period. On the left, veterans played instrumental roles in groups organized around politics and labor, and in militant groups that fought racial inequality, such as the Black Panther Party.[3] Occasionally these left- and right-wing mobilizations would overlap and feed off one another, with white power activists robbing the same Brinks armored car company hit by the left-wing Weather Underground a few years earlier, and with the paramilitary Latino Brown Berets and the Klan Border Watch focused on the same stretch of terrain in South Texas.[4]

Throughout the twentieth century, many veterans of color understood their postwar activism as an extension of their wartime combat.[5] Veterans played key roles in fostering the civil rights and armed self-defense movements.[6] The influence of key veterans upon the white power movement, therefore, is part of a longer story about veterans' claims on society, and about the expansive aftermath of modern war.

Just as some veterans fought for racial equality, others fought to oppose it. Indeed, Ku Klux Klan membership surges have aligned more neatly with the aftermath of war than with poverty, anti-immigration sentiment, or populism, to name a few common explanations. After the Civil War, the Confederate veterans who formed the first Klan terrorized both black communities and the Reconstruction-era state. World War I veterans led second-era Klan efforts to violently ensure "all-American" racial, religious, and nationalist power. Third-era Klansmen who had served in World War II and Korea played key roles in the violent opposition to civil rights, including providing explosives expertise and other skills they had learned in the military.[7] After each war, veterans not only joined the Klan but also played instrumental roles in leadership, providing military training to other Klansmen and carrying out acts of violence.[8] The effect of war was not simply about the number or percentage of veterans involved, but about the particular expertise, training, and culture they brought to paramilitary groups. Significantly, in each surge of activity, veterans worked hand in hand with Klan members who had not served. Without the participation of civilians, these aftershocks of war would not have found purchase at home. The overspills of state violence from wars, therefore, spread through the whole of American society; they did not affect veterans alone.[9]

So, too, did the Vietnam War broadly affect American culture and politics. Narratives of the war as a government betrayal and as a source of grievance laid the groundwork for white power activism. Once again, the war story drew in both veterans and civilians. But the Vietnam War was also historically distinct; it represented loss, frustration, and doubt. By intervening to support South Vietnam, the United States sought to halt the spread of communism—and to stop the Soviet Union, which supported North Vietnam and revolutionaries in the South, from amassing global power in the midst of the Cold War. In practice, the United States found itself intervening in a local, civil conflict, one shaped by the legacy of French colonial rule. American soldiers entered a morally ambiguous proxy war and faced an enemy comprising highly motivated guerrillas, partisan soldiers, and supportive or ambivalent civilians. This, together with enormous differences in culture and climate, created high levels of despair among the troops.[10]

Combat in Vietnam often took a form unfamiliar to a generation of soldiers raised on World War II films that depicted war as righteous and tempered depictions of its violence.[11] In Vietnam, American soldiers waged prolonged, bloody fights for terrain that was soon abandoned. They often described enemies and allies as indistinguishable. Infantry patrols embarked on long, aimless marches in the hope of drawing fire from hidden guerrillas. "Free-fire zones" and "strategic hamlets"—designations that labeled as enemies anyone who did not evacuate from certain areas—placed civilians in the path of war. And because success was often measured in the number of people killed, rather than in terrain held, a mix of circumstances in Vietnam created a situation in which violence against civilians, mutilation of bodies, souvenir collecting, sexual violence, and other war crimes were not just isolated incidents but ubiquitous features of war that permeated the chain of command.[12]

The United States and its people had understood the wars of the first half of the century as shared civil projects, but the Vietnam War undermined this notion.[13] When the commitment of soldiers, bombs, and money failed to produce decisive victories in Southeast Asia, civilians at home grew increasingly disenchanted with the war, helping to foster the narrative of abandonment that white power activists such as Beam would later exploit.[14] Mobilizations of protest in the United States, particularly the mass antiwar movement, openly questioned the war's morality by critiquing American involvement as an imperialist exercise.[15] Television broadcasts of wartime violence created what the writer Susan Sontag called a "new tele-intimacy with death and destruction."[16] Many returning veterans denounced the quagmire of war both in the streets and in the halls of government, and journalists documented wartime atrocities.[17] As the war dragged on, victory in the realm of public perception seemed less and less possible.

Defeat in Vietnam represented a cataclysmic break in several registers: it upended notions of the triumphant American warrior, presented a perceived threat to the balance of world power, and, for some, intensified a fear of communism.[18] The loss in Vietnam by a superpower threatened the reputation of the U.S. military. The Vietnam War was the first real test of an integrated army, and the racial violence that plagued soldiers of color in combat and at home signaled the incompleteness of this transformation. The move to the all-volunteer force in 1973—the army abolished the draft in part because of mass opposition to the Vietnam War—was followed by several years of crisis for that institution as measured by public perception, levels of enlistment, and the percentage of recruits that met the army's racial, class, and educational preferences.[19]

The frustrations and failures of the Vietnam War also defined the home front. In 1967 the artist Martha Rosler began making collages transposing the violence of warfare from *Life* magazine photographs to the suburban domestic spaces of *House Beautiful;* she titled that series "House Beautiful: Bringing the War Home." Leftist Vietnam veterans and other activists used the slogan "Bring the War Home" to illustrate the distance between the violence of warfare and those who waged or supported war from the comfort of the home front—and to call for left-wing political violence at home.[20]

Indeed, the gulf between the violence and hardship that soldiers witnessed in Vietnam and the society to which they returned motivated radical responses aimed at divergent political goals. Veterans in the early 1970s—

most prominently Vietnam Veterans Against the War—led antiwar demonstrations, denounced the war, mobilized to provide assistance for those suffering physical effects from the chemical defoliant Agent Orange (widely used in Vietnam), and urged better Veterans Administration support.[21] Some veterans groups—most notably the prisoners of war / missing in action (POW / MIA) movement—gained major political lobbying power in this period, in part because of their attempted co-optation by the Nixon administration, and in part because of their own success in framing their appeals.[22]

In the 1980s, the discourse generated in novels, memoirs, and medical and journalistic accounts alike shifted to emphasize the mistreatment of veterans by the government and by civil society. The idea that the nation had wrongly rejected, failed to honor, and impugned veterans created an emphasis on healing and memorialization. This discourse papered over a critique of the war itself by foregrounding the wounded and wronged veteran.[23] Meanwhile, a systematic accounting of wartime atrocities—including official apologies for events such as the massacre of hundreds of civilians at My Lai—came to be seen as an open threat to an ascendant neoconservative worldview. For the war to be remembered as a "noble cause," as presidential candidate Ronald Reagan called it in 1980—or even to sustain the narrative that its veterans had been honorable men "denied permission to win," as he said after he became president—required the systematic exclusion of an antiwar critique and transformed what appeared to be an apolitical, intimate style of memoir and narrative into a conservative political project.[24]

Some veterans, though, insisted upon a direct connection between their grievances and political action. The small and influential group of veterans that unified, armed, and radicalized the white power movement invoked the Vietnam War specifically to decry the Reagan-era federal government even as they invoked some of its language. They told this story about the Vietnam War: the corrupt government sent American boys to Vietnam and then denied them permission to win by limiting their use of force against a beastly, subhuman enemy. Many met gruesome injury and death, and all faced hardship, insects, abandonment, rot, and disease. After American soldiers came home, people spat on them and called them baby-killers. No one appreciated the service they had given their country. Those left behind as prisoners of war were abandoned and forgotten, and those who returned were denied both homecoming parades and their proper place in public memory. This series of betrayals, the narrative concludes, shows the irredeemable corruption of the American government but proves the valor of soldiers and most of the military.

Parts of this Vietnam War story are historically valid, appearing in memoirs, oral histories, and scholarly accounts. Other elements remain widely regarded as factual even though they are contested by historical evidence. Popular accounts of the Vietnam War continue to take as fact that soldiers were spat upon by protesters as they returned home, that the war could have been won if not for the betrayal by corrupt or cowardly politicians, and that politicians abandoned large numbers of living prisoners of war in Southeast Asia. Yet all of these claims have been challenged in the historical literature.[25]

The Vietnam War story served a vital role in the white power movement. Its precise function changed over time, often following generational shifts. A first wave of activists, including Beam, sought to continue the war they had fought in Vietnam in the United States and beyond. To take a few other examples, Tom Posey served in the Marines in Vietnam, and then in the Alabama National Guard. He flirted with the John Birch Society and violent Klan action before founding a mercenary group, Civilian Military Assistance, which carried out acts of violence in Central America and on the U.S.-Mexico border.[26] Glenn Miller claimed twenty years of army service, including two tours in Vietnam as a Green Beret, before he was discharged for distributing racist literature.[27] He subsequently organized a major paramilitary white power group that obtained stolen weapons and matériel from military installations, enlisted active-duty troops as members and trainers, and declared war on the government.[28] Such activists often referred to their own experiences in the Vietnam War as justification for perpetrating racist violence at home. The war provided a narrative that supported the selection of communists as their scapegoats and supported revolution against the state that had failed them in wartime. They drew upon their wartime experiences for tactical guidance, weapons expertise, and rhetorical framing of their white power and mercenary activities.

Other activists came to the movement after nearly enlisting, or had an intense interest in the military but decided not to enlist because of frustration with the way the war was unfolding. Randy Weaver, who would join the movement and become part of its most iconic martyrdom story at Ruby Ridge, joined the Green Berets but resigned in frustration when he was never shipped out.[29] Bob Mathews was in a car on the way to enlist at Fort Huachuca, Arizona, when he abruptly changed his mind. He had heard a radio story about the prosecution of Lieutenant William Calley for the massacre of hundreds of Vietnamese civilians at My Lai. Mathews believed such acts of violence were justified, and saw Calley's prosecution as evidence of government betrayal of American soldiers. The episode dissuaded him from enlisting and shored up his belief in the irredeemable corruption of the state. Mathews would ultimately found the Order, a white power terrorist group, to wage war against the federal government.[30] Gary Lee Yarbrough, who was a member of the Order, had been inducted into the Marines in lieu of incarceration, but went absent without leave and ended up serving his time in prison rather than in Vietnam. While incarcerated, Yarbrough encountered another pipeline into the movement through the Aryan Brotherhood, a white power prison gang.[31]

The Vietnam War was such a powerful symbol and reference point that some activists claimed to have served when they had not. For example, Michael Perdue, who attempted to invade the Caribbean island of Dominica to create a puppet government that would funnel money back to the Klan, spoke of a military and mercenary combat record that was quickly proven false.[32] Whether they had served or not, activists took from the war a tangle of testimony and potent narratives, as well as a set of uniforms, weapons, and political rhetoric. Primarily, the Vietnam War allowed men to take on the role of the soldier as an all-encompassing identity. Randall Rader, who did not serve and did not claim to be a veteran, nevertheless came to white power activism through his keen interest in the military in general and in Vietnam in particular. He later testified that he used a close study of U.S. Army manuals, particularly those on guerrilla and counterinsurgent warfare in the Vietnam era, to become military trainer for the white separatist group the Covenant, the Sword, and the Arm of the Lord and, later, the terrorist group the Order.[33] During his term as instructor, these groups dramatically increased their paramilitarism and took up the symbols, weapons, uniforms, and matériel of the Vietnam War. And even for those who served in later wars, such as Oklahoma City bomber Timothy McVeigh, a combat veteran of the Gulf War, the Vietnam War narrative and the culture it engendered remained a major symbolic force that worked to organize ongoing acts of white power violence.[34]

For white power activists, a shared story about Vietnam outweighed the historical reality of the war itself. Nowhere in the movement was this narrative more clearly distilled than in the writings and speeches of Louis Beam, one of the movement's most well-recorded and persuasive voices. Beam's narrative, which turned on the violence of warfare, was based on his own service, but it reflected common elements of the Vietnam War experience popularized in memoirs and in movies such as *The Deer Hunter, Platoon, Apocalypse Now,* and *Full Metal Jacket.*[35] In one sense, it matters less whether things happened exactly as Beam described them, and more that he was able to articulate a story that rang true for others who fought in Vietnam.[36]

Beam was a charismatic speaker and persuasive writer who emphasized fiery rhetoric and explicit racism. Compact, dark-haired, and serious, in photographs Beam appears focused and reserved. When he wasn't in his Klan robes or fatigues, he usually looked like a working-class southern man ready for church in a pressed, button-down shirt. Beam was a natural public speaker, with a Texas accent and a metered style reminiscent of the evangelical preachers he had heard in his youth. He regularly invoked history, religion, and the founding fathers. He would start soft and measured, conversational, and then his voice would rise, and he would shout and gesticulate as though he was bringing his flock to Christ, which—as a proponent of Christian Identity—he believed he was doing.[37]

Beam's life could stand in for that of many other American soldiers. Born in 1946 in Baytown, Texas, he enlisted in the army at nineteen, the average age of soldiers who served in Vietnam. Like most of his fellow servicemen, he came from a working-class family. He had economic reasons to enlist, with a young wife and a child on the way. His father had served as a combat soldier in World War II, and Beam, following in his footsteps, volunteered early in the war.[38]

The war did not make Beam racist; he reportedly expressed white supremacist political views before he deployed, and he certainly supported fiery segregationist George Wallace while stationed in Vietnam.[39] This, too, was common in a newly integrated U.S. Army, in which some white soldiers, including Beam, hung Confederate flags in their barracks, often in opposition to the civil rights movement reshaping race relations back home.[40] But his wartime experiences—which featured exposure to racist and anticommunist ideology, violence, and a feeling of betrayal by the government—helped shape the form and magnitude of the mission Beam would advocate after homecoming.

While Beam brought his own beliefs to the war, he also enlisted in an army in which white personnel regularly used racist slurs against soldiers of color in training and in combat. Though the U.S. Armed Forces began to integrate by executive order in 1948, full implementation was not quickly achieved. Institutional practice as well as individual prejudice continued to foster inequality. As historians have shown, the draft disproportionately targeted poor black communities, and was also used as a punitive measure to send black race rioters to war in order to quell domestic dissent. Black soldiers received the fewest promotions and the most courts-martial.[41] Racial tension permeated military installations at home and in Vietnam. While white and black soldiers faced combat together, the rear echelon was intensely segregated: one black soldier described Saigon as "just like Mississippi."[42] In Beam's camp at Cu Chi in Vietnam, black and white soldiers frequently exchanged insults, slights, and blows. Beam served in the 25th Aviation Battalion at a moment of escalating racial tensions. As the language of black power circulated between home and battlefront, black soldiers created a culture of Afros and black berets, greeting each other with fist bumps. Some white soldiers in the 25th reported feeling alienated or threatened because of such actions. Klansmen serving as active-duty personnel in Vietnam announced plans for cross-burnings and spray-painted racial epithets on rear echelon buildings.[43]

 By 1970, the Marine Corps recorded more than a thousand incidents of racial violence at installations both in Vietnam and back home. White supremacist groups targeted black military personnel around domestic bases and posts. In 1964, for instance, four members of the United Klans of America—the group Beam would join after homecoming—murdered a black army reserve lieutenant colonel on his way home from training at Fort Benning, Georgia. In 1968, black and white Marines met in a series of violent altercations at Camp Lejeune, North Carolina, until the death of a white Marine caused authorities to intervene.[44]

At Camp Pendleton, a Marine base in southern California, active-duty personnel organized on-base Klan activity beginning in 1973, according to a Naval Investigative Service study and a report by the *New Times*. The Camp Pendleton chapter of the Klan had garnered some two hundred members, according to a local news report, and had participated in the systematic "kidnapping, shooting, firebombing, torturing, beating and otherwise harassing [of] black Marines" even as some officers promoted Klan members and issued, the paper claimed, "secret" clearances for six of them. The report catalogued almost two hundred racial incidents at Camp Pendleton from 1973 to 1976.[45] That November, black Marines stormed a meeting of white

Marines, stabbing six. David Duke claimed that the event was a Klan meeting and that the attacked white Marines were Klansmen.[46] Afterward, Klan Marines held "war councils," according to the *New Times,* and called for retaliatory killings. The Klan, the reporter concluded, in a play on "The Marines' Hymn," "has been successfully organizing new dens from the halls of Montezuma to the shores of Tripoli."[47]

While military service could foster opportunities for soldiers to encounter people from different backgrounds, leading to friendships that would outlast the war, it could also harden prejudices and set the stage for racial violence.[48] After Beam returned home, his invocation of the Vietnam War for the organization of white power activism built upon the racial tension of his military service, and upon the mounting resentment of some white Americans who believed their opportunities were being curtailed by the advance of civil rights.[49] His story would resonate not only with some veterans but also with many people both in and beyond the white power movement. Beam's narrative turned on stymied grief, constant danger, fixation on weapons, and betrayal, all elements that he believed were shared by fellow white Americans.

In some instances, Beam wrote on behalf of "us," meant to include all U.S. soldiers fighting in Vietnam. He wrote that he arrived at the front by helicopter and airplane transport and felt a rapid displacement intensely: "They called us up, placed a rifle in our hands, transported us 12,000 miles, planted us in the jungles, and told us to kill or be killed."[50] Even if this didn't square with Beam's record—he had served in Germany before arriving in "the jungles"—it did resonate with a prominent feature of Vietnam War deployment.[51] During World War II, soldiers had trained and served with one group, communalizing the experience of combat with a long boat ride home; in contrast, most soldiers were deployed to Vietnam with disquieting speed and upon leaving their units, rapidly returned home. Psychologists have argued that individual deployments by airplane and helicopter changed the very character of the combat unit, sometimes breaking bonds that previously had sustained soldiers in and after battle.[52] Invoking this displacement, Beam reached out to those who had experienced the same alienation from their fellow soldiers.

Beam wrote about his "Post Viet Nam Stress Syndrome," and his writings reflect many of the earmarks of post-traumatic stress disorder (PTSD).[53] After its addition to the *Diagnostic and Statistical Manual of Mental Disorders* in 1980—in part because of veterans' activism—PTSD gave a name to the combat trauma suffered by many Vietnam veterans and became part of the public discourse about the war.[54] Whether Beam sustained this injury or not, his narrative appealed to those who had PTSD.

His grievances expressed the frustrations of soldiers with the state, political leaders, and civilians who appeared to be corrupt and complicit in the failed war, and reflected feelings widely held by American soldiers in Vietnam about how retreat from combat zones frequently offered no real sense of safety, how racial tension split the rear echelon, and how the inability to distinguish allies from enemies among the Vietnamese hid the enemy. Prevalent night attacks meant that death could come for soldiers at any time. Beam wrote of the plight of the "poor grunt bastards," the foot soldiers used as bait to locate enemy positions and then call in air attacks.[55] Their most common form of engagement with the enemy was ambush, while land mines and booby traps created intense and constant fear.[56]

Dehumanizing descriptions of the enemy broadly applied to the Vietnamese during the war—and not just by a few soldiers—would reappear in white power rhetoric at home. The widespread use of body counts as a marker of success in the Vietnam War encouraged soldiers to think of the enemy as numbers or vermin, not people.[57] On a reconnaissance flight in June 1968, in "a blazing exchange of gunfire," Beam and his fellow helicopter gunner "killed five Viet Cong fleeing across a rice paddy" thirty kilometers northwest of Saigon, according to the newsletter of the 25th Infantry. As gunners opened fire, the men on the ground fired back with rocket-propelled grenades, tracers, and small arms fire. The newsletter noted that the twenty-minute engagement that day "netted 183 enemy bodies." That this language appears in an official account of the event, and not by Beam himself, shows that such attitudes had purchase far beyond radical activists.[58]

Indeed, the 25th Infantry had a troubled relationship with civilians, both in and out of the major base camp at Cu Chi. At times the army kept soldiers from associating with civilians entirely, while disparaging the Vietnamese with dehumanizing rhetoric. Some soldiers made sport of throwing rocks at civilians, shooting at them with slingshots, and pelting them with debris from passing vehicles. As one 25th Infantry soldier remembered, "everybody was a zip, gook, or animal"; another said soldiers regarded the Vietnamese as subhuman and noted that "seeing a dead gook was no big deal."[59]

To Beam, as to the broader conservative public, the Vietnam War signaled a divide between the America of the past and one transformed by antiwar protest and the rights movements that would continue to dramatically alter American domestic life over the coming decades. Antiwar protests, furthermore, had altered perceptions of the war itself, leading to rising antimilitarism. For some, the war had become something spurious and dishonorable, a perception furthered by media coverage and wartime atrocities such as the My Lai massacre.[60] "After I got home from the war . . . things didn't seem like they were before I went to Vietnam," Beam told an undercover reporter posing as a Klan recruit shortly after his return. "Everything seemed different. The whole climate of the nation had changed. Before I went over to fight, most of the people seemed behind us soldiers—but when I returned, it seemed the majority of Americans were against us, against war as a whole."[61]

Beam understood the Vietnam War as the catalyst for American decline and yearned to reclaim a time before social and political changes had transformed the nation.[62] Embattled white power activists saw the Vietnam War as emblematic of all that had gone wrong. In the lack of welcome home and shortage of jobs when they returned, they found grist for a yearning for a time of easier economic opportunity for white men, and grounds for condemning economic threats such as the farm foreclosure crisis, stagflation, and job loss. The impact of the Vietnam War was inextricably linked to all the threatening changes of the 1970s that had turned their world upside down.

Beam's writings departed from a mainstream sentimentalized veterans' discourse in openly calling for violence. There is a tension in his writing between a person trying to cope with the violence of combat and the general of a white power revolution trying to incite further violence at home. As he flew in his Huey helicopter, transporting the bodies of dead American soldiers, he wondered:

> I become engrossed in a door gunner's trance of meditation (1500 feet in the air, 80 knots air speed, distant horizon) wondering who this guy is. Is the red gore there by my feet blood from a White man, or a Black man? Or just a dead man? . . . It occurs to me that I don't really know much about this bleeding guy in the torn bag, and nothing at all about the guy next to him, in a green, heavy duty, non leaking plastic body bag.[63]

The horror of the war briefly pushed Beam to locate humanity beyond race in a world in which all men, black and white, could easily become indistinguishable dead men in body bags.

However, he consistently used the horror of blood, death, and mutilation to argue that the government and civil society had betrayed and abandoned soldiers in Vietnam, and, therefore, that civilians should face the violence of war at the hands of white power activists on the home front.[64] Beam repeatedly called for violence in his writings, both in works under his own name and in those written under pseudonyms. In 1982, he invoked the war to demand reprisal: "America's political leaders, bankers, church ministers, newsmen, sports stars and hippies called us 'baby killers,' and threw chicken blood on some of us when we returned home. You're damn right I'm mad! I've had enough! I want these same traitors to face their enemy now, the American fighting man they betrayed, all three million of us."[65] An article published under one of his pseudonyms called for resistance to a predicted seizure of guns from citizens and urged white power activists to hold on to their weapons so that newspaper headlines of the future might read,

> "Millions of Formerly Peaceful, Law-Abiding Citizens Up in Arms"— "Vigilantes of One and Two Persons Take Law into Own Hands"— "Politician Cut in Two by Shotgun Blast as He Steps from Car"— . . . "Federal Judge Killed by Bomb Blast as He Starts Car"—"Judge Found Dead, Hands Tied behind Back, Throat Cut"— . . . "U.S. Senator Found Hanging from Limb of Tree on River."[66]

In 1989, Beam promised that "although the battlefield had changed and rules were different, THE WAR CONTINUES."[67] He decried the conservatives who had risen to power: "It is time now for the voice of the radical to be heard. . . . Out with the conservatives and in with the radicals! Out with plans for compromise and in with plans for the sword!"[68] Lest his readers mistake his intent, he clarified in another essay that "the sword need not be literal, though many of us would enjoy righteous satisfaction from actually lopping off heads of the enemy. A sword in the year of our Lord 1981 can be an M-16, three sticks of dynamite taped together, a twelve-gauge, a can of gas, or whatever is suitable to carry out any commission of the Lord that has been entrusted to you."[69] Beam described wanting to machine-gun everyone who had sent American soldiers to Vietnam and everyone who had wronged them when they came home.[70] A decade after the movement declared war on the state, he called for action to recover prisoners of war and help veterans suffering from Agent Orange exposure: "Get your gear together—lock and load— move out! Let 1993 be the year we win the last battle of the war."[71]

Spanning decades, Beam's narrative of unending combat appealed to
Vietnam veterans, active-duty soldiers, and a wider audience of disaffected
white men and women. In the 1970s, the movement would begin to militarize and unify around this narrative. Klansmen would shed their white robes
to don camouflage fatigues, neo-Nazis would brandish military rifles, and
white separatists would manufacture their own Claymore-style land mines
in their determination to bring the war home.

Years after the war in Vietnam ended, the narrative of that conflict continued to shape white power activism and serve as a principal signifier of
the movement's paramilitarism. In 1989, as militias gathered in the Northwest, Beam wrote:

> Even after all this time there seems to be no way we can forget or let Vietnam
> descend into the past. . . . There is no relief, and can be none. We are forever
> trapped in the rice paddies and skies of Vietnam. We can neither go back or
> go forward, suspended for eternity in the place that they put us. . . . Forget?
> Not even if I could.[72]

2   Building the Underground

Viet-Klan.

—*Journalist Gordon Hunter, referring to Klan harassment*
of Vietnamese refugees

Paramilitary camp training, Carolina Knights of the Ku Klux Klan / White Patriot
Party, 1985. (*© Robin Rayne Nelson, ZUMA Images*)

IN 1977, Louis Beam used a Texas Veterans Land Board grant—a program
designed to provide economic benefits to returning veterans—to purchase
fifty acres of swampland.[1] On a landscape that recalled the rice paddies of
Vietnam, Beam built Camp Puller, a Vietnam War–style training facility
designed to turn Klansmen into soldiers.[2] Over the next few years, Beam
would climb from participation in a small Klan group to leadership of a

national, unified white power movement that shared a paramilitary orienta-
tion and adopted violent methods. Beam would implement a Klan Border
Watch to target undocumented immigrants at the U.S.-Mexico border, and
he would recruit active-duty military personnel. He would create an elite
Special-Forces-style unit within the Klan, and proceed to build a network
of paramilitary training camps. He would call upon his soldiers to foster a
harassment campaign against Vietnamese refugee fishermen on the Texas
coast, whom he deemed enemies. Later, through the intervention of the
Southern Poverty Law Center (SPLC) and a trial that banned paramilitary
training in Texas, Beam would find himself temporarily halted—but the
strategy of warfare honed from this frustration would inflame the white
power movement and further shape the history of domestic terrorism.

At every step, Beam invoked the violence and loss of the Vietnam War to
justify his worldview and to structure his actions. At every step, the exercise
of violent action formed the community that would give rise to the white
power movement.[3] Violent rhetoric worked to indoctrinate activists through
boot-camp-like experiences at paramilitary training facilities, and shared acts
of violence such as the Klan Border Watch and the harassment of Vietnamese
refugees bound them in common purpose.[4] The movement arrived at this
exercise in violent community formation through a long buildup that would
connect the Texas coast to the 1979 shootings in Greensboro, North Carolina, and to a transnational circuit of antidemocratic mercenary soldiering.

Paramilitary camps emerged directly from the combat experiences of key
activists in Vietnam. Beam, who would participate in the building and operation of at least four paramilitary camps, returned home, decorated, in
1968 and joined the United Klans of America, pinning his military decorations onto his crimson Klan robe.[5] He quickly grew frustrated by "government subversion" of the Klan, however, and began looking for other
opportunities. He tried the anticommunist John Birch Society, a local
anti-integration Citizens Council, the anticommunist Minutemen, the American Nazi Party, and the National States Rights Party, but he bristled at
the overemphasis on secrecy, "ridiculous" tactics, and extreme antisemitism
that occluded what he saw as larger, common issues affecting all white
people. Soon Beam set out to form his own group.[6]

He began with sporadic violent activity, all of it anticommunist or white
supremacist. He was arrested for disrupting a communist protest, dynamiting
a Houston radio station that broadcast what he called "Hanoi news," and

blowing up the local Communist Party headquarters. In each case, charges against him were dropped or never filed.[7] In another incident, Beam was charged with possession of an illegal or unregistered handgun; he later testified that this charge arose from his abduction of a white woman in an interracial relationship, which he said he had done at the behest of her parents and which he called an act of "chivalry and honor." In 1979, Beam threatened a visiting vice premier from communist China by lunging at him in the underground parking lot of a Houston hotel, but once more he was not charged.[8]

Concurrent with these early actions, Beam sharpened a Vietnam War story that called for racist and anticommunist violence at home. "I knew the battle wasn't over," Beam told an undercover reporter disguised as a Klan recruit. "The mere fact that I had returned from Vietnam didn't mean the war was over. It was going on right here in the States. I knew right then and there I had to get engaged again and fight the enemy." This new, domestic front of Beam's war collapsed wartime and peacetime, battlefield and home front. "Over here, if you kill the enemy, you go to jail. Over there in Vietnam, if you killed the enemy, they gave you a medal," Beam said. "I couldn't see the difference."[9]

Using the Vietnam War as his framing narrative, Beam organized his own, independent Klan. By 1975 he had affiliated his group with the rapidly growing Knights of the Ku Klux Klan (KKKK), helmed by David Duke and rising as a national-level organization. The KKKK had membership strongholds in Louisiana, North Carolina, and Southern California, in addition to Beam's followers in Texas.[10]

Duke advanced a new public image of the Klan, one that was better-educated and genteel. He gave witty talk-show interviews wearing a suit and tie, claiming to be not racist but "racialist," and advocating separatism rather than violence. His Klan advocated not for the denial of minority rights, he explained, but for the right of Klansmen to associate only with whites. Duke explained that people of color weren't the enemy but merely childlike dupes of Jews and, especially, communists. Racism, although still a major motivating force of KKKK members, slipped behind the veil of Duke's softened language. He and his associates attempted to appeal to the mainstream in the New Right, where libertarian ideas of choice and coercion had found traction. They also spoke to a centrist silent majority that mobilized around contemporary issues such as busing and housing segregation. Although this group discussed such issues through ideas of consumerism and meritocracy—for instance, arguing that their hard work and success should allow them to maintain their property values through neighborhood segregation and opposing school integration through busing— they accorded with white supremacist political goals.[11]

Public interviews, mainstream outreach, and political campaigns represented only one arena of Klan strategy. Even as they presented a softened public front, the same activists built an underground of violent, overtly racist activity utterly at odds with many of their public statements. They constructed a paramilitary infrastructure and expanded their membership through violent training and action. Beam's Camp Puller in Double Bayou, one of at least four Klan camps in Texas and many more around the country, explicitly copied military training. Participants donned fatigues. In exercises at Camp Puller, Beam carried an AR-15, a civilian, semiautomatic version of the M16 soldiers carried in Vietnam. He talked about "kill zones" in the United States, modeled on those that had structured combat in Vietnam, and told his trainees about the excitement of ambushes, the Vietnam War's most frequent type of engagement.[12]

Klan paramilitary camps attempted to duplicate both the indoctrination and the violence of the experience of army boot camp, which sought to remake recruits and inculcate a disposition toward violence.[13] The violence Klansmen used as a hazing and community-building ritual sometimes referenced similar group acts carried out by American soldiers during the Vietnam War.[14]

Beam knew that wartime experiences had shaped Klan violence throughout history, and he regularly invoked these lessons of the past.[15] When Confederate veterans of the Civil War founded the first Ku Klux Klan in 1866, they sought to relive "the excitement of army scenes."[16] They did so through the increasingly systematic and violent harassment of black communities in the South. Group participation in such acts of violence ensured loyalty to the cause.[17]

The Klan's second rise followed the national consolidation of a Civil War narrative that valorized the violence of the first Klan, capitalized on the high-profile lynching of Leo Frank, and then drew in returning veterans from World War I.[18] It reached its largest membership in 1924, at some four million nationwide. The second Klan, led by a Spanish-American War veteran, drew white Protestants, opportunistically capitalizing on local tensions in multiple regions of the country. Anti-black in the South, the second Klan was also anti-Catholic in Protestant Indiana, anti-immigrant on the East Coast and on the U.S.-Mexico border, and anti-labor where unions had radicalized the Pacific Northwest. The Klan's decline in the late 1920s followed the failure of key leaders to act within the group's strict moral codes, most particularly in a widely publicized rape, mutilation, and death of a white schoolteacher at the hands of an Indiana Klan leader.[19]

The third Klan resurgence, which trailed the return of veterans from combat in World War II and Korea, mobilized in opposition to the civil rights movement of the 1950s and 1960s. As in the white power movement, the involvement of veterans was instrumental in acts of Klan violence, and showed the early stirrings of paramilitary formation. Paramilitarism was a feature of Klan activity and also appeared in neo-fascist groups such as the Columbians and the American Nazi Party, both of which featured veteran participation in this period.[20]

To be sure, so many men had fought in World War II that the involvement of veterans is hardly surprising. However, not only did some veterans participate in the third-era Klan, but a number of those, according to an undercover reporter observing one group, wore their military insignias and made up a higher percentage of paramilitary Klan units, such as the elite "storm troopers," than the general membership. This, too, would recur in the white power movement. Wearing their military uniforms, such units carried out anti-black and anti-civil-rights violence.[21]

Air Force veteran Robert Shelton's United Klans of America (UKA)—the group Beam would join when he came home from Vietnam—sometimes paraded in military uniforms, and undertook an anti-civil-rights bombing campaign. In the most widely known act of UKA violence, Klansmen acting under the direct guidance of a navy veteran with explosives expertise bombed the Sixteenth Street Baptist Church in Birmingham, Alabama, in 1963, killing four black girls.[22]

Beam's organizing activities reflected his dissatisfaction with the infiltrated and ineffective vestiges of the third era, hobbled by the late 1960s by informants and agents provocateurs working under the FBI Counter-Intelligence Program (COINTELPRO).[23] He implemented the Texas Emergency Reserve, a Special-Forces-style Klan unit with extensive weaponry and rigorous training. When Beam and Duke spoke at a 1979 rally near Dallas, they did so "guarded by Klansmen from Fort Hood who were dressed in

paramilitary garb and armed with pistols, rifles, and bayonets."[24] This recruitment strategy linked military and paramilitary ideas, movements, and
memberships.

The year Camp Puller opened, Beam also created a Special-Forces-style
Klan Border Watch, with elite training, to intimidate undocumented immigrants. Its patrols formalized actions undertaken a few years earlier by
Tom Metzger, Beam's counterpart in the California KKKK. The patrols
functioned both as a publicity stunt and as a way to inculcate real anti-
immigrant hostility and encourage acts of violence. Some patrols worked as
photo opportunities for the press: in one such incident, Duke and California
KKKK members hung "Klan Border Watch" signs on their cars and drove
to the border near San Diego and Tijuana. When no undocumented immigrants appeared, Duke boasted to reporters, "I think some Mexicans are
afraid to enter the country because of the Klan."[25]

By participating in the Klan Border Watch, Klansmen claimed to be doing
the work of the state by enforcing laws already in place and augmenting the
U.S. Border Patrol. Beam described his patrols as vigilantism in the service
of the state. "When our government officials refuse to enforce the laws of
the country," he told a reporter, "we will enforce them ourselves."[26] Strad-
dling the line between the public and private faces of the Klan, the Border
Watch rehearsed more extreme forms of paramilitarism to come, such as the
turn to revolution after 1983.

Beam told a *Dallas Morning News* reporter that the patrol had caught and
illegally detained undocumented immigrants in South Texas.[27] While the
U.S. Border Patrol and several U.S. newspapers dismissed such efforts by
the Klan as a publicity stunt, their intimidation tactics were described in
newspapers in Mexico and as far away as Nicaragua, where one story recounted Beam's claim that Klansmen surveilled the border with private airplanes. An undercover American reporter who posed as an undocumented
immigrant to make the crossing during this period reported, "On the bus,
stories of violence by the Ku Klux Klan at the border—20 murders and the
numerous rapes of women who dared to cross the border—circulated freely.
Such stories, although untrue, aroused fears among the passengers that they
would have to avoid not only the U.S. Border Patrol but the Klan as well."[28]
Whether or not the reporter was too quick to dismiss rumors of Klan violence as patently "untrue," the Klan Border Watch worked to intimidate
crossing migrants—and to bind the patrol's participants in common cause.[29]

Beam's paramilitary methods—as well as a major scandal involving the alleged sale of secret Klan membership information that led to Duke's resignation from the KKKK in 1980—paved the way for his rapid advancement as a Klan leader. Camp Puller alone had trained some 500 men from the KKKK and other groups, and Beam prepared to expand.[30]

Growth depended upon the social and financial investment of a close cohort of Klan supporters, tied to Beam and his growing movement through violent activism as well as through family relationships facilitated by women's participation. Dorothy Scaife, mother of a Klan security forces member, trained at Camp Puller and then purchased adjacent land, which she donated to expand the facilities in 1980. She worked as a trainer and reported to Beam. Besides Scaife, who described herself to a reporter as a former Klan member, several other women helped to run Camp Puller.[31] Beam's younger brother, Phillip Beam, was a co-owner of the Double Bayou land. A third co-owner of the camp's original fifty acres, Robert Sisente, would later say that Phillip Beam ran scuba instruction for trainees at nearby Camp Winnie. Sisente was a forty-nine-year-old Korean War veteran who named Camp Puller after his commanding officer in the Marines. He participated in the Klan Border Watch and worked the security detail at Klan rallies, a position usually held by elite soldiers. Although he was head of the Texas Emergency Reserve and Beam's second-in-command, Sisente claimed to have no knowledge of Klan activities in the camp and said that he was not a Klansman. Louis Beam, on the other hand, spoke freely about Camp Puller as a Klan facility after its presence became public knowledge.[32]

Camp Puller attracted attention in the fall of 1980 with a series of undercover reports and parental complaints. Klansmen had used the facility to instruct a group of high-school-age Explorer Scouts on strangulation, decapitation using a machete, hijacking airplanes, and firing semiautomatic weapons. Trainers at the camp had come close to taking the young Scouts on a Klan Border Watch patrol. As one trainer explained to reporters, they had restaged their own Vietnam War boot camp training for the teenagers.[33]

To Beam and others in the camp, paramilitary training had just as much validity as a military boot camp, and served the same anticommunist mission. Although the publicity generated by the Explorer Scouts fiasco caused Sisente to briefly close Camp Puller in November 1980, Beam expressed no remorse. "Instead of playing baseball or . . . kicking a football around they are learning how to survive," Beam said. "We are operating just as legally as the Boy Scouts . . . or the United States Army."[34] Beam felt he had the right to recruit and train an army to defend his race from the threat of immigration, and to carry out border enforcement on behalf of the state. And as with a military boot camp, violence was meant to do the work of shaping foot soldiers who would be loyal to one another and to his cause.[35]

However, the camps also prepared participants for future antigovernment combat. Beam believed that the United States and the Soviet Union would soon engage in a nuclear struggle but would lack the military strength to follow missile attacks with a land invasion. He planned to wage race war at that moment of vulnerability, after the missile strikes. A white separatist army, he said, could take control of the United States—or at least Texas— expelling all nonwhite people to create a white homeland. It would be convenient that their vehicles, uniforms, and weapons looked like those issued by the U.S. government, with their original army paint and markings; as Sisente told an undercover reporter posing as a recruit, "We may need to pass for National Guardsmen or Army guys someday."[36] "We'll set up our own state here and announce that all non-whites have 24 hours to leave," Beam said to a group of recruits that included the same undercover reporter. "Lots of them won't believe it or won't believe us when we say we'll get rid of them, so we'll have to exterminate a lot of them the first time around."[37]

By 1980, Beam and Sisente were well on their way to collecting enough equipment to outfit and command a paramilitary army. Beam kept a grenade launcher attached to his AR-15 assault rifle, and he had distributed twelve radiation detectors to his troops.[38]

Though Beam and the Texas KKKK dreamed of race war and a white homeland, they did not immediately declare open war on the government. Instead, they chose an enemy that would allow them to frame their violence as serving the state by continuing the Vietnam War against Asian enemies. Following a long history of Klan opportunism, they used local tensions to conscript new recruits in the work of shared violence against a minority group. For this, they looked across Galveston Bay. There, along the Texas coast, the white fishing community had grown increasingly anxious about the arrival of Vietnamese refugees.[39] The white fishermen turned to the Klan for help waging a campaign of intimidation against the Vietnamese.

Although many Americans initially responded to the arrival of Vietnamese refugees with enthusiasm, particularly in the case of refugee children, unease grew as the number of arrivals increased. The refugees arrived in the middle of an economic crisis. By 1974, economic shock had produced stagflation, the perilous combination of rising inflation rates, slow economic growth, and growing unemployment. Gasoline was scarce and expensive, the auto and steel industries struggled, unemployment rose, and hourly wages dipped for the first time in a quarter century. By 1982, nine million Americans were out of work.[40] Although the Sunbelt, including Houston and the nearby Texas coast, fared better than other regions, still people struggled.[41] Under these conditions, Vietnamese refugees—displaced from their homeland by the same military engagement that fomented Klan paramilitarism—looked to some like economic competitors.[42]

Many refugees knew how to shrimp and crab, having done so in waters much like those of Galveston Bay. Moving to the Texas coast from the places where they had been officially resettled by government and sponsor organizations, they arrived in extended families and shared their resources, pooling their money to buy boats. They frequently didn't understand the many official and unofficial rules governing where, when, and how they could fish, and many spoke little or no English. They worked twelve-hour days regardless of the weather, and frequently netted larger catches than their white counterparts. They lived frugally and worked together. As one white fisherman said in frustration, "They ain't beating us with brains . . . they're beating us with a lifestyle. They live eight or ten to a trailer and eat only what they catch. How do you compete with that?" Many white fishermen believed their livelihoods were threatened by the sudden increase in competition, which simultaneously overfished the harbor and flooded the local seafood market, driving down prices.

In Seadrift, Texas, a town of 1,000 people, the arrival of 100 refugees profoundly altered local culture: suddenly, some 10 percent of the population spoke Vietnamese and lived in a very different way than the town's other inhabitants.[43] In August 1979, after a misunderstanding about the acceptable distance between crab traps, a fight in Seadrift ended in the shooting death of a white crabber. Two Vietnamese fishermen were acquitted on self-defense grounds. As tensions increased along the coast, the white fisherman's brother and father told the press that Viet Cong lurked among the refugees.[44]

A white power periodical, the *Thunderbolt,* soon picked up the story, circulating a widely held belief that as the shrimp population dwindled, the federal government was financially supporting the Vietnamese but leaving white fishermen to fend for themselves. False rumors flew that the refugees lived on hefty welfare checks, as well as having smuggled stolen gold out of Vietnam, and bought their boats with their ill-gotten cash. Tensions about refugee resettlement flared nationwide, including on the Texas coast.[45]

For many veterans, economic instability mapped onto an emerging narrative of the lost Vietnam War and its uncelebrated soldiers.[46] "There was a time that I was proud to wear my uniform and ribbons to show I fought in Vietnam. But now I'd be ashamed to because I was a fool," said Gene Fisher, a veteran and Seabrook shrimper who would lead a coalition of frustrated white fishermen. "Uncle Sam has broken his promise to the Vietnam veterans and kept his promise to the Vietnamese."[47]

Fisher's story of government betrayal in Vietnam blended with a lack of government and social support for veterans at home. The government's simultaneous support of Vietnamese refugees fit seamlessly into a worldview compatible with the Klan's anticommunism and racism. Immediately after his tour in the Marines—when he returned to Seabrook on convalescent leave with six wounds from a Claymore land mine—Fisher had been treated like a hero. But as public opinion of the war soured, his life became increasingly difficult. He landed in prison for burglary and assault on a police officer in Nebraska, and served part of a second sentence for interstate transportation of stolen motor vehicles. Two marriages ended. He held unsatisfying jobs, such as working on other people's boats. By 1979, he told the *Houston Post,* he was through with all those troubles and ready for his share of the American dream. But he couldn't become rich because of the refugees, who were in the bay each day, outfishing him and his friends and, significantly, reminding him of the war. He experienced the refugees themselves as "one of those nightmares . . . you can't move and you can't scream."[48] His language pointed to a distress far out of proportion with simple economic anxiety. Fisher came to believe that the refugees were counterparts of the same enemy soldiers who had wounded him in Vietnam.

In fact, the Vietnamese refugees on the Texas Coast represented one of several populations that came to the United States because they were displaced by U.S. military and economic interventions abroad.[49] Ironically, while the white fishermen and Klansmen painted the refugees as Viet

Cong—and the mainstream media picked up this rhetoric in a more tangential way by characterizing the dispute as a continuation of the Vietnam War—several of the Vietnamese fishermen had fought as American allies during the war. Nguyen Van Nam, who would lead the Vietnamese Fishermen's Association, had served twenty-two years in the army of South Vietnam, where he rose to the rank of colonel. He later received American military training at Fort Benning, Georgia. Another had enlisted in the South Vietnamese marines, although he had not seen combat. Ngyuen Luu, association secretary, served twenty years in the South Vietnamese navy, where he was a captain; another fisherman also served in that branch. They, like many other refugees on the Texas coast and nationwide, had come to the United States to avoid reprisals against those who had been American military allies.[50]

In 1980, the first Vietnamese in the area earned their citizenship. The violence rapidly escalated. Three Vietnamese boats and a mobile home were firebombed; two Vietnamese shrimpers were beaten.[51] Guns were fired out in the bay.[52] A group of Vietnamese fishermen were pelted with beer bottles thrown from a speeding car as they walked home from the docks one night. A boat was set adrift.[53] Someone pulled a gun on a Vietnamese fisherman walking across a dock without permission and shot him in the leg. The incident was listed as a "mishap" in later FBI reports, which noted that no "complaint" was filed.[54]

It was not just economic anxiety and mistaken identification of Viet Cong enemies that drove demonization of Vietnamese refugees. The Klan and neo-Nazis also pushed explicitly racist tropes. In their periodicals, the groups accused "boat people" of carrying tuberculosis, malaria, and other diseases to the United States. At times, the articles linked the threat of disease to the threat of sexual violence, as in a widely circulated story of four Vietnamese refugees found guilty of the abduction and gang rape of seven white women in Orange County, California. One of the assailants had leprosy in remission, but the reports in white power publications claimed he had infected his victims. This story tapped into a history of white supremacist rhetoric revolving around the defense of white women from rape by men of color, a theme that would profoundly shape the white power movement in years to come.[55]

Klansmen and fishermen used gendered language and the specter of sexual violence to describe the territory they hoped to defend. Sisente would later testify that the Klan Border Patrol had been named "Operation Hemline" in 1978, evoking both a purported sexual threat of undocumented immigration and the way that the Klan saw white women—conservatively dressed—as embodying a racial nation.[56] Shrimper and Klansman James Stanfield, who had introduced Fisher to Beam at the Klan bookstore in Pasadena, told a reporter, "Galveston Bay is just like a fine woman. . . . If you rape her, she's never good anymore." To Stanfield, the actions of the refugees in securing their livelihoods constituted a sexual violation of American territory.[57]

Sensational reports on Vietnamese refugees in white power publications highlighted radical cultural difference to foment violent responses. Such stories consistently described the refugees as a "flood" that threatened to wipe out white jobs, and claimed refugees were eating neighborhood pets. In one 1980 *National Association for the Advancement of White People News*—the mouthpiece of the new eponymous organization led by David Duke—an article accused the refugees of destroying a San Francisco park by eating its plants and animals, claiming that the refugees ate rats caught in peanut-baited traps.[58]

The most damaging rumors, however, alleged that the refugees were welfare cheats and wards of the state. Anger at these supposed freeloaders provided a bridge between Klan and neo-Nazi publications and a strongly anti-statist current of anti-welfare discourse in the mainstream New Right.[59] As one article in the *Thunderbolt* put it, the "most sickening aspect of all of this" was the idea that white American taxpayers would have to pay for the welfare illicitly received by the single Vietnamese men who were outfishing them. "While welfare is only available to families," the *Thunderbolt* explained, "the 1980 federal refugee assistance program money is granted to aliens for up to three years even if they are single men. . . . Vietnamese are experts at milking such giveaway programs and stay on relief even when making huge sums from fishing."[60]

The rumor that Vietnamese refugees received large welfare payments or came to the United States with smuggled gold shaped the Texas coast community's understanding of them before they even arrived in the area, and affected their treatment once there.[61] When arriving refugees wanted to buy old boats, white fishermen charged them dramatically inflated prices, as much as $10,000 for an old shrimping boat worth perhaps a third of that. Jim Craig, an ally of the refugees, owned a wharf informally known as Saigon

Harbor, where some thirty-five Vietnamese boats docked. "The Americans laughed at them," Craig said, "and sold boats to them for more than the Americans thought they were worth because the Americans thought (it) . . . was 'government money' anyway, because the Vietnamese had received aid." Less than 9 percent of the 23,000 to 25,000 refugees in the Houston-Galveston area, however, received any kind of welfare, and those who did collected $36 per month on average. In Kemah, Texas, at the heart of the conflict, only five refugee families received aid.[62]

As the economic situation continued to tighten along the Gulf Coast, the harassment of Vietnamese fishermen—and those white members of the community who supported and traded with them—further intensified. Whites drove by the homes of the Vietnamese fishermen, throwing beer cans and eggs. Many refugees received death threats. One woman answered repeated telephone calls from an anonymous person who whispered, "Do you know where your children are?" This harassment continued in Seabrook and Kemah, on and off, through the winter of 1980 to 1981. One person pointed a gun at Vietnamese people; someone brandished a pistol in an immigrant's face.[63] The moment was ripe for Klan intervention.

On the night of January 10, 1981, someone ignited a fire on the Vietnamese-run forty-three-foot shrimping boat *Trudy B.* while it was docked in Seabrook. The next night, directly across the channel in Kemah, another fire was set on a Vietnamese-owned shrimping boat. Neither boat was destroyed as a result of the arson.[64] Off-duty police officers reported to the FBI that they had seen three cars with their lights off driving slowly along the docks. The last car, carrying four white males, stopped by the site of the second fire. The occupants got out, donned Klan robes, stood in a group for about twenty minutes, then removed the robes and left. The Houston Arson Task Force assigned to the case believed white fishermen were responsible for the fire, and that both local and Louisiana Klansmen were involved. The FBI's interest in the situation pointed in the same direction.[65]

At first, some local authorities, including Seabrook police chief Bill Kerber, seemed to blame the Vietnamese fishermen, attributing the fires to insurance fraud. But very few Vietnamese-owned boats had any insurance at all.[66] Kerber pointedly mentioned that the Vietnamese had purchased their boats with large sums of cash. "The boats they bought were American boats. They were in very poor condition," Kerber told a reporter. "The Americans saw someone to put it to, and they did. What the Americans saw was a lazy, stupid individual with a lot of money."[67] Clearly, some local officials held their own prejudices against the Vietnamese refugees.

According to FBI interviews, the Texas KKKK had been attempting to intervene in the fishermen's conflict since 1979. Beam later said that the white fishermen had believed the government would arbitrate in their favor, but after two years without action, they finally turned to the Klan for help. The Klan used the moment to solidify a narrative of government failure first in Vietnam and now on the Texas coast.[68] By February, the Texas KKKK had begun its campaign in earnest, deploying paramilitary training and tactics to escalate existing tensions into a ruthless campaign of harassment and arson against the refugees.[69]

On February 14, between 300 and 400 people attended a Klan rally in Santa Fe, Texas.[70] There, Beam burned a small rowboat. He ignited the vessel with a torch, and flames licked across the side where someone had painted "U.S.S. Viet Cong." He did this, he later testified, to demonstrate the correct method for destroying a boat by arson.[71] One of the men attending the rally wore a Klan hood sewn from camouflage fatigues. He embodied the merging of Vietnam War symbols and the local problems of the white fishermen. At the rally, the Klan announced publicly that the government had until May 15—the first day of shrimping season—to get the Vietnamese fishermen out of the Gulf. If the government failed, Klansmen threatened, they would take action.[72]

Klansmen were not the only ones to understand this conflict as part of the Vietnam War. News coverage across the nation, and in major daily newspapers, described the events this way, too. The *New York Times* characterized the Klan harassment of refugees as "one of the last pitched battles of the Vietnam War." The *Houston Chronicle* called an ensuing trial that pitted the Vietnamese fishermen against their harassers the "Viet-Klan proceedings." A *Los Angeles Times* headline described it as a war in its own right: "Texas-Asian Fishing War Heating Up on Gulf Coast."[73] This last might have come closest to the truth. Not only were the symbols, weapons, uniforms, landscapes, and presumed enemies of the Vietnam War framing the latest battle, but a new conflict was beginning. However, these media portrayals fundamentally misconstrued the situation, in which the violence went in only one direction, from white fishermen and Klansmen to the Vietnamese refugees.

In the Klan, white fishermen found sympathy, vitriolic rhetoric, guns, paramilitary training, and an ongoing battle that could frame their struggle. Fisher told the *Los Angeles Times* that fifty-two white fishermen planned to take survival and weapons training from the Klan, presumably at Camp Puller. On March 15, 1981, robed Klansmen went on an armed boat patrol of the bay, carrying long guns and "semi-automatic military rifles," and with a lynched Vietnamese refugee hung in effigy on the rigging.[74]

The boat patrol signaled a move from paramilitary preparation to action by an emboldened white power movement prepared to publicly threaten violence. Months before, a caravan of Klan and neo-Nazi gunmen had opened fire on communist demonstrators in Greensboro, North Carolina—an event that signaled the unification of Klansmen with other white power activists. Now the Greensboro gunmen were rising to celebrity status within the solidifying movement, with one participant joining the armed boat patrol in Texas.[75]

Although some boat patrol participants equivocated about the violent intent of that action, the meaning was clear to the refugee community. The Vietnamese-language local newspaper reported both the boat-burning at the Santa Fe rally and the armed boat patrol. The Klansmen hung "the Vietnamese effigy just like a bag of shrimp," testified Thi D. Hoang. "I understand it as a warning that they would do that to the Vietnamese if they do not do what they want them to do. . . . [M]y boat can still be threatened of destruction. And also I'm also afraid of body injuries, threats to my life." One Vietnamese woman said that she saw one of the Klansmen on the boat point at the house where she was standing. She grabbed her infant niece and ran out of the house. "I don't spend the night in that house anymore," she testified weeks later.[76]

A few weeks later, the *Trudy B.* was ignited again; this time, the blaze destroyed the boat. The Klan burned a cross in Seabrook. Individual threats continued and intensified: someone threatened to burn down one woman's house, others menaced Vietnamese refugees with guns. White harassers threw eggs. A white businessman who traded with the Vietnamese fishermen told the FBI that he was under pressure from the Klan, and that someone had tampered with the brakes on his car. "Unless the authorities do something," the businessman said, "there will be killings."[77]

In the face of this threat, the Vietnamese refugee community came together as the Vietnamese Fishermen's Association and filed a harassment suit with the help of the SPLC on April 16, 1981.[78] Houston attorney David H. Berg appealed to the FBI for a full investigation, and for protection. "It is clear the Klan intends to do harm," Berg wrote. "They are training in paramilitary camps around the State of Texas in the use of automatic and semi-automatic weapons, explosives and other methods of causing mass destruction and death."[79]

Meanwhile, across the bay in Double Bayou, Camp Puller quietly re-opened in April 1981. Sisente continued to publicly disavow his connection to the Klan, although his well-documented involvement in the movement would continue. By the time the Vietnamese Fishermen's Association filed suit, Beam and Sisente had more than doubled the camp's facilities. On one April weekend in 1981, thirty paramilitary soldiers bugled, raised and lowered the flag, paraded in uniform, and held a big Sunday barbeque.[80]

Neighbors knew the camp was open by the bullets flying past their doors. A community of black families lived on one side of the camp, and the white trainees aimed their guns in that direction during target practice, although white neighbors on the opposite side of the camp also reported errant bullets. The local sheriff said that none of the trainees came from the area, and that they were "mostly ex-Marines and all ex-military." The sheriff said his hands were tied. "No one has filed a complaint," he said, "they won't file complaints because they fear reprisal, or potential reprisal."[81]

During the early months of 1981, Beam called for a mediating board to attempt to deal with the conflict on the Texas coast. According to the Klan newspaper *White Patriot,* he wanted the board to include two fishermen, one American and one Vietnamese; one representative of the governor; and "one American and one Vietnamese veteran of the Vietnam war."[82]

Beam's proposal was further evidence of his view that the conflict on the Texas coast restaged the Vietnam War.[83] As Fisher put it in an April 21 press conference, Viet Cong and communist spies had infiltrated the Vietnamese fishermen. Another white fisherman chimed in, "North Vietnamese communists are infiltrating the ranks of the Vietnamese relocated in the Kemah-Seabrook area whose sole purpose is to cause discontent, create fear and conflict among the Vietnamese and stir up incidents with the American fishermen." Prominent Klansman James Stanfield also spoke of communist infiltration.[84] Fisher would later say that this fear of communism, read here specifically as the fear of the Viet Cong, was the reason white fishermen turned to the Klan for support. "We were seeing Communists under every bush then," Fisher testified. Therefore, he argued, the white fishermen were simply continuing a defensive battle against the Viet Cong, waging the war the government had abandoned.[85]

Occasionally other American veterans challenged the way the white fishermen used the Vietnam War to rally support for their cause. For example, when Fisher went before the Seabrook City Council to criticize its condemnation of the Klan, he gave a fiery speech that turned on patriotism, his service in Vietnam, and his war injuries. One city councilman, also a veteran, told the press that Fisher was misusing patriotism. However, the Klan invocation of the Vietnam War often garnered community support.[86] One threatening phone call to the Seabrook Police Department put these sentiments plainly. Although the caller claimed he didn't hate anyone because "he had the love of Jesus in his heart," he said "the only good . . . Viet Cong" was "a dead one."[87] The caller painted all ethnic Vietnamese as Viet Cong. Sometimes this racial confusion extended even further. One white fisherman called Craig's dock "Pearl Harbor" rather than "Saigon Harbor," revealing a slippage between wars, between enemies of Asian ancestry, and between enemies and allies.[88]

Beam looked to the federal government to rectify the situation, demanding that it purchase the boats and resettle their refugee owners elsewhere.[89] The Texas governor, Beam said, should also prevail upon the Coast Guard and the state Parks and Wildlife Department to enforce fishing regulations, but the claim that the Vietnamese fishermen didn't obey fishing laws had lost validity by the spring of 1981. A Texas game warden testified that while the Vietnamese were initially "problem violators" of fishing and safety laws due to language barriers and cultural difference, by 1981 they had "learned the laws very well" and had proportionally fewer violations than U.S.-born fishermen. An FBI background memo filed in May 1981 further noted that the U.S.-born fishermen "only selectively obeyed some of the laws and some of their own customs." Anticommunism, racism, and invocation of the lost Vietnam War fueled the white community's resentment of the refugees—not failure to follow fishing laws.[90]

Many of the Vietnamese fishermen—representing sixty-nine boats—tired of living under such harassment and offered in March 1981 to leave on the condition that the white fishermen buy back the boats. Many even signed bilingual English-Vietnamese documents declaring their willingness to sell, including a clause stating, "I guarantee that, after the boat is sold, I will not buy another one and will not engage in fishing or shrimping activity." However, since the white fishermen had systematically overcharged the refugees—as Craig noted, $3,000 boats had been sold to the refugees for $10,000, and the Vietnamese had then made repairs and improvements that increased the vessels' value—few white fishermen could afford to buy back the boats. So most of the Vietnamese stayed in Galveston Bay.[91]

By this point, depositions had begun in the Vietnamese Fishermen's Association lawsuit against the white harassers, and attorneys for the Vietnamese fishermen filed various motions and complaints that focused on continued Klan involvement. On Beam's instructions, "a robed, pistol-carrying leader of the Ku Klux Klan and a self-described Nazi" took photographs of the Vietnamese as they gave their depositions. Judge Gabrielle McDonald—a young black woman with a strong civil rights background—confiscated the film, but the act was clearly intended to intimidate witnesses. Lawyers claimed that Beam, who arrived to give his deposition in a Klan robe, was visibly armed with a pearl-handled pistol. Beam scornfully denied this, saying the object under his robe was a Bible, all the protection he needed. He added, "Only prostitutes and pimps carry pearl-handled guns and I'm neither."[92]

The SPLC leveraged the trial to bring national attention to the Klan's paramilitary camps. Morris Dees, lead attorney for the plaintiffs, showed the court two videotapes of Beam conducting guerrilla training, saying that several white shrimpers had attended Klan camps "to learn tactics for possible use against the immigrants." One tape was widely played by the mainstream press, airing on NBC's popular show *Today*. At least one expert witness testified that the videos showed Beam "training a viable military organization."[93]

Called to testify, Beam referred to the armed patrols of the bay as "protest," adding, "I like the hell out of the Vietnamese. I think they deserve to get their country back." Implicit in this comment was the idea that the refugees belonged in Vietnam, not in Texas. Beam emphasized the Vietnam War as the context for and validation of his actions, and his own service record as proof of good character. When McDonald rebuked Beam for cursing on the stand, he replied, "I'm sorry, it's the soldier in me."[94]

Meanwhile, Beam continued to spearhead the Klan campaign. A second Santa Fe rally on May 9 was smaller than the February rally, with only about 100 participants. Rain prevented the scheduled cross-burning. Despite the small crowd, new alliances were emerging that signaled the unification and further paramilitary organization of the white power movement. One of the speakers at the rally was Jerry Paul Smith, who had personally shot several communist demonstrators in Greensboro. "I have invited the Greensboro hero from that shooting," Beam said. "You may remember that the Klan lawfully and with the will of God behind them executed five communists in Greensboro." Publicity pamphlets for the rally dubbed Jerry Paul Smith "Greensboro's answer to John Wayne." Also in attendance at the rally were ten blue-uniformed members of the Idaho-based neo-Nazi and Christian Identity group Aryan Nations, including leader Richard Butler. The presence of both Aryan Nations leadership and a Greensboro gunman signaled the growth and national reach of the new movement prepared to wage war on American soil.[95]

Five days later, the court ruled that the Klan did indeed pose a threat to the Vietnamese fishermen. On May 14—the day before the shrimping season would begin in Galveston Bay—McDonald granted an injunction that specifically forbade the Klansmen and white fishermen from carrying guns, wearing Klan robes when in groups of two or more, or burning crosses "where Vietnamese shrimpers live or work around Galveston Bay." The judge also prohibited boat burning, armed boat patrols, threats, assaults, or any other unlawful conduct that could be reasonably foreseen as likely to intimidate the Vietnamese. McDonald backed the injunction by promising to hold violators in contempt of court, and ordered the notice posted at the Klan bookstore and headquarters in Pasadena, Texas, and around the docks on the coast.[96]

Shortly after the ruling, McDonald received a threatening letter from Post Falls, Idaho, not far from Hayden Lake, where Aryan Nations had begun to form. On the letterhead, the sending group called itself the Social Nationalist People's Party, but used the sword logo later made famous by Aryan Nations. The letter, addressed "To YOUR HONOR?," berated McDonald for her ruling in favor of the Vietnamese fishermen. "As a Viet Nam veteran and a white man I am appalled at your conduct from the bench," it declared. Enclosed in the envelope was a widely circulated white power image, a poster titled "Running Nigger Target," featuring an offensive caricature and text endorsing the murder and torture of black people.[97]

Despite the hate mail, tensions on the Gulf Coast quickly subsided after McDonald's injunction. Texas district attorney Mark White intervened in the case in June, shifting its focus away from the specifics of the fishermen and toward the larger problem of the paramilitary camps. At that time, Beam freely admitted to having between one and three operational paramilitary training camps in Texas, including Camp Puller. He would later specify that some of these camps might have been mobile and therefore much harder to regulate.[98]

White issued an injunction stating that the KKKK had "associated themselves together as a paramilitary organization" in violation of a state law that said, in part, "No body of men, other than the regularly organized State Military Forces of this State and the troops of the United States, shall associate themselves together as a military company or organization or parade in public with firearms in any city, or town of this state."[99] Even as White prepared to shut down the camps in Texas, many similar sites were conducting combat training across the country. The Christian Patriots Defense League trained people on hundreds of acres of land in Missouri, West Virginia, Indiana, and Colorado. Near Cullman, Alabama, the Invisible Empire Knights of the Ku Klux Klan ran Camp Mai Lai, named to laud the notorious massacre of civilians in Vietnam. Klansmen told a reporter that similar camps were operational in Mississippi, Georgia, Tennessee, and "two northeastern states," and hinted that another might be up and running in Louisiana. In Missouri, members of the secret society and paramilitary terrorist group the Order would train at a paramilitary camp conducted by the Covenant, the Sword, and the Arm of the Lord, an Arkansas-based white separatist compound—and would later purchase their own paramilitary training facility in Idaho. In North Carolina, white power activists would steal weapons from military installations, and recruit and hire veterans and active-duty personnel to train them in their use at multiple paramilitary camps.[100]

Beyond the camps created specifically for the white power movement's projected race war, others opened to a broader assortment of would-be mercenaries, gun hobbyists, and survivalists. A few camps even catered to leftist paramilitary movements, such as the Brown Berets, a Latino group. These camps often included the instrumental participation of veterans, and used the weapons, tactics, and uniforms of the Vietnam War and its paramilitary outgrowth. Camp Puller and the Klan harassment of Vietnamese refugees were a bellwether of a broader paramilitary turn.[101]

In Texas, the fishermen's dispute ended with the injunction against Klan paramilitarism and with the passage of laws in the Texas legislature putting limits on shrimping, in an effort to control overfishing.[102] On June 4, 1982, Judge McDonald made her injunction permanent. Ruling that the paramilitary training both intimidated Vietnamese refugees and violated state law banning private armies, she disbanded the Texas Emergency Reserve, ordered the Klan to "stop paramilitary training" in Texas entirely, and permanently enjoined the Klan from combat, combat-related training, or parading in public with firearms. The ruling specifically shut down Camp Puller, as well as Camp Bravo at Liberty, Texas; Camp Winnie in Winnie, Texas; and Camp Alpha, location unknown. "Regardless of whether it is called 'defense training' or 'survival courses,'" McDonald told the *Houston Chronicle,* "it is clear to this court that the proliferation of military / paramilitary organizations can only serve to sow the seeds of future domestic violence and tragedy."[103]

However, the white power movement had already garnered too much momentum to be slowed by one court decision. Camps were still up and running in Florida, North Carolina, Idaho, Missouri, Arkansas, Colorado, Mississippi, Tennessee, Indiana, West Virginia, and other states. And in July 1981—well before Judge McDonald's permanent injunction—Beam called in to a radio show on the day he was sentenced on a misdemeanor conviction for conducting paramilitary training on federally owned grasslands without a permit. He had already resigned as Texas KKKK Grand Dragon, but told the radio host that he was up in Idaho on vacation with some new friends: members of the Aryan Nations. It was a sign that the white power movement was consolidating in the Northwest. Beam—whose sentence of ten months' probation and a small fine would soon be overturned on appeal—resigned as Texas KKKK Grand Dragon but soon relocated to Idaho and continued his activities there.[104]

Those watching Beam were close behind. Just before the trial began, the FBI had declared the Texas Klan defunct and not worthy of further investigation. The Bureau closed the fishermen case in 1982, turning its gaze northwest and transferring the records from Houston to its Seattle and Butte, Montana, offices. The FBI was already monitoring Beam and his new Aryan Nations affiliates in Idaho in October 1981.[105]

In the next few years, Beam would pursue his war against nonwhites and develop the cell-style strategy of leaderless resistance. His ideas would teach white power activists how to carry out the revolution he had envisioned in Texas. Despite the court injunction, Beam still saw things the way he had four years earlier:

> We are already aware of Communist agents among the refugee community. . . . There are a number of Vietnam veterans like myself who might want to do some good old search and destroy right here in Texas. They don't have to ship me 12,000 miles away to kill Communists. I can do it right here. They trained me for it, and with sufficient motivation, I'm ready.[106]

Beam continued his war, prepared to kill communists in the United States just as he had killed them in Vietnam.

3   A Unified Movement

> If the Nazis don't get you, a Klansman will.
>
> —*Song sung to the tune of "Sixteen Tons," California Knights
> of the Ku Klux Klan rally, Oceanside, California, 1980*

Virgil Griffin (center) marches with robed and paramilitary-uniformed Klansmen to protest the imprisonment of a white man for the bombing of a black-owned newspaper, Raleigh, North Carolina, 1982. *(Bettmann, Getty Images)*

ON NOVEMBER 3, 1979, a caravan of neo-Nazis and Klansmen fired upon a communist-organized "Death to the Klan" rally at a black housing project in Greensboro, North Carolina. Five protestors died—four white men and one black woman—and many more were injured. Fourteen Klansmen and neo-Nazis faced murder, conspiracy, and felony riot charges. Although three news cameras captured the identity and actions of the Klan and neo-Nazi shooters, all-white juries acquitted the defendants in state and federal criminal trials. A civil suit returned only partial justice. The Greensboro confrontation heralded a paramilitary white power movement mobilized for violence, and also revealed a legal system broadly unprepared to convict its perpetrators.[1]

The shooting at the Greensboro rally was the logical extension of post–Vietnam War paramilitary culture and a series of increasingly violent clashes between the fractious radical left and the nascent white power movement. Sharing a common story of the Vietnam War, disparate Klan and neo-Nazi factions united around white supremacy and anticommunism, and sustained the groundswell by circulating and sharing images, personnel, weapons, and money. In 1979, North Carolina Klansmen had recently discovered a new leader in David Duke. His Knights of the Ku Klux Klan (KKKK), gaining momentum nationwide, had just secured a local foothold in an area with a long tradition of Klan activity and with other active Klan factions. In February, Duke himself came to Winston-Salem to screen *Birth of a Nation*. The 1915 film depicts Klansmen as heroically saving the South— embodied by white women threatened by interracial sex—from the ravages of blacks and northern carpetbaggers during Reconstruction.[2]

While neither the post–Vietnam War KKKK nor the white power movement was primarily southern, the film's invocation of the lost Civil War had particular resonance in North Carolina. For the South, the Vietnam War was not the only American defeat at play in the popular imagination, nor the only war that needed to be reengaged. Indeed, one illustration published in the Alabama-based KKKK newspaper *White Patriot* portrayed a Confederate veteran standing in formation with a Vietnam War–era Green Beret and a third man wearing a Klan hood.[3] At the time of Duke's visit in 1979, the KKKK showed signs of a southern membership surge as well as openness to new alliances: people wearing Nazi armbands, for instance, attended an exhibit of Klan artifacts at a county library in Winston-Salem.[4]

At the same moment, an attack waged by Invisible Empire Knights of the Ku Klux Klan upon black civil rights marchers in Decatur, Alabama, modeled a Klan strategy of forming armed caravans to carry out violence.[5] The Decatur altercation wounded four black demonstrators and resulted in a local ordinance prohibiting guns within 1,000 feet of public demonstrations. The Invisible Empire responded by driving a caravan of vehicles past the mayor's house: "If You Want Our Guns, Come and Get Them," one sign read. The local police chief made no arrests, unsure if the ordinance applied to a moving caravan of cars. The Invisible Empire, helmed by Bill Wilkinson, famously didn't get along with several other Klan factions. Nevertheless, an increasing circulation of newspapers and other printed ephemera had begun to link these groups, and articles about the Decatur clash appeared in Klan and neo-Nazi publications as well as in the mainstream press. The incident foreshadowed the caravan of Klansmen and neo-Nazis that would gun down protestors in Greensboro months later.[6]

In July 1979, local members of the Federated Knights of the Ku Klux Klan and the American Nazi Party arranged another screening of *Birth of a Nation*. This time they chose a community center in the small, working-class town of China Grove, North Carolina, about sixty miles from Greensboro.[7] Members of the Workers Viewpoint Organization (WVO)—which soon changed its name to the Communist Workers Party (CWP)—organized a rally and march in protest. A hundred self-proclaimed communists as well as black community members stormed the community center, armed with clubs. While Klansmen and Nazis stood on the porch with shotguns, a few policemen managed to keep the groups from attacking each other. The Klansmen retreated into the building as protestors damaged the structure and burned a Confederate flag.[8]

The scene was remarkably similar to the final sequence in *Birth of a Nation*, in which the southern family hides in a small cabin as the town is, as the intertitles say, "given over to crazed negroes . . . brought in to overawe the whites." As the "black mob" and the carpetbaggers wreak havoc in town, tarring and feathering Klan sympathizers and attempting to force an interracial marriage, those in the cabin are trapped, hopelessly besieged, until a large cadre of robed Klansmen rescues them, accompanied by the strains of Richard Wagner's "Ride of the Valkyries."[9]

No such rescue party appeared in China Grove. Klansmen experienced the protest as a direct attack. The women huddled in the bathrooms as the men defended the building, vowing revenge. Several Klansmen would later study photographs of the China Grove demonstrators to choose whom to "beat up" in Greensboro on November 3. In the moments before the fatal shooting, a news camera would capture neo-Nazi Milano Caudle murmuring

"China Grove" as he drove past the demonstrators, evoking that earlier clash just before the shooting began.[10]

The CWP, on the other hand, saw China Grove as a success. A Maoist Communist group that advocated political violence, the CWP was largely composed of young, earnest white and Jewish outsiders, many from New York. Several had left jobs as doctors at Duke Hospital to unionize textile factory workers in nearby Greensboro, choosing the town because of its low unionization and the persistent problem of brown lung disease acquired from inhaling cotton fibers. The group also included black activists long involved with the local civil rights movement. While the WVO/CWP claimed a long alliance with the black community in Greensboro, it was a complicated relationship characterized by misunderstanding. Black residents would later express their frustration that the CWP had turned their neighborhood into a site of confrontation without their consent. WVO/CWP leaders claimed China Grove as a victory, ignoring the fears of future violence the confrontation had raised for many group and community members. Following several other Maoist and radical left groups nationwide, the CWP took the official position that organizing against the Klan required aggressive confrontation. They mobilized against what they called a southern Klan resurgence, and against the impact such a movement might have on unionizing and racial cooperation.[11]

The Klan was, indeed, in the midst of a major membership surge. According to watchdogs, the Klan had been 6,500 strong in 1975 but by 1979 had increased to 10,000 active members plus an additional 75,000 active sympathizers. Duke, at the peak of his popularity on the talk-show circuit, boasted that the KKKK had doubled its membership between March 1978 and March 1979. A Gallup poll, furthermore, showed that the number of people with favorable opinions of the Klan rose from 6 percent in 1965 to 11 percent in 1979.[12]

While the local community and national press perceived people on both sides of the Greensboro confrontation as dangerous and violent extremists, they also remained deeply engaged in the anticommunism of the Cold War. The Greensboro community, including local media, saw the Klansmen as local boys defending the status quo and the communists as anarchist outsiders who came to town to make trouble. The communists, with their openly revolutionary agenda, were understood as traitorous, radical, and dangerous in a way that Klansmen were not.

The Greensboro shooting was the culmination of almost two years of in-tense antagonism and repeated clashes between white power groups and the radical left. In July 1978, Tom Metzger, Grand Dragon of the KKKK in California, encountered left-wing opposition when the Maoist Progressive Labor Party (PLP) and Committee Against Racism (CAR) tried to forcibly prevent Metzger's Klan from screening *Birth of a Nation* in an Oxnard, Cal-ifornia, community center. According to the KKKK newspaper *Crusader,* the communists had come to the screening prepared for a fight: "PLP / CAR put over nine police in the hospital, swinging lead pipes rolled in *Challenge* newspapers." The *Los Angeles Times* reported that forty leftist demonstrators had charged the community center, wielding clubs, bottles, and pipes. Po-lice arrested thirteen demonstrators for incitement to riot, assaulting police officers, carrying concealed weapons, and refusing to disperse. Between 180 and 300 more demonstrators—characterized by local police as "mostly Mexican-Americans"—remained on the street, shouting "Death to the Klan, Death to the Klan!" One Klansman, blindsided by a protestor's lead pipe, suffered a broken nose and lost teeth, according to police. Three law enforcement officers and four demonstrators also sustained serious injuries, and seven more policemen reported minor wounds.[13]

Similar incidents across the country showed rising tension between the left and the nascent white power movement. In August, leftists attacked neo-Nazi Michael Breda in Kansas City as he was giving a radio interview—twelve to fifteen men with clubs and pipes broke into the radio station and beat Breda and another member of his group, the American White People's Party. Although the attack lasted less than a minute, Breda and two radio station employees suffered significant head and shoulder injuries. A member of the International Committee Against Racism and the Revolutionary Communists Progressive Labor Party—iterations of CAR and PLP—took credit for the beating. Breda told the *Los Angeles Times* that the same thing had happened during a Houston radio interview.[14]

The next summer, Klansmen gathered in Little Rock, Arkansas. They intended to stage a counterdemonstration to some 1,200 to 1,500 mostly black men and women protesting the rape conviction of a mentally disabled black man. The event stirred memories of the civil rights movement: Little Rock had seen some of its most tumultuous moments around the integra-tion of the city's Central High School in 1957, when federal troops were called in to keep order. As the *Chicago Tribune* reported of the 1979 march, "To preclude violence . . . state and city officials sent in extra men and firepower, including 230 state troopers, a full platoon of Alabama National Guardsmen, two armored personnel carriers, and police from surrounding communities armed with AR-15 semiautomatic rifles and pump-action shotguns." This intense armament foreshadowed another burgeoning paramilitary culture in the escalating militarization of civilian policing.[15]

Two months later, some forty members of Metzger's Klan met to discuss "illegal aliens and Vietnamese boat people and communists and other things" in Castro Valley, California. Thirty chanting and stone-throwing CAR members stormed the meeting to break it up. The Klan swiftly responded with a fifteen-man contingent armed with clubs and plywood shields, dubbed the "Klan Bureau of Investigation." Sheriff's deputies broke up the fight, which resulted in only one minor injury. The speed of the Klan response showed both an escalation from the Oxnard confrontation the previous year and the expansion of group activities throughout California. Although Metzger had militarized his operation as early as 1974 through the Klan Border Watch and other activities, the California KKKK was now regularly prepared for violent confrontation at public events.[16]

As violence came to the fore of the movement, distinctions among white power factions melted away. Klansmen and neo-Nazis set aside their differences, which had been articulated largely by World War II veterans with strong anti-Nazi feelings, as the Vietnam War became their dominant shared frame.[17] White men prepared for a war against communists, blacks, and other enemies. As one Klansman said just after the China Grove altercation, "I see a war, actual combat, eventually between the left-wing element and the right wing."[18]

Klansmen and neo-Nazis united against communism at the same moment that elements of the left fractured and collapsed under the pressure of internal divisions and government infiltration. In Greensboro, for instance, the CWP competed locally with the Revolutionary Communist Party and the Socialist Workers Party. The members of each group refused to speak to each other and more than once came to blows while attempting to unionize the same textile mill.[19]

In contrast, white power activists bound by paramilitarism also developed a cohesive social movement managed through intimate social ties. Intermarriages connected key white power groups, and Christian Identity and Dualist pastors provided marriage counseling. White power activists, who often traveled with their families, stayed at each other's homes and cared for each other's children. They participated in weddings and other social rituals and depended on others in the movement for help and for money when arrested. They founded schools to teach their ideas. The Dualist Mountain Church, for instance, hung Nazi flags and performed cross-burnings, but also held "namegivings," weddings, "consolamentum" ceremonies for the sick, and last rites.[20]

In September 1979, two months before the Greensboro shooting, about 100 neo-Nazis, National States' Rights Party members, and Klansmen of various groups convened in Louisburg, North Carolina. Leroy Gibson, convicted in 1974 of two civil-rights-era Klan bombings, organized the meeting. Gibson, who claimed twenty years of service in the Marine Corps, said that 90 percent of his faction, the Rights of White People, was composed of veterans. Gibson described paramilitary training and free instruction for local high school students. Harold Covington, leader of the National Socialist Party of America, spoke of Nazi paramilitary training camps in two North Carolina counties. "Piece by piece, bit by bit, we are going to take back this country!" he said, holding aloft an AR-15 semiautomatic rifle.[21] A rope noose was strung from a tree outside the lodge "for purely inspirational purposes," as Klan Grand Dragon Gorrell Pierce told an Associated Press reporter.[22] Many activists attended the meeting heavily armed.

Participants called the rally the first North Carolina meeting of Klansmen and neo-Nazis, although the groups had begun cooperating as early as February. Activists understood how World War II affected relations between their groups. "You take a man who fought in the Second World War, it's hard for him to sit down in a room full of swastikas," Pierce said. "But people realize time is running out. We're going to have to get together. We're like hornets. We're more effective when we're organized." Pierce argued that urgent threats—particularly communism—required Nazis and Klansmen to band together.[23] They named their coalition the United Racist Front and pledged to share resources.

Shifting from the openly segregationist language of the civil rights era to a discourse in which anticommunism was used as an alibi for racism, Klansmen spoke publicly of race as a secondary concern. "The one thread that links all Klan factions and other extreme right-wing groups such as

Nazis is hatred of communists," one Associated Press article reported just after the shooting. "Blacks, they say, are pawns of communism, and integration is merely one salvo in the communist battle to destroy the United States."[24]

This strategy drew on a long history of Klan rhetoric that intertwined racial equality, communism, labor organization, immigration, anti-imperialism, and internationalism as threats to the "100 percent American" nationalism early Klans sought to defend. Such ideas were linked not only in Klan rhetoric but also on the left. In Alabama, for instance, the Communist Party attempted in the 1930s to mobilize the same groups targeted by Klan vigilantism and harassment. Communists called the Jim Crow South an oppressed nation, pushed for black self-determination, decried lynching, and defended black men accused of rape. They organized for shorter workdays, better labor conditions, and the right of tenant farmers to engage in collective bargaining. Those who opposed communism in the South—not only the Klan, but many southerners—explicitly associated communism with free love, assaults on the family and on the church, homosexuality, the idea of white women becoming public property, and the threat of interracial sex. In this way, communism and unionization were seen as threats to the white supremacist racial order, which the Klan purported to defend.[25]

In the days before the Greensboro shooting, the men who would join the caravan papered the North Carolina city with posters of a lynched body in silhouette, hanging from a tree. Part of the caption read "It's time for old-fashioned American Justice." (Four years later, the same language and graphic would appear on a poster for Posse Comitatus in the Midwest. The Posse would use the Klan graphic in 1983 to encourage its members to stockpile guns and ammunition in preparation for white revolution. The flier promoted its own circulation: "Reprint permission granted," it read. "Pass on to a friend.")[26]

When the Klan and Nazi caravan drove to Greensboro on November 3, its members expected to wage war on communists. The CWP prepared for confrontation as well, anticipating the brawling that had characterized such clashes in previous years. Several communists wore hard hats. Others armed themselves with police clubs and sticks of firewood. Some brought small guns to the demonstration, though these were mostly left in locked cars.[27]

But the United Racist Front in North Carolina, following the movement at large, had outfitted itself as a paramilitary force. White power activists brought three handguns, two rifles, three shotguns, nunchucks, hunting knives, brass knuckles, ax handles, clubs, chains, tear gas, and mace. Roland Wayne Wood, a neo-Nazi who had served as a Green Beret in Vietnam, had a tear gas grenade, possibly stolen from nearby Fort Bragg; he wore his army boots. They had packed several dozen eggs for heckling and "a .22 cal revolver as fresh as the eggs—a receipt for its purchase was with it." This implied that the Klansmen and Nazis armed themselves particularly for the November 3 confrontation, with plans to use the guns. They also had two semiautomatic handguns and an AR-180 semiautomatic rifle, a civilian version of a military assault rifle. The Vietnam War's guns and uniforms framed this attack, much as the war's narrative framed the larger movement.[28]

Significantly, although the Vietnam War had also impacted the left, the militarization of the left never matched that of the paramilitary right, in part because of the right's cultural embrace of weapons and in part because of the matériel and active-duty personnel that the white power movement continued to draw from the U.S. Armed Forces. Veterans led leftist groups like the CWP, continuing a legacy of protest and armed self-defense begun by veterans of color who participated in civil rights, armed self-defense, and other left movements after homecoming. In Greensboro, one of the CWP leaders, Nelson Johnson, was a local black activist who had fought in Vietnam. While some on the left advocated radical activism in the name of anti-colonial self-determination, however, many wavered on the use of violence.[29]

On the sunny Saturday morning of November 3, 1979, CWP members arrived in Greensboro's Morningside Homes, a black housing project, to stage their widely publicized "Death to the Klan" demonstration. Three television news crews arrived. At a rally preceding the march, protestors—along with a number of children wearing red berets—milled around the intersection, singing protest songs and burning a Klansman in effigy. While the group expected confrontation during the march, they did not expect it at the rally. And, due to a series of command decisions and miscommunications, local police had not provided on-site protection, but instead stationed their cars and personnel several blocks away.[30]

Meanwhile, Klansmen and Nazis convened at a member's home and talked about "getting into some fistfights" with the communists. Caudle showed people a military machine gun and told them he could get more for $280 each. Spurred on by Eddie Dawson, a longtime Klansman and some-time FBI informant, they grabbed guns and formed a caravan of cars. They intended to picket the march, taunting and throwing eggs, but they also brought the guns and planned to use them if necessary. As Klansman Mark Sherer would later testify, "By the time the Klan caravan left . . . it was gen-erally understood that our plan was to provoke the Communists and blacks into fighting and to be sure that when the fighting broke out the Klan and the Nazis would win. We were prepared to win any physical confrontation between the two sides."[31]

As the caravan of cars approached, a news camera zoomed in, refocusing on a Confederate flag license plate. The protestors took up the chant: "Death to the Klan, death to the Klan." People in the caravan screamed racial slurs. A young black man yelled, "Get up," beckoning at the Klansmen and Nazis in the cars. A black demonstrator hit a car with a stick as it accelerated at him; the car swerved wildly at the demonstrators. A teenage white girl shouted from one of the cars, calling the protestors "kikes" and "nigger-lovers." In a pickup truck, Sherer, smiling, hung out of the front window and fired the first shot in the air, with a powder pistol. The air turned heavy with blue smoke. Another Klansman fired, also pointing his shotgun in the air. Sherer fired twice more, claiming later that these shots hit the ground and a parked car.[32]

A young Klansman yelled into the CB radio, "My wife's in one of those cars!"[33] Klansmen and neo-Nazis climbed out of the vehicles and ran toward the intersection. The groups met, fighting with fists and sticks.[34] CWP member Sandi Smith screamed for someone to get the children out of the way; a black woman, eight months pregnant, lost her balance and fell while trying to run away, her legs pelted with birdshot.[35] CWP member Jim Waller retrieved a fellow protestor's shotgun from a parked car, pulled it up, and aimed it at Klansman Roy Toney. They struggled, and the gun fired twice.[36]

As the shots continued, a few communist protestors reached for their handguns. Caudle climbed out of his powder-blue Ford Fairlane and walked calmly around to the trunk, from which he distributed shotguns, rifles, and semiautomatic weapons to six men. One of these men, Klansman Jerry Paul Smith—a cigarette dangling from his lower lip—dropped one knee to the ground, a gun in each hand, as he fired into the panicking crowd. Others took aim and shot, over and over. One gunman, a survivor remembered, passed up a clean shot at a white woman in order to kill Sandi Smith, a black woman, instead.[37] Klansman Dave Matthews, firing buckshot, would later recount, "I got three of 'em";[38] neo-Nazi Roland Wayne Wood, who had a 12-gauge pump shotgun, would claim, "I hit four of the five that were killed and wounded six more."[39] Three minutes after the first shot, twelve Klansmen and neo-Nazis, including Jerry Paul Smith, Wood, Matthews, Harold Flowers, Terry Hartsoe, and Michael Clinton, climbed into a yellow van and drove away. The police didn't arrive until the gunfire had subsided and the yellow van had fled the scene. By then, five protestors lay dead or mortally wounded; as many as seven more protestors and one Klansman were injured, and damage to the Morningside Homes community would reverberate across generations.[40] The dead included Cesar Cauce, shot by a .357 Magnum in the neck, heart, and lungs. Michael Nathan had "half his head shot off." Jim Waller lay dead with fifteen bullets in his body. Bill Sampson was shot in the heart; Sandi Smith was shot between the eyes. Paul Bermanzohn, who survived, was shot twice in the head and once in the arm. He underwent major brain surgery and spent the rest of his life in a wheelchair.[41]

Despite the threats and altercations leading up to the clash, the shooting took Greensboro by surprise. A town of textile mills, rapidly developing Greensboro had a reputation for progressivism but low rates of unionization. The city prided itself on its civil rights history—the Woolworth's of the first lunch counter sit-in of the civil rights movement, in 1960, would become a designated landmark downtown. Greensboro's civil rights record, however, turned on a "progressive mystique" that placed a premium on civility, consensus, and paternalism. While protestors experienced a notably lower level of violence in the Carolinas than in the Deep South, North Carolina was still a stronghold of civil-rights-era Klan activity.[42]

The Greensboro shooting briefly garnered national attention, making *Time, Newsweek,* and the front pages of several major papers including the *Boston Globe, Miami Herald, New York Times,* and *Times-Picayune.* President Jimmy Carter ordered an investigation into Klan resurgence on November 5, and his press secretary announced that a special unit of twenty-five FBI agents had been assigned to the case. Also on November 5, however, the Iran hostage crisis took the front page and held it for some fourteen months.

Greensboro became a strange aside, lost in the inner pages of national newspapers.[43]

But within the white power movement, Greensboro served to energize activists. A few months later, Metzger's KKKK organized another march in Oceanside, California. Local police had to separate Klansmen from counterprotestors, who shouted "Death to the Klan!" as both sides threw rocks and bottles. Klansmen kicked and beat one member of the Revolutionary Socialist League until blood covered his head and face.[44] As they marched, wielding bats, the Klansmen sang a song to the tune of "Sixteen Tons" that lauded the altercation in Greensboro and ended with the refrain, "If the Nazis don't get you, a Klansman will."[45] The U.S. Department of Justice marked 1979 as a particularly violent year, noting that serious Klan violence had increased 450 percent.[46]

The movement drew on anticommunism to classify that violence as self-defense. Klansmen and neo-Nazis involved in the November 3 shooting almost uniformly invoked the Vietnam War to justify their actions. As Klansman Virgil Griffin—the Imperial Wizard of the Invisible Empire KKKK, who had brought a semiautomatic handgun to the November 3 march[47]—said in a public statement long after the shooting:

> I think every time a senator or a congressman walks by the Vietnam Wall, they ought to hang their damn heads in shame for allowing the Communist Party to be in this country. Our boys went over there fighting communism, came back here and got off the planes, and them . . . that they call the CWP was out there spitting on them, calling them babykillers, cursing them. If the city and Congress had been worth a damn, they would've told them soldiers turn your guns on them, we whupped Communists over there, we'll whup it in the United States and clean it up here.[48]

Griffin saw the Vietnam War not only as a war between nations but also as a universal, man-to-man conflict between communists and anticommunists. He had tried three times to enlist, he said, but doctors declared him unfit for duty because of his asthma. Griffin's Vietnam War, real to him, was in the realm of a popular narrative. Within that story, he equated all antiwar protestors with the CWP and all veterans with the Klan.[49]

Michael Clinton, a Klansman who rode in the yellow van on November 3, had a good record of army service, his wife told a reporter. He was drawn into the Klan because of its anticommunism and its paramilitarism. And the wife of caravan member Harold Flowers, the only Klansman injured on November 3, expressed her anticommunism as a common view: "Everybody has concerns."[50]

Following the shooting, the local district attorney's office pressed charges against all fourteen of the Nazis and Klansmen who had been arrested after the melee. Charges included four counts of first-degree murder, one count of felony riot, and one count of conspiracy.

The defendants called upon the Vietnam War story to raise money for their defense. Several of the men from the caravan posed for a photograph in front of the local Vietnam War memorial. The signed photo circulated in the *Thunderbolt* under the heading "Dangerous Communists Killed" and was reprinted in other white power publications. In an attempt to raise money for the defense and awareness for their cause, the photo also appeared in the *Talon*, a white power periodical that made its way—free of charge—to prison inmates.[51]

Trial proceedings began on August 4, 1980, and from the outset reflected the entrenched racism of the North Carolina judicial system. The allowance of peremptory challenges—dismissal of jurors without explanation—meant that the defense could easily select an all-white jury. With fourteen people on trial, the defense had a total of eighty-four peremptory challenges to use at its discretion: defense attorneys dismissed fifteen black jurors for cause and another sixteen peremptorily. This system so clearly produced racially biased juries that North Carolina would abolish it in 1986.[52] In this case, it ensured a jury sympathetic to the defendants.

The all-white jurors were all Christian and therefore likely to be fundamentally opposed to communism, understood in 1979 as a threat to any organized religion and, in the South, tinged with the threat of race mixing. Jurors repeatedly voiced anticommunist rhetoric. Foreman Octavio Manduley, who had fled Fidel Castro's Cuba in the 1960s, spoke frequently to the press about his strident anticommunism, allegedly telling a reporter that the CWP was like "any other Communist organization" and needed "publicity and a martyr." He implied that the CWP had staged the November 3 altercation with the intention of getting one of its members killed in order to bring attention to its cause. His view resonated with a summary presented in the *Thunderbolt*:

"The hitch came when they got more martyrs than they intended." The *Thunderbolt* also reported that Manduley called the Klan "a patriotic organization."[53]

Manduley quickly became a favorite of the white power movement, held up as an example of white, anticommunist, first-wave Cuban immigration. Slain CWP member and fellow Cuban Cesar Cauce, on the other hand, was painted as "a pro-Castro enemy agent" of questionable whiteness. Cauce had come to the United States later than Manduley; the *Thunderbolt* claimed Cauce was "on the first boatlift of so-called refugees. Fidel Castro used the boatlift to empty his prisons and insane asylums of thousands of undesirables to further destabilize America for his planned communist overthrow of the U.S. Government in the future." This passage conflated Cauce's arrival with the 1980 Mariel boatlift, which Castro had indeed used to move inmates to the United States. The white power focus on immigrants as communists and as threats to whiteness was a thread that connected the Greensboro shootings to the Klan harassment of Vietnamese refugees on the Texas Coast.[54]

Although later proceedings would cast doubt on whether Manduley had really expressed views that the Klan was "patriotic" and the neo-Nazis were "strongly patriotic," at least one juror did make those comments.[55] Other jurors and potential jurors expressed sympathy with the defendants or distrust of the CWP. One prospective juror said of the gunmen, "I don't believe that they were guilty of anything but poor shooting." Another said of the slain, "I think we are better off without them."[56] One juror, the wife of a sheriff's deputy, commented after the not-guilty verdict, "I'm really worried about the spread of communism."[57] A man who was chosen as an alternate juror said he believed that it was less of a crime to kill a communist than to kill someone else. According to the *Thunderbolt,* another juror "stated that the communists got themselves in too deep when they challenged the Klan to attend their 'Death to the Klan' rally. . . . The Klansmen were simply the superior marksmen."[58]

Those responsible for the prosecution of the gunmen also reportedly expressed prejudice. Even district attorney Mike Schlosser drew connections between peacetime communist protestors in North Carolina and communist soldiers abroad; when asked by a reporter about his ability to objectively prosecute the Klan and neo-Nazi gunmen, Schlosser referenced his own experience fighting in Vietnam and added, "And you know who my adversaries were there." In another public comment, Schlosser reportedly said that the Greensboro community felt the CWP members got what they deserved.[59]

Besides the anticommunism that framed the proceedings, the state trial failed to take into account the role of two government informants who had foreknowledge of the Greensboro shooting and may have actively incited the altercation. Neither prosecution nor defense called them as witnesses. Two other key witnesses against the white power activists also refused to testify because of their fear of reprisal, surrounded as they were by a paramilitary and demonstrably lethal white power movement.[60]

Public distrust of the CWP mobilized sympathy for the white power gunmen. Furthermore, CWP members repeatedly undermined their chance at what justice the court could offer. Several of the women widowed on November 3 confounded the Greensboro community when, instead of weeping or grieving, they stood with their fists raised and declared to the television cameras that they would seek communist revolution.[61] Days after the shooting, an article appeared in the *Greensboro Record* that was titled "Slain CWP Man Talked of Martyrdom" and implied that the CWP had foreknowledge of the shooting and that some planned to die for the cause. This damaged what little public sympathy remained. In language typical of mainstream coverage, the story described the CWP as "far-out zealots infiltrat[ing] a peaceful neighborhood." Even two years later, when the widows visited the Greensboro cemetery and found their husbands' headstone vandalized with red paint meant to symbolize blood, they would not be able to effectively mobilize public sympathy.[62]

Community wariness of the CWP's militant stance only increased after the CWP held a public funeral for their fallen comrades and marched through town with rifles and shotguns. The fact that the weapons were not loaded hardly mattered: photographs of the widows holding weapons at the ready appeared in local and national newspapers. In the public imagination, these images inverted the real events of November 3, when a heavily armed white power paramilitary squad confronted a minimally armed group of protestors. The defendants, depicted as respectable men wearing suits in front of the Vietnam War memorial, stood in stark contrast to the gun-toting widows.[63]

National and local CWP members took up a campaign of hostile protest of the trial itself. The day before testimony began, the CWP burned a large swastika into the lawn of the Bureau of Alcohol, Tobacco, and Firearms director, and hung an effigy on his property with a red dot meant to convey a bullet wound. In the trial itself, CWP members refused to testify, even to identify the bodies of their fallen comrades. CWP widows who shouted that the trial was "a sham" and emptied a vial of skunk oil in the courtroom were held in contempt of court. Although the actions of the widows may have "shocked the court and freaked out the judge," as the CWP newspaper *Workers Viewpoint* proudly reported, the widows' "bravery" didn't translate as such to the Greensboro community.[64] Even those who may have sympathized with the CWP after seeing the graphic footage of the shooting soon found that feeling complicated by the group's contempt for the justice system, however problematic that system was.

With the CWP widows refusing to tell their stories, attorneys for the defendants built a self-defense case by deploying two widely used white power narratives: one of honorable and wronged Vietnam veterans, and the other of the defense of white womanhood. The defense depended on the claim that CWP members carrying sticks had threatened Renee Hartsoe, the seventeen-year-old wife of Klansman Terry Hartsoe, as she rode in a car near the front of the caravan. Terry Hartsoe testified that he could see the communist protestors throwing rocks at the car and trying to open the door. Such a statement can be seen as alluding to the threat of rape of white women by nonwhite men, a constant theme throughout the various iterations of the Klan since the end of the Civil War.[65] White supremacy has long deployed violence by claiming to protect vulnerable white women.

To bolster the claim that the CWP had started the fight, and that the Klansmen and Nazis had acted in self-defense, attorneys called an expert witness from the FBI. Based on the locations of the news cameras that had recorded the altercation, he said, he could pinpoint the origin of each shot with new sound-wave technology. Using this new and insufficiently tested method—later broadly discredited—he testified that the CWP had fired several of the first shots. In other words, the defense convinced the jury that the CWP had started the fight. However, under North Carolina law, the claim of self-defense should have been limited to defendants free from fault in planning or provoking a confrontation. Even had the CWP fired first, the Klansmen and Nazis intended to incite a fight, and had planned it in advance. Their armament alone, and the receipts that showed the timing, indicated as much.[66]

Meanwhile, some defendants showed little or no remorse for the five deaths and numerous injuries that resulted from the shooting. Defendants testified at the trial that members of the white power movement had displayed autopsy photographs of the CWP victims at a Klan fundraising rally on September 13, 1980. Jerry Paul Smith had obtained copies of the autopsy photos, as well as photos of the dead and mutilated victims taken just after the shooting, from the office of one of the defense attorneys. Smith said someone had displayed the photos at the Klan rally without his knowledge, and that he asked for them to be put away when he saw them.[67]

The jury spent long hours watching the footage of the shooting—forward, backward, and in slow motion—and witnessed the raw violence of the event. However, jurors heard nothing of the Klan's use of graphic photographs of the victims for fundraising; they were out of the courtroom when this information came to light. Prosecutors argued that the "jury should hear the testimony, saying it shows the Klansmen acted with malice and have no regrets about the deaths of five Communist Workers Party members," but the judge disagreed. The jury deliberated without accounting for the continuing violence manifested in the circulation of those images, including profiting from the photographs of the wounded, mutilated, and dead. Such action recalled a long history of circulating lynching photographs. The white power movement was using the pictures to raise money not only for the defense of the "Greensboro 14" but also for acquiring weapons to use in future violent actions—including a projected race war.[68]

On November 17, 1980, the jury arrived at a unanimous not-guilty verdict after six days of deliberation and twelve major votes. Surprised Klansmen and neo-Nazis wept. The verdict was a national news story. *Saturday Night Live* even ran a sketch depicting the opening day of "Commie Hunting Season." The performance received little laughter and scant applause from the live studio audience, and NBC received 150 phone complaints that it was offensive. Perhaps the accuracy of the sketch, despite its overwrought redneck accents and heavy-handed satire, rendered it humorless. The basic point, that a court had effectively condoned the intentional killing of communists, rang true.[69]

After the acquittal, the white power movement amplified its praise of the Greensboro 14. The *Thunderbolt* reported at length that the men showed courage during the long trial, from praying and singing "God Bless America" in jail to their heroic homecoming. Family, neighbors, and fellow

Klansmen cheered for Smith when he returned home, where "he proudly wore a [Confederate States of America] belt buckle and flew the Confederate flag over his house. One neighbor . . . remarked: 'I've said all along they ought to pin a medal on those boys.'" A journalist reported that Smith's "feelings toward blacks have softened, partly because of black prisoners he met in jail." His alleged contrition didn't last long. Two days later, Smith crashed his car after exchanging gunshots with an unknown person.[70]

Smith had testified in court that, after a blow to the head, he had no memory of firing into the crowd in Greensboro with a gun in each hand. But he soon traveled to Texas to recount the shooting as a guest speaker at a rally of Klansmen mobilizing against Vietnamese refugees. By 1984, members of the movement could buy a ninety-minute interview of Smith on audiocassette, in which he retold the shooting in detail. The story he allegedly didn't remember became his currency and celebrity within the movement.[71]

Indeed, the white power movement took the acquittal as a green light for future action. The Aryan Nations organ *Calling Our Nation* ran photographs of neo-Nazis in Detroit marching with signs reading "Smash Communism: Greensboro AGAIN." To some, the trial stood as one battle won in a global war against communism, the same war they had fought in Vietnam. As Klansman and defendant Coleman Pridmore remarked: "This is a victory for America. Anytime you defeat communism, it's a victory for America. The communists want to destroy America, to tear it down, and they should be tried for treason."[72]

The Greensboro case went to trial again on January 9, 1984, this time under civil rights laws in federal court. Although an appeals court blocked a court-ordered federal investigation into "charges of high-level government involvement" under the Ethics in Government Act, this time the court did allow investigation into the role of government informants who provoked or failed to prevent the altercation.[73] The FBI and ATF had long used undercover agents in attempts to arrest members of fringe groups on both left and right, and would continue to do so in the years that followed. However, the 1971 end of COINTELPRO made it illegal for undercover operatives to act as agents provocateurs or to initiate or incite violence. The first man in question, Eddie Dawson, was a longtime Klansman who had occasionally reported information to the Greensboro Police Department and FBI. The second, Bernard Butkovich, was a career ATF agent working undercover.[74]

According to three neo-Nazis and one Klansman, Butkovich—posing as a trucker interested in the movement—had foreknowledge of the Greensboro caravan and did not report it to other agents, his superiors, the FBI, or local law enforcement. He allegedly suggested several illegal activities, encouraging people to get equipment used to convert weapons to fully automatic function and suggesting the assassination of a rival Klan leader. Group members also said Butkovich advised white power activists to harbor the November 3 fugitives after the shooting. The Klansmen and Nazis didn't take any of his suggestions. Butkovich defended his actions—with the support of his superiors in the ATF—by saying that these statements were necessary to establish him as a credible member of the group for future intelligence-gathering purposes. Butkovich had met Covington and Wood at a White Power Party rally in Ohio in June 1979, but his wire had gone dead, failing to record a lengthy section of their meeting.[75]

Eddie Dawson, on the other hand, actively worked to plan and provoke the November 3 clash. Dawson gave speeches to fire up the Klansmen and Nazis to protest the CWP rally, according to Klansman Chris Benson's later trial testimony. And police knew that Dawson was bringing the Klan to confront the CWP. They knew the Klansmen had eggs and planned to heckle, and that they had guns. They knew Virgil Griffin was involved, that he had "a hot head with a short fuse," and that he frequently carried weapons.[76]

Dawson obtained a copy of the CWP parade permit prior to November 3 and so he knew where to find the communists. That day, he urged the caravan members to hurry to the CWP rally. At the same moment, the Greensboro Police Department ordered two officers on an unrelated call away from the neighborhood, and sent the rest of the force to lunch. As a result of this sequence of events—as well as prior confrontations between the CWP and the local police that had led the latter to decide that officers would protect the demonstration from afar—no police officers were on the scene when the shooting began.[77]

The evidence in the federal trial clearly established that the earlier claim of self-defense could not stand. As one prosecutor noted, the Klansmen and Nazis "fired 11 shots before any shot was fired in return," by which point they had wounded several people. Mark Sherer, who had by then quit the Klan, testified that Griffin had planned to incite a race war in North Carolina and that Smith had experimented with making pipe bombs. Butkovich had overheard a Klansman say the explosives would "work good thrown into a crowd of niggers," but had failed to mention bombs in his ATF paperwork. Sherer now indicated that the Klansmen and Nazis fired the third and fourth shots, which had been attributed to the CWP by faulty sound analysis in the state trial.[78]

Despite substantial evidence to discredit the claim of self-defense—and despite the full cooperation and testimony of the CWP—the federal trial exonerated the Klansmen and neo-Nazis a second time. Prosecutors sought to prove that by shooting and killing them, the Klansmen and neo-Nazis denied the CWP members their civil rights for reasons of race. To make this case, the jury instructions specified, the prosecution had to show that race was the "substantial motivating factor" behind the violence. The defense countered that the Klansmen and neo-Nazis acted on political, not racial, motives. They were, as they had said repeatedly, trying to defend the United States from communism. And since the connection between anticommunism and racism in the ideology of white power activists went unexplained, the Klansmen and neo-Nazis walked free again in April 1984.[79]

The third and final trial began in March 1985. In a civil suit, the CWP widows and eleven injured demonstrators sought monetary damages from the Klansmen, the neo-Nazis, Dawson, Butkovich, the Greensboro Police Department, the City of Greensboro, the State Bureau of Investigation, the FBI, the ATF, and more. The judge dismissed several of these defendants, including the federal agencies that had sovereign immunity, and also dismissed a number of unknown "John Does" because charges against them were too vague. The case went to trial with sixty-three defendants.[80]

Attorneys for the plaintiffs called seventy-five witnesses over eight weeks; the defense lasted four days. In the most dramatic moment of the trial, former Klansman Chris Benson testified that he had previously lied in court because he feared retaliation. Benson had been the second-highest-ranking Klansman in the Greensboro caravan, and in earlier trials had maintained that the CWP demonstrators provoked the violence. Now he said that white power activists had intended to provoke a confrontation. In cross-examination by Klansmen and Nazis representing themselves, Benson "said he had particularly feared the 'underground Klan,' which he described as a paramilitary group that would 'carry out acts to intimidate people.'" Benson named members of the paramilitary Klan, including co-defendant Dave Matthews, and added, "I saw Mr. Matthews shooting at people in Greensboro who were running away from him."[81]

Benson, reformed and contrite, stood in stark contrast with most of the other defendants. On the first day of the trial Roland Wayne Wood wore "an olive drab T-shirt with the phrase 'Eat lead, you lousy red' printed next to an image of a man in camouflage fatigues spraying automatic weapon fire." Because Wood chose to represent himself in the civil trial, he wore the shirt in court while acting as a part of the U.S. justice system.[82]

Despite compelling evidence, the jury, which this time included one black member, delivered only partial justice. In June 1985, it found some of the absent policemen and some of the white power gunmen—Dave Matthews, Jerry Paul Smith, Roland Wayne Wood, Jack Fowler, and Mark Sherer—jointly liable for one of the five deaths and two of the many injuries. Significantly, the only death found wrongful was that of Michael Nathan, the only one of the five people killed who was not a card-carrying CWP member. It might be wrong to shoot bystanders, the decision confirmed, but there was nothing wrongful about gunning down communists. The City of Greensboro paid the full amount of the settlement, covering the costs for Klansmen and neo-Nazis.[83]

Once again, the white power movement took the settlement payment as endorsement of violent action. As Klansman and *Thunderbolt* editor Ed Fields wrote in his 1984 personal newsletter, "We must increase activity while we are still free—while juries made up of God fearing White people will free our street activists such as in the Greensboro case."[84] Louis Beam, too, saw Greensboro as a success for the movement. In a film of Beam's paramilitary camps in Texas circa 1980, he told the camera, "When the shooting starts, we're going to win it, just like we did in Greensboro."[85]

The Greensboro shooting had the effect of consolidating and unifying the white power movement. Most directly, caravan participant Glenn Miller would use the shooting to leverage state leadership in the North Carolina Knights of the Ku Klux Klan, which would soon change its name to the White Patriot Party, uniform its members in camouflage fatigues, and march through the streets by the hundreds. In his increasingly revolutionary *Confederate Leader,* Miller expressed pride about the shooting even six years afterward.[86] A veteran who served two tours in Vietnam as a Green Beret, Miller used paramilitary camps to prepare his new white army for race war, recruited active-duty soldiers, and obtained stolen military weapons. Soon he would align his force with the white power terrorist group the Order.[87]

The idea of worldwide struggle against communism also aligned the Greensboro gunmen with antidemocratic paramilitary violence in other countries. *Thunderbolt,* for instance, called it "very strange" to hear President Ronald Reagan "pleading for money to send to guerillas" fighting against communists in Nicaragua and El Salvador when "right here in America we have a clear case of White Christian family men being shot at by communists who returned fire in a perfect case of self-defense."[88] To the movement, there was little difference between white power gunmen at home and paramilitary fighters who worked to extend U.S. interventions abroad.

Harold Covington, an American Nazi Party Leader and veteran who claimed to have been a mercenary soldier in Rhodesia, did not participate in the Greensboro caravan, but sent several of his men to the skirmish. Shortly before the shooting, Covington wrote a letter to the Revolutionary Communist Party, which he mistook for the CWP. "Almost all of my men have killed Communists in Vietnam and I was in Rhodesia as well," he wrote, "but so far we've never actually had a chance to kill the home-grown product."[89] Covington, who saw himself as a person who killed communists—he killed them abroad and he intended to kill them at home—showed how violence at home and anticommunist interventions abroad would link white power organizing with a network of mercenary soldiers who waged war in Central America and beyond.

4   Mercenaries and Paramilitary Praxis

> Wild men . . . doing wild things.
>
> —*State Department official on mercenaries in Nicaragua*

Frank Camper instructs trainees in use of machine guns at a camp for prospective mercenary soldiers, Alabama, 1985. (© *Eli Reed, Magnum Photos*)

TOM POSEY WAS so eager to fight communists that he attempted to join the Marines early, at sixteen. When he came of age in 1964, he did enlist in the Marines and served in Vietnam, rising to the rank of corporal by 1966. He also joined the Alabama National Guard and explored right-wing groups, having become a member of the anticommunist and ultraconservative John Birch Society in 1963.[1] After coming home from Vietnam, Posey found that life as a wholesale grocer bored him: "Peacetime is miserable, sitting on my butt."[2] He considered several avenues for paramilitary activism, both racist and anticommunist. In 1979 Posey attended a Klan action in Decatur, Alabama, his hometown. There, around 100 members of the Invisible Empire Knights of the Ku Klux Klan, armed with bats, clubs, and guns, attacked a civil rights demonstration. They inflicted major injuries and shot two civil rights demonstrators in the head and face. While the FBI did not find sufficient evidence to charge the Klansmen, the Southern Poverty Law Center would file a civil lawsuit that reopened the case. Four Klansmen were later found guilty of criminal charges, and ten were bound by consent decrees in settling the civil suit.[3]

Instead of delving into the domestic white power movement, however, Posey took a different route. He formed a new group that used similar guiding principles for violent action, Civilian Military Assistance (CMA). Drawn largely from Vietnam veterans and active-duty National Guardsmen in the South, CMA described itself as a civil organization dedicated to supporting anticommunist combat in Central America with supplies, weapons, and manpower.[4] CMA conducted vigilante patrols of the U.S.-Mexico border, adopting the tactics of the earlier Klan Border Watch, and contributed mercenary soldiers to the Contras, a loose alliance of paramilitary groups that sought to overthrow the leftist Sandinista government in Nicaragua after the 1979 revolution. In Nicaragua, CMA acted covertly on behalf of the U.S. government—it was funded by the CIA and supplied by the U.S. military.[5] Under President Ronald Reagan, the state's semi-official interventions would swell into a bustling, multilayered network of mercenary soldiers, CIA operatives disguised as rogue mercenaries, and civilian veterans doing the work of state military advisors, all participating in a frenzied effort to circumvent public opinion and congressional checks, to contain or roll back communism, and to redeem the loss in Vietnam.[6]

Posey's engagements are one example of the complex interconnections between U.S.-sanctioned covert intervention in Central America, white power activism, and the actions of independent mercenary soldiers. He formed the CMA as an alternative to, but in common cause with, the domestic white power movement. He used his organization to move the soldiers, weapons, and symbols of the Vietnam War to the fight against communism in Central America. He saw himself as more than a "standard mercenary" who fought without "scruples or morals"—Posey's battle cries featured a strong belief in God intertwined with virulent anticommunism. He would gladly shoot any American citizen who aided the cause of communism. "I wouldn't shoot them as individuals," he explained. "I would be shootin' them as communist."[7] For Posey, as for the Greensboro shooters and others in the white power movement, killing communists provided an opportunity for like-minded combatants to join forces. Mercenary soldiers—civilians who fought for money and for free in the anticommunist skirmishes of the Cold War—honed an antidemocratic praxis some would later use to structure acts of violence on U.S. soil.

In parallel with the way white power activists in Greensboro understood themselves as participating in a global war against communism, mercenaries such as Posey expressed approval of acts of white power violence at home.[8] Links between white power activists and mercenaries were strong and sustained. In Rhodesia, where between 1965 and 1980 as many as 2,300 American mercenaries defended the white minority-rule government, soldiers for hire included John Birch Society members and neo-Nazis.[9] One gun dealer and former Klansman who later sold a cache of fourteen AR-15 assault rifles to the white power terrorist group the Order claimed to have been "approached by people in Alabama who I am now told were undercover agents for the government about engaging in gun running to South America," presumably CMA. Although he declined the sale, the attempt reveals continued interconnection between the CMA and the white power movement.[10]

White power activists focused keenly on Central America, traveling there with frequency. Louis Beam, a national-level movement leader, made several trips to Mexico and Costa Rica for reasons ranging from evading arrest to obtaining cheap medical care, participating in business ventures, and possible money laundering and arms deals.[11] Members of the Order had supplied the Contras and reportedly guarded a Costa Rican gold mine secretly owned by the Covenant, the Sword, and the Arm of the Lord, an Arkansas white separatist group. The story about the mine may be apocryphal, and cannot be verified in the archive. But by the mid-1980s, the Order did regularly produce false Costa Rican identification for its members, as one member had spent time there. Movement interest in the region was marked and intense, if not fully illuminated by archival sources.[12]

Although the number of veterans who became mercenary soldiers represents a very small percentage of the men who served in the Vietnam War, their activities made a profound impact—both in politics and in violence— in countries throughout the Third World. Veterans who used their combat training in Vietnam to act as mercenary soldiers elsewhere brought the war's violence to new battlefields and new enemies. Between the 1960s and the end of the Cold War, American mercenaries fought to preserve white minority-rule governments in Rhodesia and South Africa, and in Latin America and the Caribbean they propped up U.S.-supported regimes, opposed leftist movements, and attempted to overthrow leftist governments. Some traveled back to Southeast Asia, where they supported anticommunist actors and regimes, and to Angola and the Congo, where they augmented U.S. support of guerrilla factions that opposed the Soviet Union.

Posey saw himself and CMA as protecting the United States from a threatening Red menace. He believed the government wasn't doing the job because politicians refused to deploy sufficient force to let soldiers win. He invoked a series of failed military actions in Korea, Vietnam, and the Middle East that he attributed to half-hearted U.S. commitment.[13] Posey's Vietnam War memories structured CMA and, by extension, shaped a significant element of the CIA involvement in Central America. Others, too, perceived the American mercenaries as continuing the Vietnam War. In Rhodesia, for instance, one author described the civilian-targeted violence carried out by mercenaries as "transplanted American methods of dealing with the Viet Cong in Vietnam."[14]

The circuit that brought mercenary soldiers to the Third World moved other vestiges of the Vietnam War as well: weapons, technologies, strategies, and slang. The struggle to continue white minority rule in Rhodesia deployed planes and helicopters left over from Vietnam, as well as field cannons, rifles, tanks, and 900 tons of small arms and mortars. An estimated 15,000 mercenaries accounted for as much as 60 percent of Rhodesia's white army, and included soldiers from around the world. The contingent of Americans was relatively small—between 40 and 2,300—but left an indelible cultural imprint. Elite fighting units within the Rhodesian army were modeled after the U.S. Army Special Forces. Even the word "gook" had made a transnational circuit—beginning as "gugu" to describe territorial subjects during the U.S. conquest of the Philippines, the term "gook" migrated to the anticommunist war in Korea, was widely used to disparage enemies and civilians alike in Vietnam, and eventually became shorthand for the enemies of mercenary soldiers in various African countries.[15]

The linkage between domestic anticommunism, white power organizing, and intervention abroad found more public backing in some conflicts than it did in others. For instance, U.S. foreign policy did not support the white supremacist wars in Rhodesia and South Africa, at least in part because of President Jimmy Carter's commitment to human rights and his dedication to race-neutral democracy as a moral issue at home. Although some people in and beyond the white power movement organized to support overtly white supremacist conflicts in southern Africa, it was difficult for many Americans to reconcile these with the new, post-civil-rights racial mores. The Carter administration also argued that transition to majority rule in southern Africa would better prevent communist revolution there in the future.[16]

Central America provided an opportunity with wider appeal. There, mercenaries were only one weapon in an extensive arsenal of covert Cold War strategies. In the years before the Iran-Contra scandal became public in 1986, the United States co-opted, advised, funded, condoned, and created an assortment of local actors, mercenary soldiers, and CIA operatives that worked to support anticommunist regimes, unseat leftist governments, and keep right-wing, military, and counterrevolutionary governments in place throughout the region.

Mercenaries fought in places where they believed they could redeem the defeat of the Vietnam War, this time against new communist enemies. Posey spoke of the enemy in Vietnam as indistinguishable from civilians, and largely saw communists in other sites as interchangeable with those he had fought under more official auspices. Speaking of Central America, he said:

> I take it for granted that if we're down there and we get shot at, those other people must be the communists. If somebody's shooting at you, they sure as heck ain't your friend. . . . In Vietnam . . . who were the soldiers? Who was the [Viet Cong]? The ones in pajamas? Everybody wore black pajamas. You didn't know until after the battle. If they was laying there with a rifle in their hand that was made in Russia and you got men laying down here dead with Russian bullets in them, then they must have been the communists.[17]

Anyone who fired at Posey was, to him, a communist. A banner in the background of an iconic press photo of Posey vividly summarized this worldview: "Kill 'Em All, Let God Sort 'Em Out."[18]

Mercenary combat made visible the interchanges between white power activism and more mainstream paramilitary culture. For instance, the slogan "Kill 'Em All, Let God Sort 'Em Out" appeared regularly in the paramilitary magazine *Soldier of Fortune.* Founded in 1975 by Special Forces veteran Robert K. Brown, *Soldier of Fortune* had 35,000 subscribers, 150,000 newsstand sales, and an estimated 300,000 casual readers in the mid-1980s. The magazine's content appealed to a readership that included gun hobbyists, hunters, survivalists, and armchair adventurers. While it did not espouse white power rhetoric, it did appeal to activists through its extensive coverage of issues relevant to the movement, such as white minority rule in Rhodesia, and its many articles on weapons and matériel, martial arts, urban warfare, survivalism, and other skills relevant to the white power reader.[19]

Similarly, Posey's stance reflected not only the thoughts of mercenaries on the fringe but an interventionist current in mainstream conservatism that gave rise to increasing paramilitarism within the Reagan administration itself. In the 1980s, Central America became the testing ground for an escalation in anticommunist foreign policy pursued through a series of brutal covert interventions. The policy came under intense public scrutiny when the Iran-Contra scandal broke in 1986. While those in government shied away from public statements using the kind of directly dehumanizing language that mercenaries would employ so freely, U.S. foreign policy in Central America nevertheless generated a civilian-targeted, body-count-oriented violence that recalled popular representations of combat in Vietnam.[20]

The paramilitary turn, in both popular culture and foreign policy, built upon decades of counterinsurgency strategy and crystallized around the loss of the Vietnam War. The public at large hesitated to engage in new wars, and members of Congress elected by the antiwar and leftist social movements of the 1960s and 1970s sought to limit presidential power to send troops into action. The War Powers Resolution, passed over President Richard Nixon's veto in 1973, set strict limits on when, how, and for how long the executive branch could send American soldiers to war. Advocates of intervention believed that waging new wars that could redeem the loss in Vietnam could stop the spread of communism. However, they faced a major obstacle in the public and legislators' reluctance to commit the country to new conflicts. Antiwar attitudes from the defeat in Vietnam softened in the 1980s, but the public remained resolutely opposed to a draft and to any tax increases needed to pay for large-scale military operations. Instead of big war, the United States increasingly fought communism through covert interventions and the support and use of U.S.-trained local counterinsurgent units.[21]

A fundamental contradiction of the Cold War was that the United States frequently allied with antidemocratic governments to carry out a foreign policy that purported to protect freedom and democracy. Containment under Presidents Richard Nixon and Jimmy Carter sought to stop the spread of communism. President Ronald Reagan adopted a more aggressive roll-back policy that sought to unseat communist and leftist governments where they already held power. In practice, this meant opposing anticolonial revolutions and struggles for self-determination that swelled through the Third World in the 1970s and 1980s. Increasingly, America's attempt to protect democracy at home by preventing communism from approaching its borders resulted in the violent suppression of democratic and popular political change abroad.[22]

This contradiction employed a definition of democracy that broke a long bond between the notions of liberty and social responsibility. Instead, liberty was linked with free enterprise. Revolutions for self-determination were often deemed communist, and thus threats to be contained. Not only did this occlude a long American intellectual tradition joining democracy with social welfare—an idea codified during the New Deal, refined by the emergent discourse of human rights after World War II, and embraced in the social movements of the 1960s—but it further aligned U.S. democracy with aspirations to global dominance.[23]

Indeed, Nicaragua became a stark example of the contradiction between U.S. intervention in the name of preserving democracy and opposition to popular revolutionary movements. President Anastasio Somoza Debayle was a U.S.-supported dictator notorious for the kidnapping, torture, and assassination of his political opponents, although he was friendly to U.S. business and political interests in the region. The Somoza family had ruled Nicaragua since 1934 with U.S. military and economic support (though the Carter administration stopped aid to Somoza because of his human rights record), and many Nicaraguans suffered from poverty, illiteracy, and high infant mortality even as the Somozas amassed a fortune—as well as control of Nicaragua's banks, airline, television stations, industries, and one-third of its land. A people's movement dedicated to a leftist state and named after Augusto César Sandino, the popular leader who had opposed a U.S. occupation of Nicaragua in the 1930s, sought Somoza's overthrow. The Sandinistas hoped to free Nicaragua from the influence of U.S. government and businesses, renegotiate foreign debt, and address social inequality by providing health care, creating jobs, instituting land reform, providing food subsidies, and supporting education. Rather than being simply communists, the Sandinistas represented a political coalition of Marxists, socialists, Catholics, and progressive capitalists.[24]

American mercenaries in Nicaragua who worked to prop up the Somoza regime arrived there through the School of the Americas, a military training institution run by the U.S. Army. Founded in the Panama Canal Zone in 1946 and later relocated to Fort Benning, Georgia, the School of the Americas worked to circulate U.S. military tactics, training, and weapons to Latin American allies, building military and police institutions through which the United States could exercise absentee regional influence.[25]

Somoza sent his son Anastasio Somoza Portocarrero to the United States in 1977 for college and military training. Somoza Portocarrero spent time at West Point and Harvard University, and then trained at Fort Leavenworth and Fort Benning. At the U.S. Army Special Forces training school in Fort Bragg, North Carolina, he met Michael Echanis, who became a mercenary soldier for the regime.[26] Echanis, a twenty-seven-year-old decorated Vietnam veteran, had a marketable skill set, according to a lengthy *Soldier of Fortune* profile. He had served in the infantry, suffering major injuries that hospitalized him for eight months; after his recovery he became an accomplished hand-to-hand fighter and prolific writer of martial arts manuals. Besides training SEALs, Army Rangers, and Special Forces units at Fort Bragg, Echanis was also a member of the *Soldier of Fortune* editorial board and was frequently pictured in its pages wearing camouflage fatigues, often in action shots.[27]

Somoza Portocarrero recruited Echanis—and another veteran, Charles Sanders—specifically to teach the skills they had learned in the Vietnam War. In 1977, Somoza Portocarrero took command of the Basic Training Infantry School (EEBI) within the elite Nicaraguan National Guard. U.S. advisors had formed the National Guard to quell the nationalist insurrection led by Sandino in the 1930s; by 1972, the U.S.-trained unit had claimed the lives of more than 30,000 of Somoza's political opponents.[28] Indeed, Somoza kept control of the National Guard even during his brief ouster as president, thus retaining control of Nicaragua itself. In a 1978 series of candid interviews given on the condition that they could be published only posthumously, Echanis told the *Los Angeles Times* that he had risen to a position of leadership within the National Guard and the EEBI. "I run all unconventional warfare training for the guard," Echanis told the reporter. "I run all operations and intelligence on counter-operations against the Sandinistas. I have a $5 million budget and I just got another $1 million and six colonels to set up a special antiterrorist intelligence division." Echanis also described his long personal war against communism. "I hate Communists for what they did to my people in Vietnam," he said. "I've got six AK-47 holes in my body."[29]

Memoirs by Nicaraguan National Guard members verify Echanis's involvement but argue that he exaggerated his position and influence.[30] One National Guard member, Henry Briceño, wrote that the guardsmen referred to Echanis as a "trainer" rather than by a military title, but added that he was still considered a high-ranking man and accompanied Somoza Portocarrero wherever he went. Briceño described Echanis as "a hero of the Viet Nam war" and the best instructor of "a mountain of methods to kill, kill, and kill some more."[31]

Echanis played a crucial role in guiding the implementation of American methods and weapons on Nicaraguan soil. He claimed approval from the U.S. government and cited a letter from the secretary of state asking him not to violate human rights or kill noncombatants. He "interpreted this to mean that it was all right to kill combatants."[32] In September 1978, Echanis died when his private plane, belonging to the commander of the National Guard, crashed into Lake Nicaragua. In a *Los Angeles Times* article about his death, State Department officials were quoted as saying that the government knew mercenaries were fighting to support the Somoza regime in Nicaragua, but could do little to stop them.[33] Indeed, the American state's reaction to mercenary combat in the 1970s and 1980s ranged from inconsistent prosecution to tacit non-action to overt approval.

The government also failed to take seriously the links between American mercenaries and the white power movement. One example of this is the story of Operation Red Dog. On April 27, 1981, FBI and ATF agents arrested a group of ten men on their way out of New Orleans. Authorities seized their cache of weapons and supplies: eight Bushmaster automatic rifles, ten shotguns, five rifles, ten handguns, ten pounds of dynamite, 5,246 rounds of ammunition, Nazi and Confederate flags, the neo-Nazi newspaper *National Vanguard,* and various military manuals. Investigation eventually revealed that the men were participants in a plan to send mercenaries by boat to the small Caribbean island of Dominica to overthrow the government there and set up a puppet regime that would funnel millions of dollars to the Klan in the United States.[34]

The would-be invaders of Dominica included Don Black, a high-ranking Klan leader of the Knights of the Ku Klux Klan, the organization with chapters led elsewhere by Louis Beam and Tom Metzger that had militarized on a national scale. The leader of the mercenaries, Michael Perdue, was, as one follower said, "obsessed with the league of Aryan Nations thing"—a reference to the unifying white power movement and specifically to Aryan Nations in Idaho, where Louis Beam had relocated after an injunction barred him from running paramilitary camps in Texas.[35] Five of the mercenaries had military training, and all but one had affiliations with U.S. or Canadian Klan and neo-Nazi groups. One of them, Bob "Mad Merc" Prichard, would later be diagnosed with post-traumatic stress disorder from his harrowing tour in Vietnam, where he was shot twice and wounded a third time by the shrapnel of a rocket-propelled grenade. Prichard had trained at a paramilitary camp run by Glenn Miller's Carolina KKKK—soon to be renamed the White Patriot Party—that was associated with the Klan and neo-Nazi shooting of communist protestors in Greensboro, North Carolina, in November 1979 and later with the large-scale theft of military weapons.[36]

Though their end goal was to funnel money to the Klan, likely to facilitate the race war for which Klansmen had started to prepare, the Dominica mercenaries framed their actions as a defense of the United States from communism. Even though they sought the overthrow of a Dominican prime minister who opposed communism, they saw the island as ripe for takeover by either American or Soviet communist interests, and claimed they were working to forestall a Soviet victory. When they rented the boat for their mission they claimed to be CIA operatives, and perhaps some even believed this to be the case.[37]

The first iteration of their plan revealed that the Operation Red Dog mercenaries saw themselves as acting in service of the state. Though they quickly abandoned this plan for lack of manpower, they had hopes of invading Grenada. The Reagan administration itself would invade Grenada just two years later under more official auspices, but using a notably similar anticommunist ideology.[38] Black frequently spoke of the similarity in rhetoric and objectives that he thought connected the Klan with the Reagan administration, always claiming that he had acted patriotically even when he broke the law. "We were military advisors, and our purpose was to stabilize and secure the island against communists," Black later told a reporter. "Had we been successful, it would have been in the best interests of the United States."[39] Black's comment about Dominica echoed Reagan's talk of stabilizing and securing Grenada when referencing successful U.S. interventions.[40] In other words, white power mercenaries positioned themselves within a state ideology of covert action that itself constituted a form of paramilitarism.[41]

Reagan would later describe the Grenada invasion as the beginning of the end of American "self-doubt and national confusion" in the wake of the Vietnam War.[42] Indeed, while the Dominica mercenaries came from a variety of political, economic, and cultural backgrounds, they shared both intense anticommunism and deep identification with the Vietnam War story. Some had served in Vietnam, while others fashioned their identity around their participation in paramilitary combat. Group leader Michael Perdue falsely claimed Green Beret experience in Vietnam—he was convicted of petty theft and thrown out of the Marines before he could be deployed overseas—and boasted of a long and fabricated record of mercenary combat in Uruguay, Rhodesia, and Nicaragua.[43]

Charged with violating the Neutrality Act, which prohibited American citizens from engaging in combat in countries with which the United States had not declared war, most of the ten would-be Dominica mercenaries pleaded guilty. Of three who did not, only one walked free, twenty-one-year-old Alabaman Michael Norris. Although Norris had been affiliated with both the KKKK and the neo-Nazi group National Alliance prior to the Dominica attempt, his defense was gullibility: he claimed he didn't know any better and stumbled into mercenary action by accident.[44]

Norris's acquittal revealed a legal system unprepared to understand or curb the white power movement's paramilitary violence. The plot looked unrealistic and badly managed—a *Los Angeles Times* headline, for instance, called it "A Tragicomedy of Errors," and ATF agents jokingly referred to it as "the Bayou of Pigs"—but its significance should not be minimized. The plot revealed a rapidly militarizing white power movement. And in the case of Norris, who was effectively acquitted on the basis of his claim that he hadn't known any better, the U.S. court system underestimated the risk he posed: in the two years following his acquittal, Norris—and another Dominica mercenary, Wolfgang Droege—would work with the Order, a terrorist group that carried out counterfeiting, armed robbery, and assassinations in attempts to wage race war.[45]

The invasion attempt also demonstrated that Dominica was just one of several countries in the Western Hemisphere that these activists understood as the front lines of a global war against communism. Two longtime mercenaries who had been enlisted for the Dominica plot, Frank Camper and Robert Lisenby, had run multi-week mercenary camps for years, recruiting trainees through *Soldier of Fortune*. In March 1981, the month before the planned Dominica invasion, they were arrested with a dozen mercenaries-in-training when they conducted paramilitary training exercises that ventured too close to a Central Florida nuclear reactor for the comfort of the local police. They were carrying military-style identification in Spanish when they were arrested, and Lisenby told a reporter for the *Los Angeles Times* that they were preparing for "deep jungle" warfare. Seeking out combat was "a holdover from Vietnam, I guess," said Lisenby. "We are soldiers. It's in our blood."[46]

Released after the Central Florida incident, Lisenby and Camper began preparing for Operation Red Dog, but they never made it to the embarkation point. Two weeks before the other participants were arrested in New Orleans, Lisenby and Camper were arrested in Miami. They had illegal weapons and explosives in their car—including a bomb—and a map marking the location of the Miami consulate of the Dominican Republic. Officials released Camper, later revealed to be an FBI informant, but detained Lisenby on explosives and weapons charges. Initially, the press and police called the connection between the failed Dominica invasion and the apparent attempt to bomb the Dominican Republic consulate a product of ignorance at best and lunacy or stupidity at worst; apparently the assumption was that Lisenby had intended to bomb the embassy for the island of Dominica and didn't know the difference between that country and the Dominican Republic.[47]

The incident yields more insight if taken seriously. An anonymous source told one reporter that the mercenaries did know the difference, and that anticommunism connected the two sites. In each case, mercenaries hoped to send the message that they would not tolerate communism in the Caribbean. In other words, the Operation Red Dog mercenaries saw Grenada, Dominica, the Dominican Republic, Nicaragua, and El Salvador as the front lines in a war against communism.[48]

The specter of the Vietnam War appeared regularly in characterizations of Central America, and not just among those on the right. The Sandinista newspaper *La Barricada* published an uncaptioned, stand-alone front-page photo of street graffiti reading "Yankee, we will bring you hell, just like in Vietnam." A Workers' Front pamphlet in Nicaragua echoed the same language, opposing what the party saw as an "imperialist campaign" for "the Vietnamization of Central America." An American journalist wrote of El Salvador: "For both opponents and proponents of the Reagan administration's policy towards Salvador, Vietnam provides the emotional kindling, the passion, as well as the frame of reference." Neoconservative William F. Buckley printed a column titled "Nicaragua, Another Vietnam" in the *National Review*. As the administration received thousands of letters against intervention in Central America, some opponents distributed a popular bumper sticker that read, "El Salvador is Spanish for Vietnam."[49]

By the 1970s, with multiple guerrilla groups in El Salvador opposing an increasingly militarized, corrupt, and ultraconservative government,[50] U.S. militarists saw another opportunity to relaunch, redeem, and hone Vietnam War methods. American military advisors, largely from Special Forces, guided the Salvadoran army in implementing counterrevolutionary tactics. Congress imposed a limit of fifty-five advisors, but the actual number reached as many as twice that at any given time, augmented by more than a hundred CIA agents. The war in El Salvador would rage for twelve years.[51]

It was this El Salvador, torn by low-intensity and civilian-targeted warfare, which *Soldier of Fortune*–affiliated mercenaries entered in 1983. Small teams of ten to twelve men—largely composed of the magazine's editorial staff—worked to train the Salvadoran army in "everything from counter-ambush to field medicine," according to one report. They brought with them the technologies, uniforms, and language of the Vietnam War and, although they claimed neutrality, by February 1983 they were close enough to combat to receive fire.[52]

Like Posey—who participated in at least one *Soldier of Fortune* trip to El Salvador—the magazine's founder and his compatriots saw themselves as doing the work the U.S. government should do, but was unable or unwilling to carry out. "I keep saying, the only reason we're down there [in Central America] is because the Congress won't let anyone else do the job," Brown said. "If Washington would get its act together we wouldn't have to do it for them." Brown claimed that the cap on advisors set by Congress necessitated the intervention of private mercenaries. By 1984, the *Soldier of Fortune* teams were regularly teaching small-unit tactics, including marksmanship with small arms and mortars, to Salvadoran troops.[53]

Mercenaries involved in El Salvador sometimes acted as state agents by meeting with official U.S. military advisors to report on Salvadoran performance in the field. In this way, U.S. military advisors barred by their superiors or by congressional restraints from traveling into combat areas could still judge the Salvadoran performance in battle by the reports of experienced Americans. Roberto D'Aubuisson, ultraright leader, death squad commander, and School of the Americas alumnus, went so far as to say that he preferred mercenaries to the official deployment of more advisors.[54]

The presence of mercenaries in Central America often correlated with violence against civilians. In El Salvador, *Soldier of Fortune* teams worked most closely with the Atlacatl Battalion.[55] Between its official U.S. military training and the arrival of the *Soldier of Fortune* teams, the battalion had massacred nearly 1,000 civilians, more than half of them children, in the village of El Mozote. Battalion members stabbed and decapitated some victims, and shot others with bullets manufactured for the U.S. Army and stamped "Lake City, Missouri."[56] The Salvadoran military encouraged these abuses with its own anticommunist training, but the presence of American mercenary trainers correlated with civilian-targeted violence. In 1983, a story in the *Washington Post* anticipated the impact of the kind of dehumanizing rhetoric espoused by the mercenaries. The reporter recounted a *Soldier of Fortune* issue documenting the El Salvador trips.

> One picture . . . showed a smiling Salvadoran soldier draped in sashes of machine-gun bullets. The caption read, "Airborne gunner after he blew away two Gs." In the magazine's parlance, "Gs" are enemy guerrillas. Another picture on the same page showed a Salvadoran soldier and two members of the magazine group crouching in the brush around the bodies of two dead "Gs." The picture clearly resembled photographs that hunters take after they have bagged a deer.[57]

Far from decrying such practices, some mercenaries boasted about their association with brutal regimes and units. At a 1985 *Soldier of Fortune* convention, firearms editor Peter Kokalis proudly introduced himself as a member of the Atlacatl Battalion to roars of approval from the crowd.

Kokalis alluded to killing communists as target practice. "Remember, when it comes to police brutality, that's the fun part of police work!" Kokalis joked. Then he brandished a short-barreled assault rifle: "I'm going to take it down to El Salvador to try it out on a variety of targets."[58] Kokalis and his contemporaries spoke of guerilla insurgents as targets, gooks, and animals rather than human beings, recycling the body count rhetoric of the Vietnam War in a renewed anticommunist mission.[59]

After the Sandinista revolution of 1979 and Reagan's inauguration in 1981, the United States continued to provide advice and supplies in El Salvador but increasingly adopted more direct strategies in Nicaragua. Mercenary activity adapted to this change. In September 1984, a Huey helicopter carrying American mercenaries crashed in Nicaragua after receiving fire. Four CMA mercenaries escaped, and two died on the scene: Dana Parker and James Powell were both thirty-six-year-old Vietnam veterans on what CMA called a "rescue operation," soon revealed to be an attack on a Nicaraguan military school that killed three young girls and an old man.[60] Parker and Powell were typical CMA members: Powell had served as a helicopter pilot in Vietnam, where he was shot down in combat three times. Parker had served as a Green Beret.[61] He was also on leave from the Special Forces unit of the Alabama National Guard, deployed at the time of his death to Panama to "plan and conduct unconventional war operations" there.[62] The Reagan era fostered a rise in special-operations-style units in all branches of the military as well as civilian police forces, and CMA actions showed the easy slide from Special-Forces-style units to paramilitary CIA missions to rogue mercenary involvement in the Third World.[63]

The helicopter crash was a precipitating event in the public's discovery of the Iran-Contra scandal. The Reagan administration sought to unseat the Sandinistas as part of a new rollback policy that committed the United States not only to containment, or stemming the tide of communism and leftist governments to new countries, but also to violently removing them from territories already won. In the legislative branch, however, Congress attempted to stop the Reagan administration from waging war on the Sandinistas. Congressional limits and public reluctance drove the administration to increasingly covert methods. Through the CIA, the executive supported the Contras even as Congress passed a series of laws restricting U.S. military intervention in Nicaragua. Three Boland Amendments, passed between 1982 and 1984, prohibited direct attempts to overthrow the Nicaraguan government, in particular limiting CIA covert action. They restricted and then prohibited funding for the Contras. Significantly, Congress only set partial limitations, allowing a continuation of "humanitarian" aid even though it prohibited direct military support.[64] To circumvent congressional limitations on intervention, Reagan administration officials funneled the proceeds from arms sales to Iran to illegally fund the Contras. Iran-Contra, as this deal became known, became a widely reported public scandal in 1986, with trials of high-placed Reagan administration officials stretching through the years that followed. Although the systematic destruction of documents occluded a full accounting of the deal and those who approved it, several officials were indicted. George H. W. Bush later pardoned several of those convicted in the final years of his presidency.[65]

The Iran Contra scandal revealed rising paramilitarism in the nation itself. Hawks in the Reagan administration saw the executive as the head of a Cold War military chain of command rather than as one branch of a three-part government limited by checks and balances. The CIA, newly incorporated into Reagan's cabinet, now functioned as part of the executive. The administration also further expanded army Special Forces and navy SEAL units, and militarized SWAT teams and other civilian police units as well as the National Guard by providing these agencies with military weapons and training.[66]

The intense media attention in the United States following the 1984 helicopter crash did not stop CMA activity. The Nicaraguan opposition newspaper *La Prensa* reported the next week that a U.S. Army official had used CMA to move military equipment to the Salvadoran army. Posey anticipated the group would double or triple over the next few months because of increased interest generated by the crash.[67]

Before CIA involvement became public, Senator Patrick Leahy (D-Vermont) called for an investigation, saying that the CMA mercenaries surely would have had to use U.S. government-constructed trails in Honduras to launch their attack. He was quickly overruled. But Posey proudly claimed the support of the U.S. government, including assistance from U.S. embassies in Honduras and El Salvador. Posey did say the FBI had warned him about violating the Neutrality Act, but he insisted that he had permission from the U.S. Department of Treasury to buy guns and send them to El Salvador. Since January 1984, Posey said, CMA had delivered more than

$70,000 worth of military equipment and at least fifteen American instructors to the Nicaraguan Democratic Force (FDN), the main Contra group launching attacks from Honduras.[68]

The State Department made a statement immediately after the CMA helicopter crash claiming that the CIA did not send the mercenaries and suggesting that the Contras might have turned to them "to fill battlefield shortages caused by a congressional cutoff of U.S. aid in May."[69] While this language of "shortages" hinted that the mercenaries unofficially furthered the Reagan administration agenda, it also allowed the CIA to avoid taking any direct responsibility for mercenary violence. As a State Department official told the *Los Angeles Times*, "There was no connection between the raid and the U.S. government. We can't prevent wild men from doing wild things."[70] By writing off the mercenaries as "wild"—insane, uncontrollable, and beyond the limits of society—the administration disavowed the agents of its own violence.

Indeed, the CIA employed the trope of the insane mercenary soldier to hide its involvement in the region. The CIA had hired Parker and Powell and the U.S. Army had loaned them the Huey helicopter, but the agency claimed that the mercenaries were what one former CIA agent called "disposable assets." The state could employ them and then make them disappear, erasing questions of accountability. Paramilitary romanticism and emotional instability worked to discredit operatives who chose to go public. As a former CIA case officer noted, "The agency likes things that way. . . . The wilder and crazier and sillier the story, the more they like it. The agency indulges people to come up with that. It's the best defense."[71]

Meanwhile, mercenaries set their sights on increasingly ambitious targets, and their actions became more and more visible. Just after the helicopter crash, the story broke that Posey and a CMA team had undertaken a major arms trafficking trip to Honduras the previous fall. They arrived with a trunk containing their "personal arms," which included two heavy machine guns, a flamethrower, and a bazooka, and which customs agents admitted with no delays. Posey carried a letter offering his services to Honduran army commander General Gustavo Álvarez—head of Battalion 3-16, a School of the Americas–trained and CIA-aided death squad within the Honduran army that carried out most of that country's assassinations and disappearances throughout the 1980s. As *La Barricada* reported, Posey was leading "an organization that the [CIA] created as a screen to funnel millions of dollars from official channels in the Reagan administration to [supporters of Somoza] so that they can develop their campaigns of terror."[72]

Posey's group signed in at the U.S. embassy in Tegucigalpa upon arrival in Honduras and openly declared themselves to be mercenaries. The embassy staff recorded them without objection. Posey described "Tegooch" as a city "full of Americans who may or may not be with the CIA." Also at the embassy, Posey made contact with a Salvadoran colonel in order to send military supplies to that country. A Nicaraguan journalist asked if Posey "was just a brutal and bloodthirsty mercenary" or if he worked for the CIA. Posey dodged the question. The reporter described Posey's mission as traveling to "machine-gun children and murder women." Posey described it as, "for our boys, something like a well-deserved vacation."[73]

As the *New York Times* reported mounting State Department and CIA concern about American mercenaries, Reagan commented publicly that aiding the Contras, whom he consistently characterized as freedom fighters, was "quite in line with what has been a pretty well established tradition in our country" and that he would "be inclined not to want to interfere with them." However, the CIA and State Department worried about rogue mercenaries provoking a diplomatic crisis. Although Posey maintained that CMA and its members would not participate in combat, a series of investigative articles in the *Memphis Commercial Appeal* claimed that teams of thirty Americans and seventy Nicaraguans planned to carry out a series of raids on strategic Nicaraguan military targets.[74]

Around the same time, CMA became larger and less centralized. Membership had blossomed in the two months following the helicopter crash: Posey reported new chapters in multiple regions. CMA claimed more than 1,000 members in 1985, and some number of those members had connections to the white power movement: they belonged or had belonged to the Klan, the John Birch Society, or both. One local director of a CMA chapter, for instance, said he had chosen to join CMA instead of the Klan, again signaling their common cause and memberships.[75]

The U.S. government stepped in to regulate CMA only after the group received enough public attention to force an investigation. In April 1985, five CMA mercenaries were arrested in Costa Rica. In a raid on an FDN Contra camp near the Nicaraguan border, authorities confiscated a large cache of arms and ammunition including grenades, bazookas, rifles, and machine guns. Interviewed after the bust, the mercenaries spoke of the startling ease of trafficking weapons, manpower, and matériel to Central America. They said they had flown from Florida to El Salvador on a plane loaded with weapons, including M-16 automatic rifles, 20-millimeter cannons, .50-caliber machine guns, and 60-millimeter mortars—a total of six tons of military supplies. During the trip, one mercenary said, "there were no customs checks, and nobody asked any questions."[76]

Posey confirmed that CMA sent the mercenaries, but denied giving them weapons. According to a CMA affiliate attempting to gain immunity from prosecution, the mercenaries plotted to blow up the U.S. embassy in neutral Costa Rica and to frame the Sandinistas for the attack. They intended to create outrage in the United States that would lead to public pressure for invasion.[77] Soon after the CMA investigation began, American mercenary and former Marine Eugene Hasenfus was shot down over Nicaragua while supplying the Contras. Hasenfus said he had been hired by a mercenary organization "to do what I did in Vietnam."[78] The subsequent investigation, and the following Iran-Contra hearings, revealed that he was working for the U.S. government in delivering the weapons. Hasenfus's mission, and the spotlight it brought to the circulation of mercenaries, marked the end of their widespread employment as covert state agents in Central America.[79]

The CMA, one of the most visible examples of mercenary activity in Central America, worked to unite fringe and mainstream supporters of intervention. CMA was linked to *Soldier of Fortune* through images, personnel, and rhetoric: the magazine gave posthumous heroism awards to Parker and Powell at its 1984 convention, which Posey accepted on their behalf.[80] And, as noted before, while the magazine did not endorse the white power movement, some of its subscribers, readers, and convention participants were members of the movement. The camouflage fatigues later worn by members of the Order when training for overt race war were purchased at a *Soldier of Fortune* convention. There, Randall Rader, head of paramilitary training for the Order, said he spent between $10,000 and $15,000 obtained through armored car robberies on uniforms, boots, "military goods and sophisticated equipment of different sorts. . . . It all fell right into the military science and the guerilla warfare I was teaching."[81]

The violent white power movement roundly supported mercenaries fighting in Central America. Just after the helicopter crash, Dominica mercenary Don Black told a reporter that the Reagan administration condoned

CMA actions. "It's clear to me that the United States is passively supporting rebels to overthrow the government of Nicaragua," Black said.[82] This tacit support, to Black, meant as much as an official mission. He spoke of his plans for future mercenary projects abroad and concurrent white supremacist paramilitary training at home. On parole for his attempt to invade Dominica, he could not leave the United States himself. Nevertheless, Black said he planned to send 125 Klansmen to advise the Contras. Black intended to name them the Nathan Bedford Forrest Brigade, after the Confederate lieutenant general and first Grand Wizard of the Klan, who "pioneered guerrilla warfare." To train them, Black promised to reopen a defunct Klan paramilitary facility—Camp Mai Lai, named for the My Lai massacre— near Cullman, Alabama.[83]

Black's brigade either never materialized or was inconsequential enough to avoid archival documentation. Nevertheless, his remarks explicitly linked Central America–bound mercenaries to the Vietnam War: "I think a lot of Klan members will be enthusiastic about taking part in this. . . . Many of our members have military experience and some are Vietnam vets." He also told a reporter, "I suspect there are several hundred Americans down there [in Central America]."[84]

Black very likely drew support for his belief that the United States government backed the Contras from Reagan's soaring rhetoric about the dangers of communism "in our own backyard."[85] The president spoke frequently of Nicaragua's proximity to the United States, and of the necessity of defending the U.S. border from an impending communist flood as the Sandinistas would "ultimately, move against Mexico."[86] Reagan warned that Managua, Nicaragua, was just a two-day drive from Harlingen, Texas.[87] As he told the nation in 1986, "If we don't want to see the map of Central America covered in a sea of red, eventually lapping at our own borders, we must act now" by supporting the Contras.[88] On other occasions, he made the same argument about the rest of the region, claiming that the Soviet Union and Cuba were trying to "install communism by force" throughout the Western Hemisphere. "What we see in El Salvador is an attempt to destabilize the entire region and eventually move chaos and anarchy toward the American border."[89]

By invoking both Reagan and Forrest, then, Black attempted to identify himself with the freedom fighters, and to collapse the distinction between official state action and rhetoric. Black told *White Patriot* that if he had violated international law in Operation Red Dog, then so had Reagan, and so had an entire generation of American soldiers. The administration, after all, had invaded Grenada and supported the Contras, both without official declarations of war from Congress. If the Neutrality Act were enforced, Black argued, "every soldier who served in Korea and Vietnam would be guilty." Black equated his interventionist mercenary force with a series of undeclared wars waged by the United States. With no official declarations of war issued since 1941, Black reasoned, all military actions following that date had the same degree of legality as his invasion of Dominica. The Vietnam War itself, in other words, validated his mercenary action.[90]

Conservative and white power ideologies alike linked fears of communism abroad—especially in the Western Hemisphere—with threats to the southern border of the United States that included rising immigration.[91] In addition to warning about communism potentially moving up through Central America and Mexico toward the United States, Reagan had also expressed concerns about a wave of Nicaraguan refugees coming into the United States across the southern border. "If the Communists consolidate their power, their campaign of violence throughout Central America will go into high gear, bringing new dangers and sending hundreds of thousands of refugees streaming toward our 2,000-mile long southern border," Reagan told the nation in a 1986 radio address. "We cannot and we must not permit this to happen."[92] Here, Reagan interwove anti-immigration rhetoric with fears about communism and race.

Members of CMA took it upon themselves to confront this perceived threat at the border, following more than a decade of similar Klan Border Watch actions.[93] In July 1986, nineteen CMA members in camouflage fatigues left Tucson, Arizona, to patrol the Lochiel Valley, three miles north of the border and thirty miles east of Nogales. By this time Civilian Military Assistance had changed its name to Civilian Materiel Assistance, but its mission and leadership remained the same. Armed with semiautomatic weapons and night vision goggles, the patrol members ventured two and a half miles into Mexico before returning to the United States. There, they set booby traps for, fired upon, and stopped two vehicles transporting undocumented immigrants. They detained sixteen men, women, and children, forcing them to stand at gunpoint for ninety minutes with their legs spread and their hands over their heads.[94]

J. R. Hagan, a "burly" thirty-seven-year-old Vietnam veteran and former Army boot camp sergeant, led the patrol. Hagan said CMA planned the

border action for "defensive" reasons, in an attempt to stop the drug smug-
glers they believed financed the Sandinistas.[95] Hagan added that some CMA
members carried AK-47 assault rifles and versions of M16s because they were
veterans, and therefore wanted the best guns available. He saw the paramilitarism of the group, from uniforms to semiautomatics, as a direct result of
its members' combat in Vietnam.[96]

Hagan denied that CMA had booby-trapped the vehicles' route, detained
people, entered Mexico, or fired weapons. But some group members—
themselves veterans—thought the group had gone too far, and blew the
whistle to journalists. Floyd Blaylock, a Vietnam veteran who had also fought
as a mercenary in Central America, resigned in protest, saying "I feel that
the well-being of civilians and CMA members was endangered. . . . Weapons
were handed out to people who in my opinion were not competent." Brad
Wright, a twenty-five-year-old former Marine who was on his first CMA
outing that night, added, "I can't trust them. They lied about what happened.
If our mission was to report, document, and observe, why do we need military codes and guns?"[97]

By contrast, Tom Posey told the *New York Times* that he was "proud as a
peacock in a cornfield" of the Arizona CMA branch, "because it's Americans standing up and doing something."[98] CMA had by then grown to claim
5,000 members spanning all fifty U.S. states and eight countries. According
to Posey, veterans accounted for 75 percent of the group; he claimed the
rest included active-duty military personnel.[99] Opposition to immigration
had rapidly gained traction nationwide, with a particularly strong foothold
in the Southwest. The Arizona border had, by 1986, undergone a series of
transformations that increased its militarization and surveillance. Only
four days before the CMA border action, Congress had finally passed the
long-debated Immigration Reform and Control Act. The measure granted
amnesty to some three million undocumented immigrants, but also strengthened the Border Patrol, made it illegal to knowingly hire undocumented
immigrants, further militarized the border, and criminalized so-called illegal
aliens. Ultimately, the act made Latinas and Latinos in the United States—
whether recent immigrants or longtime residents—less able to secure full
civil rights.[100]

The legislation followed widespread anti-immigrant sentiment during the
economic strife of the 1970s, as well as increasing concern over the drug trade
nationwide. The mercenaries had embarked from Tucson, Arizona, the epi-

center of the Sanctuary Movement that provided refuge to victims of the very anticommunist guerrilla wars they had waged in Central America. The immigrants opposed by mercenaries and white power activists on the fringe had arrived in the United States in large part because of the violent impact of U.S. covert interventions in their home countries. While migrants from Mexico were still largely impelled by economic inequality, most other immigrants to the United States in these years came from Nicaragua, El Salvador, Vietnam, and other countries where the United States had carried out military actions.[101]

The U.S. legal system broadly failed to respond to the CMA incident, which theoretically constituted both kidnapping and a violation of the Neutrality Act. The undocumented immigrants detained by CMA were immediately deported. Then the Cochise County attorney, Alan Polley, decided not to prosecute the CMA mercenaries. Before being elected county attorney, Polley had served as defense attorney for three men accused of torturing, robbing, beating, and shooting at three undocumented immigrants trespassing on their ranch in 1976, in the Hanigan Case. Although the U.S. Department of Justice investigated the possibility that CMA had violated the civil rights of the immigrants, the case could not be prosecuted because a government official with a history of defending vigilante violence declined to enforce the law. Key witnesses—the undocumented immigrants who had been apprehended by the CMA patrol—disappeared after being deported. However, the two leaders of the CMA border patrol were indicted on firearms charges in December 1986. Both of them were felons, convicted on minor drug charges in the early seventies that made it illegal for them to carry guns.[102]

By 1987, Posey, subpoenaed in the Iran-Contra investigations and under threat of indictment for gunrunning and Neutrality Act violation, also found himself the target of a civil suit.[103] Significantly, Posey and his codefendants successfully argued in late 1988 that they could not be guilty of violating the Neutrality Act because the United States was, in fact, at war with Nicaragua, even if that war was covert and undeclared. In dismissing the case, a federal judge wrote: "The court finds overwhelming evidence that the United States was not 'at peace' with Nicaragua during the time charged in this indictment." Posey was cleared of all charges.[104]

Both CMA and *Soldier of Fortune* retreated from militant activity in the late 1980s, and so their members came to be perceived as armchair adventurers who did little more than participate in annual conventions.[105] This characterization gave insufficient credence to the real wars enabled by these formations, and the acts of mercenary violence that ventured far beyond weekend hobbies and warrior fantasy. Even the annual *Soldier of Fortune* conventions, as the Order's purchases of uniforms and weapons show, contributed to real paramilitary intentions.[106] Such actions were gaining a new momentum on the domestic front as the white power movement declared war on the state.

PART II   **THE WAR COMES HOME**

5   The Revolutionary Turn

> Let us be . . . weapons of war.
>
> —*Membership oath, the Order*

Order members Gary Lee Yarbrough (left) and David Lane at the Aryan Nations compound in Hayden Lake, Idaho, December 1983. *(Patrick Cunningham, Associated Press Photo)*

IN 1983 THE WHITE power movement declared war on the state. This marked a tectonic shift for the movement, which until then had featured populist and reactionary Klan mobilizations and vigilante violence.[1] Rather than fighting on behalf of the state, white power activists now fought for a white homeland, attempted to destabilize the federal government, and waged revolutionary race war.

To be sure, a long and messy ramp-up led to revolution. In the Texas paramilitary camps before the fishermen's dispute, Louis Beam had speculated to an undercover reporter about how he would use his paramilitary infrastructure for eventual race war.[2] The early 1980s were characterized by small-scale violence waged by local groups, and by the first stirrings of the terrorist group the Order. And some movement documents about the revolutionary turn—including the Order's Declaration of War in December 1984—appeared a full year after the shift, and were written only when federal agents began to close in on white power operatives.[3] FBI records and the testimony of a few key activists point to the Aryan Nations World Congress in July 1983 as the moment of formal declaration of war—but the FBI informants were not in the room when this discussion purportedly took place, and the activists who spoke about it were testifying for the state and may have had their own reasons to overstate the importance of the World Congress and to support prosecutors' theories.[4]

But certainly something happened in July 1983. The archive clearly shows that before that date, Klansmen on the Texas coast, Klan and neo-Nazi gunmen in Greensboro, and mercenaries in Central America had justified their violent actions by claiming to serve state and country. Even as they targeted new communist and racial enemies at home and abroad, they claimed to be continuing the work of the state. After the Aryan Nations World Congress, where white power leaders purportedly made a formal declaration of war, the movement shifted nationwide to call for revolution against the Zionist Occupational Government (ZOG), bombing of public infrastructure, undermining of national currency, assassination of federal agents and judges, and attempts to break away into a white separatist nation. The movement after 1983 was decidedly revolutionary. As Beam wrote in the introduction to his widely circulated *Essays of a Klansman* that year, "The old ways have failed miserably. . . . Out with the conservatives and in with the radicals! Out with plans for compromise and in with plans for the sword!"[5]

The 1983 World Congress wasn't the first gathering of its kind. Aryan Nations leader Richard Butler had convened white power activists at the group's compound in Hayden Lake, Idaho, every summer since 1975. The gathering was part organizing meeting, part church service, part summer picnic. Attendees listened to racist speeches and cemented social ties over a big spaghetti dinner.[6] Nazis, Klansmen, and other believers from the United States, Canada, Germany, and beyond drove narrow dirt roads up to the property, nestled between farms under the big skies of northern Idaho. Towering ponderosas and squat evergreens bordered the main field, blocking sight lines and making the place feel more remote. Some participants bedded down in the bunkhouse designated for young, single men recruited as Aryan soldiers. They met women their age through the Congress, played volleyball, and watched television. Others pitched tents with their families, drying their laundry on lines hung between the trees. Alongside Butler's modest, flower-ringed house, the compound featured a high watchtower manned by armed guards, a church with a stained-glass Aryan Nations sword logo, and an outdoor platform where speakers could address the crowd.[7]

The two activists who later testified for the state claimed that there was a private, heavily guarded meeting at the 1983 Congress at which white power leaders and elite activists discussed organized revolution and the articulation of a major change within the movement.[8] A precise list of people in the room, and what they discussed, remains contested. Richard Butler, by his own testimony, convened the closed meeting, informally described some tourist attractions in nearby Coeur d'Alene, and then left the room.[9] Louis Beam and Robert Miles were both present at the Congress—Beam gave a speech exhorting the defense of an innocent white Rhodesian girl against racial peril,[10] and Miles conducted a cross-burning and a "blessing of the sword" that included firearms[11]—so either or both could have been there. Order members including Bob Mathews, David Lane, and Bruce Pierce certainly attended the World Congress, and might have been in the room.[12]

Following the convention in Idaho, activists widely adopted two new strategies: using early computer networks to mobilize and coordinate action, and "leaderless resistance," cell-style organizing in which activists could work in common purpose without direct communication from movement leaders. Both strategies facilitated greater connection between white power activists while making their movement activities less visible. Both served to occlude direct orders from movement leadership. Cells and individual white power activists determined their actions and targets through a set of common cultural narratives obtained through speeches, relationships, movement publications, and new computer message boards.[13] The Vietnam War was the major frame that organized these narratives and the ensuing campaign of violence.

In some ways, the revolutionary turn within the white power movement paralleled a concurrent, widening fissure in the mainstream right between patriotism and support of the government. The 1980 election of Ronald Reagan elevated the antistatism that had long characterized New Right grassroots activism to the White House itself.[14] From the 1970s forward, ideas of individualism and freedom broke loose from their Cold War counterbalances of social responsibility, morality, and justice.[15] As Reagan said in his inaugural address about the nation's ongoing economic problems, "In this present crisis, government is not the solution to our problem; government is the problem."[16]

White supremacist violence has had a complex relationship with state power throughout U.S. history, and the precursors of the white power movement have varied greatly in their character. Vigilantism should be understood as violence that served to constitute, shore up, and enforce systemic power, that is to say, not only overt power wielded by the state, but also the many informal structures that upheld law and order. Because white supremacy undergirded state power throughout U.S. history, vigilantes most often served the white power structure.[17] Vigilante violence such as lynching served to bind settlers into a unified white polity in the colonial period, and to target racial others and strengthen the state's development in early America.[18] It often stood in for a weak state during the westward expansion of the nation's frontier.[19] During World War I it worked to shore up nationalist fervor and generate the second-era, popular and mainstream Ku Klux Klan.[20] Spectacle lynchings in the South between 1890 and 1930,[21] and in Texas around 1915,[22] propped up Jim Crow segregation laws and helped to ensure the docile labor pools necessary for the nation's entry into corporate-commodity capitalism. Vigilante violence demarcated whites as separate from and more powerful than not only blacks but also Mexicans and Mexican Americans. To be sure, it also targeted white victims, particularly social outcasts, religious others, and unruly women, but for the most part—and often even when its victims were white—vigilantism simultaneously served white supremacy and the state.[23]

At some moments, violent white supremacists had sought to subvert or overthrow state power. In these cases, their violence does not properly qualify as vigilantism because it no longer worked to support the state: it is better understood as revolutionary violence.[24] The first era of the Ku Klux Klan sought to undermine the federal government through violence against freed slaves and supporters of Reconstruction. Klan violence dissipated only after the end of the system it had sought to overthrow. As lynching became more visible and public, Klan terror gave way to violence that worked to uphold the new Jim Crow social order—vigilante violence.[25]

The third-era Klan, too, worked against some aspects of the federal state during the civil rights movement, using acts of violence to confront demonstrators, but also to prevent the enforcement of laws prohibiting segregation and disenfranchisement. Both prosecution and the changing tide of public opinion eventually curtailed violence, driving the Klan underground before it reemerged as one element of the white power groundswell after the Vietnam War. Significantly, though, neither the first- nor third-era Klan sought to overthrow the federal government itself. Both groups had limited and local objectives, seeking to regain local power or prevent federal influence in local contexts.[26] Although white power activists used prior Klan mobilizations to conceptualize and shape their actions, and although some continuity in membership has connected Klan surges from the first era forward, the post-1983 white power movement represented a major break with prior Klan activity.[27]

Three veterans shaped a new wave of coordinated—though "leaderless"—revolutionary action nationwide. Louis Beam had served in Vietnam, and Richard Butler and Robert Miles claimed to have fought in World War II, Miles with the French Foreign Legion. Butler, a tall, tanned man who chain-smoked Pall Mall cigarettes, led Aryan Nations. He lived on the Hayden Lake, Idaho, compound with his wife, and preached there at the Church of Jesus Christ Christian, a Christian Identity congregation. Beam had resettled in Hayden Lake as Aryan Nations Ambassador following the 1981 court-ordered halt to his paramilitary Klan activities in Texas. This title referred to his work in outreach from the Hayden Lake compound to other white power groups. Miles was a gray-haired man in his late fifties, released from prison in 1979 after serving six years for a plot to blow up school buses in an attempt to halt integration. He ran the Mountain Church, a Dualist white power congregation in Cohoctah, Michigan, affiliated with a chain of fifteen autonomous churches. All three men were compelling speakers and prolific writers. They helmed such publications as Butler's widely distributed *Calling Our Nation,* Miles's regular and lengthy *From the Mountain,* and Beam's sporadic but inflammatory *Inter-Klan Newsletter and Survival Alert.*[28]

The movement's new strategy of cell-based organization was intended to conceal the movement's organization and protect its leaders, make it difficult for agents provocateurs to infiltrate the movement, limit the government's ability to prosecute movement members for incidents of white power violence, and forestall public opposition. Beam, Butler, and Miles had learned much about defense from the ongoing prosecutions of the Greensboro gunmen, the court order that halted paramilitary training in Texas, and the presence of government informants and agents provocateurs within white power groups—efforts that, while delivering few real restraints on white power violence, did hamper movement organization and cost white power leaders time and money. For some time they had been chafing at the presence of undercover informants at their meetings and ceremonies, and they had come to realize that they would never achieve their aims through electoral means. "It is . . . pure fantasy," Beam wrote in 1983, "to imagine the Klan as a broad-based political movement that will obtain the numbers requisite to effect peaceful political change."[29]

Miles proposed an organized network of white power cells: 600 centers, positioned 100 miles apart and outside of the range of likely Soviet nuclear strikes against the United States. In one sense, Miles's formulation was a preparation for something still to come rather than the war at hand: he wrote of an apocalyptic battle or post-nuclear moment, a forced evacuation, a mandatory seizure of guns—or simply a call to concentrate white power members through migration in order to found a white homeland. The centers could respond after an apocalyptic crisis. Meanwhile, he wrote, they should focus on knowing their local areas and local enemies, and also on preparing supply and escape routes.[30] In another sense, Miles laid the groundwork for something larger. As he wrote in 1984:

> You are the organization. You alone. You with others. It all begins with you. You are the keystone, the nucleus and intersecting point in the web. You must plan, act and believe that it all now depends upon you. You alone can triumph. You alone can endure and survive. . . . Five kinsmen can be a highly efficient and effective intelligence team.[31]

Miles proposed that small five-man cells of white power soldiers could create a nationwide network, connected with one another by a common mission and family-like social ties. The infiltration or prosecution of any one such cell would remove only five activists from the greater struggle.

Leaderless resistance, the movement's name for cell-driven revolutionary violence, was not an altogether new concept, and white power leaders were aware of this. The John Birch Society had used a similar method of expanding and proliferating secret chapters, although they credited their strategy directly to methods lifted from their communist opponents.[32] Beam claimed to have developed his version of the strategy from a 1962 tract by Colonel Ulius Louis Amoss, which laid out hopes that an army of communist exiles would one day take up arms against the Soviet Union in alliance with the West, led not by orders but by "leading ideas."[33] At Camp Puller, Beam was thinking in terms of how to capitalize on a Soviet-U.S. showdown and how to seize a white homeland.[34] Beginning in 1983 and intensifying with the fall of communism in 1989, however, he would shift his target to the state.[35] As he wrote in 1992, "Col. Amoss feared the Communists. This author fears the federal government. Communism now represents a threat to no one in the United States, while federal tyranny represents a threat to *everyone*." Seeking to avoid "government infiltration, entrapment, and destruction of the personnel involved," Beam envisioned a cell-based terrorism that drew both on the American Revolution and, significantly, on strategies successfully deployed by communists.

> Participants in a program of Leaderless Resistance through phantom cell or individual action must know exactly what they are doing, and how to do it. It becomes the responsibility of the individual to acquire the necessary skills and information as to what needs to be done . . . all members of phantom cells or individuals will need to react to objective events in the same way through usual tactics of resistance. Organs of information distribution such as newspapers, leaflets, computers, etc., which are widely available to all, keep each person informed of events, allowing for a planned response that will take many variations. No one need issue an order to anyone. Those idealist[s] truly committed to the cause of freedom will act when they feel the time is ripe, or will take their cue from others who precede them. . . . It goes almost without saying that Leaderless Resistance leads to very small or even one man cells of resistance.[36]

Cell warfare without direction from movement leadership depended upon commonly held cultural narratives and values, and shared texts and symbols, to motivate and coordinate activity. In this new climate, movement texts that had already captured the imagination of white power activists came to play a major role in shaping action. The racist utopian novel *The Turner Diaries*, perhaps the most prominent white power text, was one that served this function. It first appeared in serial form in *Attack!*, the newspaper of the neo-Nazi group National Alliance, in 1974. Group leader and author William Pierce published it in paperback under the pseudonym of Andrew Macdonald in 1978.[37] Over the next twenty years, *The Turner Diaries* sold some 500,000 copies, gaining tremendous popularity both in the white power movement and around the mercenary soldier circuit. It was advertised in *Soldier of Fortune* magazine and sold in bookstores as far away as South Africa. That *The Turner Diaries* popped up over and over again in the hands of key movement actors, particularly in moments of violence, reveals its utility in coordinating acts of underground resistance. Louis Beam would use "Turner" as one of his many aliases. Glenn Miller would later say he handed out some 800 free copies of the book while leading the White Patriot Party, and an undercover informant verified that he received the book during his induction to that group. Order member Bruce Pierce would be arrested carrying a copy, and Order member Randall Rader would say the group kept a stack of twenty to thirty copies in the bunkhouse at Bob Mathews's farm. Timothy McVeigh would sell the novel on the gun show circuit prior to his bombing of the Oklahoma City federal building.[38]

The Turner Diaries worked as a foundational how-to manual for the movement, outlining a detailed plan for race war. Presented as a diary found and published after a white racist revolution has overthrown the U.S. government, it describes an all-white utopia. It recounts a series of terrorist attacks leading up to the partitioning of a white homeland in California and the use of nuclear weapons to clear first the United States and then the world of nonwhite populations. In the future world, in which the diary serves as a historical artifact of the revolution, the white supremacist army, called the Organization, has abolished the dollar, started a new calendar at year zero, and made women subservient. At various moments, the novel describes the forced migration of all people of color out of California, the genocide of Jews, the nuclear bombing of high-density black populations in the South, and the public lynching of all people in interracial relationships.

The book drew heavily on the idea of veterans as white power soldiers and on the utility of paramilitary violence. The protagonist, Earl Turner, implies that many Organization members were military men. Turner says, "We have decades of guerrilla warfare in Africa, Asia, and Latin America to instruct us," and he warns that the white supremacist movement will force the public "into the front lines, where they must choose sides and participate, whether they like it or not."[39]

In the novel, set in the late 1980s and early 1990s, Earl Turner works as a soldier in the racist movement attempting to overthrow the government, which he calls the System. An engineer handy with weaponry, Turner advances quickly through the ranks; after he blows up FBI headquarters, the Organization inducts him into the Order, a secret society of key soldiers. He then performs the Test of the Word, proving his knowledge of movement ideals, and the Test of the Deed, proving himself through violent action. He vows to kill himself before giving away the group's secrets. The Order, he writes, "will remain secret, even within the Organization, until the successful completion of the first phase of our task: the destruction of the System." When Turner is arrested, he breaks his vows by failing to kill himself with a cyanide capsule prior to interrogation. Although the group breaks him out of prison, they decide to punish him for his failure by assigning him a suicide mission. The diary ends as Turner prepares to fly a small plane— loaded with a sixty-kiloton nuclear warhead—into the Pentagon. A small afterword, in the voice of someone who has found Turner's diary, describes the ensuing revolution and white victory after his death. This narrative, outlining a strategy that is dependent on secrecy, loyalty, and violence, would become the sustaining myth of a real-life Order dedicated to a violent war on the state, and a guidebook for decades of white power terrorist violence.[40]

Beam, too, wanted white power activists to organize as a guerrilla army. For the cell structure, he drew both on the organization of counterinsurgency combat troops and on the organization of the communist revolutionaries they faced in wars and mercenary interventions around the world. He called for a network of cells organized not by direct orders from leadership, but by a common set of worldviews, logics, and a violent repertoire of action held in common by movement members. Much as the white power movement used racism, anticommunism, and frustration over the experience and loss of the Vietnam War to bind together previously disparate groups, leaderless resistance factions could use that same narrative to operate on their own, with only minimal coordination from leadership. *Essays of a Klansman,* printed at Hayden Lake in 1983, contained a two-part piece, "Understanding the Struggle," that began to outline this strategy. In an undated essay, likely published shortly thereafter, Beam named this approach "Leaderless Resistance" and further refined the idea:

> Any one cell can be infiltrated, exposed and destroyed, but this will have no effect on the others; in fact, the members of the other cells will be supporting that cell which is under attack. . . . At first glance, such a type of organization seems unrealistic, because the natural question is, how are the cells to cooperate with each other, when there is no intercommunication or central direction? The answer to this question is that participants in a program of Leaderless Resistance through phantom cell organization must know exactly what they are doing and how to do it. This is by no means as impractical as it appears, because it is certainly true that in any movement, all persons involved have the same general outlook, are acquainted with the same philosophy, and generally react to given situations in similar ways. As the entire purpose of Leaderless Resistance is to defeat the enemy by whatever means possible, all members of phantom cells will tend to react to objective events in the same way, usually through the tactics of resistance and sabotage.[41]

In other words, Beam's strategy relied on the viewpoint, values, and predictable reactions shared by white power groups to form them into an army. The Vietnam War narrative was critical here, as it framed both the general outlook and philosophy of white power paramilitarism, and because it provided the repertoire from which activists and cells might select violent actions.[42]

This guerrilla war on the state was never intended to succeed through an outright coup aimed at overwhelming the military and police, at least not in the early stages. The overwhelming militarization and armament of the state discounted such a strategy even for those who dreamed of race war. Instead activists in resistance cells hoped to follow the model of *The Turner Diaries* in mounting a campaign of violence designed to awaken a sympathetic white public. They hoped that acts like destroying infrastructure, poisoning water, assassinating political targets, and undermining public confidence in currency would reveal the problems with "the System." They thought people of color, race traitors, Jews, communists, journalists, academics, and other enemies were lost causes. But they hoped that they could sway a white public in their favor, make small territorial gains, and eventually seize movement objectives ranging from a white homeland in the Pacific Northwest, to a white America, to a white world secured by the annihilation of all people of color. *The Turner Diaries* provided an outline for each step of this plan.[43]

The recruitment efforts, publications, and training infrastructure of the pre-1983 white power movement paved the way for the formation of resistance cells on the ground. Now the movement required foot soldiers to fill its cells, and a network of communication to connect their acts of "resistance and sabotage" in a common mission. In addition to a sustained focus on recruiting veterans and active-duty military personnel, in the late 1970s and early 1980s Aryan Nations adopted an aggressive strategy to recruit activists directly from prisons. Butler focused on detention facilities with visible racial tensions. So did other white power leaders, with one Texas Aryan Nations and Klan leader claiming that more than 300 inmates subscribed to his mailing list in a single Texas prison.[44] Miles began the Mountain Church's prison outreach program in 1970 and increased his emphasis on prison recruiting in 1978. By 1988 he included a special section for prisoners—"Beyond the Bars . . . the Stars!"—in his *From the Mountain* newsletter, which he claimed had a total circulation of 5,700 copies a month.[45]

Butler undertook his campaign to recruit current and former prisoners openly, and spoke about such activity as Christian Identity proselytizing. "All three Northwest state penitentiaries are prime targets for tracts, leaflets, posters and letters extolling segregation and the supremacy of the white race," he told the *Oregonian* in 1984. "They write in. They want to know, and so as a service we are expanding and telling the gospel of the Kingdom by sending them a sample packet. . . . We send out thousands of them."[46]

Within prison walls, the violent white power gang Aryan Brotherhood rapidly accrued members and power, acting as an auxiliary of Aryan Nations on the inside and influencing its parent organization. "Aryan Nations . . . will not do anything with the prison population without the [Aryan Brotherhood]'s sanction," the FBI reported in 1984. The Aryan Brotherhood, with members suspected in various murders of guards and inmates, also was involved in loan-sharking, gambling, extortion, and gun and drug trafficking, and sent a substantial portion of their illicit profits to Aryan Nations, often disguised as religious offerings.[47]

Key white power activists moved directly from prison to underground white power cells. Gary Lee Yarbrough, for instance, came from "one of the most notorious families" in Pima County, Arizona. His parents frequently fought each other with knives, and three of their four sons had long criminal records. Convicted of grand theft, burglary, and possession of marijuana, Yarbrough served the full eight years of his sentence, since his numerous assaults on guards and other inmates and his possession of marijuana, homemade weapons, and white power literature did not recommend him for early release. Yarbrough later said he was in an isolation cell, praying for a sign from God, when the guard handed him an Aryan Nations recruitment letter. He spent his last three years inside as a leader of Arizona State Prison's Aryan Brotherhood.[48]

Not only did recruitment mobilize both prisoners and, if Yarbrough can be believed, some of their guards, but it also emphasized a lifelong commitment to the movement by articulating a permanent state of war. The Aryan Brotherhood inducted members for life, and failure to keep group secrets was punishable by death. "On entering this family, we pledge our blood," members swore; "on leaving, it will be shed." The group's bylaws spelled out that "the [goal] and purpose of this organization is to instill and maintain respect and pride of/ and for the white race. And to become a major power in this prison and state." In Arizona, this would be realized by hundreds of gang members, including current and former inmates, involved in a broad range of criminal activity outdistanced only by prison gangs in California. The Arizona Aryan Brotherhood's organized crime extended statewide and included murder, kidnapping, armed robbery, burglary, drugs, assault, rape, child molestation, and child prostitution. Law enforcement officers formed a special unit to deal with Aryan Brotherhood after seven members in Phoenix, Tucson, and Arizona State Prison were indicted on charges of conspiring to smuggle weapons into the prison. In a three-month trial, four convicted Brotherhood members testified that they sent a full 25 percent of the crime ring's profits to Aryan Nations as religious offerings.[49]

While Aryan Nations claimed to endorse a simple, wholesome lifestyle at its compound—defined by the absence of popular media, abstinence from drugs and alcohol, subservience of women, race-based education of children, and a strict morality grounded in the Christian Identity interpretation of the Bible—its members accepted ill-gotten funds as well as recruits with long criminal records. Movement leaders spoke of the state of emergency necessitated by impending race war to justify this contradiction.

A broad call for migration to establish a white homeland drew white power activists to the Northwest. Yarbrough traveled to Idaho immediately after his 1979 release. He quickly became an Aryan Nations Color Guard Leader and a model member of the group.[50] Two men from Tom Metzger's California KKKK, Frank Silva and Randy Evans, made the trip north, and soon regularly attended target practice sessions at the Aryan Nations compound.[51] Bruce Carroll Pierce, enthralled with the West, moved to Montana and stumbled on Aryan Nations.[52] Richard Scutari made his way to the Northwest from Florida, bringing his wife and children after becoming involved with the movement there.[53] David Lane traveled up from Colorado. He was a Denver-area white supremacist whose wife of fourteen years had left him after his arrest for distributing hate literature.[54] Lane became "a pitiful, lonely, sexually frustrated figure at neo-Nazi meetings," according to one journalist, and soon earned the nickname "Lone Wolf."[55] David Tate, on the other hand, had grown up in the Aryan Nations compound, where his entire family lived and worked. "Vigorous and attractive, [Tate's] love of weaponry and militant action became public knowledge when he posed on the cover of a *Seattle Times* supplement wearing a 'White Power' T-shirt and holding a Mini-14 rifle," the *Rebel* reported in 1984. Tate worked the Aryan Nations printing press with Yarbrough, turning out propaganda leaflets and, later, counterfeit bills.[56]

Just across the state line, Robert Jay "Bob" Mathews had migrated to the Northwest from Arizona, where his father had brought him into the tax protest movement at age fifteen. Mathews's father, who was in the Air Force Reserve, was also a member of the anticommunist and ultraconservative John Birch Society. At twenty-one, Mathews formed the Sons of Liberty, a paramilitary, anticommunist, and survivalist group, and got in some minor legal trouble for tax evasion. He moved to the Northwest in 1974, settling in Metaline Falls, a small, quiet, and very remote town in northeastern Washington. He also helped one of his old friends from the Sons of Liberty escape the FBI with a phony passport; the friend traveled to Rhodesia as a mercenary soldier. This friendship connected Mathews not only to the tax resistance movement but also to the mercenary soldier circuit. He soon joined the National Alliance, run by leading white power movement thinker and *Turner Diaries* author William Pierce. Mathews read *The Turner Diaries* as a member of the National Alliance, possibly in installments as it was first printed in *Attack!* He met a woman through a personal ad in 1975 and married her in 1976, but his new wife, Debbie Mathews, could not have children. In 1981, they christened an adopted son at Aryan Nations, but Bob Mathews remained deeply frustrated about his failure to contribute to the white race through procreation.[57]

At the Hayden Lake compound, Beam, Mathews, and other migrants met lifelong Aryan Nations members such as Tate. Butler acted as the public and religious head of the organization, leaving Beam and Mathews free to build an underground. Mathews founded the Order—also called Bruder Schweigen, or Silent Brotherhood—as both secret society and paramilitary strike force, intended to carry out the most difficult criminal acts envisioned by movement leaders and by its commander, Mathews. It included fewer than ten men in the beginning, but it quickly grew to fifty members, organized in cells.

Modeling its name, structure, rituals, and actions on *The Turner Diaries,* Mathews outlined the Order's six-step strategy. First was paramilitary training in the camps in Idaho and Missouri. Second, "fundraising"—robbery and counterfeiting. Third, the purchase of weapons. Fourth, distribution of stolen and counterfeit money to other white power groups. Fifth, "security," or the assassination of individuals on a circulated hit list. Sixth, expansion into cells to avoid prosecution. The Order's ultimate goal was to create a white separatist nation in the Northwest, and later to expand this territory into an all-white homeland encompassing all U.S. and Canadian soil north of the U.S.-Mexico border.[58]

Order members pledged their lives to race war until victory or until death. They took their induction oath on Mathews's farm. They stood in a circle around a white female infant, who symbolized the race they sought to protect. They raised their arms in a "Hitler salute." "I, as a free Aryan man," they recited, "hereby swear an unrelenting oath upon the green graves of our sires, upon the children and the wombs of our wives." They swore that they had no fear of death or foe, but had "a sacred duty to do whatever is necessary to deliver our people from the Jew and bring total victory to the Aryan race." They pledged secrecy about all activities to follow. They swore to rescue any of their number taken prisoner. "Should an enemy agent hurt you," they promised their silent brothers, "I will chase him to the ends of the earth and remove his head from his body." Their oath recognized them as racial warriors, but also transformed them into weapons. "My brothers, let us be [God's] battle ax and weapons of war. Let us go forth by ones and by twos, by scores and by legions, as true Aryan men," they vowed. "We are in a state of war and will not lay down our weapons until we have driven the enemy into the sea and reclaimed the land which was promised to our fathers of old, and through our blood and His will, becomes the land of our children to be."[59]

As younger activists joined the white power movement in this period, the Vietnam War narrative became increasingly unmoored from a lived experience of combat. The war had provided the fuel and the frame of reference for the formation of the white power movement in the late 1970s, and in the 1980s continued to work as a narrative and set of symbols that shaped claims of authenticity, tactics, modes of violence, and paramilitary structures within the movement. This iteration of white power valued, but did not require, the participation and stories of veterans. Several members of the Order were too young to have served, but the Vietnam War story still shaped their actions, and veterans played an instrumental role in guiding the group's violence. Randy Duey was an Air Force veteran and an instructor at the survival school at Fairchild Air Force Base in Spokane, Washington, at the time he joined the group. While his position did not constitute active-duty status, Duey was an employee of the Air Force when he became a soldier in the war on the government.[60] Other members had come close to serving: Yarbrough was inducted into the Marines as an alternative to incarceration, but shortly thereafter went AWOL in Hawaii and wound up serving his prison sentence back in Arizona. Mathews intended to enlist but changed his mind because of the prosecution of Lieutenant William Calley for the massacre of Vietnamese civilians at My Lai, an act Mathews thought justified. Regardless of their individual veteran or nonveteran status, Order members entered a movement energized by and united around the symbols, uniforms, weapons, and strategies of the Vietnam War. The Order's Declaration of War in November 1984 would name congressional betrayal of soldiers in the Vietnam War as a key justification of their violent campaign.[61]

In the Order and throughout the broader movement, white power activists adopted and recognized the weapons and uniforms of the U.S. military. The Aryan Nations uniform—most of which could be obtained from a department store—included a Marine Corps cap dyed blue.[62] Randall Rader, who had never served in the military but who taught military tactics to the Covenant, the Sword, and the Arm of the Lord (CSA) and then to the Order, consistently used military standards for his decisions about methods and armament.[63] He referred to the M16, the preferred weapon of the Order, as "the standard general purpose machine gun of the U.S. Armed Forces." He called the AR-15, another commonly chosen weapon, the "Civilian model of the military M16." Rader described the AR-180, a third common weapon, as "a predecessor to the AR-15 or M16. It was designed by the same man, except it's just a later model."[64] Later, when members of the group were prosecuted under racketeering laws, Rader would testify that the Order's strategy came entirely from U.S. Army training manuals and books about U.S. military strategy.[65] Although the Order's guerrilla-style warfare might have resembled the tactics of communist guerrilla fighters, the man in charge of its implementation took the specifics directly from the U.S. military.

According to Rader, Mathews had a long-term plan for bringing the broader white power movement together under the command of the Order, and this plan rested specifically on battle-ready white power activists. Mathews told Rader that members of Aryan Nations, the Mountain Church, the National Alliance, the White Patriot Party, White Aryan Resistance, and the Christian Identity congregation led by Pastor Dan Gayman in Missouri had already completed paramilitary training. As Rader would later testify, Mathews thought that "each of these organizations, or most of them, had trained military people in the organizations and because we had founded them in these organizations, would fall under our military command . . . he told me that these groups would provide recruits to The Order out of their ranks."[66]

In its first year, the Order funneled money through Mountain Man Supply Company to operate two paramilitary training camps—270 acres total—in Idaho and Missouri. The FBI would track 137 separate shipments of matériel and supplies to Priest River, Idaho, including guns, ammunition, all-terrain vehicles, Rottweiler dogs, army K-rations, and Apple computers. The same kind of supplies flowed to the camp in Missouri.[67]

Mathews, who cemented the Order together, insisted on high morality in its acts that distinguished the group from organizations such as the Aryan Brotherhood. They thought of themselves as an elite military force, but also as the men responsible for protecting and propagating the white race. They followed *The Turner Diaries,* which instructed that for the public to support a racist revolution, all violence would have to be strictly moral: "We couldn't use means which contradicted our ends. If we begin preying on the public to support ourselves, we will be viewed as a gang of common criminals, regardless of how lofty our aims are."[68] In April 1983, Mathews and the Order, still recruiting members and refining strategy, undertook the robbery of a small pornography store in Spokane, Washington—choosing that target rather than, say, an upstanding family grocery store because they believed that the owner and clerk deserved violence. Duey punched the clerk, and the group stole a paltry $369.[69]

The robbery illustrated another important fact: although federal prosecutors and the FBI would later argue that the Order had been formed during the Aryan Nations World Congress in July 1983, this minor action shows that the group was operational prior to that meeting. Instead of being a rogue splinter group of Aryan Nations, the Order included members from several different white power organizations and belief systems, and intended to recruit even more broadly. "The Order" simply gave a name to first one, and then many, underground resistance cells within the unified white power movement, acting in concert but without direct communication with leadership.[70] Instead of being the site of the Order's founding, then, the July 1983 World Congress appears to have served as an opportunity to codify some aspects of the group's organization and augment the group's violence.

Another major event in 1983 sent shock waves through the white power movement, calling the movement faithful to revolution. In February of that year, a radical tax protestor, self-proclaimed racist, and decorated World War II veteran named Gordon Kahl killed two federal marshals and injured three others in a firefight that had erupted as he left a meeting to organize a Posse Comitatus group in Medina, North Dakota. The Posse, another white power faction, recognized no authority higher than the local sheriff and advocated vigilante violence, tax evasion, and frivolous lawsuits designed to hamper the legal system.[71] While on the run, Kahl issued a statement that equated shooting the marshals with his military service during World War II:

> I want the world to know I take no pleasure in the death or injury of any of these people any more than I felt when I was forced to bring to an end the fighter pilots' lives who forced the issue during WWII. When you come under attack by anyone, it becomes a matter of survival. I was forced to kill an American . . . pilot one day over Burma, when he mistook us for Japs. I let him shoot first, but he missed and I didn't. I felt bad, but I knew I had no choice. I would have liked nothing other than to be left alone, so I could enjoy life, liberty, and the pursuit of happiness, which our forefathers willed to us. That was not to be, after I discovered that our nation had fallen into the hands of an alien people.[72]

Kahl continued his statement with further antisemitic rhetoric, arguing that the white race and Christianity would have to stand or fall together. He evaded authorities for several months, despite a nationwide manhunt, until June, when he died in a showdown at a cement bunker in northern Arkansas. Pursuing agents fired into the bunker, which then caught fire, incinerating Kahl's body. His fiery martyrdom at the hands of federal agents became part of a white power call to arms against the state.

This call, and the organization of leaderless cells more broadly, required communication between the network of groups and activists that constituted the white power movement, and for this Louis Beam turned to a new technology: computers. His idea of organizing groups, cells, and individual white power activists through the early Internet emerged directly from the 1983 World Congress. It would turn out to be the most radical, and the most wildly successful, idea proposed that weekend. Minicomputers, which after the refinement of the microchip were finally small enough to fit in a home office, were mass-distributed by Apple and Microsoft from 1977 to 1985. *Time* magazine named the computer Man of the Year—rather, Machine of the Year—in 1983. A loose network of small, informal computer-to-computer linkages had begun to form; by the mid-1990s, it would become the World Wide Web. Beam set out to use this nascent network to coordinate white power cells.[73]

Decades before the popularization of social media as a method of organizing, white power activists used computers to connect with one another personally, and to coordinate violence and radical activism. In one of the first effective deployments of computer networks for social mobilization, Beam created a series of code-word-accessed message boards that linked the white power movement around the country and beyond. Liberty Net, implemented in 1984, featured recruitment materials; personal ads and pen pal match programs to connect white power activists; and messaging about targets for sabotage and assassination. It enabled the forging and maintenance of the social connections that sustained white power activism and violence.[74]

Liberty Net also furthered the strategy of leaderless resistance by coordinating action without creating a paper trail of evidence, especially over the two years before the FBI decrypted the network's messages. "Finally, we are all going to be linked together at one point in time," Beam wrote after setting up the network nationwide. "Imagine, if you will, all the great minds of the patriotic Christian movement linked together and joined to one computer. Imagine any patriot in the country being able to call up and access these minds. . . . You are online with the Aryan Nations brain trust. It is here to serve the folk."[75] In other words, an activist could check in and learn movement objectives from the computer message boards without ever having contact with leadership, and thus avoid implicating leadership in any ensuing crimes in the insurgent war on the state.

One overtly violent component of the network, a "computer index on traitors," sometimes corresponded to an assassination point system Beam had purportedly outlined at the Aryan Nations World Congress.[76] It listed the names and addresses of anti-Klan groups and spokespeople; those who had informed on the movement to the FBI; and targets such as federal judges and agents.[77] It also worked to further bind disparate groups in common cause. *"It is time!"* Beam and Miles wrote jubilantly in the *Inter-Klan Newsletter and Survival Alert.* "Time for a voice unhindered by loyalty to a single Klan group or leader."[78] The unified white power movement, suddenly connected by Liberty Net, sought to rise above factionalism and leader-driven group structures.

Beam was proud of the new technology—a product, he said, of "American know-how"—that would allow the white power movement to reclaim the country from the corrupt federal government. "It has been said that knowledge is power, which it most assuredly is," Beam wrote. "The computer offers, to those who become proficient in its use, power undreamed of by the rulers of the past."[79] The newly connected white power movement was poised for coordinated war, and its leaders spoke with candor about their plans to unseat the federal government. "Looking down the road, the Aryan movement is going to make the Third Reich look like a third-grade school party," Butler told a reporter. "We are just on the very outer edge of tremendous violence."[80]

Liberty Net provided immeasurable benefits to the movement. Beam immediately began to send electronic hate literature into Canada, bypassing laws prohibiting such materials from crossing the border. Klan chapters around the country began to dial in to the computer network: the Texas Klan was online by 1984, and others soon followed.[81] The Aryan Brotherhood was using Liberty Net by 1986.[82] What Liberty Net required, though, was cash. Initial startup costs came in at a substantial $3,500.[83] Each additional Apple minicomputer cost around $2,000, and the movement needed to equip its factions all around the country.[84]

While Beam worked on messaging and connection at a national level, the Order supported the Liberty Net project with robberies and counterfeiting.

No longer satisfied with the small proceeds of raiding porn stores, Mathews robbed a bank near Seattle, Washington, in December 1983, coming away with a more lucrative haul of $25,952. Still moralizing their violence, Order members understood bank robbery—and later, armored car robbery—as a way both to fund their war on the state and to target what they saw as corrupt, Jewish-controlled banks.[85]

The Order continued its robbery campaign in January 1984, when Yarbrough and Order member Bruce Carroll Pierce stole $3,600 from the Mutual Savings Bank in Spokane.[86] They sent $200 to Miles and dropped $100 in the collection plate at Aryan Nations. In April, Yarbrough bombed the Embassy Theater, a Seattle pornography house, in another act of moralized violence.[87] Then the group turned to armored car robbery. In March, Mathews, Pierce, and Duey robbed an armored car in Seattle and netted $43,345; the next month, Mathews and five others robbed more than $500,000 from an armored car parked outside a Seattle department store.[88]

At the same time, the Order refined its counterfeiting operation. Early failures, such as Pierce's arrest for passing a phony fifty-dollar bill near Yakima, Washington, in December 1984, didn't concern them. Pierce simply pleaded guilty and then failed to report to serve his sentence.[89] The Order altered its methods so that its fake bills would be caught less frequently. For this, members recruited a meticulous ex-Boeing engineer and sometime Contra supplier, Robert Merki.[90] As did the Organization in *The Turner Diaries,* the Order regarded counterfeiting not only as a source of income but also as a way to wage war on the Federal Reserve by flooding the market with fake money. Eventually the Order hoped to undermine public confidence in paper currency, fomenting revolution.[91]

Meanwhile, the group set its sights on other, more violent goals, particularly the assassination of opponents. For years, dating at least to 1979, Denver talk radio host Alan Berg had clashed on-air with members of the white power movement. An outspoken and confrontational commentator on KOA-AM radio, Berg was the kind of prominent Jewish and liberal voice that the Order sought to silence. Berg had argued on his show with local Klan leader Fred Wilkins, paramilitary trainer Jack Mohr, and Pete Peters, the pastor of a small but influential Christian Identity congregation in LaPorte, Colorado. In February 1984, Order member David Lane, who had lived in Denver prior to migrating to the Northwest, phoned in to Berg's show to recount his belief in a Jewish plot to take over the world. "I think you're sick, you're pathetic," Berg told Lane, and hung up on him. Lane's coworker at a Denver title insurance company would later testify that Lane called Berg "a filthy Jew," adding, "Somebody ought to shoot that guy."[92]

The Order found help through Peters's LaPorte Church of Christ, where Mathews recruited fifty-year-old Jean Craig. Mathews, eager to propagate the white race, had set up a second home with her twenty-eight-year-old daughter, Zillah, in Laramie, Wyoming, while still married to Debbie Mathews. In doing so, Mathews took part in a newly condoned polygamy within the movement, whose leaders put aside some ideas about traditional family structure in order to encourage the birth of white children.[93] Mathews recruited Jean Craig to spy on Berg for the Order. For a few months, whenever she could get down to Denver, the unassuming Craig tailed his movements, learning his routines. She visited KOA-AM radio, taking photographs of the security cameras. She researched Berg at the public library. She then reported back to the Order, presenting Mathews with a folder detailing Berg and his daily routine.[94]

Order member Andrew Barnhill, using money from an armored car robbery, purchased a gun from Randall Rader, the leader of paramilitary instruction for the CSA, who had just moved to Hayden Lake to train Order members. The submachine gun he sold Barnhill, a MAC-10 with silencer, could fire 900 rounds per minute. The weapon could be had for as little as $595, or even less—and with hardly any regulation—if someone bought the parts separately. Assembly presented no challenge, even for someone who didn't have the Order's extensive paramilitary training. "There are a lot of parts floating around," a local gun dealer would later tell the *Denver Post*. "Anybody that's handy can put a MAC-10 together by himself."[95]

Armed, several members of the Order drove to Denver via Laramie. At 9:15 P.M. on June 18, 1984, Pierce fired the MAC-10 as Berg stood in his driveway, cutting him down with a one-second burst that lifted him off the ground and riddled his body with bullets. Berg died instantly. Mathews and Richard Scutari, another Order member, acted as lookouts; Lane drove the getaway car. Zillah Craig would later say that Mathews had told her that he, Pierce, Lane, and Scutari were going to Denver to kill Berg. She said Mathews left their home in Laramie early on June 18, 1984, and came back the next day at 1:00 A.M. "Later, he went out to buy newspapers," Craig said, "and he, Pierce and Scutari sat around reading accounts of the Berg killing."[96] At the time of those reports, the press had not yet connected the string of robberies with the assassination, nor had reporters connected either kind of crime with the white power movement's political goals. All of these acts seemed, instead, a chaotic and random assortment of violent crimes.

Yarbrough maintained long afterward that he was not part of the Berg shooting, but his position as leader of the Order's assassination cell pointed to his involvement. One witness testified that she had seen Yarbrough running away from Berg's apartment several hours prior to the shooting; Yarbrough, nicknamed "Yosemite Sam" for his red hair and beard, was perhaps one of the most identifiable Order members.[97] Whether or not he had been there, Yarbrough became fixated on the murder weapon, which had jammed, ominously, on the thirteenth round. He decided to keep it, leaving a trail of evidence for agents to follow later.[98]

The FBI got a break in the counterfeiting case in June 1984, the same month as the Berg assassination. Order member Tom Martinez—a working-class Philadelphian who stridently maintained that his Hispanic surname came from white, Castilian origins—bought a fifty-cent lottery ticket with a ten-dollar bill counterfeited by the Order. Surprisingly, given the preparation and training of Order members, Martinez did the same thing in the same store the next day; Secret Service officers arrested him on the spot. Eventually Martinez pleaded guilty to counterfeiting and then turned informant, passing Order secrets to the FBI. Using his testimony, the Bureau would make significant progress in the counterfeiting investigation. Just after his arrest, however, Martinez had wavered about becoming an informant. "Do you think I want to die?" he asked the agents.[99] His terror revealed the possible consequences for betraying the group.

Meanwhile, movement leaders reconvened in Hayden Lake for the 1984 Aryan Nations World Congress in July, making plans to further ramp up war on the state. According to FBI affidavits, Beam gave lengthy presentations—assisted by a man named Mosby, an active-duty soldier from Fort Bragg, North Carolina—on how to build and detonate explosives, concentrating on infrastructure targets such as utilities, railroads, and bridges. The idea was that after attacks on infrastructure, the black community would begin to loot, creating a diversion during which "the white supremacist organization" could assassinate federal judges.[100]

The use of the phrase "the white supremacist organization" was an acknowledgment that the many disparate Klan, neo-Nazi, and other groups nationwide were functioning as a unified movement. The reference to "the organization"—intact even when filtered through the hearsay and transcription of FBI paperwork—came directly from *The Turner Diaries*. Indeed, during one of the sessions at the 1984 World Congress Beam and Mosby laid out a similar strategy as the plan of operations for the next year of racist violence. "Beam and Mosby stated that it is their intention to form operational units which would become involved in this sabotage operation independently using guerrilla warfare tactics throughout the United States," the affidavit read. In this session they instructed white power activists on how to shoot and kill FBI agents and other law enforcement personnel wearing body armor.[101]

Extant FBI documentation indicates that undercover informants had infiltrated the World Congress and observed the imminent danger of white power revolution. Despite this, the strategy of coordinated cell violence without direct orders from leadership was working. Hate-group incidents had already increased more than 500 percent in Idaho between 1980 and 1984.[102] The World Congress itself generated immediate violence. During the meeting, seven arson fires occurred in Spokane, Washington, the nearest large city. Just afterward, Klansmen linked to Aryan Nations firebombed the SPLC headquarters in Montgomery, Alabama. The white power movement had reached an unprecedented level of violence, funding, and purpose in its commitment to wage war on the state. As the resources of the Order grew, so did its manpower, as it accepted new members from a wide array of white power groups.[103]

The eventual arrest and prosecution of Order members depended upon evidence provided by informants. Given the Order's demand for total and lifelong loyalty from every cell member and the promise in the induction oath to find anyone who had hurt another member and "remove his head from his body," turning informant was a terribly risky endeavor. Martinez had good reason to worry about informing on the Order. As in *The Turner Diaries,* members who talked too much were to be sent on suicide missions or, more simply, killed.[104] In late summer 1984, Order member Walter West was accused of talking too much about the group. A four-man team, Randy Duey, David Tate, Jim Dye, and Richard Kemp, took West deep into Kaniksu National Forest, where Kemp struck him twice on the head with a three-pound sledgehammer and then shot him in the head. Afterward, Kemp would reenact this killing when his associates whistled or sang the popular Beatles song "Maxwell's Silver Hammer."[105] In the song, Maxwell kills two women with repeated hammer blows to the head and then, later, stands before a judge to answer for his crime. Two women cry from the gallery that he should be freed, but before the judge can rule, Maxwell kills him with the hammer, too. The Order members' invocation of the song referenced not only West's murder but also their plans to murder federal judges.[106]

The Order continued to carry out robberies using the model of *The Turner Diaries*. In July 1984, an Order robbery yielded a stunning payday that would catapult the war on the state forward. Twelve Order members and associates including Mathews, Scutari, Yarbrough, and Pierce robbed a Brinks armored car near Ukiah, California, with the help of a sympathetic employee. According to later affidavits, "approximately 12 men wearing white T-shirts and red bandanas riding in two pickups forced the armored car onto the shoulder of the road. . . . After firing several shots into the truck, a sign was displayed reading 'Get Out or Die.' The men got inside the truck and took the bags of money."[107]

The Ukiah heist netted $3.6 million in cash, a dizzying sum compared to their early robberies and enough to send them into ecstatic philanthropy. All of the participants received $40,000 in stolen cash as salary. Mathews and Zillah Craig, heavily pregnant with his child, embarked on a trip around the country to distribute large sums of money to both established leaders and rising stars of the white power movement. They went to Cohoctah, Michigan, where Mathews gave some $300,000 to Robert Miles. Miles wrote them a letter of introduction to White Patriot Party leader Glenn Miller, and they headed south. Mathews and Craig stopped in Ohio, Philadelphia, and then Arlington, Virginia, where they met with *Turner Diaries* author William Pierce. Next was Benson, North Carolina, where they met up with Miller and Order members Scutari, Barnhill, and Artie McBrearty. Barnhill and McBrearty had just come off their own distribution trip, funneling $145,000 to Rader to buy more military supplies and equipment, and then distributing $10,000 to Missouri Christian Identity leader Dan Gayman.[108] According to Rader, the Order also tithed 10 percent of all its ill-gotten income to Aryan Nations.[109]

As the distribution trips began, the Order refined its paramilitary procedures with read-and-destroy official plans, safe houses, and code names referring to icons, personal traits, and criminal records. David Lane was code-named "Lone Wolf," drawing on his existing nickname. Pierce chose "Brigham," after the polygamist Mormon leader Brigham Young. Yarbrough, with his red hair and beard, was "Yosemite Sam." Rader was known by a trainer's title, "Field Marshal," until he killed and ate his pet dog to prove a point about survivalism; then he became "Big Boy." Barnhill was "Mr. Closet," because he had a record of seeking out and hurting homosexuals. Kemp, who had killed Walter West with the hammer, went by "Jolly." Louis Beam's code name, "Lone Star," paid tribute to his home state. Beam also had a medallion given only to Order members.[110]

Although the aim of the leaderless resistance strategy was to obscure the coordination behind white power violence and limit attempts at prosecution, its success was only piecemeal. Indeed, federal agents at the FBI and ATF were working to document white power movement intergroup relationships, plans, and circulations of weapons, as evinced by federal efforts to decrypt Liberty Net and prosecute the Order. Agents would present extensive evidence of white power as a movement not only in the trials of Order members under new federal anti-racketeering laws but also in a federal sedition trial held at Fort Smith, Arkansas, in 1987–1988. Nevertheless, strategies to insulate leaders proved enormously effective in other ways. Even if federal agents and a few journalists were aware of the white power movement, the mainstream public continued to see most white power violence as the work of errant madmen. The phrase "lone wolf," previously used to describe criminals acting alone, was employed increasingly in the 1980s and 1990s to describe white power activists. This played into the movement's aim to prevent anyone from putting together a cohesive account of the group's actions. The white power movement's cell structure stymied the kind of public understanding that had worked to limit the civil-rights-era Klan, as well as the political will that could have brought about real change in how the judicial system responded to violent white power activism.[111]

The public might have been largely unaware of the extent and activity of the movement, but federal law enforcement was not. A massive federal manhunt drew together the resources of the FBI, Secret Service, and ATF. On October 18, the FBI raided Yarbrough's house in Sandpoint, Idaho. Inside, they found the MAC-10 semiautomatic that had killed Alan Berg, as well as two shotguns, two rifles, and five semiautomatic rifles. They also found 100 sticks of partially deteriorated dynamite, a three-foot-high shrine to Adolf Hitler, fragmentation grenades, night vision scopes, more than 6,000 rounds of ammunition, four loaded crossbows, police scanners, booby traps, and Aryan Nations uniforms. There was also a disguise kit, as recommended in *The Turner Diaries*. Rounding out the arsenal was a pound and a half of C-4 plastic explosives—enough, *Harper's Magazine* reported, "to blow up the federal courthouse in Boise." Yarbrough and Mathews fled the scene.[112]

A month later, Martinez, now an FBI informant, met Yarbrough and Mathews in Portland. Martinez contacted the FBI, and agents surrounded them at the Capri Motel, near the airport. Agents apprehended Yarbrough. Mathews escaped by shooting his way out, but, enacting another scene from *The Turner Diaries,* did not shoot the agent pursuing him because the man was white. Mathews fled to a safe house on Whidbey Island, a short ferry ride from Seattle. There he wrote a last letter to the movement, promising death for Martinez—"the traitor in room 14"—and asserting that his war on the state was just beginning.

> Up until now we have been doing nothing more than growing and preparing. . . . [T]he government, however, seems determined to force the issue, so we have no choice left but to stand up and fight back. Hail Victory! . . . I am not going into hiding, rather I will press the FBI and let them know what it is like to become the hunted. Doing so it is only logical to assume that my days on this planet are rapidly drawing to a close. Even so, I have no fear. For the reality of life is death, and the worst the enemy can do to me is shorten my tour of duty in this world. . . . As always, for blood, soil, honor, for faith and for race.[113]

Mathews described his life as war—a "tour of duty"—and himself as a perpetual soldier. The movement's Vietnam War story lay just behind this rhetoric: Mathews, who had never served, framed his war on the government with the same ideas about tours of duty, combat zones with no safe retreat, and perpetual readiness for combat that regularly appeared in the writings and speeches of veterans like Beam. The movement continued to reference the war not only in rhetoric and written documents, but also in its symbolic material: that Yarbrough's cache of weapons included Vietnam War–style fragmentation grenades and C-4, for instance, signaled plans for paramilitary warfare well beyond the robbery of banks and armored cars.

When federal agents found the safe house on Whidbey Island, Mathews would engage in a fiery last stand and ultimately die. Stories of Mathews's lone stand and death reached mythic prominence in and beyond the movement, and have been used to bolster an analysis of warrior culture and paramilitary masculinity as a defining force of the 1980s.[114] However, although the white power movement organized around the symbols and legacy of the Vietnam War and deployed notions of paramilitary masculinity, the revolutionary turn that necessitated cell-style organizing—the use of social networks and relationships to connect and coordinate activists—relied on the work of female activists. Although Jean Craig was widely described in court and in journalistic and scholarly accounts as the only woman in the Order, this was far from true even if she was the only one tried for her involvement. The wives, daughters, and girlfriends of Order members brokered social relationships and performed supportive work for white power cells. They disguised male activists and drove getaway cars, trafficked weapons and matériel, created false identity documents, destroyed records when pursued by federal agents, and helped to produce the symbols and rhetoric that defined the group.[115] At one point, as one Order member testified, Zillah Craig—having recently given birth to a daughter with Mathews—dressed in his clothes to lead pursuing agents away from their house in Laramie so he could evade arrest.[116]

Women, as both bystanders and actors, significantly shaped the events at Whidbey Island. The safe house there sheltered not only Order members but their wives and young children as well. Michelle Pardee, wife of Richard Scutari, would later testify that she and her two-year-old daughter lived in the Whidbey Island house just before pursuing agents discovered Mathews there. There she did support work for the Order: "[I c]ooked and cleaned for all the people at the house. . . . I went out to buy some vehicles one night. I collated some paperwork. . . . I counted some money. . . . Approximately ninety to ninety-five thousand [dollars]." She also dyed Mathews's hair to disguise him, and wrote out coded telephone numbers at Scutari's request. In late November 1984, Mathews and other Order members finally drafted a formal Declaration of War that referenced, over and over again, the protection of white children. Here, too, the work of women was not only symbolic but material and instrumental. Pardee testified of the Declaration, "They asked me to proofread it for them."[117]

As the manhunt for Mathews tightened, the wives and children, and other Order members, left the safe house. Alone, Mathews engaged in a thirty-six-hour standoff with the FBI. With 100 agents surrounding the house, Mathews returned fire effectively enough to hold them off. He had a substantial arsenal and refused to surrender. He attempted to call Zillah Craig and Debbie Mathews but could not reach either woman. After several hours, four agents approached the house and entered the first floor; Mathews, upstairs, fired through the floor with an automatic weapon. In the end, agents called in a helicopter to drop illumination flares. Mathews attempted, unsuccessfully, to shoot down the helicopter. The flares ignited something in the house—possibly a stockpile of explosives like those seized during the arrest or apprehension of nearly every other Order member—and the house went up in "a huge red fireball." White power activists, men and women, watched, horrified, as the Whidbey Island house burned. As *Harper's Magazine* reported, "They recovered what was left" of Mathews "in the morning, when the ashes cooled."[118]

Beam later testified that after Mathews's death, he "went to the closest church and started praying for [Mathews's] family." Rader's wife recorded the coverage on the local news. The movement quickly canonized Mathews as a martyr. Activists made annual pilgrimages to the site where the Whidbey Island house had stood, laying flowers, candles, and photographs where Mathews had died. Women's groups talked of creating a map for commemorative white power pilgrimages, to memorialize the site of Mathews's last stand alongside the places where others, such as Gordon Kahl, had died for the cause. "We Love the Order" slogans became common at rallies, in illustrations, and in white power publications, as did photographs of Mathews and articles honoring him. As arrests mounted, Miles started a Spring Aid Fund to support the wives and children of fallen and incarcerated Order members.[119]

The *Harper's* article postulated that Mathews, "an uncomplicated, friendly, and murderous man with a genuine talent for leadership," was simply a man out of his time, a man without a war to fight. "Once, and not long ago, society would have known exactly what to do with the likes of . . . Mathews," the article claimed. "It would have sent him somewhere and encouraged him to kill people. He would have been given an Alamo to defend or an Indian tribe to exterminate; in the slack season, he could have been sent to sea or dispatched to some distant turbulent colony where there existed ample scope for his peculiar talents." The article bemoaned the fact that Mathews had not fought in Vietnam, saying that war could have given him a legitimate outlet for his violence and bitterness. However, this notion presented too narrow a definition of war. Mathews had elected not to enlist in the military sent to fight the Vietnam War, or in the government's covert interventions in Central America—the sorts of imperial project that could be described in the language of the *Harper's* article as the policing of "distant turbulent colon[ies]"—but instead chose to wage war at home, and on his own government.[120]

Mathews's death did not slow the Order, which continued to operate and expand into new cells. Over the next few months, the FBI worked to round up Order members and associates, forming a joint task force with the Secret Service, the U.S. Marshals Service, the ATF, the Internal Revenue Service, and the Bureau of Prisons. Agents arrested Barnhill and Kemp in the middle of a poker game in Kalispell, Montana, linking them to weapons found in a commercial storage unit. They nabbed Jean Craig in Boise, Idaho, for receiving $10,000 stolen in the Ukiah holdup. And they arrested other Order members in North Carolina, near Miller's White Patriot Party operation, and near the Arkansas compound of the CSA. For a time Miller harbored Pierce and Lane as fugitives. In March, FBI agents arrested Pierce in Tennessee; he was carrying receipts for twenty gallons of nitroglycerin, an explosives component. Four days later, they caught Lane as he left a Winn-Dixie grocery store in Winston-Salem, North Carolina. A document found in his possession, "Lane's Laws," called for splitting the Order into six-member cells, each armed with two .308-caliber automatics, two rifles, and two .45-caliber automatics. "You cannot afford to engage in a chase scene," Lane wrote to prospective operatives. That was "the reason for the .308": to disable pursuing police cars. Pierce would later testify that some of the stolen money had gone to finance these new cells. The seizure of four such arsenals with the arrests of Order members made one FBI agent wonder if the group was already in the process of recruiting soldiers for its six-man cells, and therefore already in a phase of major expansion. Indeed, the archive supports this speculation.[121]

The FBI intended to vigorously prosecute the Order; its director told Congress that the group represented the most violent manifestation of the white power movement to date. On April 15, 1985, after four months of secret hearings, a federal grand jury issued a twenty-one-count racketeering and conspiracy indictment against twenty-three members of the Order, alleging that the group constituted a criminal enterprise and therefore fell under the scope of the 1970 Racketeer Influenced and Corrupt Organizations Act. Six Order members were still on the run, including Tate and Scutari. The day of the indictment, two troopers stopped Tate in a routine traffic check near the

Order's training camp in Missouri. Tate shot them both with an illegally automated MAC-10 submachine gun like the one that had been used to murder Alan Berg, killing one and injuring the other, and then fled on foot into the Ozarks. He left behind his brown 1975 Chevy van, outfitted as a mobile repair station for automatic weapons and containing enough firepower to arm another of the six-man cells called for in "Lane's Laws." He was eventually arrested after a five-day search.[122]

The arrest and prosecution of the Order members shook the white power movement from foundation to rafter. The FBI had seized a significant amount of stolen and counterfeit money, straining the movement's resources, and critical media attention suddenly focused on paramilitary white power activity. Aryan Nations cancelled its 1985 World Congress "due to unprecedented events beyond our resources." Besides convictions, the government also sought forfeiture of property acquired with stolen and counterfeit money, including caches of weapons, computers, cars, electronics, the land used for paramilitary camps in Idaho and Missouri, and Pierce's $3,000 Rottweiler.[123]

On December 30, 1985, after fifty-four hours of deliberation over eight days, a Seattle jury convicted Lane, Pierce, Craig, and others of racketeering and conspiracy. The judge sentenced Lane and Craig to forty years each, and Pierce to a hundred. The jury did not, however, return a verdict on Berg's murder. Scutari stayed on the run until the following March, when he was arrested in San Antonio; he pleaded guilty to racketeering and was sentenced to sixty years.[124]

In 1987, a federal court in Denver indicted Craig, Lane, Pierce, and Scutari on charges of "interfering with a federally protected right"—freedom of speech—"resulting in a death" in the Berg shooting. The trial began in Denver the following October, and Pierce and Lane were convicted. The district court judge added 150 years onto each of the sentences handed down in the Seattle trial, and also required that the defendants serve fifty years before consideration for parole. "Noting that there is no federal death penalty, the judge said he imposed the extraordinary sentences to make sure the parole commission doesn't make a 'mistake' that leads to their release," Denver's *Rocky Mountain News* reported.[125]

The judge in the Berg murder trial clearly believed that Order members presented an ongoing threat. However, the trials of Order members represented only a minimally effective prosecution of the white power movement.

While those found guilty received substantial sentences, fewer than half of the group's members stood trial at all; the others remained free to continue their war. Beyond the Order itself, a multitude of other cells, activists, and groups continued to function. No national-level leaders such as Beam were indicted. The absence of direct ties between cells and leadership worked to stymie prosecution, and white power activists continued to carry out violence, even as the trials progressed.[126]

Federal authorities turned their attention to the problem of the stolen and counterfeit money, much of which remained missing. All told, the Order had stolen more than $4 million, and counterfeited an unknown additional amount. At time of the 1985 indictment, however, the FBI reported recovering only $480,000 in cash. The indictments claimed that Jean Craig had received $10,000, for instance, but Craig pleaded innocent despite "earlier court affidavits and hearings" in which "FBI agents said Craig admitted receiving the robbery money from Mathews . . . in part to set up a message operation center," likely as part of Liberty Net. Pierce testified that some of the stolen money had gone to white power leaders around the country. He also testified, after fifteen hours of interrogation, that the cash went to finance "'a new Order' made up of six-man 'cells' with plans for more mayhem."[127]

The testimony about distribution of funds revealed a nationally connected and unified white power movement. Bruce Pierce, based in Idaho, said he had given $300,000 to Glenn Miller in North Carolina, $300,000 to Metzger in California, $100,000 to the CSA in Arkansas, $50,000 to William Pierce in Virginia, and $40,000 to Butler in Idaho. Rader said Mathews had told him that $300,000 went to Miles in Michigan. Order member Denver Parmenter testified that he gave an additional $1,000 to Miller, that Yarbrough gave $40,000 to Butler, and that the group planned to distribute another $250,000 to $500,000 to Miles, Gayman in Missouri, Beam in Idaho and Texas, and William Pierce in Virginia. Although several of these numbers were not substantiated, it was clear that large sums were involved.[128]

A Philadelphia Order member said he dug up $100,000 hidden on a farm in Washington and delivered it to Beam in August 1984. Two months later, Bruce Pierce gave $6,000 in marked bills from the Ukiah heist to someone in Kalispell, Montana, where Barnhill and Kemp were later arrested. Someone said Mathews had tried to give $500 to Joseph Paul Franklin, a Utah man convicted in the sniper killing of an interracial couple following the model of William Pierce's second novel, *Hunter*.[129]

Still, much of the money eluded the FBI. Two informants said Mathews had sent between $1 million and $2 million in stolen money to a Denver attorney to invest for the movement. The attorney was not identified. Because this claim was included in a ninety-four-page affidavit attempting to get court approval for a wiretap of Miles's phone, Miles found out about the transaction in pretrial discovery and was himself trying to figure out who the attorney was and where the money had gone, informants said. Newspapers reported $1 million of the stolen money still missing in April 1988. More than ten years later, in 1997, the FBI could still account for only $600,000 of the $3.6 million stolen in the Ukiah robbery.[130]

Even with plentiful evidence, the arrest of people clearly still engaged in illegal activities, and intent to prosecute, the innovations of the white power movement insulated both the leadership and the broader movement from legal culpability. While the Department of Justice shifted its strategy, beginning to consider the prosecution of movement leaders on seditious conspiracy charges, the movement redoubled its efforts, recruiting more Aryan soldiers to aid the cause and continuing its cell-driven violence. In Arkansas, the CSA stored cyanide intended to poison the water supply of a major city. In California, White Aryan Resistance began the targeted recruitment of young urban skinheads. And in North Carolina, the White Patriot Party stole weapons and matériel directly from military posts and armories as activists prepared to escalate their war on the government.

The necessary material to begin this revolution.

—*Glenn Miller, "Declaration of War," 1987*

Glenn Miller (far left) and the White Patriot Party march in camouflage uniforms, bearing the Confederate battle flag, North Carolina, 1985. *(© Robin Rayne Nelson, ZUMA Images)*

IN 1986, INVESTIGATORS for the United States Congress and Department of Defense reported growing concern in the U.S. Armed Forces over missing weapons. Hundreds of millions of dollars in military arms, ammunition, and explosives had disappeared. The military supply system had grown so large, officials told the *New York Times,* that matériel could be lost "without anyone knowing the items were gone." Scrutiny quickly turned to Fort Bragg, an army post in Fayetteville, North Carolina. The command there, the Army

Audit Agency found, had routinely assigned security guards for the armory without proper background checks. With large, open areas and regular comings and goings of all sorts of people, the post was easy to rob.[1]

A congressional report on Fort Bragg cited a large amount of missing ordnance recovered around the post, including 148 pounds of plastic explosives, 142 pounds of TNT, 1,080 feet of detonating cord, 13 hand grenades, and 35 antipersonnel land mines. Some of the weapons and explosives turned up in private homes. Children found more of it around the post, discarded or cached there. The extensiveness and capacity of this arsenal signaled more than bad record-keeping or a few soldiers out to sell unused equipment for extra money. Indeed, the thirty-five land mines—a figure representing only those recovered, rather than the whole of those missing—had the capability of inflicting mass violence on civilians. If a pound and a half of C-4 had raised concerns about the Order blowing up a federal courthouse in Idaho, 148 pounds of plastic explosive surely constituted a wartime arsenal.[2]

In the wake of the bad press around the discovery, Fort Bragg instituted surprise inspections by the military police, as well as classes for officers on managing munitions. Both of these measures, officials reported, "appeared to be bringing the problem under control." By the time the military noticed that weapons were going missing, however, the scale of the problem was staggering. In 1986, a Pentagon official estimated, $900 million in arms, electronic components, parts, and other equipment and supplies disappeared nationwide.[3]

But by then, the white power movement had developed a paramilitary network so effective, sophisticated, and dedicated to war on the state that military action to resolve the missing weapons problem came too late. The new movement used military weapons and manpower, having perfected an earlier strategy of recruiting active-duty military personnel to its cause. At least $50,000 worth of the missing weapons and explosives—almost certainly much more—had fallen into the hands of Glenn Miller's White Patriot Party (WPP), a local white power group dedicated to war on the federal government. An active-duty soldier from Fort Bragg had traveled to the Aryan Nations compound in Idaho to advise members on how to carry out a war on the state using explosives, assassination, sabotage, and guerrilla warfare. Active-duty personnel at Fort Bragg were photographed participating in white power rallies.[4]

In the post-1983 movement, the overlap in membership between white power and the U.S. Armed Forces had new implications. The active-duty soldiers who had joined Louis Beam's Texas KKKK during the fishermen's conflict in Texas had described their actions as serving the state by continuing the Vietnam War's anticommunist stand on the Texas coast. Active-duty personnel who joined the white power movement after 1983 could make no such claim. Instead, they joined a movement that openly advocated war on the state and the overthrow of the federal government. By becoming part of the movement, U.S. soldiers and Marines broke their induction oath to protect the United States from "enemies foreign and domestic." As the movement organized a campaign of domestic terrorism in its war on the state, active-duty personnel who joined its ranks sought to become those enemies.

To be sure, a 1986 directive from Secretary of Defense Caspar Weinberger decreed that "military personnel must reject participation in white supremacy, neo-Nazi and other such groups which espouse or attempt to create overt discrimination. Active participation, including public demonstrations, recruiting and training members, and organizing or leading such organizations is utterly incompatible with military service."[5] However, the directive said nothing about other kinds of actions that undergirded white power activity—such as membership excluding "organizing or leading," distributing propaganda, or displaying white power symbols. Active-duty personnel continued both passive and active participation in the white power movement. It would take until 1996—after Gulf War veteran Timothy McVeigh bombed the Alfred P. Murrah Federal Building Oklahoma City in April 1995, and after the December 1995 murder of two black people by a group of active-duty skinheads at Fort Bragg—for the military to forcefully prohibit active-duty personnel from joining white power groups.[6] Even then, the effort to bar active-duty troops from participating in the movement was not wholly successful.[7] The reluctance of the military to take rapid and decisive action regarding either the theft of military weapons or the recruitment of active-duty personnel showed an inability to accept that the white power movement was no longer a collection of hate groups but rather an organized war on the state.

After the revolutionary turn in 1983, as Aryan Nations members declared war on the government in Idaho and the Order went about amassing and distributing weapons, computers, and cash, a decentralized network of local groups carried out white power actions on the ground. Located in all regions

of the country, these groups followed the strategy of coordinated underground resistance, subscribing to movement rhetoric and aligning around
common objectives without receiving direct orders.

Among the many local-level white power factions that supported the vision of the Order, the stories of three intertwine and show how the federal
government was able to pursue charges including seditious conspiracy against
movement leaders and rank-and-file activists, mounting a major trial that
began in 1987. In North Carolina, Glenn Miller, a Vietnam War Special
Forces veteran previously stationed at Fort Bragg, had used the momentum
of the 1979 Greensboro shooting to form the Carolina Knights of the Ku
Klux Klan, later known as the Confederate KKKK (CKKKK) and, finally, the
White Patriot Party (WPP).[8] The WPP would eventually disintegrate under
legal pressure from the Southern Poverty Law Center (SPLC), a watchdog
organization that hoped to cripple white power movement activity by filing
civil suits. Miller, arrested after declaring war and going underground, would
testify for the state. In Arkansas, a member of the Covenant, the Sword, and
the Arm of the Lord would kill a state trooper, bringing a siege to the compound and revealing a massive and illegal arsenal that prosecutors used as
leverage to force leader James Ellison to testify for the state.

In California, though, Tom Metzger's California Knights of the KKK,
renamed White Aryan Resistance (WAR)—which contributed two prominent soldiers to the Order—managed to avoid prosecution in the short
term. In December 1983, WAR held a rally and cross-burning attended by
Metzger, Aryan Nations leader Richard Butler, and Order members Frank
Silva and David Tate. Silva had been a California KKKK member, but the
presence of Butler and Tate, both from Aryan Nations, reaffirmed strong
movement ties connecting the groups. In 1984, WAR became active in San
Francisco, Los Angeles, San Diego, and Sacramento, working from its base in
Fallbrook, California. It expanded the distribution of its eponymous newspaper and opened hate lines—phone numbers set up with prerecorded
racist messages—in eight cities. In November, Metzger began a talk show
titled *Race and Reason* on public access television; in January 1985, Silva, by
then a fugitive, appeared on the show and described the Klan as a "guerrilla
organization." In February, someone saying he represented WAR threatened to bomb the College of Ethnic Studies at San Francisco State University. By summer 1985, WAR had seen its membership increase 400 percent
over the previous few months.[9]

That summer was violent in California. In May, the promised bomb—undetonated—was found in a San Francisco State classroom, set to go off during a black studies class. In September, bombs were found at the home of a rabbi and at an attached Jewish school; another bomb detonated a few hours later outside the Humanist Party offices in San Francisco. Swastikas appeared on a Berkeley synagogue. Despite all of this, Metzger would not face a trial limiting his activities until 1990, when a civil suit found him and WAR jointly liable in the murder of an Ethiopian student by skinheads in Portland.[10]

The CSA, on the other hand, faced intensive prosecution. The group's name—the Covenant, the Sword, and the Arm of the Lord—referred to the hopes of compound residents that they would become the avengers of the Christian Identity God, Yahweh, in the final stages of an apocalyptic battle. Surrounded by low, wooded mountains, Bull Shoals Lake, and the Arkansas border, the 224-acre Zarephath-Horeb compound could be accessed by only one road. On the compound, seventy to ninety members lived and married, delivered babies, attended church and school, and worked in factories on the premises. As did the residents of the Aryan Nations compound in Idaho, they attempted in many ways to live simple, highly moralized lives. However, after the compound militarized in 1979, violence became part of their day-to-day routine. Their homes had kerosene lanterns and wood-burning stoves, but in their workshops they built silencers, converted weapons from semi- to fully automatic, and produced high-tech homemade hand grenades and Claymore-type land mines. They wore camouflage field fatigues and prepared to fight. The camp, leaders said, could take in 5,000 people in an emergency. They also stocked light antitank weapons (LAW rockets) and military-grade explosives such as C-4. The CSA residents had thoroughly armed themselves with the weapons of the Vietnam War.[11]

The CSA was deeply intertwined in the larger movement. It provided paramilitary training, according to trainer Randall Rader, to "several hundred" activists from other groups, including the Klan, the American Pistol and Rifle Association, and the anticommunist Christian Patriots Defense League. Aryan Nations representatives visited the CSA convocation early, in 1981. Ellison, however, openly took a second wife and declared himself the divinely ordained King of the Ozarks. This turn, along with a practice called "Plundering the Philistines" that justified robbery and theft from non-Identity Christians as permissible, caused fractures within the group.[12]

Following an infusion of money from the Order in 1983, the CSA purchased an additional 160-acre tract of land in southern Missouri, where the two groups set up a paramilitary training camp. As later investigation and prosecution would reveal, that July the CSA firebombed a synagogue and some local Jewish businesses. The next month, the group firebombed a gay community church in Springfield, Missouri. In November, CSA member and army surplus dealer Richard Wayne Snell blew up a natural gas pipeline in Fulton, Arkansas, which he thought was a feeder line to Chicago. Snell also participated in the murder of a Texarkana pawnshop owner in 1983, and killed a black Arkansas state trooper during a routine traffic stop in 1984. Agents arrested Snell as they laid siege to the CSA compound. Reflecting the connections within the white power movement, Snell had Beam's book *Essays of a Klansman* in his trunk, along with "three hand grenades, a .45-caliber machine gun, and two .22-caliber pistols with silencers" and literature and tapes from CSA and a Christian Identity church.[13]

The four-day siege of the CSA compound began when ATF agents tried to serve Ellison with a warrant "in connection with the manufacture and transportation of a silencer for an automatic weapon." In an action that would prove fruitful for the prosecution of the white power movement, agents stormed the compound on April 19, 1985. The CSA surrendered to a heavily armed force of 300 federal and state agents, who found inside the compound a 30-gallon drum of sodium cyanide, enough to kill 440,000 people. They also found what one ATF agent called "a small but efficient bomb factory," four fugitive Order members, and $40,000 in South African Krugerrands, illustrating the movement's continued common cause with the mercenary soldier circuit. Ellison testified for the state after being charged with a three-year conspiracy to manufacture and sell illegal weapons.[14]

In North Carolina, however, the CKKKK/WPP went a step further by employing the soldiers and weapons of the state itself as it waged war on the federal government. Riding the momentum generated by the Greensboro shootings, Glenn Miller had formed the CKKKK in 1980. Miller had served twenty years in the U.S. Army and was last stationed at Fort Bragg. He was discharged in 1979 for distributing racist literature, though his own account claimed that he retired in 1979 with the rank of master sergeant, having served two tours in Vietnam and racking up fifteen years as a paratrooper and Green Beret.[15] He had a stronger military bent than some other local leaders of the white power movement, and readily employed the narrative, symbols, and weapons of the Vietnam War to shape his group, which he would later describe as a military organization.[16] He outfitted CKKKK members in uniforms consisting of camouflage fatigues, black combat boots, an "Army-type pistol belt," and camouflage baseball caps. "A 2 × 4 inch Confederate Battle Flag patch is worn on the left shoulder, and a 'CKKKK' patch is worn over the left shirt pocket," Miller specified. "Military Veterans may wear duly earned and authorized U.S. military patches."[17] This use of military uniforms appealed both to veterans and to active-duty servicemen at nearby training facilities. It also meant that by joining the CKKKK, someone who had not gone to war in Vietnam could claim a small piece of a veteran's identity.

Immediately after founding the CKKKK, Miller undertook a recruitment drive targeting active-duty military personnel at Fort Bragg, Marine Corps base Camp Lejeune in Jacksonville, and the adjoining New River Air Station. In 1981, Miller staged a Jacksonville rally attended by hundreds of Marines protesting the U.S. military's ban on open racism. Miller complained that Marines stationed at New River had their barracks ransacked and printed Klan material confiscated, and that some had been dismissed on "trumped up charges." Miller said that he had more than a hundred active-duty members stationed at New River and Camp Lejeune. Although this number may have been inflated, the targeted recruitment of these active-duty troops demonstrates Miller's mobilization of a local community centered on military service to serve the goals of the larger white power movement.[18]

According to his later self-published autobiography, Miller himself had joined the Klan as an active-duty soldier stationed at Fort Bragg. His activism intertwined with his Vietnam War story. After his father gave him a copy of the racist periodical *Thunderbolt* in 1974, he wrote, "I blamed the Jews directly, for the successes of Blacks in their Civil Rights struggles, and for the loss of the Vietnam War, the latter because I believed the national media and especially the TV news destroyed the American will to win that war." Miller joined two neo-Nazi groups, first the National States Rights Party and then in 1976 the National Socialist Party of America. In 1979 he read *The Turner Diaries,* and the next year he established the CKKKK. During these years, Miller was plagued with personal problems—he lost his driver's license in 1976 for driving drunk, and his wife left him, he said, after the Greensboro shooting brought "dozens of telephoned death threats against myself and the family."[19]

Miller got the CKKKK off the ground by distributing copies of the *Thunderbolt* inscribed with the heading "Free White Power Message" and a local number where people could call in to hear a recorded diatribe. By July 1986—a period Miller called "the peak of our success"—twenty-eight such messages would be running in five southern states, getting about 5,000 calls per month, he wrote, and the group would claim 2,500 members. Messages included racist rhetoric, event details, and recruitment information.[20] In one such recording, which he reprinted in his *White Power* newspaper, Miller used the group's military uniforms as a recruitment tactic:

> The Carolina Knights of the Ku Klux Klan are trying to unite and organize white people to fight against communism and racial mixing. We're a legal organization, but we bear arms. We wear uniforms. We train our men, women, and children. If you're a patriotic white American, we offer you the chance to join with us in our holy crusade to save our country and our people. . . . White Power, the only way.[21]

By summer 1982, the group was gaining momentum, Miller's wife had returned to their home, and Miller started the CKKKK Special Forces, a program through which members could earn a green beret through loyalty and firearms training, directly invoking the military prowess and cultural cachet of the Vietnam-era Special Forces. Nearby Fort Bragg, the home of the U.S. Army Special Forces, made the CKKKK a natural epicenter of this kind of paramilitary training. The Klan group had armaments including AR-15s and 12-gauge automatics. They experimented with making Molotov cocktails and attended frequent training sessions in groups of forty to a hundred.[22]

CKKKK members spent time during 1982 and 1983 in the woods of Lee County, North Carolina, undergoing training by active-duty military personnel in search-and-destroy missions, hand-to-hand combat, escape and evasion, and ambush using an assortment of military weapons that included artillery simulators. They used this high-tech approach with the express intent of waging war on the state. Multiple witnesses later said that the group hoped to overthrow the government and establish a neo-Nazi "United State of Carolina" or a "white Southland."[23]

As their plans for race war and the establishment of a white homeland advanced, the CKKKK continued acts of intimidation against the local black population. In 1983 Bobby Person, a black prison guard in Moore County,

North Carolina, tried to apply for promotion to sergeant. CKKKK members donned fatigues, burned a cross in his front lawn, and held his family at gunpoint. The SPLC responded with a $1 million civil suit on behalf of Person—himself a Vietnam War combat veteran—and all black residents of North Carolina, opening a three-year investigation in which nearly eighty people would be deposed. In the suit, Person's legal team claimed that Miller was operating a paramilitary army with more than 300 members, based widely in eleven North Carolina counties. The suit's outcome would soon create obstacles for the movement.[24]

Meanwhile, the Order's crime spree in the Northwest had begun to generate significant funds. Andy Barnhill and Denver Parmenter, using pseudonyms, visited Miller in April 1984, bringing a cash donation. Bob Mathews himself made a distribution trip to Benson, North Carolina, on August 9, 1984. He traveled with Zillah Craig, by then eight months pregnant with his child. Miller claimed that Mathews delivered $75,000 that visit, and promised another $125,000 in six weeks. The money soon arrived, and Miller used it, as he would later testify, "to further the organization. I put four people on payroll. I bought two vehicles. I bought ten acres of land I was going to build a training camp onto. Uniforms, flags, telephone message units, the printing of hundreds of thousands of copies of my newspaper, and, you know, hundreds of other items, purchases associated with building the organization."[25]

In tandem with underground paramilitarization, the CKKKK also kept up public campaigns. Members patrolled local schools, purportedly to protect white students from black violence in integrated classrooms. They started a poll-watching service, saying they wanted to protect older white voters from intimidation at the voting booth. They undertook all of these actions in camouflage fatigues and combat boots. Miller also attempted a series of electoral campaigns, never earning many votes but garnering publicity and recruits.[26]

Soon the Order began to see Miller not just as a rising star in local leadership of the movement but as a prospective operative. At the annual Labor Day Klan rally at Stone Mountain, Georgia—an event traditionally attended by many Klan groups, including the CKKKK—Beam pulled Miller aside and took him to a nearby motel for an interview.[27] In late September, Mathews and Barnhill delivered more money and brought Miller deeper into their activities. He later wrote that Mathews had him look at, and then burn, a document outlining plans for "code names; a suggestion that my group expand to cover nine listed Southern states; a request that I maintain a record of how the money was spent; and a statement indicating how future stolen money would be divided."[28] A few weeks later, Miller attended a meeting held by Robert Miles and the Mountain Church in Cohoctah, Michigan. At least one member of Aryan Nations made the trip as well. The local police chief reported that the meeting was "some kind of quasi-military survivalist exercise," and that all twenty-five to thirty participants wore military uniforms. They displayed holsters but no sidearms; some wore swastika armbands. Many came from North Carolina. During the meeting, a few Order members conducted an interview with Miller, likely his formal initiation into the group. As an Order member, Miller took on the code name "Rounder"— "someone who gets around a lot."[29]

In November 1984—as the arrests of Order members began—Beam traveled to North Carolina. He met with Steve Miller (no relation to Glenn Miller), who was chaplain of the CKKKK, head of its paramilitary underground activities, and a Special Forces veteran, to train him and others in operating a computer bulletin board for Liberty Net. Glenn Miller later wrote that Beam received $200,000 in Order money to set up such a system nationally.

> The computers provided information such as dates and locations of meetings, lengthy propaganda articles, status of court trials, the names and addresses of anti-Klan groups, and other information deemed of interest to White racists and anti-Semites. Steve [Miller]'s job was to input his computer with local information so others around the country could keep up to date on the happenings in North Carolina and within the White Patriot Party. . . . [S]ome computer items included not only the names, addresses and locations of anti-Klan groups and leaders, but thinly-veiled threats against them.[30]

Glenn Miller later reported that he paid Beam $2,000 for a computer, plus $1,000 for expenses. Miller didn't like the computer network, he later wrote, because it left him with all the work while Beam jetted around the country in "high-style anonymity." Still, Miller got four password-protected computers up and running by August 1985, according to the *Confederate Leader,* the CKKKK newspaper, and the FBI had not yet broken the code to see what movement activists were posting.[31]

The exact amount of money transferred from members of the Order to Glenn Miller remains disputed but likely fell between $150,000 and $300,000. Miller immediately used the cash to expand the scope of his organization. He changed the name of the group to the Confederate Knights of the Ku Klux Klan—seeking to appeal to a broader population beyond the Carolinas—and then, in March 1985, to the White Patriot Party. He made plans to open new chapters. According to an FBI investigation, Miller spent more than $17,000 on publication costs that year and bought a $7,300 car, a ham radio, and an Apple IIe computer. Miller later wrote that he spent $12,000 for a ten-acre plot of land on which to conduct training exercises, and $10,000 "underground," presumably on weapons and matériel.[32]

Glenn Miller used at least $50,000 of the money to expand his armaments. Robert Norman Jones, who had lost an arm to an LAW rocket accident at Fort Bragg, would later testify that during 1984 and 1985 he sold thirteen LAW rockets, ten Claymore anti-personnel mines, 200 pounds of C-4 plastic explosives, blasting caps, weapons, ammunition, CS riot gas, TNT, and other military equipment to the CKKKK/WPP for $50,000 in cash. Jones purchased all of these from active-duty soldiers stationed in Fort Bragg, using either cash or drugs for currency. Significantly, one item from Fort Bragg—purchased by Jones and delivered to the WPP—was a set of camouflage fatigue uniforms. According to Jones and James Holder, a former group member, active-duty servicemen then helped train the camouflage-outfitted CKKKK/WPP members to use the stolen weapons. Jones testified that Order member David Lane was present for at least one of these weapons sales, one that included five antitank rockets. He said that Steve Miller attempted to purchase surface-to-air missiles following Mathews's fiery death in the standoff with the FBI, saying that with such weapons, he could have shot down the government helicopter that ignited the blaze. Around the same time, according to an ATF investigation, another WPP member attempted to buy explosives from an undercover Fayetteville police officer, and three more received M16 ammunition and gas masks stolen from the U.S. armory at Wadesboro, North Carolina. These purchases and purchase attempts indicated a clear project of outfitting the WPP as a paramilitary force, undertaken in consultation with the Order and using multiple sources for illegally acquiring military weapons and training in their use.[33]

As it armed for race war, the WPP also took up a more directly anti-government message about its intentions. "Kill the Jews and niggers, kill the President and overthrow the government," shouted members arrested for distributing hate literature in May 1985.[34] A message on one of the organization's phone-in hate lines, recorded by Miller, described the group's rejection of the "federal tyranny of Washington, D.C.," a government which he said represented everything and everyone except white people. "The federal government abandoned the white people when they rammed blacks down the throats of white people," Miller said on the recorded message. "[The government] forced integration, forced white boys to fight in the Viet Nam war, allowed aliens into the country, allow[ed] Jewish abortion doctors to murder children, and allow[ed] blacks to roam the streets robbing, raping and murdering."[35] The Vietnam War story remained a central signifier in this mix of racist, antisemitic, and anti-immigrant vitriol.

As the WPP ramped up its armament and rhetoric, the Department of Defense and Congress announced in September 1985 that tens of millions of dollars' worth of "advanced, American-made weapons" missing or stolen from military installations were showing up on the black market. The spotlight turned on Fort Bragg, from which the WPP was acquiring much of its arsenal.[36] The Department of Justice began an investigation of more than twenty people suspected of aiding in the theft of several tons of grenades, land mines, artillery, plastic explosives, and other weapons from Fort Bragg in the previous few years. Two active-duty army Special Forces soldiers were convicted in the case. During the investigation it was revealed that it was possible to obtain weapons simply by checking them out for training, but Fort Bragg officials, despite clear evidence of major lapses, planned no changes in security. The Naval Investigative Service in North Carolina also launched an investigation into whether Marine Corps equipment had been supplied to the WPP, but said it would limit its inquiry to weapons rather than examining active-duty membership in the group. These responses showed that the military administration did not yet grasp the nature of the threat posed by the white power movement, seeing disconnected paramilitary hate groups instead of a cohesive movement dedicated to antigovernment guerrilla war.[37]

The WPP, meanwhile, had reached an unprecedented level of militarization. The *Charlotte Observer* reported that a paramilitary camp in Winston-Salem known as Force Recon—perhaps the facility Miller purchased with Order money—was only one of several such sites in the state. As the FBI special agent in charge of the case commented on the growing militancy of the group: "They openly admit training operations, and have more sophisticated equipment, weapons, uniforms and computer equipment. It's overt and very obvious."[38]

Glenn Miller, during these months, harbored and aided Order members on the run from pursuing federal agents. He had recruited two lieutenants, both former members of the antigovernment Posse Comitatus in Oklahoma. Doug Sheets and Robert "Jack" Jackson had encountered the *White Carolinian,* the newspaper of the CKKKK, and had relocated to North Carolina in order to be closer to the action. They had come to town already outfitted in camouflage fatigues, and rode in on a truck "loaded . . . with shotguns and assault rifles," Miller would later write.[39]

In January 1986, Glenn Miller harbored other fugitive Order members. The public actions of the WPP continued with an anti–Martin Luther King Jr. Day rally that same month, drawing activists from several white power groups. A truck with a "We Love the Order" sign led the march. During a speech to the crowd, Miller said violence would precede a coming race war and that blood would be spilled. "Our forefathers shed some to make our country," he said, "and we're going to have to shed some to keep it, and we will."[40] After stopping a car for speeding on the way to the rally, local police discovered fifteen weapons and 1,000 rounds of ammunition in the car, which was carrying four WPP members, and arrested the four on weapons charges. Even at legal public rallies, where at least one function of paramilitarism was simply performative, WPP members were heavily armed.[41]

By July 1986, Glenn Miller was claiming 5,000 members for the WPP; journalists estimated the number at closer to 1,500. Whatever the number, all of them—including the women—were outfitted in military-style camouflage fatigues and combat boots. The FBI opened a preliminary investigation into the WPP that June, and submitted a request for a full domestic security and terrorism investigation by September. "The WPP is known to be recruiting active duty military personnel into its membership," one FBI memo from the Charlotte office belatedly advised Washington:[42]

This has sparked increased national concern that military supplies and weapons are being channeled to these supremacist groups to be used for terrorism activities. The potential harm and threat to law enforcement, as well as the general public, is great. The propensity for violence among the radical

right-wing groups has been well established. . . . It is felt that the magnitude
of the threat to society by the WPP is great and that the likelihood for violence is substantial.[43]

Despite the impending threat documented by the FBI, active-duty soldiers
remained free to participate in a movement involved in the sustained theft
of military weapons and matériel, and dedicated to the violent overthrow of
the government.

The Bobby Person lawsuit, however, had given the SPLC an opening to
pressure the white power movement. Glenn Miller had settled the case in
January 1985 by signing a consent decree to stop paramilitary activity. This
document would eventually bring down both Miller and the WPP, and
would be bitterly remembered in the broader movement. In the consent
decree, Miller agreed not to violate a state law banning the operation of
paramilitary groups with the intention of causing injury or promoting civil
disorder. But as Miller told one reporter, "We don't intend to cause any civil
disorder, so the law doesn't apply to us. The purpose is to train white people
in how to defend themselves in a crime-ridden society."[44]

The question, then, in determining whether Glenn Miller and the WPP
had violated the consent decree turned on whether the paramilitary group
intended to cause injury or to bring about civil unrest. Miller maintained
that the group was a defensive militia and therefore didn't violate the law; the
way he understood it, the group was legal as long as it wasn't dedicated to
civil disorder. His lawyer told the jury a familiar story: that Miller expected
an attempt by communist forces to overthrow the government, and that
WPP members simply wanted to be ready to defend their families. This was
the same defense Beam had mounted unsuccessfully in the earlier dispute
with the Vietnamese fisherman, and similar to the one used successfully by
the Greensboro gunmen.[45]

The prosecution, "amid an evidentiary parade of guns, hand grenades and
missile launchers," reported the *New York Times,* "painted a portrait of a
group of anti-Semitic racists who were shaped by the Christian Identity
movement, joined by active-duty soldiers and marines, and equipped with
heavy weapons stolen from Fort Bragg with the help of an Army intelligence
officer and a Special Forces supply sergeant."[46] Prosecutors claimed that
Glenn Miller was using *The Turner Diaries* as a model to take power and
establish a white separatist Southland. Miller's planned revolution would

succeed in 1992, he had claimed, the same year promised by the novel. Miller admitted to distributing hundreds of copies of *The Turner Diaries* to WPP members at rallies, meeting Mathews, and placing the slogan "We Love the Order" in the *Confederate Leader,* the WPP newspaper.[47] But under direct questioning by SPLC director Morris Dees, Miller "denied emulating The Order or being a member of it." Despite his denial, the WPP had clearly planned a race war, establishing ample evidence of intended civil disorder. Added to this, Jones testified that Miller had been directly involved in the purchase of stolen military weapons and in training Klansmen to use them for some six months after the court order, activity halted only by Miller's arrest.[48]

Regarding the law prohibiting paramilitary groups that intended to injure others, various sources reported that Glenn Miller planned, once racists had taken control of the United State of Carolina, to conduct "murder and treason trials of selected defendants," including abortion providers, "ultraliberal federal judges, neo-communist congressmen and senators, communist professors and neo-communist newspaper and television magnates." He presumed these people guilty and proposed their execution "in the tradition of the South—public hanging from a sturdy oak tree."[49]

This vivid threat of lynching, along with Jones's testimony about the tremendous quantity of stolen weapons and explosives he had sold to Glenn Miller and the CKKKK/WPP, spelled guilty verdicts for Glenn Miller and Steve Miller, delivered by a federal jury in Raleigh in July 1986. They had continued, the jury found, to operate a paramilitary organization intending "to promote civil unrest" despite their signed consent decree not to do so. With each count of criminal contempt carrying a maximum sentence of six months in jail and a $1,000 fine, Glenn Miller was found guilty on two counts, and Steve Miller and the White Patriot Party guilty on one count each. Both men had to agree to never again associate with the WPP or any members or former members, nor with a long list of white power groups and personae named by Dees. This list included the Order, Aryan Nations, several Klan factions, Tom Metzger, Richard Butler, William Pierce, James Ellison, David Lane, Louis Beam, Robert Miles, Don Black, and more. Miller was then sentenced to six months in jail, an additional six-month sentence that was suspended, and three years of probation.[50]

Glenn Miller, who believed he had been acting within the law, felt duped by the SPLC regarding the terms of the consent decree and was furious.

A dozen WPP supporters in the courtroom reacted to the verdict with sadness and shock, one woman hiding her face in her hands. The movement responded with outrage over what members perceived as heinous interference with Miller's right to free association. The *Confederate Leader* announced a rally to "protest the continuous federal harassment of patriots." Aryan Nations leader Richard Butler made the trip to speak against the verdict, as did Greensboro shooter Roland Wayne Wood. The WPP issued a $50,000 contract to kill Morris Dees. Preparing to take drastic measures, Miller sent his mailing list to David Duke, Ed Fields of the National States Rights Party, Pierce, Metzger, Miles, and Butler in the hope that the momentum of recruitment and action would continue.[51]

Cecil Cox, an active-duty Marine stationed at Camp Lejeune, took over leadership of the WPP but in October 1986, under legal pressure, disbanded the organization and closed *The Confederate Leader*. He reestablished the WPP as the Southern National Front. There would be no uniforms, Cox promised, and the group would be "pro-white" rather than anti-black and antisemitic. The SPLC estimated that membership had fallen to 1,000; Cox claimed that the group held strong at 4,500.[52]

Eventually the case brought scrutiny to the problem of active-duty military personnel participating in the white power movement's war on the state. In September 1986, Defense Secretary Caspar Weinberger issued his memorandum discouraging—but not prohibiting—service personnel from joining hate groups. As North Carolina commanders implemented this new policy, Cox and a fellow former WPP member were discharged in December 1986 for their involvement in the movement. "As a practical matter, you cannot have a racist Marine in an integrated organization and expect to train and eventually fight together as a unit," said Camp Lejeune spokesman Lieutenant Colonel David Tomsky, who remembered the Vietnam War as the time of the worst racial tension in his branch of the U.S. Armed Forces. "We don't think in terms of white, black, Hispanic, we think in terms of being good Marines."[53]

In seeing white power movement membership as a political statement, rather than participation in a war on the federal government, military leadership once again failed to acknowledge the danger posed by active-duty personnel in such a movement. Not only were such troops violating their oath to protect the country against enemies foreign and domestic—engaging as they were in a project of explicit domestic terrorism—but they also brought with them training, skills, and weapons. Active-duty troops, together with veterans, played instrumental roles in energizing the movement.

In January 1987, the FBI, ATF, and U.S. Army criminal division concluded its domestic security and terrorism investigation of the WPP, and a federal grand jury indicted five members—Steve Miller, Jack Jackson, Tony Wydra, and two others—on charges of conspiring to steal U.S. military weapons "by whatever means necessary, including robbery and murder, in order to maintain, train and equip a paramilitary armed force." They also summoned Doug Sheets as a material witness and brought the total number of Klan and WPP members charged to twenty-nine.[54]

The indictment further stated that the WPP had planned Order-style armed robberies in order to finance its paramilitarization. It pointed to an impending crime spree, stating that Steve Miller and others had planned to rob motorists on Interstate 95, and had discussed plans to rob a Pizza Hut manager in Fayetteville. It also alleged that he had conspired with Wydra and others to attempt to blow up the SPLC offices in Montgomery, Alabama. This crime spree fit the Order's ideas of moralized violence in that the "motorists" targeted were very likely drug runners who frequently used I-95, and in that the SPLC was a target.[55]

The problem of weapons theft was broad-scale and entrenched. Even as the trial unfolded, two .45-caliber submachine guns went missing at Fort Bragg; the weapons were recovered, but three soldiers would face charges. An FBI investigation, aided by the Naval Investigative Service and the Marine Corps, resulted in the conviction of 134 Marines and weapons dealers in "a national network trafficking in stolen military gear."[56] As the FBI worried about continued active-duty membership in the white power movement, agents circulated requests for information on "any recent efforts by the [National Socialist Liberation Front (NSLF)] at recruiting active duty military members, and if such activity could have been coordinated with similar membership recruiting by the WPP."[57] The NSLF, led by Karl Hand, also shared close ties with the Order. Hand was a longtime movement character and had circulated extensively through its factions. He had spoken at the Aryan Nations World Congress in 1984 and had been director and national organizer of the Knights of the Ku Klux Klan under Duke. At Hand's 1986 wedding, Tom Metzger of WAR stood up as best man and Robert Miles of the Mountain Church officiated. Standing before an altar bedecked with a swastika banner, the bride held a "beautiful bridal bouquet" donated by a local Dualist church and the couple exchanged vows and "a reaffirmation of the couple[']s faith and allegiance to their Race and its leaders," Miles reported to the readers of his newsletter. Hand's connections showed how North Carolina activists were deeply connected with Michigan, California, Louisiana, and Idaho white power groups. Stopping the flow of military weapons and active-duty personnel to the WPP had hardly stopped the movement at large from acquiring them, as its social networks and trafficking networks alike remained strong.[58]

In spring 1986, Glenn Miller had made a surprising announcement: he would run as a candidate for U.S. Senate in North Carolina. He gave interviews trying to soften his position. One article on his candidacy reported that "active-duty military personnel were not allowed to be members of his organization, to spare them from 'harassment and persecution' by military officers." Miller characterized the attention on active-duty WPP membership as "a witch hunt looking for white patriots under every rock on the military bases in this country."[59]

Still under his suspended sentence even as he sought public office, Miller was relatively certain that he would be served with weapons charges like Jackson and Steve Miller. Eventually he decided to forgo his campaign for office and "go underground and wage war against the Jews and the federal government." As he would later write, "Since they wouldn't allow me to fight them legally above ground, then I'd resort to the only means left, armed revolution." He took out a life insurance policy and said goodbye to his family.[60]

Miller drove to Oklahoma City to rendezvous with his most trusted lieutenants. In addition to the charges they faced for possession of stolen military weapons, Jackson and Sheets were also slated to stand trial for a triple murder and armed robbery at the Shelby III, a pornographic bookstore in Cleveland County, North Carolina. Three armed and hooded men had rushed into the bookstore on the night of January 17, 1987, forcing four customers and the clerk to the floor and then shooting each in the head. The attackers subsequently blew up the store with several firebombs improvised from plastic jugs and gasoline. Three of the five victims died. Sheets's trial was scheduled first, on sixteen counts including murder, kidnapping, armed robbery, and conspiracy. Before the Shelby incident, he had been serving time in a federal penitentiary for illegal firearms and explosives charges. Jackson was supposed to appear in court in the stolen military weapons case, and then for the Shelby murders. Neither man had much to lose by going underground with Miller.[61]

On April 6, 1987, Glenn Miller issued 5,000 copies of a Declaration of War, sent to the SPLC, radio stations, and everyone on his mailing lists.[62] Then he disappeared. The Declaration of War demanded, among other things, that the government revoke the consent decree limiting Miller's freedom of association with people in the white power movement, and that there be a federal investigation of Dees. Other demands included:

> Total and complete amnesty and immunity for all white patriots who are presently underground from any government prosecution . . .
>
> Promise to allow white patriots to wear camouflage uniforms, to conduct public marches and demonstrations, to train with legal firearms for defense purposes, to publish "The Confederate Leader" newspaper.
>
> The overturning of my conviction and Stephen Miller's conviction and the White Patriot Party's conviction [for contempt of court] of July 25, 1986.
>
> The payment in cash of $888,000 for damages done to myself and the White Patriot Party in these past three years.

If his demands were not met, Miller threatened, he had "eight teams of freedom fighters prepared to start a race war nationwide. We have the necessary material to begin this revolution."[63] Miller claimed that Order-directed cell organization was already in place, and referenced the stolen military weapons.

The Southern National Front, which the FBI characterized as operating with "despondency and confusion" after the name change and courtroom defeat, responded to Miller's Declaration of War with a hopeful, if short-lived, increase in militancy. Its members suddenly appeared in uniform again, even for a birthday party. The leadership personnel disappeared from FBI surveillance for days at a time, and wore sidearms.[64]

A massive manhunt for Glenn Miller and his accomplices followed. The day after the Declaration of War, three individuals robbed an armored car in an Order-style heist in Delaware. Miller had been living in Virginia, and officials assumed a connection. On April 19—the anniversary of the CSA compound bust—someone bombed an unmarked police car in Missoula, Montana. Though an Aryan Nations member took credit for the bombing, agents were initially concerned that Miller was acting as Mathews had before his fatal standoff with the FBI. A warrant for Miller's arrest for violation of bail conditions was issued on April 20, but FBI agents worried that they might not be able to apprehend him alive. The Declaration of War had been "characterized by many as a viable suicide note," wrote a Richmond FBI agent in a memo sent to the director and all branch offices.[65]

Authorities noticed that Sheets and Jackson had failed to appear in court on the same day as the Declaration of War, and Jackson sent a letter to the court explaining his absence bearing the same postmark as the Declaration. Jackson was tried in absentia and convicted on possession of illegal weapons charges. Steve Miller—who did appear in court—was convicted as well; two others plea-bargained and testified against Steve Miller, saying he had planned to use an antitank Dragon rocket against Dees.[66]

By the end of the month, U.S. marshals and the Kansas City branch of the FBI had caught up with Glenn Miller, Jackson, Sheets, and Wydra (also charged in the weapons case) at a small trailer park in Ozark, Missouri. Government agents surrounded the trailer at 6:08 a.m. and announced repeatedly that the occupants had two minutes to surrender. At 6:10, agents fired four Ferret gas rounds into the trailer and one into a nearby van. Within a few minutes, four men exited the trailer, yelling "We surrender, don't shoot, we surrender."[67]

The agents called in a U.S. Army team from nearby Fort Leonard Wood to enter the trailer, anticipating booby traps. The trailer and van held a vast weapons stockpile, including several AR-15 and M16 guns and bandoliers. Two of the guns had been converted to shoot in both semi- and fully automatic mode. There was also a stock of C-4 plastic explosives, hand grenades, pipe bombs, detonator cord, switches, and military gear, as well as thousands of rounds of ammunition. The FBI search of the premises turned up $13,880 in $20 bills, possibly from the Order's robberies and counterfeiting operations.[68]

On May 5, 1987, Glenn Miller was charged with mailing a threatening communication and possession of illegal weapons. In a plea bargain that would destroy his reputation within the movement, Miller pleaded guilty and testified against Lawrence and Sheets and—much worse, to white power activists—divulged information about the Order. The dejected Southern National Front promptly voted to disband. According to Miller, trying to justify his plea deal a decade later, no one served a longer sentence because of his testimony, and he made the exaggerated claim that the bargain reduced his sentence from a hundred years to five.[69]

In fact, Jackson and Sheets would serve only six and a half years each for the possession of illegal weapons. Even the massive and sustained theft of weapons from a U.S. military post over three years—with the express intention of violence against both the state and its civilians, and accompanying murders at the Shelby III—held only six years' worth of consequences.

Glenn Miller also testified that he had received $200,000 from Mathews, that he was told it came from armored car and bank robberies, and that he used the money to purchase facilities for military training, hire staff, and buy uniforms and vehicles. He said Mathews told him that Miles, "the number two man of the Aryan Nations," was leading "this thing," referring to a war on the government. Miller also said that members of the Order were still at large, planning a big "inside" job that would net $50 million, but did not disclose details. Judge Earl Britt sentenced Miller to five years instead of fifteen for his plea bargain—a hundred-year sentence was never on the table—and freed him on $50,000 bond until the sedition trial. All in all, Miller's testimony against white power leaders was damaging enough that he had to enter the witness protection program.[70]

Glenn Miller's testimony, however, would not be enough to curb white power activism in the sedition trial to come. The white power movement—nationally and locally—was conducting an organized war on the federal government, as demonstrated through the advent of cell terrorism, recruitment of soldiers and prisoners, the theft and procurement of stolen military weapons and matériel, and the Liberty Net computer network. Despite this clear evidence, however, the jury would acquit all thirteen white power defendants. Although the same jury selection procedures that hampered justice in the Greensboro trials would shape this verdict, acquittal would turn on the work—both real and symbolic—of white women in the movement.

7   Race War and White Women

The mothers of future Aryan warriors.

—Confederate Leader, *July 1985*

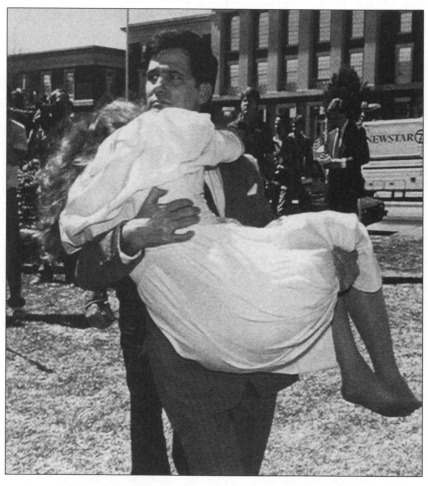

Louis Beam carries his wife, Sheila Beam, after his acquittal on federal seditious conspiracy charges, Fort Smith, Arkansas, 1988. *(Danny Johnston, Associated Press Photo)*

IN 1987, the federal government indicted fourteen white power movement leaders and activists on federal charges including seditious conspiracy. To convict, the prosecutor would have to prove that "two or more persons . . . conspire[d] to overthrow, put down, or destroy by force the Government of the United States, or to levy war against" it.[1] At the ensuing trial in Fort Smith, Arkansas, prosecutors presented extensive evidence of linkages between white power groups and of their plans for violence. Witnesses testified that the movement had declared a race war that targeted both civilians and the federal government. Attorneys presented physical evidence including stolen military weapons, extensive armament, and more.[2] Despite a compelling case, the jury delivered no convictions, and white power activists proclaimed a major victory. The 1988 acquittals at Fort Smith were, in one sense, a product of the organization and strategies of the white power movement, including cell-style organizing and a broad paramilitary infrastructure. But they also indicated the centrality of women to the movement. The trial revealed the movement's deep dependence on social connections, often brokered by women. Acquittal also turned upon the systematic invocation of a primal American story about defending white women. The Fort Smith acquittals can be better understood through a close analysis of the symbolic invocation of women within white power ideology, and the activism and performance—that is to say, the public actions that embodied symbolic and political meaning—of women in the movement.

The defendants, many of whom represented themselves, tapped into a deeply rooted and powerful rhetoric about protecting white female bodies, one that found easy traction not only in the white power movement but among many other Americans. In the purportedly colorblind 1980s, the rhetorical defense of white women from miscegenation, racial pollution, and other dangers continued to structure the worldview not only of white power movement activists but also of several jurors as well as the mainstream media coverage that shaped the trial's public perception. Danger to civilians, though clearly evinced, failed to move the jury as much as the rhetoric deployed by the defense. That the war on the state would be told as a love story within the white power movement is hardly surprising: narratives of the defense of white women and, by extension, white children and domestic spaces have been deployed to justify violence throughout U.S. history.[3] That two defendants formed romantic relationships with jurors after the trial indicates that white power rhetoric held a romantic appeal for some people in broader American society.

To be sure, the symbolic function of white female bodies was more starkly rendered in white power publications than in the mainstream. In one representative example, a 1985 white power pen illustration reimagined the nativity, showing a blond and blue-eyed Mary, Joseph, and infant Jesus surrounded by white-robed Klansmen on one side of the manger and uniformed neo-Nazis on the other. In the background, a burning cross and a swastika flag framed the Star of Bethlehem. Distributed by Aryan Nations and signed by a woman, the sketch placed the Virgin Mary at the epicenter of the unified white power movement. It used the white female body, powerful through its fertility, to symbolize a mythologized white history and theology.[4] Indeed, a cult of motherhood framed a wave of cultural representations of women in the white power movement and their real and imagined place within a movement usually understood through the lens of paramilitary masculinity.

However, the work of real white women was equally important both to movement formation, activism, and violence and to the outcome of the Fort Smith trial. Women's activism, while consciously antifeminist in the sense that women almost uniformly avoided leadership roles and combat, worked to forge the social ties that bound the movement, to support the war on the state waged through men's violence, and to perform white womanhood in ways that carried direct appeals both to the mainstream and to juries.

White power activists codified their ideas about gender in the middle of a nationally charged debate about the place of women in American society. The women's movements of the 1960s and 1970s had put forward radical claims for equality in the home and workplace, reproductive rights, and freedom from sexual violence. The Equal Rights Amendment (ERA), passed by Congress in 1972, failed to receive ratification by the states in no small part because of its purported threat of drafting women into military service and emasculating men, and by the early 1980s, its ratification seemed increasingly unlikely in the face of an ascendant conservative movement.[5] The 1973 *Roe vs. Wade* Supreme Court decision had legalized abortion but had also inflamed a debate about that issue that would prove enormously generative for social conservatives and a rising tide of evangelical voters.[6]

Ideas about women, sexuality, and birth in this period were deeply intertwined with racial ideology, and not just on the fringe. American white supremacy had long depended upon the policing of white women's bodies. In order to propagate a white race, white women had to bear white children. While white men's sexual relationships with nonwhite women mattered less to white supremacists, especially if such activity was secretive, profitable, or part of systematic violence against communities of color, for a white woman to bear nonwhite children was tantamount to racial annihilation.[7] The prohibition of interracial marriage has defined the world's most entrenched racist regimes, and sexual threats to white female bodies have been used to justify the strictest anti-miscegenation laws in the United States. Such bans multiplied and intensified through the first half of the twentieth century, with legislation and enforcement peaking when their intended subjects were white women.[8]

Before the white power movement's unification, the civil rights movement had dismantled legal segregation and made overt racism and segregation less socially acceptable. The landmark *Loving vs. Virginia* Supreme Court decision rendered anti-miscegenation laws unconstitutional in 1967, and public opinion polls showed that Americans not only rapidly came to disapprove of such bans but also quickly forgot that a majority had held them dear just a few years earlier. However, social issues that were related to white women's sexuality, reproduction, and motherhood but typically described without explicitly racist terminology—including opposition to busing, abortion, contraception, welfare, and immigration—appealed well beyond the white power movement. They extended to the mainstream New Right base and mobilized suburbanites in the political center. The continued focus on policing white women's sexuality and reproduction in the post–Vietnam War era indicates the tacit presence of white supremacy in many social issues that remained important to the New Right in the 1980s and 1990s, and belies the idea of a colorblind mainstream.[9]

In white power publications, social issues with implicit relationships to white women's bodies in mainstream society were made emphatically explicit. White power activists claimed that the Zionist Occupational Government (ZOG) wanted to abort white babies, admit immigrants, allow people of color to have unlimited children on the government's welfare dime, allow black men to rape white women, and encourage interracial marriages—all of this, they said, to destroy the white race. In this context, the wombs of white women became battlegrounds.[10]

Rather than weakening or disappearing after the legislative and social changes of the civil rights and women's movements, ideas of the pure and chaste white female body remained powerful in the 1980s. The accompanying mythic villain, the black rapist, still appeared regularly in post–Vietnam War white power publications, even as movement rhetoric and violence increasingly used anticommunism as an alibi for racial violence. The Klan newspaper *Thunderbolt,* among others, ran a regular column featuring true-crime stories of the gruesome rape and murder of white women and girls at the hands of black assailants. This feature ran next to a "Sick Photo of the Month," which usually pictured interracial couples or biracial children, implying the interchangeability and equal repulsiveness of rape, miscegenation, and interracial reproduction.[11]

Protection of white women and their reproductive capacity represented one ideology motivating white power activists to wage war. The future of the white race, activists believed, rested with the mothers of white children. In the movement, this went far beyond anti-miscegenation to the demand that every white woman attempt to bear children. One widely circulated photograph portrayed a white woman sitting on a sand dune before a bank of reeds, long hair draped over her shoulder, nursing a white infant. The sun-drenched, tranquil image appeared with a bold-faced headline: "What We Fight For" or "Fight for White Rights!" The innocent white mother and child symbolized the race under siege. As one caption in the neo-Nazi newspaper *White Power* declared, "If this woman doesn't have three or more children during her lifetime she is helping to speed her Race along the road to extinction."[12]

Significantly, members of the terrorist group the Order encircled a white female infant as they took their membership oath; her body symbolized innocence, but also future fertility. As one Order pamphlet read, "It is recommended that no kinsman be put in combat situations, i.e. raise their sword against ZOG, until he has planted his seed in the belly of a woman. The same for kinswomen, if possible, they should bear at least one warrior before putting their own life on the line." Characterizing birth as intimately tied to the battle at hand, the pamphlet worked to increase the policing of white female bodies, positioning women as mothers first and race warriors second.[13]

White power leaders embraced this pro-natalism with urgency, going so far as to advocate polygamy in hopes of an increased birthrate among movement women. Order leader Bob Mathews, for instance, could not have biological children with his wife, Debbie Mathews, and started a relationship with Zillah Craig, eventually having a child with her. As the movement turned toward open war on the state, several of its leaders emphasized that pro-natalism had become more important than a traditional family structure, and even described the birth of each white child as an act of war.[14]

In the early 1980s, a key development in movement strategy would intensify the emphasis on the reproductive capacity of white women. Activists and leaders called for a "Northwest Imperative," urging white separatists to migrate to the Pacific Northwest and establish an all-white homeland there by producing a large white population. The idea of separatism attempted to appeal to a broader audience. People could say they were "separatist," rather than use older, volatile labels such as "segregationist" or "white supremacist," just as they could replace "racist" with the pseudo-scientific "racialist."[15] Many people across the political spectrum shared the white power movement's concerns about demographic shifts and about the waning white majority. The idea of separatism facilitated recruitment even as the movement prepared for and waged race war.

White power activists had long proposed sites where they might attempt to establish a white homeland. *The Turner Diaries* had outlined a California enclave reaching from the U.S.-Mexico border to 150 miles north of Los Angeles, bounded by the Sierra Madre and the Mojave Desert. Activists in the South called for a "Carolina Free State" that would unite North and South Carolina and expel all people of color. The paramilitary Christian Patriots Defense League, likely in affiliation with the white separatist compound the Covenant, the Sword, and the Arm of the Lord, proposed a "Mid-America Survival Area" that would extend from eastern Colorado to West Virginia and Georgia, and between latitudes drawn just south of Chicago to the southern border of Oklahoma. David Duke advocated a more comprehensive racial partitioning, with designated areas for a black "New Africa" in the South; a Jewish "West Israel" on the East Coast; a Latino/a "Alta California" in the Southwest; and a designated "White Bastion" in the remainder of the country.[16]

White power leaders in the 1980s, however, set their sights on something simpler, a territory they believed they could realistically seize, populate, and defend. "All we heretics ask for is the northwestern part of the USA," wrote Mountain Church leader Robert Miles. "Let us pull away in peace. . . . We are not asking for very much. Just ten percent. Just a geographical tithe in return for which, you have peace and so do we." Miles implied that the state would have to concede a white homeland in order to avoid race war.[17]

The Northwest, Miles claimed, was the only section of the nation that could still be salvaged for the white race. He argued that Washington, Oregon, Idaho, Montana, and Wyoming, at 493,782 square miles, had a population of less than ten million people, mostly white. He proposed a refuge for white separatists, "a sanctuary for our Folk . . . since we are an endangered species in America." Miles wrote that the Northwest had everything the movement required: space free of "hostiles, indifferents or aliens," a coast, mountains, water, vacant land, a definable border, and "the warmth of the temperate zones but the cold which our Folk require in order to thrive." He believed that Mexicans were overrunning the Southwest in a peaceful but "total and final" invasion, and that the South was already lost—too racially mixed and too close to the Jewish- and politician-dominated East Coast. Meanwhile, a territory in the center of the country would be militarily indefensible, with no outlet to the sea. The Northwest was not just the white separatist homeland of choice, then, but the movement's last hope.[18]

White power leaders and activists across the country embraced the idea of Northwest migration and the founding of an all-white nation. Miles claimed his call to migrate was reprinted in "a dozen different publications," including *Calling Our Nation,* the *Inter-Klan Newsletter and Survival Alert, Instauration,* and *National Vanguard,* and was reprinted as a standalone pamphlet with 15,000 copies.[19] Richard Butler advocated the migration, as did the movement faithful to whom he preached at the Aryan Nations compound at Hayden Lake, Idaho.[20] White Aryan Resistance (WAR) leader Tom Metzger echoed Miles in romanticizing the Northwest. "To the eyes of WAR members from Southern California, the Northwest area was a truly refreshing and beautiful site," Metzger wrote. "The spirit of the cowboy and the woman pioneer are everywhere evident as tall, mostly Nordic Aryans ranch and farm while their children ride horseback. . . . [T]he prices for food and clothing are fully 10 to 40% cheaper than in other areas."[21]

Just as Metzger's invocation of "the cowboy and the woman pioneer" reinscribed gender expectations for women in the white power movement, it also fit into a longer narrative of romanticization of the West. In its mainstream use, this story elided the genocide of Native Americans by describing the West as an empty land ripe for those who sought economic opportunity and didn't fear hard work and harsh conditions.[22] Movement leaders who chose the Northwest ignored long-established chains of migration that had shaped the region and which would continue to bring Asians to Seattle and Portland and Latinas and Latinos to agricultural areas such as Washington's Yakima Valley through the 1980s.[23] Instead, the movement focused on largely white areas like northern Idaho. Butler built the Aryan Nations compound in Kootenai County, where, according to the 1980 U.S. Census, the population of 59,770 people included only 39 black residents, 197 Asians, 753 Hispanics, and 467 Native Americans. The director of the Chamber of Commerce in nearby Coeur d'Alene estimated "maybe half a dozen" Jewish residents.[24] White power leaders waxed poetic about the beautiful scenery— winding mountain roads, pine-covered hills, and brilliant blue lakes. So did journalists covering the movement migration:

> Here . . . nature has crafted a landscape beautiful enough to make you weep. Tall pines scrape the sky, reflected in cool, mirror-clear lakes. Mountains and valleys are dusted in Christmas-card snow, like powdered sugar. Everything is dipped in a piercing blue light, at rest and quiet.[25]

White power migrants worked as loggers, in mines and cement plants, and in the small economy of publication, recruitment, and armament generated by the Aryan Nations compound itself.

At the 1986 Aryan Nations World Congress, Miles pressed activists to pack up and move. He preached that the Northwest nation for whites would be won not by violence or treaty but by migration and reproduction.[26] Revolution, he said, would be made "not with guns, not with violence, but with love for each other. We will flood the Northwest with white babies and white children so there is no question who this land belongs to. We are going to outbreed each other." Miles added that this strategy should allow "as many husbands and wives as required" for each white woman to bear five to ten white children.[27]

According to movement rhetoric, white women would be delighted with their task of bearing and raising white warriors. As Butler wrote in 1984, "The thoughts of Aryan woman are dominated by the desire to enter family life. Aryan woman brings true love and affection and a happy, well-run home to refresh and inspire her man. The world of contented womanhood is made of family: husband, children and home . . . No Equal Rights Amendment or National Organization for Women buttons allowed." This antifeminist, domestic, and subservient role for white women was paired with strictly white-only sexual relationships. "Miscegenation," Miles admonished, "is the ultimate abomination and violation of the law of God."[28]

In some ways, the white power movement's emphasis on motherhood mirrored similar currents in both mainstream New Right conservatism and American culture at large. The American housewife had become iconic in the 1950s as Cold War conservatives intertwined populism and antistatism with domesticity. These roles shaped and delimited the grassroots women's activism that gave rise to the New Right.[29] Populist housewives framed essentialist notions of gender, particularly in their claim that mothers were uniquely suited to the task of vigilance in crusades against the conflated enemies of communism, internationalism, expert knowledge, and race-mixing.[30] The housewife populists of the Cold War had, by the 1980s, influenced and populated the New Right.

Between 1960 and 1980, meanwhile, motherhood itself became a central and highly racialized issue in American Cold War politics. A lower average age of marriage and rigid gender norms harmonized with a nationalist push for white women to stay home and reproduce. Bearing and rearing free white children defined good citizenship for American women, and proponents of hereditarianism and population control sought to limit birth rates among women of color. Those who supported school segregation, restrictions on welfare and public housing, tough-on-crime policing, and mandatory sterilization (largely aimed at poor women of color), as well as those who opposed immigration and overpopulation, all justified their positions by invoking the hyperfertile bodies of nonwhite women. Anxieties about rising nonwhite birth rates mingled with those about school desegregation and the sexual revolution.[31]

White power pro-natalism and the symbolic importance of women's reproduction became distilled in Order member David Lane's slogan, penned in prison and widely circulated within the movement: "We must secure the existence of our people and a future for white children." This reproductive mandate, which quickly became known as "Fourteen Words," was linked to the sexual availability of white women. After Lane's arrest, Butler offered white women as a reward for his activism, assuring the Aryan Nations congregation that "there will be many wives waiting for Brother Lane when he walks out of ZOG's prison."[32] Indeed, while incarcerated, Lane married and also wrote several poems for the *White Aryan Resistance* about the beauty of white women.[33]

The Turner Diaries also offered a template for white power women's activism within a cell-style organization and race war. The novel described a role of subservience and purity for white women, often by drawing on familiar tropes. One pivotal scene—the public lynching of men and women in interracial relationships, the women marked with "race traitor" signs—emphasized the violent policing of sexually transgressive white women. The novel's protagonist, Earl Turner, begins his racist activism as part of a cell including two other men and one woman, Katherine. She comes to life as a character only through her sexual relationship with Turner—he never speaks to her or thinks about her until then. Turner describes her as an ideal racist woman, devoted both to him and to race war: "She is an affectionate, sensitive, and very feminine girl beneath the cool, professional exterior she has always maintained." Katherine, though an activist, resides in a terrain demarcated as female, writing and editing her own women's quarterly.[34]

Although Katherine soon refuses to be "nothing but a cook and housekeeper" for the rest of the cell members, gender norms—and the expectation that her ultimate function will be to sexually reward Turner and bear white children—shape her role as revolutionary combatant.[35] She takes supportive rather than violent action: disguising the men and driving getaway cars. Meanwhile, sexual danger to white women is the force that drives the Organization to race war. At one point, a black man accosts and nearly rapes Katherine. Her monogamy and her protection by white men mark Katherine as a good woman; she remains safe from assault, and when Turner lands in prison, she waits faithfully for him.[36]

Symbolic invocations of endangered white women by male leaders and activists provided a crucial rhetorical tool for consolidating and directing white power activism and for making appeals to the mainstream. Several accounts of paramilitary masculinity examine women only in this symbolic register.[37] While male movement leaders wrote romantically about the beauty of white women and made pen sketches of topless white women bearing semi-automatic weapons for recruitment stickers, however, the cause required the work of women themselves.[38]

To be sure, the paramilitary structure of the movement meant that men held all leadership roles and that women's activism was circumscribed.

Movement discourse regularly objectified women. Even when women donned their own camouflage fatigues and marched for themselves, as they did in the White Patriot Party, leaders still viewed them as "the mothers of future Aryan warriors" and objects of sexual reward. "Look-a-here, yaw'll," proclaimed one caption in the *Confederate Leader* under a photograph of a blond woman in camouflage fatigues. "We've got the best looking gals too. 20% of the White Patriot Party is female—Serving proudly to further our cause."[39] The double meaning of "serving" emphasized both military and sexual service by women. This recruitment tactic, which may have overstated the female membership of the group, appealed to men but foreclosed the possibility that women might become white power soldiers in their own right.

Although movement rhetoric often reduced women to mute symbols, maternal or sexual, male activists within the movement needed real white women to validate men's activism both rhetorically and practically. The wives of white power activists played critical roles in establishing the credibility of their husbands. Butler and Miles both used their long marriages as evidence of good character within the movement and, when prosecuted, in court. Butler said he once discovered an informant because the man, suspiciously, didn't bring his wife to church on the Aryan Nations compound.[40] So, too, could women jeopardize the war on the state: the wife of Order member Denver Parmenter, for instance, disapproved of her husband's activism and criminal activities. She prohibited the Order from using her infant daughter in the membership oath ritual—and she may have eventually influenced Parmenter to testify against the group.[41]

For some women who rose to prominence within the movement during these years, relationships to men worked to validate these roles: some spoke as widows, others as wives, and others as promised objects of sexual reward for white male warriors. Debbie Mathews, for instance, became a regular speaker at white power events as the honored widow of Bob Mathews after his death; David Lane's wife, Katja Lane, rose to prominence in the movement after their marriage by trading heavily on his status as a "prisoner of war."[42]

Some wives of prominent leaders also rose in the movement by forming racist women's organizations affiliated with groups run by their husbands, following a long tradition of Klanswomen's auxiliaries.[43] Kathleen Metzger ran the suburban Aryan Women's League in the late 1980s, which published a considerable amount of material in its own name while her husband Tom

Metzger's WAR dominated white power activities in California. Several of her publications referred to the frustration of league members at getting "no respect from the men" and having "no place in the movement." However, the league still proposed activities that hinged on traditional ideas of a woman's sphere and—even more important, as one flier proclaimed—as "BEARERS OF THE FUTURE WHITE RACE!"[44]

The Aryan Women's League located its concerns within the bounds of home and family, a terrain marked in the movement as feminine.[45] Members started a coupon-sharing program to lower grocery bills in order to raise contributions for the race war, and produced racist and antisemitic coloring books for white children. They advocated homeschooling, fearing corruption, Jewish content, and race-mixing in public schools. They discussed memorialization for fallen movement soldiers.[46]

The league strongly emphasized the support of white infants. One flier showed a white child in pajamas, standing on top of a tiny Earth, holding a teddy bear in one hand and giving a Nazi salute with the other. The flier had blank spaces in which to write the name of a newborn white child and his or her parents, and instructed supporters to send them a dollar, thus creating a network of economic support for new families. The league followed these announcements with courteous thank-you letters about the development of each sponsored child, also enclosing more birth announcements and calling for further donations. "Yes, the baby boom for the Aryan race is here!" the letter declared. "Let us promote it!"[47]

In addition to running their own organizations and producing their own printed materials, women in the white power movement worked extensively in the social sphere, contributing to the building and maintenance of social networks, recruitment, the production and circulation of family-oriented cultural products like recipes and homeschooling materials, and the social normalization of young activists.[48] However, their role remained limited by the rigidly patriarchal and paramilitary structure of the white power movement, both in top-down leadership by men like Beam, Butler, and Miles, and in local operations of male-led cells.

In the war on the state, women were expected to bear future white warriors, train as nurses to heal the wounded, prepare stores of food and other supplies to sustain white people through apocalyptic race war, and carry out support work. Women attended—and even co-owned—paramilitary camps, but while the men trained in weapons, urban warfare, and demolition tactics, most of the women learned survivalist strategies such as canning, making their own soap and shampoo, and how best to prevent radiation poisoning in the event of nuclear war.[49] In cells, women did support work including disguising male activists and driving getaway cars, destroying documents, transporting people and weapons, designing medallions meant to identify group members, and proofreading major movement tracts such as the Order's Declaration of War (a role that may also have created opportunities for women to make substantive contributions to such writings).[50]

Women's participation worked to broaden and reaffirm the wide variety of activists incorporated within the unified white power movement, even bridging cultural divides between separatist housewives (survivalist and Christian Identity rural and suburban activists) and younger, urban skinheads. The separatist housewife discourse as written by women appears most clearly in *Christian Patriot Women,* published regularly in the late 1980s by June Johnston, a homemaker in rural Wyoming. Notably, neither Johnston nor her husband has an archival presence beyond this publication, and she may have been an invented character or a pseudonym. Nevertheless, *Christian Patriot Women* was intended for real movement women; like the Aryan Women's League, it framed its message with images, language, and topics defined by the movement as feminine and included practical information for survivalist homemaking. Johnston adorned her photocopied publication with clip-art roses and butterflies. She ran inspirational quotes and witticisms— "What to wear for 'safe sex'? A wedding ring!"—and a regular column of charming things her children said, titled "From the Mouths of Little Aryans." She also coordinated a letter-writing and fundraising campaign to support the widows of white men killed or imprisoned in the war on the state, and wrote and republished articles on a host of incendiary rumors such as stories of white women being forced to have abortions and claims that oral contraception advocates plotted to lower the white birth rate. *Christian Patriot Women* opposed the ERA and abortion and defined good womanhood through Proverbs 31, a biblical passage that outlines the attributes of a submissive, godly wife and emphasizes obedience.[51]

Johnston also sought to prepare her readers for apocalyptic race war as foretold by Christian Identity. She shared recipes for food, but also for soap, lotion, and other things women would need to make for themselves. "We must get this knowledge back . . . or we'll never be free of 'the system,'" she wrote, self-consciously quoting *The Turner Diaries*. Johnston regularly entreated readers to grow and can their own food, and to hoard store-bought food and clean water: "Life could get pretty [bad] in a very short period of time. We need food, clothing, shelter, and . . . arms!" Johnston framed this call by referencing the "New World Order," connecting the paramilitary white power movement of the 1980s to the budding militia movement that used the term much as the old guard had used "ZOG" to claim that an international conspiracy had taken control of the government. Despite the feminine aesthetic and domestic slant of the journal, it attempted to prepare women for an apocalyptic "hideous upcoming battle." Johnston conceded that even her women readers must prepare to bear arms: "Probably more of us will have to 'man the guns' than has been the case back through history. . . . We must be prepared, WELL PREPARED."[52]

As survivalist housewives like Johnston prepared for a coming apocalyptic battle with the state, women also appeared among the groundswell of skinhead activists drawn to the movement in the late 1980s. Skinheads presented the most direct cultural challenge to white power leadership. Leaders who had long abhorred drugs, alcohol, and tattoos had to adjust their rhetoric to appeal to this new group of urban recruits. Skinhead women typically wore their hair short or shaved, wore heavy makeup, and adopted androgynous postures and behaviors. Strikingly, even within skinhead publications, both male and female white power activists insisted on motherhood as a woman's most important contribution to the movement, although they rendered it differently. In 1991, for instance, the neo-Nazi SS Action Group advertised with a pen drawing of a skinhead couple and child. The woman wears a plaid miniskirt; though a mother, she holds the baby against her flat, muscular chest. Her face signals nothing soft or nurturing about motherhood.[53]

Even violent skinhead fighters defined themselves as mothers. In one interview with the Chicago zine *Right as Reina,* skinhead woman and *Bay Aryan* publisher Jessica (no last name given) recounted an incident in which a man attacked one of her friends with a loaded gun. Only sixteen years old at the time, she rushed the attacker, daring him to shoot her. She proudly remembered getting a reputation for being "crazy," a positive attribute in violent skinhead culture. "But my primary interests lie closer to the heart," Jessica said, to conclude her story. "I take care of my family (husband and baby) and try to be a model Aryan wife and mother."[54]

The emphasis on white women's reproduction was so powerful that it worked as a unifying force for activists with dramatic—perhaps otherwise insurmountable—cultural differences. Motherhood spanned the distance between housewife populism and paramilitary violence. Even *Right as Reina,* which often included semi-sexualized images of young girls and was by no means directed toward women, carried birth announcements.[55]

Women in the white power movement would shape the sedition trial, both because of the symbolic invocation of their bodies as terrain in need of defense, and because of the work real women did in forming the movement, furthering its war on the state, and performing white womanhood to garner sympathy from jurors and the public. This worked precisely because the movement story about women's purity resonated with mainstream Americans. White power women were both symbols of and actors in a common struggle: to protect white women's chastity and racial reproduction and, with it, the future of whiteness itself.

The Fort Smith trial represented a major change in the prosecution of white power violence. Before 1985, those who committed such acts of violence were often either not prosecuted by local, state, or federal authorities or acquitted at trial. The failure to convict the Greensboro gunmen in two criminal trials or to levy any real penalties upon them in a civil trial showed this most clearly.[56] Indeed, efforts undertaken by outside groups—namely, the lawsuits filed by the Southern Poverty Law Center—had done far more to slow the white power movement than had any criminal trial or state action. While criminal proceedings against violent racist actors failed to produce convictions in Greensboro, and racketeering prosecutions of Order members resulted in only piecemeal success, civil proceedings more effectively hobbled hate group activity. It was an SPLC lawsuit on behalf of the Vietnamese Fishermen's Association that had stalled Beam's paramilitary organization in Texas in 1982, albeit temporarily. In February 1987, the SPLC won a $7 million lawsuit against the United Klans of America, an old-guard group connected only loosely to the paramilitary white power movement. The court ordered the UKA to surrender its Alabama headquarters to the mother of Michael Donald, a nineteen-year-old black man two of its members had lynched in 1981. While local criminal courts frequently declined to prosecute or returned short sentences, judges in civil cases—where there was a lighter burden of proof and where the plaintiff's case could be bolstered by the resources of the SPLC—could levy fines, seize assets, reveal mailing lists, and even bar white power association and organization.[57]

The criminal justice system's failure to significantly slow the white power movement did not go unnoticed, especially by some federal agents dissatisfied with the outcomes of criminal trials involving movement defendants. According to FBI affidavits, agents felt the trial of the Order had resulted in convictions of merely "entry-level soldiers and non-coms," while the leaders— Beam, Miles, Butler, Metzger, Pierce, and others—avoided charges.[58] To some extent the strategy of leaderless resistance had worked as intended, both in protecting leaders from prosecution and by isolating cells infiltrated by informants. In 1985, the Department of Justice began Operation Clean Sweep, a massive investigation with the goal of a major court case against white power movement leaders.[59]

In recognizing the linkages between seemingly disparate white power groups, Operation Clean Sweep had several early victories. These included stopping a 1985 plot by an Aryan Nations member to kill an informant; arresting Posse Comitatus leader William Potter Gale in 1986 and convicting him of plotting to attack the Internal Revenue Service; and arresting eight members of the Arizona Patriots on gun and conspiracy charges related to a planned bank robbery in 1986 and preventing imminent acts of violence by that group.[60] On the connection between the Arizona Patriots and several other groups—Posse Comitatus, Aryan Nations, and the Order—one anonymous official told the *Arizona Republic,* "It's like one guy is in the Army and the other is in the Navy. . . . They both belong to the military." If this description alluded figuratively to the movement's actions as warfare, the evidence found upon the group's arrest established the veracity of this comparison. The Arizona Patriots had blueprints for two major dams and a power station, as well as a cache of weapons and explosives. The compound was low-tech, apart from its arsenal, with no plumbing or electricity beyond a portable generator they used to screen *Red Dawn,* a film depicting guerrilla resistance to a Soviet invasion. "They're cavemen with bombs," one federal agent told a reporter.[61]

The indictments in the Fort Smith trial, issued on April 21, 1987, used years of FBI investigation, surveillance, and wiretaps to allege that the white power movement had attempted to overthrow the government through outright revolution.[62] To be sure, the FBI had an interest in finding conspiracy, and some parts of this evidence were more reliable and better interpreted than others. However, the Fort Smith trial represented the only attempt at prosecuting white power as a coherent social movement, and the scope of the proceedings reflected this goal. Fourteen men faced indictment on charges of interstate transport of stolen money, conspiracy to manufacture illegal weapons, conspiracy to murder federal officers, and seditious conspiracy. The extensive indictment listed 119 acts to establish grounds for seditious conspiracy, including the 1981 attempted invasion of Dominica by white power activists; the firebombing of a Jewish Community Center in Bloomington, Indiana, in August 1983; the CSA destruction of a natural gas pipeline in Fulton, Arkansas, in November 1983; the theft of more than $4 million by the Order in 1983 and 1984; the purchase of guns and explosives in Oklahoma and Missouri; bank robberies in Illinois, Missouri, and North Dakota; and Liberty Net, Beam's computer network that linked white power groups and listed the names and addresses of their enemies.[63]

The indictments also revealed that war on the government had not slowed with the trials of Order members. An FBI affidavit on October 2, 1986, revealed ongoing plots to "rescue" white supremacists from incarceration at various prisons—another strategy taken from *The Turner Diaries*. Eleven friends and family members of movement leaders, recruited as FBI informants, stood ready to testify that "the top echelons had developed a plan to set off bombs at federal buildings in five cities"—including Denver, Minneapolis, St. Louis, and Kansas City—"and then threaten to bomb more buildings unless several members of The Order were released from federal prisons." Informants said that Beam, Miles, and paramilitary instructor Jack Mohr met in Harrison, Arkansas, in May 1986 to discuss a jailbreak of Order members that was to be financed with counterfeit money. Wiretaps of hundreds of calls between Miles and racist groups nationwide revealed the mechanics of movement unification.[64]

The indictment targeted white power leaders Beam, Butler, and Miles, but also a number of mid- and low-level activists: CSA member Richard Wayne Snell, who blew up the natural gas pipeline to Fort Smith and killed a state trooper; and Order members Bruce Pierce, Andrew Barnhill, David Lane, Ardie McBrearty, and Richard Scutari. All of these men were charged with attempting to overthrow the U.S. government. CSA members Lambert

Miller, David McGuire, and two more casual participants who had come to the movement through the farm foreclosure crisis, William and Ivan Wade, were charged with plotting to kill a federal judge and FBI agent. Fort Smith gun dealer Robert Smalley was also indicted, but charges were quickly dismissed for lack of evidence. Neither Tom Metzger nor William Pierce was charged; Glenn Miller and James Ellison would testify for the state under plea bargains.[65]

After many years of ineffective, smaller prosecutions, the Fort Smith trial marked the first serious attempt by the federal government to recognize the unification of seemingly disparate Klan, neo-Nazi, and white separatist groups in a cohesive white power movement, and to prosecute the movement's leaders in light of this understanding. Affidavits documented nearly a decade of control by Beam, Butler, and Miles, and also named Miles's home as the command center for the Order.[66] "They preached war, prayed for war and dreamed of war," said Justice Department prosecutor Martin Carlson. "And when war came, they willingly accepted war."[67] The indictments presented a serious enough threat to white power leaders that Beam decided to flee the country, setting off a series of events that would shape the outcome of the trial.

Before Beam fled he married a woman whose martyrdom would later rally the movement and appeal to the mainstream. After the fishermen's dispute, Louis Beam had led a chaotic personal life. He separated from his third wife in 1981, and an ugly custody battle followed the split. Beam took his young daughter to Costa Rica for two years. After his return to Texas in late 1984, he moved permanently to the Aryan Nations compound. He didn't break his Texas ties, however, and took long trips there frequently.[68]

Sheila Toohey was a pretty, blond twenty-year-old Sunday school teacher at the Gospel Temple, a Christian Identity congregation in Pasadena, Texas. Beam's young daughter was one of her students. Perhaps Beam met the Toohey family during the fishermen's dispute: his Texas Knights of the Ku Klux Klan had run a bookstore in Pasadena. Toohey came from a family that lived in a trailer in nearby Santa Fe, Texas—the site of the Klan rally where Beam had burned a boat painted "U.S.S. Viet Cong" during the fishermen conflict in 1981.[69]

"Louis fell in love with Sheila immediately," wrote J. B. Campbell, a white power movement activist who also claimed mercenary service in Rhodesia.[70]

Campbell's laudatory essay later appeared on Beam's personal website under the heading "Love" and framed with images of roses:

> [Beam had] been visiting her father, talking politics, and couldn't believe his friend could have such a beautiful, sweet and unaffected daughter as Sheila, who lived at home with her parents and brothers in Santa Fe, Texas. Sheila taught Sunday school. She'd had to wear a back brace from a recent car accident and was in constant pain, although she would never burden anyone by mentioning it. In the following weeks Sheila noticed that Louis was coming over for dinner quite frequently and that he was talking with her more than with her father. He actually likes me, she realized. Within a few months Louis asked Sheila to marry him.[71]

The passage focused on Toohey as a vulnerable white woman—in constant pain but never mentioning it—and subservient to the man who "actually like[d]" her. Her position as a Sunday school teacher confirmed her innocence, presumed virginity, fitness for motherhood, and, since she taught children at a Christian Identity church, subscription to a white power political theology. That she lived surrounded, and presumably cared for, by her father and brothers emphasized her movement from one set of male guardians to another. It also highlighted the twenty-year age difference of the newlyweds. Toohey was Beam's fourth wife; the first three had each been around sixteen years old when they married and around twenty years old when they divorced.[72]

Beam and Toohey married at a Christian Identity church in Pennsylvania in April 1987.[73] After the wedding, with seditious conspiracy charges issued, Louis and Sheila Beam traveled to Mexico to avoid trial, taking his seven-year-old daughter with them, though without the proper documents. They settled in Chapala, near Guadalajara, in a community of white American expatriates. Beam spent four months on the FBI's Ten Most Wanted list before authorities caught up with him in November 1987.[74]

One night the Beams returned home after grocery shopping. While the couple was unloading the food from the car and his daughter was still sitting in the vehicle, authorities apprehended Louis Beam. Sheila Beam "glanced out the kitchen window down at the car and was appalled to see Louis bent over the hood with a gun to his head," according to Campbell's narrative. Sheila Beam would later say that the officers never identified themselves as policemen and she assumed the attack was a robbery or kidnapping. Purportedly defending herself, she grabbed her husband's weapon and shot a Mexican federal officer three times, wounding him. Authorities detained her in Mexico for ten days while they extradited Louis Beam to the United States, where he spent the next five months in prison during the sedition trial. A Mexican judge found Sheila Beam not guilty for reasons of self-defense in November 1987, and she was released and deported back to the United States. The officer she shot in the chest and abdomen remained hospitalized.[75]

To white power activists, this story was about endangered white women, but it was also about government betrayal. Rumors flew that federal agents had used phony drug charges as a pretense for the arrest, in order to extradite Louis Beam to the United States. This narrative placed innocent Sheila Beam in the crosshairs of a renegade state.[76] However, Beam would most likely have been subject to extradition in any case, with or without drug charges.[77]

In an affidavit, Beam presented herself as an innocent white woman in need of the protection of white men. She said that she sustained an abdominal injury when the arresting officers threw her over a chair, and was then taken to jail and kept handcuffed for five days. She also said that the chief of police threatened her with torture, and that she was forced to sign documents in Spanish that she couldn't read. She testified:

> While I was in the Guadalajara jail, I was physically and psychologically mistreated. I was kept with my wrists handcuffed behind my back for five days; my wrists were so swollen that my hands were turning colors and my watch was cutting off the circulation. I was hand-fed by a little Mexican boy with his dirty fingers. Officers would come into my cell and leer at me and caress their weapons. I was chained to the bed, which had a filthy, rotten mattress, and when I would try to sleep, they would kick the bed to jar me awake and keep me from sleeping. I was refused water for extended periods and medication for my back injury or my back brace. I was denied medical attention for my abdominal injuries and suffered from vaginal bleeding for several days afterward.[78]

Her testimony positioned her as endangered. It placed her in peril and in the presence of male racial others—the "Mexican boy" feeding her with "his dirty fingers," and the officers. It presented men of color "caress[ing] their

weapons" as they "leer[ed]" at her, invoking masturbation.[79] It also placed
her in a violated bedroom space, "chained to the bed, which had a filthy,
rotten mattress." Within the broader frame of pro-natalism, this language
positioned Sheila Beam's body as vulnerable to attack by men of color, and
emphasized it as a site of combat where battles might be won or lost through
the birth or absence of white children. The vaginal bleeding she said she suffered after her imprisonment hinted at both rape and miscarriage of a white
child, and would have signified a double martyrdom.

Jailed at the moment when the state had finally turned to the prosecution
of the white power movement, Sheila Beam acted the martyr in a way that
further united activists and appealed to people beyond the movement. Her
wounded body served as a constant symbolic reminder of state failure and
betrayal. Metzger lobbied for her release; Kirk Lyons, who represented Beam
in the sedition trial and would become the go-to attorney of the white power
movement over the next decade, sent an associate, Dave Holloway, to help
the Toohey family advocate for her return. Back home, the Tooheys answered
the phone with the entreaty, "Save Our Sheila."[80] After her release Lyons told
one reporter, "It made a Christian out of me again. Her being freed was a
miracle to me."[81]

In the mainstream press, too, Sheila Beam became a sympathetic figure
in local newspapers and major publications alike. A series of articles in the
Galveston Daily News focused on her injuries, stating as fact that she had
been "severely beaten" and raising the possibility that she "may have been
sexually assaulted." The same reporter uncritically repeated white power
claims that FBI agents had refused to arrange her release to the United States,
and described "physical and psychological coercion" during her ten-day imprisonment.[82] Other articles linked her faith in God to her hopes for the
acquittal of all the trial's defendants,[83] and mentioned her pain and injuries
with no mention of the reasons for Louis Beam's arrest or Sheila Beam's actions in shooting and wounding the officer.[84] The *Houston Chronicle* reported
that she returned to the United States sobbing and limping, escorted by her
father and an associate of Lyons, and was met by her mother and three
brothers at the airport. The article emphasized that Sheila Beam had a swollen
abdomen and walked with such a pronounced limp that two people had to
support her.[85] A photograph of Sheila's return in the *Miami News* featured
a flattering photograph of her leaning against her brother's chest, holding
flowers and flanked by a pretty, smiling, female friend. The caption referred

to her "break[ing] out in tears" upon her return, and to her being "charged with shooting a Mexican federal police officer during the arrest of her husband at their . . . home." It elided any reference to Christian Identity or participation in the white power movement, either by Sheila Beam or by her husband. It didn't even name Louis Beam, much less discuss his pending seditious conspiracy charges or his stint on the FBI's Ten Most Wanted list. Nevertheless, it made clear that Sheila Beam shot the officer at her home, emphasizing domestic defense beneath a photograph that portrayed her as vulnerable, small, and feminine.[86]

For her own part, Sheila Beam delivered a political performance of martyrdom both in comments to the press and in her actions. After her release, she flew directly to Fort Smith, where Louis Beam had been transferred to a federal prison hospital following a weeklong hunger strike. White power leaders praised her selfless devotion. "Despite her severe internal injuries and equally severe psychological damage," Campbell wrote, "Sheila postponed her required emergency surgery and flew to Ft. Smith to reassure her husband."[87] Sheila Beam went to her husband's side despite her severe pain, the story had it, illustrating the sacrifice of the white female body to the needs of the movement.

During the trial, the presence of Sheila Beam's wounded and wronged body entered the official record in several ways. Lyons invoked her injuries regularly, interrupting testimony about her arrest to ask the pursuing FBI agent what had happened to her back brace and conspicuously leaving court to pick her up at the airport. Sheila Beam continued to speak about her injuries and abuse to the press, and claimed her husband's innocence with the simple position that since he had quit the Klan in 1981, he couldn't now be guilty of sedition. In truth, he had quit the Klan to join Aryan Nations and lead the white power movement on a larger scale. She also reminded newspapers that her husband held the Distinguished Flying Cross, the Army Commendation Medal, and the Air Medal for Heroism, staking out his moral authority as a hero of the Vietnam War.[88]

It is difficult to gauge the impact of such performative acts on the outcome of a jury trial, but Sheila Beam's symbolic work toward acquittal should not be discounted. Even in the pages of academic accounts that have argued that white power paramilitarism partially or wholly excluded them, women nevertheless appear as historical actors who impact events. In Rafael Ezekiel's widely cited ethnographic study, for instance, which includes his observation of the Fort Smith trial, he notes that "a sister appears for a young fellow who is already serving a long term for involvement in The Order's robbery of an armored car . . . entering the court, she touched her brother's arm, quietly, as she passed him."[89] With these actions, the "sister"— no name given, as she did not qualify as an activist in this study, but perhaps it was Brenna or Laura Beth Tate, sisters of David Tate—conferred humanity upon her brother, appealed to the jury, and neutralized the racism of the movement.[90] Similarly, Ezekiel recounts the presence of Louis Beam's "young new wife," Sheila Beam, although she isn't named in his account.[91] Ezekiel describes how the couple

> make frequent eye contact across the room. She had been the Sunday school teacher of Beam's daughter. A reporter ungraciously described her to me as "a Yahweh freak." Here in court she wears a frilled white blouse; during Beam's arrest in Mexico, she shot an armed *Federale* who had failed to identify himself.[92]

In other words, Sheila Beam played her part as a movement activist by creating and embodying a particular narrative of her innocence, the arrest, the justified shooting of the Mexican officer, and her husband's wrongful detention—one persuasive enough to be accepted uncritically by journalists and academic observers.[93]

Beyond the symbolic impact of women and their courtroom performances, several problems plagued the trial's prosecutors. The decision to hold the proceedings in Fort Smith, Arkansas, meant drawing on a jury pool near the CSA, close to the headquarters of the Populist Party, and near the place where radical tax protestor Gordon Kahl died in a shootout with pursuing federal agents. One juror would later go on record saying he admired Beam's racist views and that the Bible prohibited race-mixing. The court completed a rushed jury selection process in one day, rather than the two to three weeks customary for similar trials. In a jury pool narrowed by peremptory challenges to eliminate six black prospective jurors—the same strategy used to ensure all-white or majority-white juries in the Greensboro trials—the judge questioned jurors himself, rather than allowing the usual practice of scrutiny by attorneys. He quickly appointed an all-white, working-class jury. FBI agent Jack Knox, who had led the investigation of the white power movement following Kahl's death, would later say that the judge jeopardized the outcome by pushing the trial too fast toward completion, eliminating professionals from the jury, and excusing all jurors who had even heard of white power groups operating locally, where local news media had thoroughly covered the CSA bust just a few years earlier.[94]

The judge also greatly constricted the case planned by the prosecution, in part because of Beam's flight. He quickly excluded half of the prosecution's 1,200 pieces of evidence and half of its 200 witnesses. Beam had been arrested in Guadalajara with forty-eight pieces of evidence, but these were excluded because Mexican officers had not followed U.S. protocol. Evidence ruled inadmissible included Beam's deliberate attempt to falsify his identity with multiple blank and partially blank Texas birth certificates; false identification and military documents in the name of his alias, Jerry Wayne Clinton; a passport application; two Texas death certificates for Louis R. Beam Jr.; a California driver's license application; and instructions for filling out false identification papers. Inadmissible, too, was a medallion proving that Beam was part of the Order.[95]

The trial was lengthy and complex, with several defendants representing themselves. Movement-associated people who testified as witnesses for the prosecution frequently undermined their own credibility, whether deliberately or not. Ellison, the star witness for the prosecution, delivered large quantities of incriminating and alarming information including details of a plot to poison the public water supply of a major city. But he also referred to levitation and to speaking directly with God, which, as one newspaper reported, "may have reduced his credibility with the jury."[96] Many elements of Ellison's testimony, however, are confirmed elsewhere in the archive. Successful delivery of those thirty gallons of cyanide to the water supply of Chicago, New York, or Washington would have killed almost half a million people, according to the FBI and independent reports. A witness for the prosecution also pointed out that when he blew up the natural gas line outside of Fort Smith, Snell had intended to destroy a much larger line running from Texas to Chicago. Clearly, civilians were in the crosshairs of the white power movement's war on the state.[97]

According to assistant U.S. attorney Steven Snyder, it was this threat to the civilian population—a threat now dramatically amplified by the training and weapons of the Vietnam War and the paramilitary culture that blossomed in its wake—along with the unification of the white power movement that justified the rare seditious conspiracy charge. During the trial, the

Houston Chronicle reported, Snyder "wheeled into the courtroom two huge laundry hampers jammed with rifles, submachine guns, a shotgun, a rocket launcher, grenade launchers and grenades allegedly used at the CSA compound to train the Aryan Warriors for rebellion."[98]

The prosecution needed to establish that white power leaders were in contact with one another and involved with shaping the violence carried out by cells and individual activists. They spent significant time on the creation of a hit list that included Alan Berg, the progressive activist and controversial television producer Norman Lear, and SPLC head Morris Dees, among others.[99] They also presented data from the FBI wiretap of Miles's phones. Between March 8, 1985, and November 7, 1985, Miles had made sixty-three calls to Butler, twenty calls to CSA member David Moutoux, fourteen calls to Metzger, and assorted calls to William Pierce, Don Black, Glenn Miller, *Thunderbolt* publisher Ed Fields, and other activists. Not only did the list of individuals he called clearly illustrate a unified, connected, and coordinated white power movement, but the volume of calls indicated continued activity.[100]

The social relationships cemented by women's participation further revealed the interconnectedness of Klan, neo-Nazi, and other groups in a cohesive, antigovernment white power movement, although only some of them were mentioned in trial testimony, and they were not fully mobilized in the prosecution's argument. Marriages were an important way of forging alliances between groups and of reaffirming loyalty within factions. While marriage records are not available for most white power unions—perhaps because some of them were deliberately conducted outside of state auspices—a thorough reading of sources across several archives yields a startling picture of movement interconnections.

Limiting such examples to those immediately pertinent to the sedition trial: The daughter of the Order's chief counterfeiters, Robert and Sharon Merki—who, with her parents, had attended the LaPorte Church of Christ—married an Order member and received some of the Order's ill-gotten funds. After members of the Order assassinated their own Walter West for talking too much, another Order member, Thomas Bentley, married West's widow. Carl Franklin Jr., the leader of the Pennsylvania branch of Aryan Nations, married Order member David Lane's adopted sister, Jane Eden Lane, before becoming heir apparent to Aryan Nations founder Richard Butler; Butler officiated at their wedding.[101]

Marriages bore out intergroup connections relevant to the sedition trial even after the acquittals. Ellison, leader of the CSA, would later marry the daughter of Robert G. Millar, head of the white separatist compound at Elohim City. Dave Holloway, who traveled to Mexico to advocate for Sheila Beam's release, married twice: to the daughter of Robert Sisente, second-in-command of the paramilitary Klan group that had harassed Vietnamese fishermen under Louis Beam's direction, and to the daughter of Order member James Wallington. Wallington had evaded pursuit by FBI agents, including Knox, by hiding at Elohim City. Kirk Lyons, who represented Louis Beam in the sedition trial, would also marry within the movement in a 1990 double wedding. In a ceremony at Aryan Nations and officiated by Butler, with Beam as best man, Lyons married eighteen- or nineteen-year-old Brenna Tate—daughter of an Aryan Nations leader and sister of Order member David Tate. Her sister, Laura Beth Tate, married Neill Payne, a Houston man who had hidden the Beams when they were on the run to Mexico. And David McGuire, one of the sedition trial defendants who would become romantically involved with a juror, was previously married to Joahanna Ellison, the daughter of Jim Ellison; Ellison participated in the marriage ceremony.[102]

Romantic relationships also cast doubt upon the acquittal. Two female jurors became involved in public romantic relationships with defendants following the trial, raising questions about whether the Fort Smith proceedings met the constitutional mandate of an impartial jury and signaling the continued importance of white women to the movement. According to the *Houston Chronicle,* one juror, Carolyn S. Slater, thirty years old, entered into a relationship with acquitted CSA member David McGuire, twenty-five, following the trial. She married him after the trial, and they planned to sell their story to *People* magazine. Slater and McGuire also set up another female juror, Mary B. Oxford, age twenty-four, in a pen-pal romance with incarcerated Order member David Lane, fifty. Oxford called Lane "a little too old for me" but showed no ethical hesitation about carrying on the relationship. Both jurors said they had been attracted to the defendants during the trial. In these cases, the romantic availability of jurors signaled the defendants' innocence and, by extension, provided a kind of social credibility to the movement itself.[103]

With white power social networks only partially exposed, the Fort Smith proceedings faced another hurdle in the charismatic testimony of white

power leaders. Men such as Beam, Butler, and Miles had risen in the movement precisely because they were compelling speakers. Beam, representing
himself, invoked two rhetorical devices in his opening statement: his defense
of white women and his Vietnam War service. He said he would continue
to fight for his innocent seven-year-old daughter and portrayed his flight to
Mexico not as a criminal act but rather as an imposition upon his innocent
daughter and his wife, whom he called "Little Sheila." "My wife up until
April of this year had never been out of her father's arms," he testified, "and
it was just terrible on both of them."[104]

Then he pivoted to his Vietnam War story, and testified that he had come
home from war believing it was his duty to kill enemies, foreign and domestic. According to the trial report, Beam ended his statement with the
story of a "soldier being burned to death in the armored personnel carrier
and how he was reminded of that when he came home to see protestors
burning flags," and said this was the reason "that he turned to the politics
that he did." Beam and his attorney, Lyons, listed his many military decorations as part of a defense aimed at establishing his good character. Far from
a passing reference, Beam's testimony about the Vietnam War would fill several pages of the trial transcript.[105]

Indeed, the promise of a continued fight and a strong current of
antistatism—or at the very least a belief in popular sovereignty that super-
seded the authority of the federal government—was perfectly clear in Beam's
testimony. In cross-examination by Carlson, Beam pledged to continue his
fight. "If it comes to it, Mr. Beam, would you kill these enemies?" asked
Carlson. "To defend my country, I would continue to perform my duties as
a soldier, yes," Beam replied. "I'll do anything I can to defend the Constitution of the United States." "Including kill?" asked Carlson. "If so directed,"
Beam replied, and clarified that he took such directions from the "government
of the people. All law and authority rest in the people."[106]

On April 8, 1988, after three days of deliberation, the jury found all the
defendants not guilty on all counts. This meant that Butler, Beam, and
Miles, along with Order members Bruce Pierce, Barnhill, Lane, Scutari,
and CSA member Richard Wayne Snell, were found "not guilty of attempting
to overthrow the government." It meant McGuire and three other CSA
members were found "not guilty of plotting to kill a federal judge and FBI
agent." Most incredibly, it meant that Barnhill and Scutari were found not
guilty of transporting the money stolen by the Order and using it to finance

the white power movement. The men walked free and, with the government consenting, the judge ordered "the firearms in question returned to the person who turned them over to the government."[107]

The trial's most iconic moment occurred just after acquittal. Louis Beam, just released, spoke to reporters outside the courthouse. Beam thanked the jury for his acquittal, and declared: "To hell with the federal government." Then he said he was "out of the movement. From now on," he added, "I'm just going to write books and raise blond-headed children."[108] Surrounded by journalists and photographers, Sheila Beam collapsed into his arms.[109] A photographer captured the moment for the *Kansas City Times:* Beam, dressed in a suit, holds his wife. She wears a demure, light-colored dress that covers her arms and falls below the knee. She rests her head on his shoulder, her blond hair falling over his arm. Her feet are bare. Louis Beam's head inclines slightly toward hers, but he fixes his gaze on something farther away, and the light emphasizes his resolute expression. Sheila Beam, barefoot and limp in her husband's arms before the Confederate memorial, embodied old stories of vulnerable white women in need of protection.[110] As Campbell wrote, "Sheila fainted from the pain she was in and from the incredibleness of their stunning victory."[111]

Immediately after the acquittal, jubilant white power leaders touted this victory loudly and movement-wide. Miles said the verdict "restore[d] my faith in the people."[112] FBI agent Knox resigned in frustration. Beam founded a new publication, *The Seditionist,* and published a second edition of *Essays of a Klansman.*[113]

White power activists used the trial victory to enhance and encourage further underground operations and hone their appeal to the mainstream. In the post-1988 period, the movement would incorporate new legions of skinhead members, reemerge as the purportedly nonracist militia movement, and guide a new generation of activists, including Timothy McVeigh, to white power movement violence. And the work of white women, both as symbols and as activists, continued unabated. Indeed, when the movement used the federal sieges of two separatist compounds to fuel its militia groundswell, the stories it told to new recruits would be about women. Louis Beam would rehash the story of Sheila Beam's arrest and detention to relaunch his writings on leaderless resistance and widen the appeal of the strategy in 1992, both before and after the federal siege of a white separatist family at Ruby Ridge, Idaho.[114] The death of another martyred white woman there—this time killed by a federal sniper—would inflame the white power call to arms. "When the Feds blew the head off Vicki Weaver, I think symbolically that was their war against the American woman, the American mother, the American white wife," said Carl Franklin, the new pastor at Aryan Nations. "This is the opening shot of a second American revolution."[115]

PART III   **APOCALYPSE**

8 Ruby Ridge, Waco, and Militarized Policing

Vietnam-style assault.

—*Description by a journalist of federal actions in Waco, Texas, 1993*

White power activists and neighbors hold a vigil at a federal roadblock after learning of Vicki Weaver's death at Ruby Ridge, Idaho, 1992. (*Anne C. Williams,* The Spokesman-Review)

ON AUGUST 22, 1992, Vicki Weaver died behind the door of her crude mountaintop cabin near Ruby Ridge Creek, Idaho, holding her ten-month-old daughter in her arms. Federal agents had already killed one of her children. She held the door open as her husband, Randy, ran toward her, fleeing the shots of government snipers. A stray bullet passed through the door and struck her in the head. For days, her husband and children waited with her body, under siege by a fully militarized police force, as horrified white power activists and others held vigil at the foot of the mountain.

Within and beyond the white power movement, the siege at Ruby Ridge—along with the 1992 Los Angeles riots that preceded it and the fiery, catastrophic end to the Waco standoff that followed in 1993—inflamed a renewed apocalyptic imaginary, a worldview characterized by intensifying urgency that would eventually lead to the 1995 bombing of Oklahoma City.[1] If guerrilla war on the state characterized white power movement activity in the 1980s, spectacular state violence defined the early 1990s. White power activists reacted to these events with ideas of apocalypse on their minds.

Significantly, the apocalyptic imaginary of the early 1990s coincided with the end of the Cold War, a historical shift that rendered obsolete much of the anticommunist rhetoric that had structured white power activism through the previous decades. Apocalyptic rhetoric augmented violence and separatism within the white power movement, but also worked as a bridge issue with the evangelical right, creating opportunities for recruitment. Both constituencies had been preoccupied with the idea of apocalypse following Soviet nuclear attack. People in both groups after the end of the Cold War were, in a way, in search of a new enemy to fight in their foretold end-times battle.[2]

White power activists used antistatist currents from earlier formations to refine the idea of a Jewish-controlled Zionist Occupational Government, increasingly referring instead to a "New World Order"—an alliance of malevolent internationalist forces—as an agent of the coming end times.[3] Their apocalyptic vision motivated and shaped white power violence, using the symbols and strategies of the post–Vietnam War moment in new ways. White power activists experienced apocalyptic threat both through the perceived peril of racial extinction and through catastrophic, violent events at Ruby Ridge and Waco that reaffirmed the state as inherently evil, supplanting communism as an irredeemable enemy and giving rise to a new surge of militia organizing.[4]

The Weavers did not have the homemade Claymore land mines, C-4 explosives, or stolen military machine guns routinely found in larger white separatist compounds. However, neither were they innocent rural survivalists: they were longtime participants in the movement. Vicki Weaver's death inflamed the movement at a key moment of transition. Its activists invoked her as a model white woman they failed to protect from a rampant superstate. Whereas the white female body had previously been seen as at risk of being violated by men of color, now the risk of violation came from the state, via the brutal technologies of late twentieth-century warfare, now used by the federal government against its own citizens.

In confrontations with separatists at Ruby Ridge and Waco, local police and federal agents used military units, weapons, strategies, and technologies to unleash violence on American civilians. Hundreds of federal agents outfitted in military gear descended upon a remote Idaho mountaintop to stake out one white separatist family holed up in a cabin on Ruby Ridge. National Guardsmen participated in the standoff; military technologies included two armored troop carriers, helicopters, and the construction of a command post.[5] ATF and FBI agents deployed military technologies to close down a paramilitary separatist compound in Waco, Texas. Agents used military helicopters, body armor and shields, armored personnel vehicles, Abrams M-1 series tanks, and M-60 combat engineering vehicles equipped with tear gas. They also used military strategies including psychological warfare.[6] The white power activists enthralled by the Vietnam War now confronted another sphere in which the spillover of wartime violence had militarized domestic life: paramilitary civilian policing.

Before Ruby Ridge, the state had wielded military strategies and weapons against American citizens countless times. The civilian-targeted violence that became a feature of combat in the Vietnam War had been generated, at least in part, by policing tactics in urban communities of color. After the war, military training of police departments and paramilitary units such as Special Weapons and Tactics (SWAT) teams brought violence home once again and disproportionately targeted the same communities.[7] Paramilitary police units, implemented in Los Angeles to quell racial protest after the Watts riots in 1965 and used repeatedly to suppress dissent, would grow exponentially, even as federal police agencies, including the FBI, ATF, and DEA, militarized along the same lines. Almost 90 percent of cities with 50,000 or more residents would have paramilitary police units by 1995. The use of such units would grow 538 percent for "call-outs" (responses to emergency service calls) and 292 percent for "proactive patrols" (including the suppression of communities of color) between 1982 and 1995.[8]

Civilian policing increasingly bore the same markers of paramilitary culture that defined white power activism: the presence of both veterans and active-duty soldiers in training and patrols, secrecy about operations, and, as sociologists have documented, "changing uniforms, weaponry, language, training, and tactics."[9] Paramilitary police wore "battle dress uniforms" and the combat boots and body armor of soldiers. They defined themselves as "heavy weapons units"—a military term—and armed themselves with military-grade weapons, including submachine guns, M16s, grenades, C-4 plastic explosives, and armored personnel carriers. They organized themselves on the model of military special operations and frequently received direct training from such military units. The vast majority of SWAT team and other paramilitary police deployments responded with military force to nonviolent drug crimes. Weapons and money seized during such actions often went toward the purchase of equipment and weapons for further paramilitarization.[10]

Beginning in the early 1990s, the 1033 Program of the National Defense Authorization Act arranged for the free or low-cost transfer of surplus military weapons, gear, and other equipment such as vehicles to local police departments. Tanks, military assault rifles, grenade launchers, body armor, and more became routinely used in policing civilians at home. The war on drugs also promoted collaboration between the military and civilian police forces. In the early 1990s, the Department of Defense worked with the Department of Justice to coordinate paramilitary responses to civilian crime. As the historian Kimberley Phillips has argued, by the early 1990s "policing had become a war," largely waged against communities of color.[11]

Before Ruby Ridge and Waco, however, the rhetoric of the war on drugs and policing strategies that brought the full force of military violence down on civilians had targeted people of color in urban areas. Ruby Ridge and Waco were notable because of their rural locales, sensational media coverage, and the deaths of white women, children, and men at the hands of the militarized state. To white power activists, these confrontations— especially alongside the 1993 Brady Bill and the Violent Crime Control and Law Enforcement Act of 1994, each of which imposed restrictions on gun purchases and ownership—signified an ever more urgent need to wage race war.

Some have argued that a period of white power inactivity followed the acquittal of thirteen white power movement activists in the Fort Smith sedition trial. Similarly, many have argued that the militia movement was distinct from the white power movement that preceded it: some acknowledge a paramilitary movement in the 1980s but argue that it disappeared in 1988. They claim that something wholly new was born when the militias organized.[12]

To the contrary, white power activists understood the sedition trial acquittals as a green light for future violence, just as they had understood previous acquittals such as those in Greensboro. Indeed, the archive indicates continuous momentum from the sedition trial to the Oklahoma City bombing, revealing the militia movement as the outward growth of the paramilitary white power movement. The militia movement shared its leaders, soldiers, weapons, strategies, and language with the earlier white power mobilization. Ethnographic interviews with activists in the early 1990s showed that the movement remained fully focused on war against the state following the trial.[13] A period of intense production of white power women's publications from 1988 to 1995 revealed that such activity continued, even though it was largely out of view of scholars and journalists.

Militias appeared in the Northwest at least as early as 1989, and shared personnel, funds, images, and ideologies with the established white power movement. John Trochmann, for instance, founded the Militia of Montana in the late 1980s after involvement with Aryan Nations, and his ties to white power continued after that: Trochmann spoke at the 1990 Aryan Nations World Congress.[14] Wayne Gonyaw, head of the Tennessee State Militia, had also been an Aryan Nations leader, as had E. Tom Stetson, leader of the Unorganized Militia of Idaho. Bob Holloway—a former mercenary and white power activist—led the Texas Light Infantry, a major militia organization in Texas.[15]

Despite this clear continuity in personnel and resources, various commentators tried to draw distinctions between militias and groups such as Aryan Nations. As the *New York Times* postulated,

> Some experts say that the militia members, despite their tough talk, are not as dangerously militant as the small movements of other armed conspiracy theorists, like the Aryan Nation [*sic*] and Posse Comitatus. But, by all accounts, the militia movement is a much more widespread phenomenon, involving many more people in every region of the country, linked together by computer networks, fax, shortwave radio, home-produced videos and desktop publishing.[16]

While the *Times* was correct about the large number of militiamen across the country, the remainder of the report was misleading. Militias were indeed "dangerously militant," as later standoffs would show. And the white power movement had used a far-reaching computer network since at least 1984, to say nothing of the explosion of printed materials it had generated for decades. The earlier white power movement was also a "widespread phenomenon" that bridged regional and class identities. And, most crucially, the "small movements of other armed conspiracy theorists"—dismissed here as a coherent social movement in their own right—were root and branch of the militia groundswell.

Significantly, the *New York Times,* as well as other major newspapers around the nation, had covered the white power movement closely during the 1980s. Each of the movement's major events appeared in national news stories and became part of public discourse. The Greensboro trials generated a *Saturday Night Live* sketch; video of Louis Beam's paramilitary Camp Puller appeared on a morning newsmagazine show. Tom Metzger and Glenn Miller ran for political office, garnering substantial publicity even when they lost. Miller and Don Black, among other movement leaders, appeared on *Sally Jessy Raphael* and other popular talk shows. Metzger ran his own public access television talk show in California. David Duke's presidential campaigns in 1988 and 1992, and his successful run for the Louisiana House of Representatives in 1989, were widely reported.[17]

Government agents, too, were keenly aware of the organization of the white power movement and its continued capacity for violence. In a 1995 *New York Times* piece, the FBI special agent in charge of the Coeur d'Alene office, Wayne Manis, called the Order "without a doubt the best organized and most serious terrorist threat that this country has ever seen."[18] Jack Knox, a career agent involved in trying to prosecute white power activists—white power activists had unsuccessfully tried to assassinate him, and he retired in frustration after the Fort Smith acquittals—made similar comments.[19] Nevertheless, in the early 1990s, the militia movement was repeatedly portrayed as a novel development.

By eliding its continuity with the white power movement, these observers missed the significance of the militia movement in historical context. Far from a new groundswell, it represented a move toward the mainstream, perhaps the most successful of many such attempts to broaden recruitment. In the militia movement, the war on the government went public.

For many militiamen, antigovernment paramilitarism was rhetorically distinct from overt racism. A recruit could, theoretically, participate in a local militia without deliberately participating in the white power movement. Nevertheless, the actions of local militia groups remained framed by the same worldview, logic, and symbols that had long structured white power activism and violence. These were the very elements Beam had counted on to coordinate underground cells in his strategy of leaderless resistance. The tactics chosen by those connected in such common cause continued to feature strategies and weapons from the Vietnam War, scenarios from *The Turner Diaries,* and a rhetoric that drew strongly on the defense of white women.[20]

A shift in language worked to broaden the appeal of the militias. Leaders and activists had begun to replace the idea of Zionist Occupational Government (ZOG) with the phrase "New World Order," which signaled an alignment of malevolent internationalist forces, including the United Nations, global finance, nations, and technology, that conspired to take over the world and would soon face the righteous in Armageddon. The phrase had long circulated among fundamentalist Christians, a group that included Identity Christians who understood the righteous as including only white people. It took on a new urgency in 1991 when President George H. W. Bush used the phrase in a speech to rally the nation for the Gulf War. Bush used it to refer to the end of the Cold War and the international role of the United States in securing the rule of law, favorable trade agreements, and the ouster of Iraqi dictator Saddam Hussein. But conspiracy theorists heard Bush's use of the phrase as a signal of imminent apocalypse. The increasing prevalence of New World Order conspiracy belief among evangelicals, together with the rising importance of social issues held in common between mainstream and fringe—opposition to immigration, gay rights, and especially abortion—indicate a narrowing gap between white power activism and a large segment of the mainstream evangelical right.[21]

To the white power movement, the concept of a New World Order included both the old idea of ZOG and a broader international conspiracy of elites (sometimes Jewish) that intended to enslave the U.S. population. Movement activists saw the New World Order as a rising global superstate, endowed with unlimited power and armaments and ready to crush white citizens under the heel of its black boot.[22] In other words, the white power movement activists who had rallied around Vietnam War veterans, symbols, weapons, and uniforms and had formed their movement from the paramilitary spillover of the war now recognized that a similar circulation had militarized state enforcement mechanisms. In the 1990s the paramilitary white power movement would face the full force of militarized civilian policing.

Indeed, the idea of the New World Order drew upon the old symbols of the Vietnam War, mixing fear of internationalism with the certainty that Huey helicopters—no longer the jungle green of the Vietnam War era, but now black—signified an impending invasion by United Nations troops and foretold the herding of white people into concentration camps. Oklahoma City bomber Timothy McVeigh and his compatriots deeply feared such camps, which they believed were already constructed and waiting; these fears mushroomed into a vivid conspiracist subculture. More than two thousand pages of Internet material attempted to locate and explain the mysterious black helicopters. The idea of concentration camps inverted the old *Turner Diaries* strategy of forcing people of color into such facilities prior to their annihilation. Meanwhile, movement leaders expressed a rising sense of urgency: despite the Northwest migration, there was nowhere left to go, no further retreat. "We have run as far as we can on this earth!" wrote Aryan Nations leader Richard Butler in a 1991 call to confront the New World Order.[23]

The white power movement was deeply skeptical of the Gulf War, which Bush declared was a victorious end to what had come to be called "Vietnam syndrome," an American reluctance to fight. "I've told the American people before that this will not be another Vietnam," Bush declared. "Our troops . . . will not be asked to fight with one hand tied behind their back."[24] Bush referenced the old Vietnam War narrative as he promised to unleash the full force of the U.S. military. Butler, on the other hand, saw the Gulf War as a manipulation designed to benefit Jews, and expressed particular displeasure that the military had changed the uniforms of the 1980s to desert hues. His disapproval highlighted the continued reference point of the Vietnam War as the primary cultural marker in the white power movement and its militia outgrowth, in which members continued to wear the tiger-stripe and woodland patterns of Vietnam War camouflage or the four-color pattern implemented in all branches of the military in the late 1970s. Skepticism about the Gulf War, however, did not stop white power activists from recruiting its soldiers to their movement.[25]

In addition to the long-held strategy of targeting veterans and active-duty military personnel for recruitment, and a more successful appeal to the mainstream through militias, white power activists also deliberately modified some of their cultural standards in order to appeal to a new pool of recruits. Beginning in the late 1980s, a large number of young people became involved in the skinhead movement, which blended racial violence with a cosmopolitan white supremacy revolving around an urban concert and drug scene. On one level, the presence of skinheads signaled the frustrations of working-class white youth at a moment of profound economic transformation that seemed to threaten their life chances. In another way, skinheads represented an increasingly strong link between white power paramilitarism and prison culture.

Longtime white power leaders, most particularly Tom Metzger of White Aryan Resistance, successfully drew skinheads into the unified white separatist movement by overlooking previously insurmountable cultural differences. Many skinheads lived in urban areas and were largely uninterested in rural survivalism and social conservatism. They typically used alcohol and drugs, both of which had been decried as immoral distractions by an earlier generation of white power activists. Skinheads often had tattoos, anathema to the teachings of Christian Identity. Despite their differences, opening the movement to include skinheads generated a new pipeline of youth recruitment that helped sustain white power movement momentum. Skinheads became regular attendees at movement meetings such as the Aryan Nations World Congress.[26]

As leaders Miles, Butler, and Beam began to age, former white power strongholds like the Aryan Nations compound became increasingly peripheral to movement activity, and those who traveled to Hayden Lake to gauge the strength of the movement did not find its center there. Miles died from a blow to the head, under suspicious circumstances, in 1992.[27] That year Butler turned seventy-four; he preached old, tired sermons to a crowd of fewer than twenty, and more than one observer concluded that the movement had withered. But, using the same adaptability and opportunism that had long characterized Klan activity, the movement recalibrated to the prevailing public sentiment. The new advance guard was in militias: paramilitary groups that frequently claimed not to be racist despite overwhelming evidence to the contrary.[28]

The continued use of underground cells meant that many white power activists didn't define success as the recruitment of large numbers of new members and were content to remain small. Many underground groups worked instead to recruit and train small numbers of committed activists. So while the Center for Democratic Renewal estimated that between 1992 and 1996 there were around 25,000 "hard-core white supremacists" and an additional 150,000 to 175,000 "active sympathizers who buy literature, make contributions, and attend periodic meetings," these figures could not measure the formation of innumerable paramilitary cells, nor forecast their future violence.[29]

Indeed, the 1992 confrontation at Ruby Ridge, Idaho, electrified the movement. There, federal agents used excessive military force—and broke government rules of engagement—to apprehend a white separatist who had sold two illegally modified weapons. Randy Weaver had enlisted as a Green Beret during the Vietnam War, but resigned in frustration when he was never shipped out. He moved his family to Idaho in 1983 as part of the Northwest migration of white separatists, and took a job at the John Deere plant in Waterloo. There he heard about Aryan Nations. An Identity Christian, Weaver spoke frequently about his belief that the Bible said black and white people should not live together, not even in the same county. He also told his neighbors that Jews were behind the New World Order.[30]

In the Northwest, the Weavers found a nearly all-white community sympathetic to white separatism. Boundary County, Idaho, had only one black family among its 9,000 residents. Looking to live off the grid and home-school their children, Randy Weaver and his wife, Vicki Weaver, bought land on a remote Idaho mountaintop called Ruby Ridge. They adopted fifteen-year-old Kevin Harris. Up on the mountain, they built a primitive cabin and a shed where the women would go when they menstruated or when Vicki Weaver gave birth to a baby daughter. Randy Weaver taught Kevin, his son, Sammy, fourteen, and his daughters, Sara and Rachel, twelve and ten, how to fire guns. They carried guns everywhere they went on the mountaintop. Randy Weaver ran for sheriff in nearby Naples, Idaho, in 1988, on a platform of enforcing only those laws the people wanted enforced, a political strategy reminiscent of Posse Comitatus.[31]

The Weavers made the hour-long drive to attend the Aryan Nations World Congress at least three times. They were there in 1986 and 1989—both moments of intense focus on war on the state—and Randy Weaver sported a "Just Say No to ZOG" T-shirt and Aryan Nations belt buckle. At the Congress, a man named Gus Magisono approached Weaver to discuss the mistakes of the Order and Order II, the latter a small cell that had blown up a few buildings and carried out some minor robberies in nearby Coeur d'Alene, Idaho. He also asked Weaver about buying some sawed-off shotguns, specifying that he needed the barrels shorter than the legal limit.

Weaver agreed, selling him two modified shotguns the following week for $400, and promising more as needed. Weaver said he hoped street gangs would use the shotguns to kill each other.[32]

But Magisono was actually Kenneth Fadely, a man the federal government had busted for gunrunning and turned into an undercover informant for the ATF. Agents intent on entrapping Weaver with the gun sale hoped to turn him into another informant, as part of a broader project of cracking down on Aryan Nations and budding militia groups in nearby northwest Montana. When Weaver refused, a federal grand jury indicted him on illegal weapons charges in December 1990. After his arraignment and release, Weaver never reappeared in court. He was given the wrong court date, but he also returned to his mountaintop with plans to hole up. Vicki Weaver supported this course of action, anticipating a standoff. In a 1991 letter to the U.S. attorney for Idaho, she wrote: "Whether we live or die we will not bow to your evil commandments." She included an attached quotation from Order leader Bob Mathews: "War is upon the land. The tyrant's blood will flow." Friends and neighbors—including militia leader John Trochmann, his wife, Carolyn Trochmann, and their son—regularly brought the family food and supplies. Again, social relationships undergirded political ones within the movement: Carolyn Trochmann had helped Vicki Weaver deliver her baby.[33]

The siege came soon. In the winter of 1992, newspapers reported that federal marshals knew Weaver was holed up on Ruby Ridge but weren't sure how to pursue him. All four children, Vicki Weaver, and Harris were also in the cabin, and none of them had been charged with any crimes. In reconnaissance flights, agents observed the three Weaver children and the baby. The cabin's residents carried guns wherever they went on the property. Agents worried about another Whidbey Island, where Mathews had died in a fiery explosion after a long standoff with the FBI. They advised using caution in attempting an arrest, even though they considered Weaver to be holding the children hostage. Weaver sent out a letter stating that the impasse would end only with the deaths of himself and his family, or if federal agents admitted that they had set him up.[34]

On August 21, 1992, the Weavers' Labrador retriever sensed intruders—federal marshals conducting routine reconnaissance of the mountaintop. The dog ran toward the strangers, followed by Randy Weaver, Kevin Harris, and Sammy Weaver. The marshals shot the dog, and the separatists returned fire, Harris killing federal marshal William Degan. Marshals returned fire, killing Sammy Weaver with a shot in the back. Randy Weaver and Harris placed his body in the birthing shed and took cover in the cabin. They kept the rest of the agents pinned down with gunfire until nightfall, when the agents had to be rescued.[35]

As the siege continued, agents brought in more personnel and more military technology. They tried to use a negotiation team, but the Weavers had no telephone. They brought in armored personnel carriers and set up roadblocks to further isolate the cabin. They surveyed the mountaintop by helicopter. At least two armored troop carriers rolled through the tiny town of Naples. Gravel-filled trucks, bulldozers, and additional heavy equipment arrived, perhaps indicating plans to improve access to the cabin in order to ease the passage of more military vehicles and equipment.[36]

When word got out that a standoff had begun, both neighbors and far-flung white power activists began to arrive to show their support for the Weavers. They camped out at the roadblock down the hill from the Weaver cabin, in what the *Washington Post* described as a "rag-tag band" of as many as 300 people, including Vietnam veterans in camouflage fatigues and skinheads in combat boots.[37] This characterization calls to mind a group of men hardened either by the combat of war or by the violence of the streets. In fact, white power women played a key role at the Ruby Ridge protests, one that mirrored common practice within the movement. Debbie Mathews, the widow of Order leader Bob Mathews, had reached celebrity status in the movement after his death. She spoke not as an activist in her own right but as an honored widow and mother. She brought their ten-year-old adopted son with her to the roadblock. Carolyn Trochmann was there, too, and defended Randy Weaver to journalists.[38] People at the roadblock held signs with slogans like "Your Family Could Be Next," mobilizing public support by depicting the siege as a violation of the white family.[39]

The white power movement tried to marshal paramilitary support for the besieged family. On August 25, officers arrested five skinheads trying to bring rifles and semiautomatic weapons to the cabin via back roads. Significantly, the arresting officers and the skinheads were wearing the same camouflage fatigue uniforms, representing the clash of two distinct paramilitarizations: white power and civilian policing.[40]

On August 28, the world learned that Vicki Weaver had died up on the mountain. Randy Weaver, Harris, and the three living children cowered on the floor of the cabin. Federal agents sent in a robot equipped with tape-recorded messages from friends and family members urging the Weavers to end the standoff. The Weavers wrote a letter to the world, believing they would die, saying they had run into a "ZOG / New World Order ambush."[41] Longtime white power movement figure Bo Gritz attempted to negotiate a surrender. Gritz was a Vietnam War veteran who had been Randy Weaver's commander in the Special Forces and had worked as a mercenary before re-turning to the United States; he claimed to have personally killed "400 communists." At the time of the Ruby Ridge siege he was running for presi-dent on the Populist Party ticket, leveraging his veteran status by telling do-nors, "I'm counting on you to serve"; when his bid failed, he would found a separatist compound.

The standoff ended without a shot fired. "He just cried his wife's name, his son's name, and he stood up tall like a man, and we marched tall down the road like we said we were going to do," said Gritz. On the way down, they passed a group of skinheads at one of the roadblocks, where encamped supporters of the Weaver family now numbered more than 300. Gritz gave them a Nazi salute.[42]

Weaver and Harris, both wounded by gunshots, received medical atten-tion and were indicted on charges related to Degan's death. The standoff and the trial became a focal point for tens of thousands of enraged militiamen. From the beginning, public sympathy was with the Weavers—all they wanted, as defense attorney Gerry Spence kept repeating, was to be left alone. The state did little to change this perception, and amplified it with missteps: FBI agents testified that they had falsified evidence, both by staging photos of the site where Degan was killed and by fabricating a photograph of a bullet. Spence was so confident that the jury would see the flagrant violence exhib-ited by the state that he did not bother to present a defense.[43]

Commentators nationwide, left and right, saw Ruby Ridge at best as a public relations disaster and at worst as a rampage by a militarized super-state. As the *New York Times* argued in an editorial:

> Randy Weaver was a white supremacist. He lived as a heavily armed recluse in a cabin on a ridge in rural Idaho. Neither of those things is against the law in the United States. . . . There are a lot of lunatics out there in the woods. But it is not the job of Federal law enforcement agencies to behave in a way that seems designed to confirm their paranoia—especially when there is no

proof they have violated any laws. . . . [There was] no indication Mr. Weaver did anything illegal until Federal agents invited him to.[44]

The idea of lunatics in the woods impeded an understanding of the complex social movement that had placed the Weavers on the mountaintop in the first place, and supported their existence there.

In the face of such a blatant deployment of militarized policing, the jury acquitted Harris and sentenced Weaver to eighteen months on the original firearms and failure-to-appear charges. The fourteen months Weaver had already served in the county jail counted against that time. But Weaver's martyrdom, which turned both on the loss of his son and on the vulnerability of white womanhood as he grieved for his wife and prepared to raise his daughters alone, appealed far beyond the movement. Public opinion in his favor, together with horror over a similar state overstep in Waco, Texas, would press Congress to investigate the FBI's conduct in late 1995. Weaver would be awarded $3.1 million in compensation for the deaths of Sammy and Vicki Weaver, and the FBI would suspend and then demote the agent who had supervised the siege.[45]

Nowhere was the horror of Ruby Ridge more acutely registered than in the white power movement. Even before Randy Weaver walked down from the mountaintop and the public learned of Vicki Weaver's death, Louis Beam and others in the white power movement mobilized around the family's martyrdom. Beam used the incident to rally not only the core of the white separatist movement but also the burgeoning militias. As Beam put it, "Ten thousand Randy Weavers are spread out from one coast to another."[46]

Beam launched the United Citizens for Justice in Naples, Idaho, and organized about forty people to press for a murder trial of the federal agents. At a rally in Sandpoint, Idaho, Beam presented himself as a new arrival to the war against the state, saying he was living innocently "in a small East Texas community raising black-eyed peas and blond-haired children until I heard about the events in North Idaho." His disingenuous claim to be newly radicalized by Ruby Ridge appealed to a broad audience of horrified observers, and used the momentum of the incident to further the formation and organization of local militias without overtly tying them to the white power movement.[47]

In October 1992, white power leaders convened an emergency summit in Estes Park, Colorado, to discuss strategies for responding to Ruby Ridge.

Pete Peters, the pastor of the tiny Christian Identity LaPorte Church of Christ near Fort Collins, Colorado, led the summit. It was the first time Peters had taken such an overt leadership role in the movement, but he had been closely involved with violent white power activism for years. He was a guest on Alan Berg's radio show before the Order's assassination of Berg. He had traveled to North Carolina to explain Christian Identity to the jury during the Shelby III murder trial of White Patriot Party members. In LaPorte, he had preached to Order members David Lane and Jean Craig, and to Zillah Craig, who would bear the child of Bob Mathews. Bo Gritz had traveled to Colorado to speak at Peters's bible camp in 1990. And Peters intended to expand his flock: by the early 1990s, his Scriptures for America was running radio "outreach" broadcasts in twenty-seven cities and small towns, following a strategy used by local white power groups in North Carolina and California.[48]

While Peters preferred a cowboy hat to camouflage, he readily employed paramilitarism. Around the time of the summit, he published a pamphlet titled *The Bible: Handbook for Survivalists, Racists, Tax Protestors, Militants and Right-Wing Extremists.* The cover showed a man in camouflage fatigues, bandoliers, and combat boots, with an AK-47 on the ground by his feet and a cowboy hat on the pack beside him. The pamphlet made a case that the Bible featured tax protestors and racists as its "heroes and even role models for our children." Peters wrote that Noah was a survivalist, Samson a vigilante, and Christ himself a militant who urged people to arm themselves—even if they had to sell the clothes off their backs to do so. Peters exemplified the new turn in the movement: a more overt paramilitarism, one that could openly march against the state by letting racism, anticommunism, and antisemitism move to the background.[49]

That the militia movement emerged from the leaders, organizations, and tactics of white power organization showed clearly in the 1992 Estes Park summit, which featured speakers Louis Beam, Richard Butler, and Pete Peters along with militiamen including Tom Stetson. Attorney Kirk Lyons spoke, too; by 1990, he had founded the Patriots Defense Foundation, filed for tax-exempt status, and raised $12,000 for the legal defense of white power activists. Beckman also spoke, as did Gun Owners of America leader, anti-abortion activist, and former mercenary soldier Larry Pratt. Leveraging his mercenary experience in Central America to advocate and organize militias in the United States, Pratt exemplified once again a circuit of combat connecting the Vietnam War with anticommunist warfare in other places. Drawing on the example of counterinsurgent death squads in Central America, he called for small paramilitary units to violently resolve social problems such as drug use, interracial marriage, and the abortion of white babies.[50]

If the speakers at the Estes Park summit showed that the unified white power movement had extended itself into the militia movement, its 160-person audience emphasized this even more profoundly. Old-guard white power movement leaders attended, including *Turner Diaries* author and National Alliance leader William Pierce and Posse Comitatus leader Jim Wickstrom. So did the militiamen: John and David Trochmann, the brothers who led Militia of Montana; and Michigan Militia leader Mark Koernke. Later, the Michigan Militia would stringently deny its involvement with the white power movement in general and the Oklahoma City bombing in particular, but as this meeting showed, ties were clear from the beginning.[51]

As the summit got under way, activists repeatedly outlined plans for antigovernment terrorism despite their awareness of undercover informants in attendance. Tax-protesting pastor Greg Dixon declared, "We are at war!" and called for the establishment of militias.[52] Beam delivered an emotional account of his apprehension in Mexico before the sedition trial, and once again spoke of his wife, Sheila Beam, to invoke the vulnerable white female body. He emphasized the continued importance of a united white power movement, claiming authority by offering a long view of his activism:

> For the first time in the 22 years that I have been in the movement, we are all marching to the beat of the same drum! . . . The two murders of the Weaver family have shown all of us that our religious, our political, our ideological differences mean nothing to those who wish to make us all slaves. We are viewed by the government as the same: enemies of the state. When they come for you, the federals will not ask if you are a Constitutionalist, a Baptist, Church of Christ, Identity, Covenant Believer, Klansman, Nazi, homeschooler, Freeman, New Testament believer, fundamentalist, or fiefkeeper. Nor will they ask whether you believe in the Rapture or think it is poppycock!

He followed this description of a unified movement with a vivid account of the Vietnam War, using mistreatment of U.S. soldiers as evidence of the government's utter corruption. He saved special vitriol for the supposed abandonment of prisoners of war in Vietnam, where, he said, they still remained "in bamboo cages." He then pivoted again, calling for the defense of white women, this time speaking of Vicki Weaver and asking his audience to imagine the "brain matter" of their own wives scattered across their doorways.[53]

Beam concluded with an idea of liberty popular among the militiamen. He spoke of the tree of liberty and the need for continued white power violence: "If you think that this generation of men will maintain its present freedoms without also having to fertilize the tree of liberty with the blood of both patriot and tyrant, then you are mistaken," he said. With this call to war, Beam sought to expand the unified white power movement to include not just a coalition of overt racists, but also a new wave of sympathetic militiamen. Again, he concluded with family and the apocalyptic threat of racial extinction: "My children and your children have the right to a place under the sun."[54]

Beam's speech, which received a long standing ovation, both elided and echoed the 1979 meeting in North Carolina that formed the United Racist Front. At that summit, Klansmen and neo-Nazis spoke about banding together for the first time since the animosities of World War II. At this one, Beam sought to expand the white power movement further. He used the main events of the previous decade of white power activism—and, still writ large, the Vietnam War and the defense of white families—to rally the militias.[55]

Indeed, the white power movement had evolved far past anything so easily recognizable as a hooded, white-robed Klan march on Main Street. At Estes Park and in the militia movement in general, Ruby Ridge codified an alliance of tax protestors, radical anti-abortionists, militiamen, racists, Identity Christians, survivalists, conspiracy theorists, and those who simply believed the U.S. government had grown too large. As anti-abortion fervor, resistance to gun control laws, and anger over big government grew among mainstream conservatives during the 1990s, the white power movement leveraged these issues for recruitment. In back rooms, Lyons and Chris Temple—affiliated with Aryan Nations and a regular contributor to the *Jubilee,* a Christian Identity periodical—argued for a two-pronged war on the state. In the first phase, they would form an alliance with people of color to overthrow the government. In the second, they would "take care" of those "strangers." In other words, the long-term goal remained war on the state, one that they hoped would end in the deportation or genocide of populations of color as framed by *The Turner Diaries*.[56]

On the record, Peters directed the formation of five committees, which the *Jubilee* claimed were "strictly defensive and advocated no aggressive actions." The Divine Committee would discuss biblical examples of "self-defense and spiritual deliverance." The Legal Committee would discuss defense strategies to defend militants in court. The Public Works Committee would cover intergroup communication about "upcoming emergencies and news." The General Committee would issue public statements to the mainstream press. And the Sacred Warfare Action Tactics Committee—the SWAT Committee—would discuss "family preparedness, communication and Leaderless Resistance—a concept wherein Yahweh gives each man his inspiration for defensive action." Rather than formulating a new strategy, white power activists in the SWAT Committee used leaderless resistance and other movement strategies from the early 1980s, but now used the language of militarized policing to frame this activity.[57]

Something new happened at Estes Park: the summit rearticulated white power tactics in such a way that they became widely available to the purportedly nonracist militia movement. Beam, for instance, reissued a call for leaderless resistance in 1992 in the *Seditionist,* as well as in leaflets distributed at Estes Park. Even as the idea circulated among militiamen and old-guard racists, then, it did so in the same publication Beam had founded immediately after the acquittal of the white power activists who used the strategy to avoid conviction in the 1988 sedition trial.[58]

Beam's 1992 iteration of leaderless resistance presented the same strategy as its earlier versions, modified to reflect the end of the Cold War and the disappearance of communism as a viable enemy. "Communism now represents a threat to no one in the United States, while federal tyranny represents a threat to *everyone*," Beam wrote. "The writer has joyfully lived long enough to see the dying breaths of communism, but may, unhappily, remain long enough to see the last gasps of freedom in America."[59] That Beam called himself "the writer" served to distance the idea of leaderless resistance from his white power movement background—the casual militia reader would know only that he was anticommunist, and not that he was a longtime Klansman and Aryan Nations member. Meanwhile, he reminded hard-liners of his long movement record.

The idea of cell-style organizing with no orders issued from central leadership, which had long permeated the established white power movement, now rippled through the newer skinhead and militia factions. In the *Oklahoma Separatist,* a skinhead zine published in the early nineties, Metzger acolyte Joe Grego argued for the strategy. "Just like in *The Turner Diaries* there must be 'legals' and 'operatives,'" Grego wrote. "You don't plow gardens with machine guns."[60] In other words, the new movement was overtly paramilitary but covertly racist. Grego, a skinhead with direct ties to the white power movement, argued for taking a strategy directly from *The Turner Diaries* and running a paramilitary underground of "operatives" simultaneously with "legal" organizing in the open. "Operatives" were expected to act on their own or in small groups in order to prevent leadership from being prosecuted, and to limit the impact of government surveillance and agents provocateurs by refusing to disclose their group memberships or even their affiliation with the movement. Later, Timothy McVeigh would follow the strategy perfectly by claiming that he acted alone in bombing the Oklahoma City federal building.

Six days into the trial of Weaver and Harris for the death of the federal marshal on Ruby Ridge—just months after the movement had organized its response system at the Estes Park summit—an even more explosive confrontation began in Waco, Texas. A long undercover operation by the ATF went wrong after federal agents stormed the Mount Carmel compound. The confrontation ended in a massive fire after a months-long siege; seventy-six compound members died, including twenty-one children. Several federal agents also died, although whether from shots fired by compound residents or from friendly fire in the confusion remained unclear.

The worshippers at Mount Carmel—Branch Davidians—belonged to a paramilitary cult organized around charismatic leader David Koresh. While their multiracial community focused more on imminent apocalypse than on politics, Waco, Texas, had a history of white power movement activity and a population sympathetic to separatism. It had an active Klan chapter that had been founded in 1986, in the heat of the war on the state, and which was aligned with the burgeoning skinhead movement.[61]

In the months before the siege, workers at a local United Parcel Service facility noticed a torn package on its way to Mount Carmel; inside, they could see a hand grenade canister. At one point, undercover agents got inside the compound and discovered "a trove of semi-automatic weapons, AK-47's, AR-15's, M16's, 9-millimeter handguns, Israeli assault rifles and other weapons that cult members had been collecting for years." The residents were also converting semiautomatic weapons to illegal automatics, as had white power separatists belonging to the Covenant, the Sword, and the Arm of the Lord a decade earlier in Arkansas. When the ATF and FBI began running drills at a nearby army post, Fort Hood, to prepare for the raid, someone tipped off the Branch Davidians.[62]

The Mount Carmel flock had long prepared for war. One survivor would later testify that Koresh regularly told his followers, "There was going to be a confrontation, a battle . . . if you can't kill for God, you can't die for God."[63] An undercover agent reported that the compound members were watching a video by Larry Pratt—former mercenary leader of Gun Owners of America—on the ATF as a threat to liberty. The compound's arsenal included "at least one tripod-mounted .50-caliber machine gun, which is illegal for civilians to possess and may have been stolen from a military supply depot," as the *New York Times* would later report. Mount Carmel was a paramilitary encampment prepared for battle.[64]

The siege would drag on for fifty-one days, with spectators and sympathizers turning up to watch. Beam and Lyons arrived about a month after it began. McVeigh also made the trip to bear witness, and to sell bumper stickers with slogans such as "When Guns Are Outlawed, I Will Become an Outlaw." Later, he watched as the siege ended on April 19, 1993—with tears streaming down his face—as news footage showed federal tanks rolling in and flames consuming the compound.[65] FBI transcripts of recorded conversations inside the compound seemed to indicate that the Branch Davidians had started the fire, but the white power movement blamed the federal agents for the inferno. Letters decrying the outcome poured into the FBI.[66]

The white power movement in general, and McVeigh in particular, understood Waco as a massacre carried out by a rampant superstate and its corrupt agents. They saw the victims as innocent women and children. In some movement accounts, the victims of the Waco compound were incorrectly portrayed as all white. Kirk Lyons's and Dave Holloway's militia-directed fundraising newsletter would feature a smiling photograph of a fourteen-year-old white girl killed in the Waco siege with the caption "Why We Fight" that highlighted her martyrdom. Similar slogans had long appeared in white power publications captioning photographs of white women with their children, and worked to link paramilitarism with the defense of white families and white reproduction.[67]

The powerful rhetoric of protecting white women blended, once again, with narratives of government corruption and the symbols of the tank and the Huey helicopter passed down from the Vietnam War to frame the standoff. As Michael McNulty, a Vietnam veteran who produced the documentary *Waco: Rules of Engagement,* said, "Every promise that's ever been made to me has been broken. . . . [Waco] starts to look like Vietnam."[68] McNulty drew on the narrative of betrayal of authority from the Vietnam War to frame this new confrontation on the Texas prairie. "Sons of bitches lied to us again," added an anonymous Vietnam veteran at the scene.[69] The press invoked the Vietnam War, too: the *Guardian* called it "the Vietnam-style assault on Waco."[70]

Waco and Ruby Ridge did more than inflame the movement; for its members, they became the standard of atrocity associated with the New World Order, by now synonymous with the federal government. In their aftermath, the militia movement surged to more than 50,000 members in forty-seven states, and focused increasingly on taking violent action to stop the rampant federal government. One SPLC analyst estimated that some five million people considered themselves part of the "patriot movement"—militias and militia sympathizers—in the mid-1990s. If correct, that number outstrips previous post–Vietnam War white power mobilization and signifies an even larger movement than the second-era Ku Klux Klan in the 1920s; the white power movement had substantial numbers in addition to its extensive underground of cells dedicated to resistance.[71]

Continued paramilitarism and proven white power movement tactics structured this new groundswell. Near Waco, the Texas Constitutional Militia claimed several thousand members, and veteran Green Berets and Navy SEALs conducted its paramilitary training. The militia Big Star One, which spanned Texas, Oklahoma, and New Mexico, included active-duty U.S. Army officers and carried out mortar and grenade-launcher exercises in west Texas. The Militia of Montana put out a handbook on "how to engage in domestic terrorism and sabotage." And the SPLC reported in 1993 that law enforcement officers had discovered thirteen explosives arsenals and six weapons arsenals tied to the burgeoning movement and intended for attacks on targets that included a public housing complex in Ohio, the National Afro-American Museum, also in Ohio, and a black church in Los Angeles.[72]

Meanwhile, the Michigan Militia, where McVeigh was attending meetings, had grown to 12,000 members. When police stopped leader Mark Koernke and three members of his security team in September 1994, they were carrying three military assault rifles, three semiautomatic pistols, and a revolver—all loaded—as well as 700 rounds of armor-piercing ammunition, twenty-one magazines, and six knives and bayonets. This armament revealed a continuing paramilitary fixation on weapons, paired with increasing rage. As militia leader John Trochmann said that December, "The battle lines are drawn."[73]

The Bombing of Oklahoma City

This kind of hell.

—*Timothy McVeigh describing the bombing*

Federal agents escort Timothy McVeigh (left) after his arrest for the 1995 bombing of the Oklahoma City federal building. *(John Gaps III, Associated Press Photo)*

ON APRIL 19, 1995, a Ryder moving truck filled with fertilizer exploded in front of the Alfred P. Murrah Federal Building in Oklahoma City. The blast ripped through its glass façade and damaged its concrete columns, collapsing much of the edifice and rendering the rest structurally unstable.

The explosion wounded more than 500 people and killed 168, including 19 young children in the building's day care center. The nation turned, horrified, to the young white veteran who quickly became the focus of the investigation and trials. In the first admission of his role in the bombing, after he was convicted and sentenced to death by lethal injection, Timothy McVeigh gave an interview saying that he acted alone. He called the dead children "collateral damage" of a military action, and would later tell a fellow inmate that he found it ironic to be imprisoned because "in Desert Storm I got medals for killing people." McVeigh said he bullied his co-conspirators into helping him by threatening them and their families, and he stridently denied his connection to any movement. He said he was not racist. "You can't handle the truth," he told two reporters, quoting the famous speech from the 1992 military film *A Few Good Men.* "Because the truth is, I blew up the Murrah Building, and isn't it kind of scary that one man could wreak this kind of hell?"[1]

Indeed, it was terrifying. Commentators searched for some psychological trigger in McVeigh's past. Was it about his mother leaving, they wondered, or his failures with women? They worried about copycats who might follow in his footsteps. The trials of the other indicted men seemed far less important than the questions of why and how McVeigh acted. For a wide variety of reasons, most journalists and law enforcement officers alike failed to follow leads about additional suspects in the bombing. McVeigh appeared to be a lone madman, acting in concert with only a few co-conspirators, and easily dismissed as a mad outlier.

However, in no sense was the bombing of Oklahoma City carried out by one man. The hell McVeigh described represented the culmination of decades of white power organizing. McVeigh, trained as a combatant by the state, belonged to the white power movement. He acted without orders from movement leaders, but in concert with movement objectives and supported by resistance cell organizing. The plan for the bomb came directly from *The Turner Diaries,* the book that had structured the activity of the white power movement since the late 1970s. The choice of target came from an earlier white power movement incident: members of the Covenant, the Sword, and the Arm of the Lord (CSA), closely affiliated with the Order and Aryan Nations, had cased the Murrah Building and attempted to blow it up with rocket launchers back in 1983 but failed. The Oklahoma City bombing represented the triumph of the white power paramilitary violence that had reverberated through the American home front in the years following the Vietnam War.[2]

The bombing became popularly understood as the work of one man, or a few men, through several processes that eroded contextual understanding. One of these was the broad historical impact of the Gulf War in the early 1990s: although politicians hoped it would vanquish "Vietnam syndrome" and end the public's reluctance to engage in militarism abroad, its legacy on the ground was more complex. The quick victory in the Gulf War cemented a right-wing narrative that the Vietnam War had been lost only through government betrayal—in other words, victory in the Gulf became, for the right, further evidence of the threat presented by the federal government even as it reasserted a positive image of the U.S. military. The Gulf War also produced a new generation of combat veterans, and a militarization of American society more broadly, that white power could exploit as it pursued its new iteration of paramilitary mobilization through militias.[3]

Another erosion of meaning arose from the lack of convictions in the 1988 Fort Smith sedition trial, after thirteen white power activists were acquitted of charges including seditious conspiracy despite overwhelming evidence of their war on the state. This failure, along with the even more damaging public relations disasters of Ruby Ridge and Waco, caused the Department of Justice and some agents in the FBI to be reluctant to portray the Oklahoma City bombing as the work of a movement and hence reluctant to pursue investigative and prosecutorial strategies based on that view. Indeed, the Bureau had institutionalized a policy to pursue only individual actors in white power violence, with "no attempts to tie individual crimes to a broader movement."[4] This strategy not only worked to obscure the bombing as part a social movement but, in the years following McVeigh's conviction, effectively erased the movement itself from public understanding.

Even the FBI's own assessment of McVeigh in a criminological study of personality types fit poorly with his portrayal as a lone terrorist acting on his own motivations. "This is an easily controlled and manipulated personality," one FBI agent would tell the *New York Times* after the bombing. "They are looking for . . . some ideology. They have difficulty fitting into groups, but they are more mission-oriented, more focused."[5] This picture of McVeigh didn't fit the man who would later speak as though he had organized the entire bombing, as though he had been "one man" wreaking "this kind of hell." But the analyst's depiction of McVeigh did fit the details of his life and personality. Such a contradiction pointed, instead, to McVeigh as a soldier of leaderless resistance, motivated by the white power movement.[6]

McVeigh was born in a small town in New York and was by all accounts a quiet kid who never showed much interest in anything but guns. His mother left home when he was an adolescent. Forgotten by his teachers and dismissed by his peers, he took a job as a security guard. He liked to brandish "a huge . . . pistol out of his car window" and came to work with bandoliers of ammunition hung across his chest, like the fictional supersoldier and Vietnam War veteran Rambo. Clearly McVeigh was deeply attached to the popular culture deployments of the Vietnam War story.[7]

McVeigh found his footing when he joined the U.S. Army on May 24, 1988. His obsessive neatness made him a model soldier—clean, in control, and quick to follow orders. In the army, he met Terry Nichols and Michael Fortier, both of whom would be involved in the plan to bomb Oklahoma City. Fortier would later say that Nichols, the platoon leader, also led them as a social group, while McVeigh was the follower.[8] McVeigh and Nichols did their basic training at Fort Benning, Georgia, the same post that housed the School of the Americas. There they chanted cadences like "Blood makes the grass grow! Kill! Kill! Kill!" and one that sounded remarkably like the famous *Soldier of Fortune* motto espoused by Tom Posey and other mercenaries, "Kill 'em all, let God sort it out."[9]

After basic training, the group transferred to Fort Riley, Kansas—a post that was somewhat segregated and racially tense. McVeigh participated in this culture, exhibiting racist behavior while in the service. He kept a copy of *The Turner Diaries* and showed it to his fellow soldiers. Some of his former army buddies would later tell the *New York Times,* "McVeigh assigned 'dirty work' around the barracks to black soldiers."[10] He also felt that young black soldiers were disrespectful to him, and at one point bought a "White Power" shirt after seeing several "Black Power" shirts around the post; he didn't wear it, but he showed it to friends. McVeigh would later claim he was not racist, and that there were a few black soldiers he respected. Still, people remember him using racial slurs and singling out black soldiers for negative attention because of their race. Around this time, McVeigh joined a Klan group in North Carolina.[11]

He served at Fort Riley until he shipped out to the Gulf War with Big Red One, the 1st Infantry Division, in which he served as an infantryman and then a gunner on a Bradley armored vehicle (similar to a tank). He clashed frequently with his Latino platoon leader but was otherwise regarded as an excellent soldier. McVeigh received a promotion to sergeant and a Bronze Star, as well as Army Achievement Medal, Army Commendation Medal, National Defense Service Medal, Expert Rifleman's Crest, and other decorations.[12]

While in the Gulf, McVeigh got a long-awaited call to try out for Special Forces. One of the sergeants who knew him in the military said McVeigh had trained for this opportunity on his own time, marching with a 100-pound pack—but that was before the war. After going to Fort Bragg for the twenty-one-day Special Forces assessment and selection course, a tired and out-of-shape McVeigh washed out on the second day. He was extremely disappointed. After that, the sergeant said, he "became involved with extreme right-wing political groups off-post."[13]

After his subsequent discharge from Fort Riley, McVeigh appeared rootless. He took another short-lived security guard job, where a coworker said, "He was a loner, a follower, not a leader."[14] His ties to the white power movement deepened. A few publications later reported that McVeigh had been a member of the Knights of the Ku Klux Klan (KKKK) branch in Zinc, Arkansas, in 1992.[15] The leader of that branch, Thom Robb, was a national-level white power movement figurehead who had taken over the KKKK from Don Black after the attempted mercenary invasion of Dominica; Black had previously taken over the leadership from David Duke. Robb also published *White Patriot,* a regular and widely read movement newspaper.[16]

McVeigh's connection to the Klan in Zinc was more than casual or local—it connected him directly to the highest levels of the white power movement's war-on-the-government leadership and messaging. In February 1992, McVeigh wrote a letter to the Lockport, New York, *Union-Sun and Journal* in which he noted that he was not surprised racism was on the rise. "Is civil war imminent?" he asked. "Do we have to shed blood to reform the current system? I hope it doesn't come to that, but it might."[17] His use of the term "system" echoed *The Turner Diaries;* at very least, McVeigh had tapped into the resources and strategies of the established white power movement, subscribing to *White Patriot* and talking with a coworker about stealing guns from a military installation.[18] The theft of weapons from military installations was a longtime strategy of white power activists, especially in North Carolina—the same state where McVeigh had written the Klan for more information and to purchase his "White Power" shirt.[19]

McVeigh took the federal civil service exam to work as a U.S. marshal and scored high but was never hired; he blamed this and other career dead ends on equal opportunity laws, and said black people had put him out of a job.[20] In June 1993, McVeigh moved to Canyon West trailer park in Kingman, Arizona. His place was clean and sparsely furnished, with guns hidden all over the trailer. One woman who spoke with him at a party said McVeigh talked a lot about the government and about Hitler. "He said he didn't necessarily agree with all those Jews being killed," she said, "but he said Hitler had the right plan." McVeigh's phone records would later reveal several different calls, placed before the bombing, to an Arizona representative of the National Alliance—*Turner Diaries* author William Pierce's white separatist organization. Although he would later claim he was just looking for a place to hide out after his attack on the Murrah Building, rather than forming a relationship with or seeking guidance from the National Alliance, these calls evinced a strong and continued connection to the movement.[21]

One newspaper would later report that authorities suspected links between McVeigh and the Arizona Patriots, the group one official described in Order-era arrests as "cavemen with bombs" who had watched *Red Dawn* over and over and had plotted to destroy dams in Arizona. Their leader, Jack Oliphant, lived in Kingman, Arizona, as well, and claimed he was a former CIA mercenary who trained guerrillas from around the world in the use of explosives. He had a mailbox near McVeigh. A neighbor saw McVeigh and Nichols with Oliphant in the winter of 1993–1994. Though Oliphant said he didn't know McVeigh, and he died before the completion of the bombing investigation, it is clear that McVeigh lived in close proximity to the Arizona Patriots, and the group shared his worldview.[22] McVeigh, like the Patriots, watched *Red Dawn* over and over. He also met repeatedly with a neo-Nazi activist, and met skinhead leader Johnny Bangerter. Fortier would later say that McVeigh wanted to start a militia in Arizona in 1994.[23] Another resident told the local newspaper that McVeigh—who regularly wore fatigues—was terrifying at the shooting range, firing hundreds of rounds. "He pretty much went crazy, emptying on anything—trees, rocks, anything there," the man said. "He just went ballistic."[24] As had earlier white power activists, McVeigh and Fortier broke into a National Guard armory in an attempt to steal guns and explosives, but they found only a few tools to steal.[25] Once again, McVeigh was drawing heavily on the experiences of the white power movement.

In 1994, McVeigh quit his security guard job at a local trucking company and moved to Michigan. There, he spent time off and on with Terry Nichols and his brother, James Nichols, who owned the farm near Decker where they stayed. An informer would later testify that James Nichols had been talking about leveling a federal building with a "megabomb" since 1988. The witness remembered Nichols saying that "a small bomb could cause such a disaster," and looking through his tool shed for a news clipping that showed the Murrah Building in Oklahoma City. When he didn't find it immediately, he began to draw a diagram freehand.[26] Thus, McVeigh lived with a militia movement member who had long fixated on blowing up the Murrah Building—enough so that he could draw it from memory.

While staying and working on James Nichols's farm, Terry Nichols and McVeigh experimented with explosives and attended Michigan Militia meetings. Terry Nichols sent a letter to the government renouncing his right to vote, participating in a widely used white power and militia movement strategy called "severation" in which members broke their official ties to the state by destroying Social Security cards, birth certificates, and other documents. Terry Nichols also subscribed to several white power publications. Michigan Militia members would later claim that James Nichols urged them all to go through severation, but that they asked him to leave because he was too radical. Still, McVeigh seems to have risen within the Michigan Militia. One newspaper reported that witnesses saw McVeigh at a militia meeting in Florida as a bodyguard to its leader, Mark Koernke. Although Koernke denied knowing him, McVeigh's promotion to security guard at such a meeting indicated that he had entered the ranks of the heavily armed upper echelons of the militia movement.[27] Throughout the history of the post–Vietnam War white power movement, private security forces had been a place to groom and train future movement leaders as well as elite paramilitary operatives such as members of the Order. A casual movement member would rarely, if ever, rise to a position of such trust.

In addition to his militia activity, McVeigh's lifelong obsession with guns also gave him entry into a national network of weapons dealers. Under the alias Tim Tuttle, McVeigh traveled the gun-show circuit, reading, selling, and distributing *The Turner Diaries* in uniform or in camouflage fatigues. He also took another page from the strategy first proposed at the 1983 Aryan Nations World Congress as the movement turned to revolution: he distributed information about movement enemies, perhaps in hopes of coordinating others in the underground. His call was heavily framed by the defense of white women: McVeigh passed out cards with the name and home address of the sniper who had killed Vicki Weaver at Ruby Ridge. At a gun show in Tulsa, Oklahoma, he met Andreas "Andy the German" Strassmeir, a German army veteran who lived in a nearby white separatist compound, Elohim City. McVeigh also read other white power publications and sent them to his sister, Jennifer McVeigh. His reading list included the paramilitary mercenary magazine *Soldier of Fortune* and the white power newspaper *Spotlight*.[28]

Zinc, Arkansas, the site of McVeigh's Klan chapter, sat between Elohim City and the CSA compound; the three groups had substantial contact over the 1980s, and the Elohim City–CSA relationship was particularly close. One can draw a triangle between Fort Riley, where McVeigh was stationed; the CSA compound near Bull Shoals Lake, Arkansas; and Elohim City, just over the Oklahoma border. The triangle included no drive longer than six hours, and included both Zinc and Fort Smith within the routes connecting those three sites. McVeigh appears to have had connections to all these places: he once received a traffic ticket in Fort Smith, Arkansas. He and his sister subscribed to *The Patriot Report*, published in Fort Smith by a white separatist who lived at Elohim City. He was cited for crossing a double yellow line less than twenty-five miles east of Elohim City on October 12, 1993, six months after the Waco siege and during a frenzy of movement activity; and in 1994 he stayed at a hotel in Vian, Oklahoma, twenty miles from Elohim City on the route back to Fort Riley. Connections between Elohim City and McVeigh were ample and sustained over at least the two years prior to the bombing, discrediting his later claim that he only wanted to hide out in the compound after the explosion.[29]

Founded by Robert Millar in 1973, Elohim City—"City of God," in Hebrew—consisted of some seventy-five white separatists living on a 400-acre wooded compound, mostly in trailers parked on cement slabs. Residents trained with homemade napalm, Claymore mines, grenades, assault rifles, AR-15s, and Ruger Mini-14s. Strassmeir would later describe it as "a mix of the Afghani mountains and the Vietnam jungle," locating the camp in a global paramilitary geography.[30] Residents called Millar—the silver-haired leader in a clergyman's shirt and stiff white collar—"Grandpa," and for thirty-four of them, this was literally true.[31] They were dedicated to what Millar called "cultural and genetic integrity," and were careful—in light of the CSA and Waco busts—to give the government no excuse to lay siege to their compound. Millar claimed the residents possessed no illegal weapons, although he refused to allow searches of the compound. He claimed he was not anti-government, although he frequently said that the ATF and FBI had "exceeded their legal mandates." In interviews, Millar called himself a voice of moderation, and denied that the community was racist or paramilitary.[32] However, several clear markers of white power movement involvement and paramilitary armament belied these claims.

Millar preached Christian Identity and separatism, and said that the wealth of the white race proved that they were God's chosen people. He foretold civil war and race riots, and talked about "black helicopters." Members of the compound brought semiautomatic weapons to church, even in front of outsiders. Elohim City residents called themselves "racialist," believed in a Zionist conspiracy to control the government, and refused to participate in Social Security. Some didn't pay taxes. One resident, a respected elder, was a Vietnam veteran who "went into the Vietnam War as a gung-ho patriot and came out feeling betrayed by his government." Three neo-Nazi skinheads lived nearby and attended church in the compound, and two worked at its sawmill. All of these factors point to a white separatist paramilitary compound consistent in its beliefs, and armament, with the broader white power movement.[33]

Although the community itself had little to offer by way of a paramilitary force—only fifteen residents were adult males or teenage boys, with most being women, children, and old men—it served as a hideout and way station for other Aryan soldiers. James Wallington of the Order had hidden at Elohim City, and Kirk Lyons traveled there frequently.[34] Elohim City regularly hosted white power movement leaders, including Tom Metzger, and had close ties with a cell of white power bank robbers called the Aryan Republican Army (ARA). Federal agents had tried twice to search the compound; on one of these occasions, related to a child custody dispute, Millar and other armed men confronted agents on the road and refused to let them in. Worried about a showdown like the one at Waco, the agents left without entering the premises. Much later, Millar's son would concede that Elohim City had periodically given refuge to Aryan Nations members and other people in the movement.[35]

Jack Knox, the lead FBI agent who resigned in frustration after the sedition trial, believed that the government should have investigated Elohim

City following the CSA bust in 1985, and later spoke about the second time federal agents were denied legal entry to the compound. Knox believed that immediately after the CSA bust, a member of the Order who had master-minded the Ukiah armored car heist holed up in Elohim City. When Knox and another agent tried to enforce a warrant for that man's arrest, Millar and his grandsons confronted them at gunpoint until they agreed to leave. Knox saw this chain of events as government failure to prevent the disaster at Oklahoma City. "I think something should have been done prior to the bombing. I think something should have been done in connection with the CSA / Aryan Nations investigation," Knox told the *Arkansas Democrat-Gazette* in 2003. "I think there should have been a thorough investigation of Elohim City."[36]

Millar claimed that there was "not a long or profound connection" be-tween Elohim City and the CSA, saying he thought his group was "labeled in with them because we are both members of the Christian Identity."[37] In fact, the connection between the CSA and Elohim City was remarkably long and profound. It was Millar who anointed Ellison "King James of the Ozarks" in the early 1980s. Ellison, Noble, and others from CSA attempted to travel to Elohim City in late December 1984, as the movement attempted to respond to the death of Order leader Bob Mathews. Federal agents called upon Millar to negotiate Ellison's surrender during the 1985 CSA bust.[38] Millar's granddaughter would marry Ellison—who, at the time of the sedition trial, had at least two other wives—at Elohim City in May 1995, just after the Oklahoma City bombing.[39]

For all that Millar touted nonviolence—"I believe destruction is coming, but I want no part in starting it," he told a *New York Times* reporter in 1985— the compound did have a thoroughly armed paramilitary force led by Strassmeir, who would later be implicated in the bombing investigation.[40] Millar claimed this was only to send "a message to the area that our little village here shouldn't be violated and we will protect ourselves."[41] Millar believed in the same impending apocalyptic race war—and the role he would play in that fight—as did Ellison and other white power activists.

Millar acted as spiritual advisor to another CSA member who, unlike El-lison, had stayed loyal to the white power movement through the Order and sedition trials. Richard Wayne Snell was the man who had blown up a natural gas pipeline in Fulton, Arkansas, in 1983, and killed a pawnshop owner and a pursuing black state trooper before hiding out in the CSA compound. He was arrested during the 1985 bust with Beam's *Essays of a Klansman* and three hand grenades in his trunk.[42] This was another strong connection between the bombing and the movement. Snell was scheduled to be executed by lethal injection on the day of the bombing, April 19, 1995. This was also the ten-year anniversary of the federal action at the CSA compound and the two-year anniversary of the fiery end to the Waco siege, which McVeigh had watched on television, weeping.

Snell and Ellison had come up with the idea to bomb the Murrah Building some ten years earlier. In October 1983, during intense Order activity, the CSA considered using rocket launchers to destroy the building's glass façade. Snell and Ellison had just attended the Aryan Nations World Congress, the meeting where Beam and others declared war on the state and laid out the strategy of leaderless resistance, and of targeting federal officials, institutions, and buildings. Kerry Noble, Ellison's right-hand man, cased the building with Snell several times that summer. They found Kent Yates, a former U.S. Army munitions specialist who claimed to have devised a system to simultaneously launch twelve to sixteen rockets from the back of a van parked on the street. They planned to carry out the attack while people were inside. "We knew people would die," Noble said. "But the war against the government meant nothing if people didn't die." They abandoned the plan when a rocket misfired, exploding in Yates's hand and burning him. "Ellison interpreted this as a sign from God that it wasn't what we [were] supposed to do," said Noble. Instead, the group attempted to assassinate Knox and others in 1983, but failed after a car accident delayed them. Charges around the attempted assassination became part of the 1988 sedition trial.[43]

In the months leading up to the 1995 bombing, the government received specific warnings about Elohim City. Undercover informant Carol Howe reported "dangerous, apocalyptic statements" from Millar, Ellison, and others. Although the government dismissed this information—the ATF and FBI said Howe was "deactivated" as an informant in March 1995—Howe said she warned the agencies that something big was coming, and her warning was substantial and specific. She heard the leaders saying that "a 'cataclysm' was pending in the spring of 1995 and that federal buildings in Oklahoma City or Texas were being targeted for a bomb that would signal a 'racial holy war' in the United States." It would coincide, Howe later said, with the second anniversary of the Waco inferno on April 19, 1995. The flock at Elohim City was preoccupied with the Waco raid, and residents held daily meetings about bombing a building in late 1994 and early 1995. Howe's former boyfriend was Dennis Mahon, a former National Guardsman who had belonged to White Aryan Resistance and the White Knights of the Ku Klux Klan and was by then living in Elohim City. Howe said Mahon had blown up a truck with a 500-pound ammonium nitrate and fuel oil bomb in 1989 or 1990 in Michigan, where he was in contact with longtime racist leader Robert Miles. Mahon and Strassmeir, she reported, were talking about bombing federal buildings in Tulsa and Oklahoma City. Howe also said that while she was never formally introduced to McVeigh—and may never have seen him—she believed he was in Elohim City prior to the bombing.[44]

Howe would later claim that the government had attempted to suppress this information, and that if she had been "deactivated," no one had ever told her so. The government said that her information was not specific enough to prevent the Oklahoma City bombing or to justify a potentially disastrous raid of Elohim City. Howe was acquitted of subsequent conspiracy charges related to an alleged bomb threat, which many saw as government retaliation for inconvenient testimony.[45] Because of this residual doubt about her credibility, the jury in McVeigh's trial never heard about Howe or what she witnessed in Elohim City. Stephen Jones, McVeigh's attorney, told the *Tulsa World* that

> throughout Howe's tenure as an AFT informant in 1994–1995, she filed 70 reports and frequently was polygraphed. . . . "They . . . found her to be a reliable, credible informant," Jones said. "The documents further show a group of people associated with Elohim City were planning, actively, to engage in assassinations, mass murder and bombings directed against the federal government. . . . She reported it. She watched while smaller bombs exploded, and reported it."[46]

Between Howe's information, which gave the nature, date, and origin of the threat—and even went so far as to specify the details of a truck bomb and a federal building in Tulsa or Oklahoma City—and the descriptive example of the bombing given in *The Turner Diaries,* state agencies did have substantial and historical information about what was about to happen. McVeigh was carrying out a planned and logical act, one that drew directly on the resources and strategies of the white power movement and targeted a building that had been at the forefront of the movement's collective conscience for more than a decade. He was motivated by the same events that drove the movement at large. After the passage of the Violent Crime Control and Law Enforcement Act in August 1994, which outlawed nineteen types of semiautomatic weapons, McVeigh wrote to Michael Fortier in exasperation: "What will it take," he asked, to foment the revolution, to spur the war on the government promised by the movement and *The Turner Diaries*? Within weeks, their plan to bomb Oklahoma City was under way.[47]

McVeigh would even carry the messages of the white power movement on his body during the attack. He bombed the Murrah Building wearing a T-shirt that depicted the tree of liberty with the slogan "The tree of liberty must be refreshed from time to time with the blood of patriots and tyrants." It was nearly the exact phrase Beam had used to rally the movement after Ruby Ridge, at the 1992 Estes Park summit of white power leaders and activists.[48]

Later, guards would say that McVeigh told them about his plans for the bombing while in prison awaiting trial. He said he had considered federal buildings and other sites in Denver, Kansas City, Texas, Little Rock, and South Dakota as potential targets. In the end, he chose Oklahoma City for the Murrah Building's architectural vulnerability. It had nine floors with large glass windows, and had no courtyard or plaza that separated it from the street. A truck could park almost directly under its expansive glass façade. His aim was to damage not just the ATF—although that agency had offices in the Murrah Building—but as many federal agencies as possible. The building also faced an open park, meaning that the blast damage would be largely confined to people in the federal building, whom McVeigh saw as complicit with the New World Order.[49]

McVeigh, Nichols, and Fortier worked as a cell, amassing the supplies and funds needed to carry out the bombing. They used the moralized robberies of the Order as their model of operations. In September 1994, McVeigh and Nichols stole blasting caps, dynamite, and fuse cords from a quarry in Marion, Kansas, not far from Terry Nichols's home. In November 1994, they carried out an Order-style robbery to support the costs of the bombing, Nichols taking some $60,000 worth of goods including guns, cash, silver bars, and gold coins from the home of gun dealer Roger Moore, who lived in a rural area near Hot Springs, Arkansas. McVeigh had stayed at Moore's home prior to the robbery, and Moore immediately suspected his involvement. Some of the stolen guns were later found in the search of Nichols's house.[50]

In the weeks before the bombing, McVeigh wrote a letter to a female friend that hinted he was going underground. *The Turner Diaries* called for a separation of legal and paramilitary wings of the movement, stating "it would be a breach of Organization discipline for a member of an underground unit to engage in any direct recruiting activity, however minimal. That function has been relegated to the 'legal' units."[51] In other words, operatives in the guerilla war were to leave the distribution of pamphlets to "legal" units while they worked on assassinations and bombings. In the letter, McVeigh told his friend he would no longer do leafleting or recruiting because he had "certain other 'militant' talents that are in short supply and greatly demanded." He encouraged her to continue leafleting in his stead.[52] McVeigh also wrote to his sister Jennifer, telling her that he had become a member of a "Special Forces Group involved in criminal activity."[53]

The Turner Diaries gave a very specific example of a truck bombing of the sort McVeigh was planning. In the novel, Turner and his cell unit bomb the FBI headquarters in Washington, D.C. They use a truck bomb with around 5,000 pounds of ammonium nitrate fertilizer with blasting gelatin and dynamite, and they drill holes so that the driver can light the fuse from the cab of the truck. They plan to drive the truck into the freight area, set the fuse, and walk away. They are fully aware that their action will hurt or kill the people who work in the building. In the novel, the bomb detonates at 9:15 A.M., catching people at the beginning of their workday and killing more than 850. Turner worries about one pretty twenty-year-old white girl trapped under a steel door.

> When I stooped to stop the girl's bleeding, I became aware for the first time of the moans and screams of dozens of other injured persons in the courtyard. Not twenty feet away another woman lay motionless, her face covered with blood and a gaping wound in the side of her head—a horrible sight which I can still see vividly every time I close my eyes. . . . All day yesterday and most of today we watched the TV coverage of rescue crews bringing the dead and injured out of the building. It is a heavy burden of responsibility for us to bear. . . . But there is no way we can destroy the System without hurting many thousands of innocent people—no way. It is a cancer too deeply rooted in our flesh. And if we don't destroy the System before it destroys us— if we don't cut this cancer out of our living flesh—the whole race will die.[54]

Even as Turner stops to help the iconic injured white woman, he insists that innocent civilians—including white women and children—must die in order to "cut the cancer" of the federal government out of the "living flesh" of white society. While Turner considers the deaths of civilians a "heavy burden of responsibility," he still sees the "pawns" killed in the bombing as unavoidable collateral damage in the cause of race war and in preventing the apocalypse of racial extinction. McVeigh would describe the civilians he killed in much the same way.

Drawing on the *Turner Diaries,* then, McVeigh drove his 1977 yellow Mercury Marquis to Oklahoma City, where he parked in a downtown garage near the Murrah Building. He called Nichols to come pick him up, and they drove north to Junction City, Kansas—the nearest city to Fort Riley, where McVeigh had long held a storage unit—and rented a Ryder truck using his 10 percent military discount. Just afterward, on April 5, McVeigh placed a two-minute phone call to Elohim City. He was trying to reach Strassmeir, who had lived there off and on since 1991 and had become head of security. This position indicated Strassmeir's involvement with the compound's paramilitary side; watchdogs have pointed out that after Waco, he was instrumental in upgrading the compound's arsenal to include assault rifles. By the time of McVeigh's phone call, however, Strassmeir had already left the compound for good because he did not approve of the imminent arrival of Ellison, who would marry Millar's granddaughter weeks after the bombing.[55]

In another connection, one that the archive does not fully explain, McVeigh also called Lyons's law office a few days before the bombing.[56] Perhaps McVeigh wished to coordinate a defense. Perhaps he was prepared to be a scapegoat after the bombing. Perhaps the cell was prepared for any man caught to take the fall for the others and go to jail. After all, McVeigh—who after the bombing was caught on a routine traffic stop—later claimed credit for the attack even as Lyons spirited Strassmeir out of the country before he could be thoroughly investigated.[57]

In the days before the bombing, McVeigh stayed on task. When Nichols and Fortier expressed doubt or reluctance, McVeigh circulated *Armed and Dangerous: The Rise of the Survivalist Right,* a book by journalist James Coates who had covered the emergence of the Order in the 1980s. A copy of *Armed and Dangerous* from Kingman, Arizona's Mohave County Library turned up in the FBI search of Terry Nichols's house in Kansas. The book included a chapter on the Order, many references to Louis Beam, material on the CSA, and a comprehensive description of the movement as a whole. Having read it and required its reading by his compatriots, McVeigh could not have been ignorant of the white power movement in which he now planned to participate.

And what would arrest matter to a soldier in that kind of war? "We are the legions of the damned," read a passage by Order leader Bob Mathews in the book's epigraph. "The army of the already dead."[58]

As they marshaled the will to carry out the attack, McVeigh and his co-conspirators continued to gather the supplies they would need. On April 17 or 18, a witness reported seeing five men with a Ryder truck parked near Geary State Lake. The site was less than a half hour's drive on the route from Junction City, Kansas—where McVeigh had rented the Ryder truck—to Oklahoma City, via US-77, a back road that passed through Herington, Kansas, where Terry Nichols lived. The witness said he saw a Ryder truck loaded down with ammonium nitrate fertilizer parked on the side of the road. Thinking the truck was stuck, he stopped to help, but he changed his mind after a menacing look from one of the men. Descriptions of the men matched those of militiamen and white power figures active in the area—and indicated that at least three other people besides McVeigh and Nichols were present. The other vehicles parked near the Ryder truck were a pickup, a large stakebed truck, and a brown car. McVeigh had already parked his 1977 yellow Mercury in a downtown garage in Oklahoma City, ready for the get-away, and had removed its Arizona license plate. Nichols drove a pickup. Federal agents never followed the lead about the other two vehicles, nor did they locate and interview these other suspects. After assembling the bomb at Geary State Lake with unknown accomplices, McVeigh drove the Ryder truck from Kansas to Oklahoma City on 250 miles of back roads, in order to avoid being pulled over.[59]

The night before the bombing, McVeigh slept in the Ryder truck with the 7,000-pound fertilizer bomb. The morning of April 19, he drove into Oklahoma City, inserted earplugs, lit a five-minute fuse and then a two-minute one as he approached the target, parked the truck in the delivery pull-off in front of the Murrah Building, checked that the fuses were burning, got out of the truck, and walked away. He made it about 150 yards before the explosion lifted him off the ground.[60]

The bomb killed 167 people, and a nurse died on the scene when she was hit by falling debris, bringing the death toll to 168. More than 500 were injured. Nineteen children died in the blast. The number of deaths in Oklahoma City exceeded the 148 Americans who had died in combat during the Gulf War. One Vietnam veteran on the scene compared the blast to war, but said that the bombing was worse. "In the war, you knew the enemy was coming after you. You were prepared. You could defend yourself. . . . We had no warning for this."[61]

Many of the victims, and most of the children, were disfigured, burned, or maimed. Parents used birthmarks to identify their dead children. "I couldn't see anything in his face at all. It was all puffed up, all bloody with scratches and stitches and black eyes," said Jim Denny, father of Brandon Denny, three, who had a strawberry birthmark on his thigh. "But his legs, his little legs. His legs were so clean." McVeigh and Fortier would both claim later that they didn't know about the day care center on the second floor of the building, directly over the place where the Ryder truck had exploded. Rescue workers lined up the small bodies in a playground.[62]

The structural instability of what remained of the Murrah Building complicated the rescue effort; falling pieces of debris and swinging electrical lines threatened rescue workers. It rained on and off during the days that followed the bombing, and crews frequently had to abandon the crane they were using because of concerns about lightning. One victim, pinioned under fallen steel, had to have her right leg amputated on the scene because moving the debris might have caused the building to collapse. An assistant fire chief spoke of the people still stuck in the wreckage. "There are places we have to crawl over bodies to get to other people," he said. "People are crying out to us. There are areas where we can reach through and try to touch their hands. There are some areas we can't get to at all." As the days passed, the presence of putrefying bodies further hampered the rescue effort, with workers slowed by the sheer volume of blood and bodily fluids.[63]

In the chaos after the blast, McVeigh got in the parked getaway car and drove slowly away from Oklahoma City, heading north. He would later say that he forgot to put a license plate on the car, and this oversight led to his arrest when he crossed a double yellow line in Perry, Oklahoma, seventy-five minutes after the bomb went off. The timing indicates that he carefully drove at or under the speed limit from Oklahoma City to Perry, on a route that would have led him back to Fort Riley. McVeigh, who owned a radar detector and frequently drove recklessly, far above the speed limit, was exercising unusual caution.[64]

When he was arrested, McVeigh had no money with him.[65] He did have a semiautomatic handgun loaded with a Black Talon "cop killer" bullet.[66] The standard protocol for white power operatives being pursued was to shoot the police officer and flee. Snell had done so, as had Order member David

Tate.[67] McVeigh, however, was polite to the arresting officer, perhaps because the policeman quickly drew his weapon. McVeigh told the officer he had a gun, and then surrendered peaceably.[68] He was arrested with Strassmeir's card in his wallet.[69] It was a strange oversight, and this—along with McVeigh's unusually strict observance of the speed limit in his getaway— indicated that he did not set out to be arrested. Perhaps he thought, when he surrendered, that he could not be linked to the bombing and would be quickly released. Indeed, only through a lucky and rapid John Doe description issued to the Perry jail was McVeigh held for anything other than the routine traffic violation and a concealed weapon charge.[70] McVeigh never attempted violent evasion or jailbreak and was consistently cooperative with his jailers.

Also in the car at the time of his arrest was a thick packet of extremist literature, quotes from Patrick Henry and Winston Churchill, and writings on Waco and on Samuel Adams. The envelope that held them was sealed; perhaps McVeigh carried them in case he was apprehended and unable to tell his story for himself. One of the items in the packet was a quote from *The Turner Diaries:*

> More important, though, is what we taught the politicians and the bureau-crats. They learned this afternoon that not one of them is beyond our reach. They can huddle behind barbed wire and tanks in the city, and they can hide behind the concrete walls of their country estates, but we can still find them and kill them.[71]

McVeigh wanted the bombing to send a message to the New World Order: that white American men could still wage war on the state.

As McVeigh sat in one lockup, perhaps wondering if authorities would release him on the traffic violation or discover his connection to the bombing, Snell awaited execution in another. There he received Robert Millar, who had come from Elohim City to counsel him as his death approached. An FBI review of the prison log would later report that Snell spent the hours before his execution lying on his bunk and watching television coverage of the Oklahoma City bombing, "smiling and chuckling." As guards prepared to administer the lethal injection that night, Snell's final words were of race war and a warning for the Arkansas governor. "Look over your shoulder, justice is on the way," Snell foretold. "I wouldn't trade places with you or any of your political cronies. Hail His victory. I am at peace." After the lethal injection at 9:10 P.M., men from Elohim City collected his body. He was buried at the compound, with a funeral officiated by Millar that revealed, again, the close ties between that community and Snell's CSA.[72]

In the days that followed, more and more links between the bombing and the white power movement emerged. Authorities transferred McVeigh to prison to await trial. They identified and located Terry Nichols after he turned himself in to the state police in Herington; a search of his house produced some thirty weapons, including a replica Uzi machine gun. In the home and car of McVeigh, officials found writings and letters about his belief in a right to carry firearms without government restraint. He also had a book, *Sinister Twilight,* and a video, *Day 51*—both about Waco.[73]

Meanwhile, doubts arose that one truck bomb could have inflicted so much damage. Two anonymous Pentagon experts said the damage was consistent with five separate bombs, but the ruins were demolished before an independent forensic team could investigate. The government cited health concerns as the reason for expediting the demolition. This part of the story generated complicated conspiracy theories, as did witness reports of a "John Doe 2," never located, described as an olive-skinned, dark-haired man.[74]

Regardless of the specifics of the explosion, McVeigh could not have acted alone. Regardless of whether only the Ryder truck bomb or an additional series of smaller explosions caused the damage, Nichols and Fortier were very likely joined by the Geary State Lake accomplices in helping McVeigh with the bombing. When McVeigh wrote that he had become a member of a "Special Forces Group involved in criminal activity," it signaled membership. Such groups, the paramilitary elite of the white power movement, were not newly wrought by the militiamen: they had led mercenary expeditions in Central America, conducted vigilante border watches, confronted Vietnamese refugees on the Texas coast, and robbed and killed in the Order and in affiliated local groups. McVeigh's membership in such a cell during these years positioned him as a soldier of the white power movement. It also pointed to the continued power of violence in binding white power actors together. McVeigh, who wanted more than anything to be a member of the U.S. Army Special Forces, instead found the equivalent position in the paramilitary war on the state, a campaign that had always been modeled on the Vietnam War story.[75]

The image of McVeigh as a working soldier was emphasized by his trial, which began on the tenth anniversary of the Fort Smith sedition trial, and that of Terry Nichols. Further links between the white power movement and the bombing emerged while McVeigh and Nichols were in jail. After authorities decided Strassmeir was a person of interest, movement lawyer Lyons helped him flee the country before the investigation could produce any more information to tie him to the bombing. And because McVeigh refused to acknowledge his role in the bombing until after his conviction, McVeigh's defense team went so far as to issue a false confession in hopes of baiting white power leaders into giving affidavits. The *Rocky Mountain News* later reported that the confession was meant to make Beam think McVeigh was acting as the perfect operative by accepting blame for the bombing. The defense team thought Beam was a possible suspect in the bombing but was unable to get him on record in a useful way. Beam, purportedly plagued with ongoing personal crises, including custody battles and health problems he attributed to Agent Orange exposure in Vietnam, had begun to quietly withdraw from the movement. During the investigation, Beam said through an intermediary that he could not be held responsible for how others might misuse his ideas.[76]

Unable to prove that McVeigh was carrying out Beam's strategy of leaderless resistance, the defense team argued that there had been a conspiracy. It was based, they said, in Elohim City, where resident "members of the Aryan Nations, the Posse Comitatus and former Kansas City Ku Klux Klan leader Dennis Mahon" assisted McVeigh. Jones argued that in the weeks before the bombing, Elohim City was "populated by individuals who previously had engaged in armed confrontation with the federal government including neo-Nazis with training manuals on how to make ammonium nitrate bombs."[77] Jones relied on the testimony of Carol Howe, allowed as a witness in Nichols's trial, who maintained that Mahon and Strassmeir cased the Murrah Building three times just before the bombing. Jones also referred to an Order-style spree of bank robberies in the area carried out by the Aryan Republican Army. That group certainly followed the directives of the Order's war on the state: it carried out a chain of bank robberies from 1994 to 1996, eventually robbing nineteen banks in eight states. Of six suspects in those robberies, four had lived at Elohim City or had close ties there. One was wanted for the triple murder of a gun dealer and his family. ARA members included Michael Brescia and Mark Thomas. Some suspected Brescia of being involved in the Oklahoma City bombing as John Doe 2, although such suspicions were never investigated or confirmed. Dennis Mahon—of Tom Metzger's White Aryan Resistance in California, and Carol Howe's former boyfriend—was close friends with Brescia and Thomas. Thomas was also the leader of the Pennsylvania branch of Aryan Nations. These connections pointed persuasively to Elohim City as a refuge and staging ground of a continued war on the state waged by the unified white power movement. "If the bombing or anything like that was planned here, it was certainly not to my knowledge," said Millar in an uncharacteristically weak denial. A local witness claimed to have seen McVeigh with one of the accused ARA bank robbers.[78]

The conspiracy defense did not succeed: McVeigh was found guilty and sentenced to death by lethal injection. Perhaps Jones lost the case, commentators ventured, because McVeigh refused to offer sufficient information to sustain the defense. Wrote author Gore Vidal, who undertook a lengthy correspondence with McVeigh after his conviction, "Jones's case led some reporters to speculate that McVeigh himself was limiting his own defense in order to prevent evidence that might implicate others in the bombing from entering the record."[79] Later, in Terry Nichols's trial, Vidal pointed out that the jury forewoman, after reporting a hung jury, told the press, "Decisions were probably made very early on that McVeigh and Nichols were who they were looking for, and the same sort of resources were not used to try to find out who else might be involved. . . . The government really dropped the ball." The forewoman received bomb threats soon after saying so. Some jurors, Vidal wrote, believed that other conspirators were still at large.[80]

Vidal also wrote, "I unearthed evidence that the FBI did not follow up on solid leads, or, if they did, failed to turn those over to the defense. I uncovered information provided to the FBI by Kansas law enforcement, and by very reliable eyewitnesses who were apparently disregarded," including the story of the five men at Geary State Lake. He also "found evidence that the FBI may have withheld certain information from the defense teams during discovery, potentially tainting the verdicts against both McVeigh and Nichols."[81] Indeed, the FBI deliberately withheld such evidence in its strategic pursuit of a single perpetrator. Attorney General John Ashcroft would delay McVeigh's execution by a month, at the end, to allow the defense to review materials not disclosed during the trial. The FBI turned over thousands of pages of documents that the agency had not revealed even under a direct order from the judge.[82] Nevertheless, McVeigh's execution in June 2001 cemented the popular perception that he had acted alone.

Meanwhile, most reactions to the bombing within the white power movement fell into two categories: those who condemned the act and believed McVeigh was an innocent scapegoat, and those who approved of the bombing as violence necessary in the war on the state. Militia of Montana leader David Trochmann said federal government operatives had carried out the bombing in order to discredit militias.[83] Incarcerated Order member David Lane published a lengthy open letter to McVeigh in his newsletter. Angry that Richard Matsch, the same judge who had sentenced him and his fellow Order members, was presiding over McVeigh's trial, Lane wrote that McVeigh had surely been set up.

> Timothy, you are dealing with a government that over the last two centuries has traveled from Dixie, to Cuba, to Mexico, to Panama to Grenada, to a dozen Latin American countries, from the halls of Montezuma, to the shores of Tripoli, to Italy, to Germany twice, to Japan, to Korea, to Vietnam, to Iraq, to Waco, to Whidbey Island, to Ruby Ridge and dozens of lesser known wars, occupations and assassinations, in pursuit of their . . . New World Order. In the process they have killed and maimed many tens of millions of very real people.[84]

Lane placed the battles of the white power movement—the standoff between Mathews and the FBI at Whidbey Island, the siege at Ruby Ridge and the fire at Waco—in a history of brutal U.S. interventions all over the world. Under the power of such a superstate, a man set up to take a fall could not expect justice. The *Jubilee,* following this line, called the bombing a tragedy, but also defended McVeigh from what it saw as unjust federal prosecution.[85]

Meanwhile, *Turner Diaries* author and National Alliance leader William Pierce lauded the bombing and promised more violence to come. "Terrorism is a nasty business. Most of its victims are innocent people," Pierce said. "But terrorism is a form of warfare, and in war most of the victims are noncombatants."[86] Other movement figures recognized the violence as part of their war on the state. The National Socialist Workers' Party said it had no connection to the bombing, but that members of the movement were probably involved. In an ethnographic interview, one white separatist woman said people in her group "were happy about what happened in Oklahoma. There's a lot of anger out there. The people, some felt sorry for the children but the rest of them got what they deserved, the government deserved. The government provoked this."[87]

Beam offered a call to action. In a long "historical analysis" of the bombing in the *Jubilee,* he decried the "horrendous explosion and senseless loss of life in Oklahoma City" and wrote that the bombing would fuel the police state, which would crack down on the militias and on gun ownership. Then, Beam asked the reader to put aside assumptions of conspiracy: what if the government had not set up the Oklahoma City bombing? What if McVeigh and Nichols were not government agents, but ordinary men? "What then would produce the amount of frustration necessary to motivate decorated Gulf War veterans to carry out such an act independent of any government collusion?" he asked. "Two things come to mind: Failure of government to punish those who killed Mrs. Weaver and her son at Ruby Ridge, and failure of government to punish those in law enforcement who murdered innocent men, women, and children at Waco." From this invocation of martyrs, Beam moved fluidly into a new call to arms.

> When the law breaks down, the vigilante is called forth. . . . To control this disease of the American spirit we must go straight for the command and control center in Washington. We still have the power to take back America so long as free elections are held. Between now and the next national election we must all arm ourselves with a voter registration slip and use it like a .308 sniper weapon to "take out" the infectious bought whores of the new world government who are now proposing to rule us all with an Orwellian iron fist—forever beating us into submission, while claiming to protect us.[88]

Likening a voter registration slip to a sniper rifle was a strangely unwieldy metaphor for Beam. Perhaps it is better read as a coded message to movement followers and to underground resistance cells. The .308 was the weapon proposed in the Order's plan for six-member cells to avoid police pursuit by killing policemen and disabling their cars. And the target, clearly embedded in the message, was "the command and control center in Washington." Beam was calling for soldiers to follow McVeigh's lead in acting against the federal government.

Indeed, the bombing launched an almost immediate and widespread wave of violence as the militia movement, and the broader white power movement, took action around the country. Four militiamen were arrested in Oklahoma, where they were allegedly planning to bomb several buildings. Federal documents said that they had planned to practice at Elohim City; while Millar admitted that he knew one of the men, he said he knew nothing about their plan.[89] Three members of the Georgia Republic Militia were convicted of stockpiling bombs. Militia members from West Virginia, Ohio, and Pennsylvania were accused of planning to blow up the FBI's national fingerprint center, another idea taken directly from *The Turner Diaries*. A federal mine inspector and his wife were injured in a copycat bombing in Vacaville, California. There was an Oklahoma-based conspiracy to blow up the Anti-Defamation League offices in Houston.[90] Bombings, bomb threats, murders, and armed protests plagued gay bars in the South and abortion clinics there and in the Midwest. Confederate Hammer Skins—skinheads armed with assault weapons—chased law enforcement officers away from a "White Man's Weekend" in Dawsonville, Georgia.[91] In 1995, seven Militia of Montana members stormed the sheriff's department to demand the return of confiscated property; five—including leader John Trochmann—were arrested on concealed weapons charges, and authorities suspected they had planned to kidnap and hang a district court judge. The *New York Times* reported on several other fugitives holed up in Idaho and Montana, each man waiting for, and perhaps even hoping for, his standoff with the feds.[92]

Several familiar white power activists reemerged after the bombing. In 1997, a jury convicted navy veteran Veren Jay Merrell of domestic terrorism bombings and bank robberies in eastern Washington, including bombing a Planned Parenthood clinic, a U.S. Bank branch, and a suburban bureau of the Spokane-based *Spokesman-Review*. Merrell, who had written for the *Jubilee*, was a member of the Arizona Patriots not convicted after the 1986 bust. The group had relocated to Idaho (possibly following Bob Mathews), had reorganized, and had continued to wage war on the state. Merrell, who practiced severation, was a nuclear expert from his time in the navy and easily translated this skill set to bomb-making.[93] Ex-mercenary and Civilian Military Assistance head Tom Posey also turned up again after the Oklahoma City bombing, and was convicted of conspiracy to sell night-vision goggles—nearly a quarter of a million dollars' worth—stolen from the army post at Fort Hood, Texas.[94] In 1999, Buford Furrow—who had married Debbie Mathews, the widow of Bob Mathews—opened fire on a Jewish community center and killed a Filipino postal worker in Los Angeles, California.

Furrow, who was using an Uzi, also wounded three children, a teenager, and an old woman. In his van, police found 2,000 rounds of ammunition and an Army Ranger handbook; he was also armed with other weapons, including hand grenades. Furrow may have been attempting to get into the Phineas Priesthood, a Christian Identity group that required its soldiers to wage acts of race war in order to gain membership. Furrow was a longtime Aryan Nations member with a history of violent activity. In an earlier court appearance for assault, he had said he fantasized about committing a mass killing: even so, he was able to obtain an Uzi and carry out further crimes.[95]

On July 27, 1996, Eric Rudolph bombed Atlanta's Centennial Park in the middle of the Olympics. Because the bomb had shifted, orienting its explosion vertically rather than horizontally, its shrapnel wounded only 111 people and killed two; the bomb had been intended for a much higher death toll. Rudolph, escaping arrest, followed with three more bombs in 1996 and 1997, targeting two abortion clinics and a gay bar. Those blasts injured another six people and killed two more. All four bombs, the FBI would later confirm, were "powerful antipersonnel devices, containing nails, that were designed to kill and maim," with secondary blasts or advance warning phone calls calculated to target rescue workers.[96] Rudolph, who signed his letters "Army of God" in reference to a violent anti-abortion crusade, had grown up around white separatism. As a freshman in high school, he wrote a paper denying the Holocaust, a common intellectual exercise for white power movement members and their children. His family lived in the North Carolina wilderness; Rudolph was anti-abortion, anti-gay, and dedicated to war on the state.[97]

Rudolph, an experienced woodsman, disappeared into the mountains of western North Carolina, where he remained on the run—and on the FBI's Ten Most Wanted list, with a reward of $1 million—for five years. He chose a region, reported the *New York Times,* where white separatist organizations were known to take refuge. And indeed, the locals did little to help authorities catch Rudolph. FBI director Louis Freeh and Attorney General Janet Reno made impassioned pleas, describing the horrific details of the Olympic Park bombing, to attempt to generate help finding Rudolph. When Rudolph was apprehended near Murphy, North Carolina, he had buried four caches of dynamite around the town, including a twenty-five-pound bomb across the road from the Army National Guard armory that served as the base for the FBI manhunt. This revealed a continued engagement with the Order's attempts to target law enforcement officers, the White Patriot Party's theft of military weapons from North Carolina armories, or both.[98] Meanwhile, a string of less publicized incidents showed a white power movement still active and violent. The Arizona Patriots plotted to blow up abortion clinics in the mid-1990s. In 1999, Benjamin Smith, linked with the white power World Church of the Creator, went on a shooting spree in Illinois and Indiana, wounding six Jews and killing two people of color before killing himself.[99]

The Oklahoma City bombing, as Beam foretold, resulted in a federal crackdown that dampened the white power movement somewhat in the late 1990s and early 2000s. Thom Robb's Klan in Zinc, Arkansas, disbanded under the pressure of the bombing investigation. In March 1996, the FBI attempted to round up the Montana Freemen at Justus Township, provoking a long siege, but one that ended peacefully and avoided creating a membership surge like the one that had followed Ruby Ridge and Waco. Lyons turned up at Justus Township to help with hostage negotiations. The *Jubilee* called the raid the culmination of three years of government harassment, political persecution, and judicial suppression. McVeigh said his bombing had curbed state violence. Perhaps he was right: after all, there had been no fiery end to the siege at Justus Township.[100]

Until his execution in 2001, McVeigh maintained that he had acted alone, with coerced help from Fortier and Nichols, in carrying out the bombing. He said that his attorney was wrong about the conspiracy idea, that he had never met Mahon, and that he had encountered Strassmeir only once, at a gun show. He said he had made calls to Elohim City and the National Alliance only to secure a place to hide after the bombing.[101] The evidence, however, from McVeigh's life history, to his associations, to the ideas that shaped his life and actions, points to his long participation in the white power movement and as a soldier of its cell-style underground. It didn't matter that McVeigh had no demonstrable contact with white power leaders. He could be no greater an acolyte had he gone into battle under direct command. McVeigh referred to the bombing as a "military action," and the bombing was indeed the culmination of decades of white power organization, bringing to bear years and years of paramilitarism. The successful strategy of leaderless resistance meant that movement leaders could never be linked to the bombing—and that even the white power movement itself could become invisible, its coordinated violence misunderstood as disconnected acts carried out by lone terrorists.

A police car decorated with the slogan "We Will Never Forget" sits before the
wreckage of the Alfred P. Murrah Federal Building in Oklahoma City, April 1995.
(Rick Bowmer, Associated Press Photo)

THE BOMB IN OKLAHOMA CITY left an eight-foot crater in the street and a massive hollow in the edifice of the federal building. Survivors spoke of the material void they encountered in the immediate aftermath of the blast: the
empty space where that part of the building should have been. "It was like
the end of the world when the blast hit, this tremendous noise and pressure
against you, and I could see everything disintegrating," said Wanda Webster, a sixty-five-year-old employee of the Office of Native American Programs. "When I finally did remove the rubble and stand up, there was
nothing there."[1]

Such descriptions of absence serve as an apt metaphor for the way the
bombing distorted, or even destroyed, what had been a popular awareness

of white power activity. From Klan paramilitary camps to the Greensboro shooting, from the Order to the Fort Smith sedition trial, white power actions made the news. Although the connections between such episodes were not always made clear, they nevertheless appeared in mainstream newspapers, on morning newsmagazine and afternoon talk shows, in movies and television miniseries, and even on the late-night comedy show *Saturday Night Live*.[2] But Timothy McVeigh's execution cemented a perception of the bombing as unconnected to the events that came before, as an inexplicable act of violence carried out by one or a few actors. This idea threatened to occlude the white power movement altogether. Leaderless resistance had triumphed as a strategy to hide the broader movement in the bombing investigation and prosecution, and in the journalistic and scholarly accounts as well. They have portrayed white power movement violence as isolated, rather than a series of coordinated acts, and its activists as madmen rather than as part of a movement.

The Oklahoma City bombing stands as the fulfillment of the revolutionary violence waged by white power activists. Gulf War veteran Timothy McVeigh carried out the bombing in connection with other activists; read and distributed the novel that had structured the violence of the Order; chose a building that white power activists had targeted since 1983, the year they declared war on the state; talked about stealing weapons from a military post; and saw civilians as "collateral damage" in a war upon the federal government.[3] His action was the work of a post–Vietnam War paramilitary white power movement that was still structuring militia violence and supposedly "lone" acts of terrorism in 1995.

That the Oklahoma City bombing, which stood as a singular event of mass-casualty terrorism on American soil—deliberate violence at a scale unsurpassed, at that time, since the bombing of Pearl Harbor—did not solidify a public understanding of the white power movement and its capacity for violence is remarkable.[4] Smaller-scale violent events earlier in the twentieth century, such as the 1963 bombing of the Sixteenth Street Baptist Church in Birmingham, Alabama, had played a role in galvanizing public opinion against the Klan and in favor of the civil rights movement.[5] Certainly such events helped tip the scale of public opinion away from overt racism and the outright support of racial violence, such that in their aftermath, even politicians who pursued policies with racial implications increasingly framed these in coded terms.[6]

What was left unfinished, unexplained, and unconfronted about white power meant that it could resurge in the years following 1995. White power should have been legible as a coherent social movement but was instead largely narrated and prosecuted as scattered actions and inexplicable lone wolf attacks motivated not by ideology but by madness or personal animus. It might have been treated as a wide-reaching social network with the capacity to inflict mass casualties, but was too often brushed off as backwardness or ineptitude. It should have been acknowledged as producing, supporting, and deploying a coherent worldview that posed radical challenges to a liberal consensus around racial and gender equality and support of institutions including the vote, courts, the rule of law, and federal legislative bodies. Instead, the disappearance of the movement in the years after Oklahoma City—engineered by white power activists but permitted and furthered by government actors, prosecutorial strategies, scholars, and journalists alike—left open the possibility of new waves of action. Even as prolonged wars in Iraq and Afghanistan shaped a new generation of white power activism, this new activity would largely continue to evade public understanding, despite the warnings of watchdog groups, until it broke into mainstream politics in the 2016 presidential campaign and election.

Although militias and copycat crimes briefly surged following the Oklahoma City bombing, white power activism underwent an inescapable shift after 1995. In the late 1990s, the movement largely relocated into the online spaces it had begun to build more than a decade earlier.[7] Continued movement activity unfolded mostly out of public view. While a few scholars joined the watchdogs in monitoring and studying websites such as Stormfront, white power was generally regarded as a fringe and untenable ideology.

While the Vietnam War story as lived experience and cultural force receded with time, the war remained relevant. New generations of activists participated in a movement with direct genealogical through-lines to the post-Vietnam white power unification, sharing organizational strategies, ideologies, resources, and personnel with the 1979–1995 groundswell. Stormfront, for instance, was founded in 1995 by Dominica mercenary Don Black; much of the contemporary "alt-right" posture was modeled on earlier political campaigns by David Duke; the acquittal of militants at Malheur Wildlife Reserve in Oregon at their 2016 trial echoed the 1988 Fort Smith sedition trial, and the action of those militants may have been an attempt to provoke federal violence reminiscent of Ruby Ridge. Consciously or not, all of these actions referenced decades of white power movement history, and several continued to employ movement networks.

The symbolic universe of the post-Vietnam movement endured in white power action. In his 2015 shooting of nine black worshippers at a Bible study in Charleston, South Carolina, Dylann Roof undertook an action that followed the movement's teachings in an attempt to foment race war.[8] He also used symbols that derived from the 1979–1995 period of white power activism. In photos he posted online, he wore a Rhodesian flag patch, which symbolized a white minority-rule government that had never existed during his lifetime and referenced a cause framed by Louis Beam at the 1983 Aryan Nations World Congress, to take one example of its invocation. Roof used 88, a code for "Heil Hitler" popularized in the 1980s by the movement at large. And he used the Confederate flag, which at the turn of the millennium increasingly symbolized a cultural stance that conflated white supremacy with opposition to a multicultural liberal consensus. Because of the Internet, Roof never had to meet another activist to be radicalized by the white power movement, nor to count himself among its foot soldiers.[9]

A brief public contestation with white power ideology and symbols followed the Charleston shooting. One activist climbed a flagpole to remove the Confederate battle flag from the South Carolina state capitol.[10] Others, including politicians on both sides of the aisle, activists, and citizens, engaged in a renewed debate about the flag, and some attempted to remove it from the places where it still flew: on college campuses, over government and legal buildings, and beyond.[11] But this attention provoked a substantial backlash and may have further galvanized and emboldened a segment of the electorate that identified more closely with white power ideologies around such symbols, and around white supremacy, revanchist notions of gender roles, belief in the inherent corruption of the federal government, and an apocalyptic future. The rise of the self-proclaimed "alt-right" from the websites and forums founded by white power activists and the explosion of such views into mainstream politics during the presidential campaign and election of Donald Trump show that—in a sense—Dylann Roof did participate in a chain of events that measurably decreased opportunity for and unleashed violence against people of color in myriad ways. Hate crimes proliferated in the wake of the election. Roof wrote in a manifesto that he wanted to provoke race war; in the most abstract sense, he might have gotten what he was looking for.[12]

There is, of course, insufficient historical distance or archival material to offer large-scale interpretations of the present moment. What is inescapably clear from the history of the white power movement, however, is that the lack of public understanding, effective prosecution, and state action left an opening for continued white power activism. The state and public opinion have failed to sufficiently halt white power violence or refute white power belief systems, and failed to present a vision of the future that might address some of the concerns that lie behind its more diffuse, coded, and mainstream manifestations.

Understanding white power as a social movement is a project both of historical relevance and of vital public importance. Knowledge of the history of white power activism is integral to preventing future acts of violence and to providing vital context to current political developments. Indeed, to perceive the movement as a legitimate social force, and its ideologies as comprising a coherent worldview of white supremacy and imminent apocalypse—one with continued recruiting power—is to understand that colorblindness, multicultural consensus, and a postracial society were never achieved. Violent, outright racism and antisemitism were live currents in these decades, waiting for the opportunity to resurface in overt form. This story renders legible the many ways that racial ideology and incessant warfare have underwritten political issues that extend well beyond the fringe. It powerfully reveals how white power rhetoric and activism, time and again, have influenced mainstream U.S. politics, and most especially in the aftermath of war.

Notes

Abbreviations

ATF	Bureau of Alcohol, Tobacco, and Firearms (Freedom of Information Act)
CRL	Center for Research Libraries, Chicago, IL
FBI	Federal Bureau of Investigation
	FBI clip Federal Bureau of Investigation, news clippings file (Freedom of Information Act)
	FBI File Federal Bureau of Investigation, collected file on particular group or person (Freedom of Information Act and FBI Electronic Reading Room)
	SAC Special Agent in Charge
GPL	Greensboro Public Library, Greensboro, NC
GTRC	Greensboro Truth and Reconciliation Commission
HH	Gordon Hall and Grace Hoag Collection of Dissenting and Extremist Printed Propaganda, Ms. 76, Brown University Library, Providence, RI
IHNCA-UCA	Instituto de Historia de Nicaragua y Centroamerica, Universidad Centroamericana, Managua, Nicaragua
LC	Elinor Langer Research Collection, Special Collections, University of Oregon, Eugene
Miles et al.	*United States of America vs. Miles et al.*, no. 87-20008 (W. D. Ark, 1988), Center for Research Libraries, Chicago, IL F-7424
Pierce et al.	*United States of America vs. Bruce Carroll Pierce et al.*, CR-85-0001M (W. D. Wash, 1985), Accession 21-95-0078, Location 823306, Seattle, WA
RH WL	Wilcox Collection of Contemporary Political Movements, Kenneth Spencer Research Library, University of Kansas, Lawrence
SC	Keith Stimely Collection on Revisionist History and Neo-Fascist Movements, Special Collections, University of Oregon, Eugene, Oregon
SPLC	Intelligence Project Holdings, Southern Poverty Law Center, Montgomery, AL
Vietnamese Fishermen's Association	*Vietnamese Fishermen's Association, et al., v. The Knights of the Ku Klux Klan, et al.*, no. H-81-895, 518 F. Supp. 198 (1982); 34 Fed. R. Serv. 2d (Callaghan) 875; June 3, 1982
WAR	*White Aryan Resistance / White American Resistance* (Fallbrook, CA)
WHC	Western History Collection, Denver Public Library, Denver, CO (Biography Clipping Files: Berg, Alan, 1934–1984)

Introduction

1. White American Resistance (Fallbrook, CA), "White Soldier Boy," *White American Resistance* 4, no. 1 (1985): 17, LC, Series XIII, Box 1, Folder 3.

2. On widespread public distrust in a variety of social institutions, see Daniel T. Rodgers, *Age of Fracture* (Cambridge, MA: Harvard University Press, 2011), 6.

3. Robert O. Self, *All in the Family: The Realignment of American Democracy since the 1960s* (New York: Hill and Wang, 2013); Patrick Hagopian, *The Vietnam War in American Memory: Veterans, Memorials, and the Politics of Healing* (Amherst: University of Massachusetts Press, 2011).

4. On conservative anxieties about the 1965 Hart-Celler Immigration Act, see Natalia Mehlman Petrzela, *Classroom Wars: Language, Sex, and the Making of Modern Political Culture* (Oxford: Oxford University Press, 2015); Alicia Schmidt Camacho, *Migrant Imaginaries: Latino Cultural Politics in the U.S.-Mexico Borderlands* (New York: New York University Press, 2008).

5. On the farm crisis, see Catherine McNichol Stock, *Rural Radicals: Righteous Rage in the American Grain* (Ithaca: Cornell University Press, 1996); Evelyn A. Schlatter, *Aryan Cowboys: White Supremacy and the Search for a New Frontier, 1970–2000* (Austin: University of Texas Press, 2006).

6. Louis R. Beam Jr., "Vietnam Bring It on Home," *Essays of a Klansman* (Hayden Lake, ID: A.K.I.A. Publications, 1983).

7. On justifying vigilante violence by claiming sovereignty outside of or superseding the state, see Lisa Arellano, *Vigilantes and Lynch Mobs: Narratives of Community and Nation* (Philadelphia: Temple University Press, 2012); Stock, *Rural Radicals;* Christopher Waldrep, *The Many Faces of Judge Lynch: Extralegal Violence and Punishment in America* (New York: Palgrave Macmillan, 2002).

8. On the 1980 election as the victory of the New Right, see Lisa McGirr, *Suburban Warriors: The Origins of the New American Right* (Princeton, NJ: Princeton University Press, 2001); Sean Wilentz, *The Age of Reagan: A History, 1974–2008* (New York: HarperCollins, 2008).

9. Michelle M. Nickerson argues in *Mothers of Conservatism: Women and the Postwar Right* (Princeton, NJ: Princeton University Press, 2012) that antiexpert and antistatist credentials permeated the earliest grassroots stirrings of the New Right. On antistatism in the New Right, see also Michelle Nickerson and Darren Dochuk, *Sunbelt Rising: The Politics of Space, Place, and Region* (Philadelphia: University of Pennsylvania Press, 2011); D. J. Mulloy, *The World of the John Birch Society: Conspiracy, Conservatism, and the Cold War* (Nashville, TN: Vanderbilt University Press, 2014).

10. This *Time* quotation and analysis of this phenomenon appear in Self, *All in the Family,* 402–403.

11. Louis R. Beam Jr., *Essays of a Klansman,* 2nd ed. (Hayden Lake, ID: A.K.I.A. Publications, 1989), 43–44.

12. Most militias adopted "Patriot" and similar terms.

13. These numbers, drawn from Southern Poverty Law Center and Center for Democratic Renewal estimates, appear in Betty A. Dobratz and Stephanie L. Shanks-Meile, *The White Separatist Movement in the United States: "White Power, White Pride!"* (New York: Twayne, 1997); Raphael S. Ezekiel, *The Racist Mind: Portraits of American Neo-Nazis and Klansmen* (New York: Penguin, 1995); Abby L. Ferber and Michael Kimmel, "Reading Right: The Western Tradition in White Supremacist Discourse," *Sociological Focus* 33, no. 2 (May 2000): 193–213.

14. Mulloy, *World of the John Birch Society,* 2–3, 15–41.

15. On the concept of "leaderless resistance" changing movement attitudes toward recruitment as a measure of success, see Dobratz and Shanks-Meile, *The White Separatist Movement in the United States,* 25. On membership numbers as secondary to a movement's structure of struggle, see Sidney Tarrow, *Power in Movement: Social Movement, Collective Action and Politics* (Cambridge: Cambridge University Press, 1994), 15.

16. Brad Knickerbocker, "New Armed Militias Recruit Growing Membership in US," *Christian Science Monitor,* April 3, 1995, 1; Wyn Craig Wade, *The Fiery Cross: The Ku Klux Klan in America* (New York: Simon and Schuster, 1987); Jessie Daniels, *Cyber Racism: White Supremacy Online and the New Attack on Civil Rights* (Lanham, MD: Rowman and Littlefield, 2009); Mattias Gardell, *Gods of the Blood: The Pagan Revival and White Separatism* (Durham, NC: Duke University Press, 2003).

17. Anti-Catholicism was not a pronounced feature of post-1975 white power rhetoric. Kelly J. Baker, *Gospel According to the Klan: The KKK's Appeal to Protestant America, 1915–1930* (Lawrence: University of Kansas Press, 2011); Kathleen M. Blee, *Women of the Klan: Racism and Gender in the 1920s* (Berkeley: University of California Press, 1991); Nancy MacLean, *Behind the Mask of Chivalry: The Making of the Second Ku Klux Klan* (New York: Oxford University Press, 1994). On the pervasive belief in a biblical foundation for segregation, see Jane Dailey, "Sex, Segregation, and the Sacred after *Brown*," *Journal of American History* 91, no. 119 (2004): 119–144.

18. British Israelism posits a theology similar to that of Christian Identity, in which British Anglos are the lost tribe of Israel. Dualism and two-seed proponents believed that white people descended from Adam and others descended from the serpent. A similar theology posits that white people descended from Noah and people of color from Ham. The World Church of the Creator's theology, Creativity, proposed that white people were superior. Odinism was a form of pagan belief based on Norse mythology. Michael Barkun, *Religion and the Racist Right: The Origins of the Christian Identity Movement* (Chapel Hill: University of North Carolina Press, 1996); Gardell, *Gods of the Blood.*

19. Some activists straddled this divide: Louis Beam, for instance, described himself as "Identity-Baptist," a term that implied an evangelical upbringing but current participation in Christian Identity. Southern Poverty Law Center, "Interview with Louis Beam, Texas Grand Dragon of the K.K.K., Leader Aryan Nations, Nazi, C.P.D.L. [Christian Patriots Defense League] Survival Conference, Licking, Missouri, June 24, 1984," SPLC.

20. On evangelicalism as a growing and increasingly politicized faith, see Self, *All in the Family,* 9; Neil J. Young, *We Gather Together: The Religious Right and the Problem of Interfaith Politics* (Oxford: Oxford University Press, 2015).

21. Somer Shook, Wesley Delano, and Robert W. Balch, "Elohim City: A Participant-Observer Study of a Christian Identity Community," *Nova Religo: The Journal of Alternate and Emergent Religions* 2, no. 2 (April 1999): 245–265.

22. Ideas about outlasting the tribulation also appeared in mainstream evangelical accounts such as Tim LaHaye's popular *Left Behind* novels, the first of which appeared in 1995.

23. Following the International Holocaust Remembrance Alliance recommendation, I adopt the spelling "antisemitism" to avoid "legitimiz[ing] a form of pseudoscientific racial classification that was thoroughly discredited by association with Nazi ideology, [and also dividing] the term, stripping it from its meaning of opposition and hatred toward Jews." See International Holocaust Remembrance Alliance, "Memo on Spelling of Antisemitism," April 2015, https://www.holocaustremembrance.com /sites/default/files/memo-on-spelling-of-antisemitism_final-1.pdf.

24. I refer here to widely held movement beliefs as set forth in major and widely circulated white power newspapers such as the *Thunderbolt, White Power, WAR, White Patriot,* and others, and in the unpublished writings and speeches of the historical actors that appear in the chapters to come.

25. On postwar remasculinization and paramilitary culture in the 1980s, see Susan Jeffords, *The Remasculinization of America: Gender and the Vietnam War* (Bloomington: Indiana University Press, 1989); Susan Jeffords, *Hard Bodies: Hollywood Masculinity in the Reagan Era* (New Brunswick, NJ: Rutgers University Press, 1994); James William Gibson, *Warrior Dreams: Violence and Manhood in Post-Vietnam America* (New York: Hill and Wang, 1994); Susan Faludi, *Stiffed: The Betrayal of the American Man* (New York: William Morrow, 1999).

26. Kathleen M. Blee, *Inside Organized Racism: Women in the Hate Movement* (Berkeley: University of California Press, 2002); Abby L. Ferber, *White Man Falling: Race, Gender, and White Supremacy* (Lanham, MD: Rowman and Littlefield, 1998).

27. Participation by women and families also characterized earlier white supremacist mobilizations, such as the second-era Ku Klux Klan, which reached its peak in the 1920s. Blee, *Women of the Klan;* MacLean, *Behind the Mask of Chivalry.*

28. Accounts that have argued for such a distinction include Ezekiel, *The Racist Mind,* xxi–xxii; Mitch Berbrier, "The Victim Ideology of White Supremacists and White Separatists in the United States," *Sociological Focus* 33, no. 2 (May 2000):

175–191; Dobratz and Shanks-Meile, *The White Separatist Movement in the United States;* Jessie Daniels, *White Lies: Race, Class, Gender, and Sexuality in White Supremacist Discourse* (New York: Routledge, 1997).

The "fifth era" was an idea with wide currency in the movement, and appeared in texts and on stickers and patches that read "33/5," signifying a numeric code for "KKK" and a "5" to denote the fifth, underground era. See, for instance, Louis Beam, "Computers and the American Patriot," *Inter-Klan Newsletter and Survival Alert,* ca. 1983–84, LC, Box 22, Folder 20; Robert E. Miles, "'Take Off the Hood' Scream Our Foes!," *Inter-Klan Newsletter and Survival Alert: Death to Every Foe and Traitor!* (A.K.I.A. Publications, Hayden Lake, ID), no. 1 (ca. 1983): 5, SC, Box 31, Folder 6.

29. Sara Diamond, *Roads to Dominion: Right-Wing Movements and Political Power in the United States* (New York: Guilford Press, 1995); Michael Zatarain, *David Duke: Evolution of a Klansman* (Gretna, LA: Pelican Publishing Company, Inc., 1990); Leonard Zeskind, *Blood and Politics: The History of the White Nationalist Movement from the Margins to the Mainstream* (New York: Farrar, Straus and Giroux, 2009).

30. On long ramifications of violence, see Kidada E. Williams, "Regarding the Aftermaths of Lynching," *Journal of American History* 101, no. 3 (December 2014): 856–858; Monica Muñoz Martinez, "Recuperating Histories of Violence in the Americas: Vernacular History-Making on the U.S.-Mexico Border," *American Quarterly* 66, no. 3 (September 2014).

31. Jefferson Cowie offers an example of characterizing the 1970s as a period of reactionary politics related to resisting the social changes of the 1960s in *Stayin' Alive: The 1970s and the Last Days of the Working Class* (New York: New Press, 2010).

32. See, for instance, Niall Ferguson et al., eds., *The Shock of the Global: The 1970s in Perspective* (Cambridge, MA: Belknap Press of Harvard University Press, 2011).

33. On the oil crisis, stagflation, and the rising cost of limited natural resources, see Meg Jacobs, *Panic at the Pump: The Energy Crisis and the Transformation of American Politics in the 1970s* (New York: Hill and Wang, 2016). On the 1970s as a moment of economic reckoning and realignment, see Jefferson Cowie, *The Great Exception: The New Deal and the Limits of American Politics* (Princeton, NJ: Princeton University Press, 2017). On the 1970s as a moment of political and cultural transition, see Self, *All in the Family.* On the limitations of the GI Bill as an engine of post–World War II economic redistribution and the ways it unequally advanced straight white men to the exclusion of other groups, see Margot Canaday, *The Straight State: Sexuality and Citizenship in Twentieth-Century America* (Princeton, NJ: Princeton University Press, 2011).

34. Cowie, *Stayin' Alive.*

35. Elaine Tyler May, *Homeward Bound: American Families in the Cold War Era* (New York: Basic Books, 1988); Self, *All in the Family.*

36. Self, *All in the Family,* 7.

37. On the democratic state as an exercise of free market ideology detached from ideas of community, responsibility, and social welfare, see Greg Grandin, *The Last*

Colonial Massacre: Latin America in the Cold War, 2nd ed. (Chicago: University of Chicago Press, 2011), xii–xiii; Rodgers, *Age of Fracture.* I owe particular thanks to the graduate students in my American Conservatism colloquium for refinement of this interpretation of the importance of the 1970s in this section.

38. See, for instance, Robert W. Balch, "The Rise and Fall of Aryan Nations: A Resource Mobilization Perspective," *Journal of Political and Military Sociology* 34, no. 1 (Summer 2006): 82; Daniels, *White Lies;* Gardell, *Gods of the Blood;* Pete Simi and Robert Futrell, *American Swastika: Inside the White Power Movement's Hidden Spaces of Hate* (Plymouth, UK: Rowman and Littlefield, 2010), 9. Gardell's account does not distinguish between primary and secondary sources, accepting Evelyn Rich, "Ku Klux Klan Ideology, 1954–1988," Ph.D. diss., Boston University, 1988, as the basis for historical and contextual information about Klan organization. Beyond many incorrect assertions, Rich's dissertation was never peer-reviewed or published, and Rich later entered into a long-term romantic relationship with a prominent white power activist.

39. Doug McAdam and David A. Snow, *Readings on Social Movements: Origins, Dynamics and Outcomes,* 2nd ed. (Oxford: Oxford University Press, 2010), 1; Charles Tilly, *Social Movements: 1768–2004* (Boulder: Paradigm, 2004), 7; Tarrow, *Power in Movement,* 6, 15.

40. See, for instance, Blee, *Inside Organized Racism;* Ezekiel, *The Racist Mind,* xxii, 321; Ferber, *White Man Falling;* Abby L. Ferber, "The Construction of Race, Gender, and Class in White Supremacist Discourse," *Race, Gender and Class* 6, no. 3 (1999): 72–73; Michael Kimmel and Abby L. Ferber, " 'White Men Are This Nation': Right-Wing Militias and the Restoration of Rural American Masculinity," *Rural Sociology* 65, no. 4 (2000): 582–604.

41. I use the concept of "repertoire" as it appears in social movement theory articulated by Sidney Tarrow and Charles Tilly, and also as a component of performance. See Tarrow, *Power in Movement;* Tilly, *Social Movements;* Diana Taylor, *The Archive and the Repertoire: Performing Cultural Memory in the Americas* (Durham, NC: Duke University Press, 2003).

42. This definition of social movement formation comes from Tilly, *Social Movements,* 7.

43. The criterion of "WUNC displays" and the delineated analysis of worthiness, unity, numbers, and commitment follow the widely adopted definition offered by Tilly in *Social Movements.*

44. Tarrow, *Power in Movement,* 17–21; Doug McAdam, John D. McCarthy, and Mayer N. Zald, *Comparative Perspectives on Social Movements* (Cambridge: Cambridge University Press, 1996), 5–6.

45. *The Turner Diaries* was first printed in serial in National Alliance, *Attack!,* 1974–1976, SC, Box 31, Folder 9, and then published as Andrew Macdonald, *The Turner Diaries* (Hillsboro, WV: National Vanguard Books, 1978).

46. Mattias Gardell argues that white power in the late 1990s is best understood as a "counterculture" defined less by a shared set of political objectives and more by a "scene" of white power relationships, worldviews, lifestyles, religions, and music. Gardell, *Gods of the Blood,* 71–73, 196–197.

47. Newspaper clippings cited in this book sometimes come from archival sources, such as FBI or SPLC clipping files or mainstream journalistic accounts reprinted in white power publications. In these cases, dates and page numbers sometimes are not available, or a page number is available that refers, for instance, to the FBI file rather than the newspaper publication. These articles are not readily available in searchable databases since most of those located this way do not yet appear in electronic form. Further, FBI files are not truly replicable sources, as pagination can change depending on the scope of each Freedom of Information Act (FOIA) request used to obtain the file. I have given the most complete information available for each clipped article cited here. There is no repository for records obtained through the FOIA process apart from published FBI files, which are referred to by their filename when available. Otherwise, records are stored by each agency and can be obtained only through FOIA.

48. The three collections are the Elinor Langer Research Collection, Special Collections, University of Oregon, Eugene; the Wilcox Collection of Contemporary Political Movements, Kenneth Spencer Research Library, University of Kansas, Lawrence; and the Gordon Hall and Grace Hoag Collection of Dissenting and Extremist Printed Propaganda, Ms. 76, Brown University Library, Providence, Rhode Island.

49. On the constitutive power of violence, see Ned Blackhawk, *Violence over the Land: Indians and Empires in the Early American West* (Cambridge, MA: Harvard University Press, 2006).

1. The Vietnam War Story

1. Louis R. Beam Jr., "Vietnam Bring It on Home," *Essays of a Klansman* (Hayden Lake, ID: A.K.I.A. Publications, 1983), 35; Testimony of Louis Ray Beam Jr., *Miles et al.,* November 17, 1988, Box 16, Volume 2; Louis Beam, "War Stories 12," posted to the 25th Aviation Battalion website, http://www.25thaviation.org/id1046.htm; "Decorated," *Tropic Lightning News,* March 18, 1968, 2.

2. Photographs of Beam in uniform in Ron Laytner, "'I Infiltrated the Ku Klux Klan . . . and Lived!,'" *Argosy* 387, no. 6 (August 1978); "Cassette Tapes," advertisement, *Inter-Klan Newsletter and Survival Alert: Death to Every Foe and Traitor!* (A.K.I.A. Publications, Hayden Lake, ID), no. 3 (ca. 1983): 1, SC, Box 31, Folder 6; Louis R. Beam Jr., *Essays of a Klansman,* 2nd ed. (Hayden Lake, ID: A.K.I.A. Publications, 1989); Louis Beam, "A Card and Cookies," *Seditionist,* no. 2 (Spring 1989): 18, LC, Series II, Box 3, Folder 8.

3. Jefferson Cowie, *Stayin' Alive: The 1970s and the Last Days of the Working Class* (New York: New Press, 2010), 33; Donna Murch, *Living for the City: Migration,*

Education, and the Rise of the Black Panther Party in Oakland, California (Chapel Hill: University of North Carolina Press, 2010), 111, 139–140.

4. For instance, information about the Weather Underground appears in the Aryan Nations FBI file because of the Brinks connection: "Aryan Nations," FBI Records: The Vault, https://vault.fbi.gov/Aryan%20Nation. See also, Jeremy Varon, *Bringing the War Home: The Weather Underground, the Red Army Faction, and Revolutionary Violence in the Sixties and Seventies* (Berkeley: University of California Press, 2004); Associated Press, "Vigilante Groups Warned against Border Actions," *New York Times,* October 29, 1977, 8.

5. As the activist and scholar W. E. B. Du Bois famously wrote of black soldiers at the end of World War I, "We return from fighting. We return fighting." W. E. B. Du Bois, "Returning Soldiers," *Crisis* 18, no. 1 (May 1919): 13. On postwar activism among other veterans of color: David G. Gutiérrez, *Walls and Mirrors: Mexican Americans, Mexican Immigrants, and the Politics of Ethnicity* (Berkeley: University of California Press, 1995); Laura Pulido, *Black, Brown, Yellow, and Left: Radical Activism in Los Angeles* (Berkeley: University of California Press, 2006); Lorena Oropeza, *¡Raza Sí, Guerra No!: Chicano Protest and Patriotism during the Viet Nam War Era* (Berkeley: University of California Press, 2005).

6. Jennifer E. Brooks, *Defining the Peace: World War II Veterans, Race, and the Remaking of Southern Political Tradition* (Chapel Hill: University of North Carolina Press, 2004); Christine Knauer, *Let Us Fight as Free Men: Black Soldiers and Civil Rights* (Philadelphia: University of Pennsylvania Press, 2014); Kimberley L. Phillips, *War! What Is It Good For? Black Freedom Struggles and the U.S. Military from World War II to Iraq* (Chapel Hill: University of North Carolina Press, 2012); Timothy B. Tyson, *Radio Free Dixie: Robert F. Williams and the Roots of Black Power* (Chapel Hill: University of North Carolina Press, 1999).

7. Kathleen M. Blee, *Women of the Klan: Racism and Gender in the 1920s* (Berkeley: University of California Press, 1991); Brooks, *Defining the Peace;* David Cunningham, *Klansville, U.S.A.: The Rise and Fall of the Civil Rights–Era Ku Klux Klan* (New York: Oxford University Press, 2012); Nancy MacLean, *Behind the Mask of Chivalry: The Making of the Second Ku Klux Klan* (New York: Oxford University Press, 1994); Evelyn A. Schlatter, *Aryan Cowboys: White Supremacy and the Search for a New Frontier, 1970–2000* (Austin: University of Texas Press, 2006); Wyn Craig Wade, *The Fiery Cross: The Ku Klux Klan in America* (New York: Simon and Schuster, 1987).

8. On the campaigns of violence enabled by Klansmen and Columbians (a neofascist organization) who had served in World War II, for instance, see Brooks, *Defining the Peace,* 60–72. The United Klans of America, the organization whose members would bomb the Sixteenth Street Baptist Church in Birmingham, Alabama, killing four black girls, learned bomb-making from a navy veteran, according to Wade, *The Fiery Cross,* 321.

9. On the aftermath of warfare and other violence, see Dane Archer and Rosemary Gartner, *Violence and Crime in Cross-National Perspective* (New Haven, CT: Yale University Press, 1984); Joanna Bourke, *An Intimate History of Killing: Face-to-Face Killing in Twentieth-Century Warfare* (New York: Basic Books, 1999).

10. Christian G. Appy, *Working-Class War: American Combat Soldiers and Vietnam* (Chapel Hill: University of North Carolina Press, 1993); Marilyn B. Young, *The Vietnam Wars, 1945–1990* (New York: HarperCollins, 1991); Mark Philip Bradley, *Vietnam at War* (Oxford: Oxford University Press, 2009).

11. See, for instance, James William Gibson, *Warrior Dreams: Violence and Manhood in Post-Vietnam America* (New York: Hill and Wang, 1994).

12. See, for instance, Nick Turse, *Kill Anything That Moves: The Real American War in Vietnam* (New York: Picador, 2013); Patrick Hagopian, *The Vietnam War in American Memory: Veterans, Memorials, and the Politics of Healing* (Amherst: University of Massachusetts Press, 2011), 406.

13. On the way war had functioned previously, see, for instance, David M. Kennedy, *Freedom from Fear: The American People in Depression and War, 1929–1945* (Oxford: Oxford University Press, 1999); James Sparrow, *Warfare State: Americans and the Age of Big Government* (Oxford: Oxford University Press, 2013).

14. Bradley, *Vietnam at War;* Appy, *Working-Class War.*

15. Hagopian, *The Vietnam War in American Memory,* 12.

16. Susan Sontag, *Regarding the Pain of Others* (New York: Farrar, Straus and Giroux, 2003), 2.

17. Andrew E. Hunt, *The Turning: A History of Vietnam Veterans against the War* (New York: New York University Press, 2001).

18. Susan Jeffords, *The Remasculinization of America: Gender and the Vietnam War* (Bloomington: Indiana University Press, 1989).

19. Phillips, *War! What Is It Good For?;* Jennifer Mittelstadt, *The Rise of the Military Welfare State* (Cambridge, MA: Harvard University Press, 2015); Beth Bailey, *America's Army: Making the All-Volunteer Force* (Cambridge, MA: Harvard University Press, 2009).

20. Martha Rosler, "House Beautiful: Bringing the War Home" (1967–1972), http://www.martharosler.net/photo/war1/index.html; Varon, *Bringing the War Home,* 61.

21. Hunt, *The Turning;* Edwin A. Martini, *Agent Orange: History, Science, and the Politics of Uncertainty* (Amherst: University of Massachusetts Press, 2012); Judith Herman, *Trauma and Recovery: The Aftermath of Violence from Domestic Abuse to Political Terror* (New York: Basic Books, 1992); Jonathan Shay, *Achilles in Vietnam: Combat Trauma and the Undoing of Character* (New York: Maxwell Macmillan International, 1994); Jonathan Shay, *Odysseus in America: Combat Trauma and the Trials of Homecoming* (New York: Scribner, 2002); Hagopian, *The Vietnam War in American Memory.* See also Kristin Ann Hass, *Carried to the Wall: American Memory and the Vietnam Veterans Memorial* (Berkeley: University of California Press, 1998);

David Kieran, *Forever Vietnam: How a Divisive War Changed American Public Memory* (Amherst: University of Massachusetts Press, 2014).

22. Michael J. Allen, *Until the Last Man Comes Home: POWs, MIAs, and the Unending Vietnam War* (Chapel Hill: University of North Carolina Press, 2012); Robert O. Self, *All in the Family: The Realignment of American Democracy since the 1960s* (New York: Hill and Wang, 2013).

23. Hagopian, *The Vietnam War in American Memory,* 18–19.

24. Ibid.; Ronald Reagan, "Peace: Restoring the Margin of Safety," speech to the Veterans of Foreign Wars Convention, Chicago, August 18, 1980; Ronald Reagan, "Denied Permission to Win: Remarks on Presenting the Medal of Honor to Master Sergeant Roy P. Benavidez," February 24, 1981. The neoconservative William F. Buckley described the Vietnam War as a failure "where the bones lie of men who trusted us"; Buckley, "On Anniversaries," *National Review* 37, no. 10 (May 31, 1985): 54. See also D. Keith Mano, "The Vietnam Veterans' Parade," *National Review* 37, no. 14 (July 26, 1985): 52–53.

25. Jerry Lembcke, *The Spitting Image: Myth, Memory, and the Legacy of Vietnam* (New York: New York University Press, 2000); Appy, *Working-Class War;* Allen, *Until the Last Man Comes Home.* The narrative that the Vietnam War could have been won with the deployment of more counterinsurgency force still appears. See, for instance, Robert Kaplan, *Imperial Grunts: On the Ground with the American Military, from Mongolia to the Philippines to Iraq and Beyond* (New York: Random House, 2005). Recent work has also focused on the noncombat experience in Vietnam, describing the massive rear echelon and its consumer comforts in contrast to the hardship of long, aimless jungle patrols. Meredith H. Lair, *Armed with Abundance: Consumerism and Soldiering in the Vietnam War* (Chapel Hill: University of North Carolina Press, 2014).

26. "'Don't Shoot Them as Individuals, Shoot Them as Communists': The Outlook Interview: Tom Posey, Anti-Sandinista Mercenary, Talks to Brian Barger," *Washington Post,* September 23, 1984, 77; Iver Peterson, "Mercenaries in Fatigues Meet in Nevada Glitter," *New York Times,* September 23, 1984, 26; Bob Dunnavant and Lee Michael Katz, "U.S. Civilians Fighting Mad: Group Seeks Vets to Advise El Salvador," *USA Today,* ca. 1983, SPLC; "U.S. Officials Concerned by Alabama-Based CMA," *Montgomery Advertiser,* reprinted wire service report from the *New York Times,* ca. December 13, 1984, SPLC; New York Times News Service, "Klan Activity Resurging In Southern States," ca. July 5, 1979, Greensboro Public Library; Mike Dunne, "Weapons Added to Klan Symbol List," *Advocate,* 1981, LC; Consent Decree, *Brown v. Invisible Empire Knights of the Ku Klux Klan,* no. 80-NM-1449-S, S.D. Ala., November 21 1989; Iver Peterson, "Mercenaries in Fatigues Meet in Nevada Glitter," *New York Times,* September 23, 1984; Dudley Clendinen, "Anti-Communism Called the Thread Binding Group That Captured Aliens," *New York Times,* July 11, 1986, A8.

27. "KKK Leader Announces Gubernatorial Platform," *Confederate Leader* 84, no. 9 (ca. 1984): 3, RH WL H149.

28. Mike McLaughlin, "Armed Soldiers and Marines Participate in White Supremacist Rallies," United Press International, April 15, 1986, SPLC; "White Patriot Commandos," *Village Voice,* May 6, 1986, 32–33, RH WL Eph 2199.

29. Philip Weiss, "Off the Grid," *New York Times Magazine,* January 8, 1995, 48, LC, Box 18, Folder 3; James Long and Stephen Stuebner, "Weaver Jurors Travel a Hard Road," *Oregonian,* July 10, 1993, A1, A12, LC, Box 18, Folder 13; Leonard Zeskind, *Blood and Politics: The History of the White Nationalist Movement from the Margins to the Mainstream* (New York: Farrar, Straus and Giroux, 2009), 301.

30. Gibson, *Warrior Dreams,* 216; Kevin Flynn and Gary Gerhardt, *The Silent Brotherhood: Inside America's Racist Underground* (New York: Free Press, 1989), 58.

31. James Coates, *Armed and Dangerous: The Rise of the Survivalist Right* (New York: Noonday Press, 1997), 59, 222.

32. Stewart Bell, *Bayou of Pigs: The True Story of an Audacious Plot to Turn a Tropical Island into a Criminal Paradise* (New York: Wiley, 2008), 208–209.

33. Testimony of Randall Rader, November 4, 1985, *Pierce et al.,* Box 6, at 6948–6953.

34. On McVeigh, see Andrew Gumbel and Roger G. Charles, *Oklahoma City: What the Investigation Missed—and Why It Still Matters* (New York: William Morrow, 2012); Catherine McNichol Stock, *Rural Radicals: Righteous Rage in the American Grain* (Ithaca, NY: Cornell University Press, 1996).

35. Similarly, Vietnam veteran and memoirist Tim O'Brien has described departures from the factual that nevertheless convey some greater reality about war as "story-truth." Scholarship about traumatic memory distinguishes between a factual record and the validity of testimony in which narrative truth may or may not correspond with verifiable fact but nevertheless describes the experience of survivors of a traumatic event. O'Brien, *The Things They Carried* (New York: Houghton Mifflin, 1990). See also Shoshana Felman and Dori Laub, *Testimony: Crises of Witnessing in Literature, Psychoanalysis, and History* (New York: Routledge, 1991). On the broader cultural production of the Vietnam War narrative, see Hagopian, *The Vietnam War in American Memory;* Gibson, *Warrior Dreams;* Susan Jeffords, *Hard Bodies: Hollywood Masculinity in the Reagan Era* (New Brunswick, NJ: Rutgers University Press, 1994); Kieran, *Forever Vietnam;* Hass, *Carried to the Wall.*

36. Beam's service record is more verifiable than those of many of his compatriots. Information about his combat experience appeared in undercover interviews, journalistic accounts, and several instances of court testimony given under penalty of perjury. Photographs of Beam in Vietnam were publicly available, and copies of his medals and decorations appeared in photographs and, much later, on his personal website. Records of his marriages and early life, as well as those of his family relationships, are publicly accessible. Beam's unusually robust archival presence offers a verified example of the interplay between combat experience and white power activism. Such a detailed story is difficult to construct for most white power activists,

because military service records from the Vietnam War remain sealed. Such records become accessible through the National Archives on a rolling basis after sixty-two years.

37. Untitled photographs, 1204.01, 1509.39, 1704.13, 3302.15, 3302.22, SPLC; Louis Beam, Estes Park Speech, October 23, 1992, video recording, SPLC. On Beam's childhood in an evangelical congregation, see "King and Queen Crowned at Lake Jackson Church," *Brazosport Facts,* April 22, 1959, 5.

38. Appy, *Working-Class War,* 18–28; "Louis Beam," Report, Anti-Defamation League, https://www.adl.org/sites/default/files/documents/assets/pdf/combating-hate /Louis-Beam.pdf; Louis Beam, "I Cried Tears for Dresden," February 13, 1997, http:// louisbeam.com/dresden.htm; National Archives and Records Administration, U.S. World War II Army Enlistment Records, 1938–1946, Record Group 64, National Archives at College Park, College Park, MD (accessed through Ancestry.com); Texas Department of Health Services, Texas Birth Index, 1903–1997 (accessed through Ancestry.com).

39. Scott Sunde, "Ex-KKK Leader Running Scared from FBI," *Times-Herald,* July 27, 1987, A1, LC, Series XIII, Box 5, Folder 12; Anti-Defamation League, "Louis Beam"; Louis Beam, "All I Got to Say Is Vote for Wallace," photograph, 25th Aviation Battalion, Little Bear Gunners 4, http://www.25thaviation.org/littlebears/id150.htm#1.

40. Phillips, *War! What Is It Good For?,* 223–224.

41. On the draft as a mechanism to target political opposition and on inequality in the ranks, see ibid., 194–224.

42. Ibid., 222.

43. Eric M. Bergerud, *Red Thunder, Tropic Lightning: The World of a Combat Division in Vietnam* (New York: Penguin Books, 1994) 10, 14, 21, 136, 287–290; Phillips, *War! What Is It Good For?,* 203, 219, 222–224.

44. Phillips, *War! What Is It Good For,* 226, 240.

45. Roger Rapoport, "The Marine Corps Builds Klansmen," *New Times,* May 27, 1977, 22, LC, Box 22, Folder 20.

46. Patsy Sims, *The Klan* (Lexington: University Press of Kentucky, 1996), 190.

47. Rapoport, "The Marine Corps Builds Klansmen."

48. Similarly, as Brooks argues in *Defining the Peace,* World War II strengthened a notion of "racialized male citizenship" in the South (60).

49. Cowie, *Stayin' Alive;* Matthew D. Lassiter, *The Silent Majority: Suburban Politics in the Sunbelt South* (Princeton, NJ: Princeton University Press, 2006).

50. Beam, *Essays of a Klansman* (1983), 33.

51. "News from the Services," *Brazosport Facts,* July 29, 1965.

52. Shay, *Achilles in Vietnam,* 55–62; Appy, *Working-Class War,* 140, 242, 308; Herman, *Trauma and Recovery.*

53. Spelled "Sindrome" in original. Louis Beam, "Forget? Hell No!," *Seditionist,* no. 3 (Summer 1989): 13–14, LC, Series II, Box 3, Folder 8.

54. American Psychiatric Association, *Diagnostic and Statistical Manual of Mental Disorders,* 3rd ed. (Arlington, VA: American Psychiatric Association, 1980); Herman, *Trauma and Recovery;* Hagopian, *The Vietnam War in American Memory;* Kalí Tal, *Worlds of Hurt: Reading the Literatures of Trauma* (Cambridge: Cambridge University Press, 1996); Robert Jay Lifton, *Home from the War* (New York: Simon and Schuster, 1973).

55. Beam, "Forget? Hell No!"

56. Appy, *Working-Class War,* 164–176; Shay, *Achilles in Vietnam,* 24; Beam, "War Stories 12."

57. See, for instance, Appy, *Working-Class War;* Philip Caputo, *A Rumor of War* (New York: Henry Holt, 1977); Turse, *Kill Anything That Moves;* Shay, *Achilles in Vietnam,* 103–106; Lifton, *Home from the War.* On similar dehumanization in World War II, see John W. Dower, *War without Mercy: Race and Power in the Pacific War* (New York: Pantheon Books, 1986), 106–107.

58. "Colonel's Chopper Hits Fleeing VC; Kills Five," *Tropic Lightning News,* June 3, 1968, 7.

59. Bergerud, *Red Thunder, Tropic Lightning,* 223–229; Shay, *Odysseus in America,* 70–72.

60. Gibson, *Warrior Dreams,* 10; Daniel C. Hallin, *The Uncensored War: The Media and Vietnam* (New York: Oxford University Press, 1986).

61. Laytner, "'I Infiltrated the Ku Klux Klan."

62. Beam, "Introduction to the Second Edition," *Essays of a Klansman* (1989).

63. Beam, "A Card and Cookies."

64. Louis Beam, "POW's and Agent Orange—The Government's Final Solution," 1996, http://www.louisbeam.com/pows.htm.

65. Beam, *Essays of a Klansman* (1983), 39; Lembcke, *The Spitting Image.*

66. Nathan Bedford Forrest (pseud. of Louis Beam), "Someday Soon," *Calling Our Nation* (Aryan Nations) 28 (1982): 28–29, HH.

67. Beam, *Essays of a Klansman* (1989), 10.

68. Ibid., 45.

69. Beam, *Essays of a Klansman* (1983), 29.

70. Beam, "Forget? Hell No!"

71. Beam, "POW's and Agent Orange."

72. "Forever" is spelled "for ever" in the original. Beam, "Forget? Hell No!"

2. Building the Underground

1. Texas Veterans Land Board, http://www.glo.texas.gov/vlb/index.html.

2. FBI clip, FBI report to Assistant U.S. Attorney Hays Jenkins copied to Houston, May 7, 1981, "Klan Gunfire Worries Neighbors," *Houston Chronicle,*

April 28, 1981, 1, 195; Texas Veterans Land Program, Contract of Sale and Purchase, 8-83244, Louis Ray Beam Jr., Travis County, September 15, 1977, vol. 405, 710, SPLC; *Vietnamese Fishermen's Association,* Deposition of Dorothy Scaife, July 6, 1981, Houston, Texas, SPLC.

3. On Beam's invocations of the Vietnam War at key moments of movement formation, see, for instance, Louis R. Beam Jr., "Vietnam Bring It on Home," *Essays of a Klansman* (Hayden Lake, ID: A.K.I.A. Publications, 1983); Louis Beam, "A Card and Cookies," *Seditionist,* no. 2 (Spring 1989): 18, LC, Series II, Box 3, Folder 8; Louis Beam, "POW's and Agent Orange—The Government's Final Solution," 1996, http://www.louisbeam.com/pows.htm.

4. On the power of violence to create and structure social orders and political formation, see, for instance, Ned Blackhawk, *Violence over the Land: Indians and Empires in the Early American West* (Cambridge, MA: Harvard University Press, 2006), 9; Jean Franco, "Gender, Death, and Resistance: Facing the Ethical Vacuum," *Critical Passions: Selected Essays* (Durham, NC: Duke University Press, 1999), 18–38; Michael Taussig, "Culture of Terror—Space of Death: Roger Casement's Putumayo Report and the Explanation of Torture," *Comparative Studies in Society and History* 26, no. 3 (July 1984): 467–497.

5. Bill Minutaglio, "Biography of a Hatemonger," *Dallas Morning News,* May 22, 1988, LC, Box 9, Folder 20; "Decorated," *Tropic Lightning News,* March 18, 1968, 2.

6. This paragraph draws from Beam's published writings and from an interview given to an undercover reporter. Louis R. Beam Jr., *Essays of a Klansman,* 2nd ed. (Hayden Lake, ID: A.K.I.A. Publications, 1989), 6; Ron Laytner, " 'I Infiltrated the Ku Klux Klan . . . and Lived!,' " *Argosy* 387, no. 6 (August 1978); *Vietnamese Fishermen's Association,* at 4, 64, 260, July 15, 1981, SPLC.

7. The details of these cases are not available in existing archival material.

8. The identity of the woman Beam kidnapped does not appear in the archival record. He clarified that in that incident, the charges of false imprisonment were dropped, but he was charged with possession of the weapon used. *Vietnamese Fishermen's Association,* Continuation of the Deposition of Louis Beam, vol. 11, May 3, 1981, Houston, Texas, SPLC; Norman Kempster, "Teng Takes 'California Flight' in Houston Space Shuttle Trainer," *Los Angeles Times,* February 3, 1979, A8.

9. Laytner, " 'I Infiltrated the Ku Klux Klan . . . and Lived!' " On the idea of perpetual combat in the twentieth century, see Mary L. Dudziak, *War Time: An Idea, Its History, and Its Consequences* (Oxford: Oxford University Press, 2013).

10. *Vietnamese Fishermen's Association* at 64, 260, July 15, 1981, 4, SPLC; James Ridgeway, *Blood in the Face,* 2nd ed. (New York: Thunder's Mouth Press, 1995), 166.

11. Ridgeway, *Blood in the Face,* 166; Matthew D. Lassiter, *The Silent Majority: Suburban Politics in the Sunbelt South* (Princeton, NJ: Princeton University Press, 2006); Michelle Alexander, *The New Jim Crow: Mass Incarceration in the Age of Colorblindness* (New York: New Press, 2010).

12. *Vietnamese Fishermen's Association,* June 3, 1982, at 3, SPLC; Minutaglio, "Biography of a Hatemonger"; Christian G. Appy, *Working-Class War: American Combat Soldiers and Vietnam* (Chapel Hill: University of North Carolina Press, 1993), 164.

13. On the role of violence in Vietnam War boot camps, see, for instance, Appy, *Working-Class War;* Joanna Bourke, *An Intimate History of Killing: Face-to-Face Killing in Twentieth Century Warfare* (New York: Basic Books, 1999).

14. Shared violence in the Vietnam War appears throughout the literature. See Nick Turse, *Kill Anything That Moves: The Real American War in Vietnam* (New York: Picador, 2013); Bourke, *An Intimate History of Killing.*

15. Beam, "Klankraft," *Essays of a Klansman* (1983).

16. Wyn Craig Wade, *The Fiery Cross: The Ku Klux Klan in America* (New York: Simon and Schuster, 1987), 33.

17. Wade, *The Fiery Cross,* 67, 76.

18. On a Civil War narrative that joined North and South, see David Blight, *Race and Reunion: The Civil War in American Memory* (Cambridge, MA: Belknap Press of Harvard University Press, 2002); Wade, *The Fiery Cross.*

19. Wade, *The Fiery Cross,* 183, 215–247; Peter N. Stearns, "Historical Interpretations of the 1920's Klan: The Traditional View and the Populist View," *Journal of Social History* 24, no. 2 (Winter 1990): 341–357; Kathleen M. Blee, *Women of the Klan: Racism and Gender in the 1920s* (Berkeley: University of California Press, 1991); Nancy MacLean, *Behind the Mask of Chivalry: The Making of the Second Ku Klux Klan* (New York: Oxford University Press, 1994); Mae Ngai, *Impossible Subjects: Illegal Aliens and the Making of Modern America* (Princeton, NJ: Princeton University Press, 2004), ch. 2; George Sánchez, *Becoming Mexican-American: Ethnicity, Culture, and Identity in Chicano Los Angeles, 1900–1945* (New York: Oxford University Press, 1993), 59. Local Klan dens attempted resurgence during the Great Depression and through the German-American Bund just before World War II, but failed to garner widespread support. During World War II, with the public and policy makers focused on antifascism and an emerging doctrine of human rights, the Klan largely went quiet.

20. On the Columbians in the postwar 1940s, see Jennifer E. Brooks, *Defining the Peace: World War II Veterans, Race, and the Remaking of Southern Political Tradition* (Chapel Hill: University of North Carolina Press, 2004), 63–69. Wade also notes that Asa Carter's Klan in the late 1940s and early 1950s adopted paramilitary uniforms; *The Fiery Cross,* 303. On the American Nazi Party, led by Pacific Theater veteran George Lincoln Rockwell, see Elinor Langer, *A Hundred Little Hitlers: The Death of a Black Man, the Trial of a White Racist, and the Rise of the Neo-Nazi Movement in America* (New York: Metropolitan Books, 2003), 124.

21. Brooks, *Defining the Peace,* 52–67; Wade, *The Fiery Cross,* 303, 321–25; Stetson Kennedy, *The Klan Unmasked* (London: Arco, 1954).

22. Wade, *The Fiery Cross,* 313–321.

23. David Cunningham, *There's Something Happening Here: The New Left, the Klan, and FBI Counter-intelligence* (Berkeley: University of California Press, 2004).

24. Max Baker, "Texas' New Right," *Fort Worth Star-Telegram*, March 18, 1990, page unclear, SPLC.

25. *Vietnamese Fishermen's Association*, Deposition of Jerry Hartless, July 7, 1981, Houston, Texas, 28, SPLC; Langer, *A Hundred Little Hitlers*, 129, 137; Bob Stertz, "KKK Chief Says Klan Patrolling Border," *Daily Dispatch* (Bisbee, AZ), November 3, 1977, 1, Papers of Tom Miller, University of Arizona Library Special Collections; "The Great White Hope," *Newsweek*, November 14, 1977.

26. John Bloom, "Secrecy Prevails in Klan Watch," *Dallas Times Herald*, reprinted in *Crusader*, no. 28 (1977): 10, Ms. 76.21, Box 21-1, HH 977.

27. Ibid.

28. Louie Gonzalez, "Perilous U.S. Border Crossing," *Chicago Tribune*, January 15, 1978, 1.

29. UPI, "Ku Klux Klan Contra Inmigrantes Ilegales," *Novedades* (Managua), October 26, 1977, 37; Bloom, "Secrecy Prevails in Klan Watch," *Dallas Times Herald*. On violence against women at the border, see Alicia Schmidt Camacho, *Migrant Imaginaries: Latino Cultural Politics in the U.S.-Mexico Borderlands* (New York: New York University Press, 2008).

30. Tom Metzger, transcript of taped message, *Aryan Update*, September 10, 1990, 12:30 P.M., LC, Series V, Box 1, Folder 14; Leonard Zeskind, *Blood and Politics: The History of the White Nationalist Movement from the Margins to the Mainstream* (New York: Farrar, Straus and Giroux, 2009), 36, 45; Langer, *A Hundred Little Hitlers*, 140; Daniel Gearino, "Texas Klan Unit Infiltrated: Secret KKK Training Camp Disclosed," *Los Angeles Times*, September 10, 1980, C10.

31. "Klan Gunfire Worries Neighbors"; "Paramilitary Training by Klan Is Banned," *Houston Chronicle*, June 4, 1982, 1, RH WL Eph 2211; *Vietnamese Fishermen's Association*, Deposition of Robert Sisente, July 6, 1981, Houston, Texas, SPLC.

32. "Paramilitary Training by Klan Is Banned"; *Vietnamese Fishermen's Association*, Deposition of Robert Sisente, July 6, 1981, Houston, Texas, Deposition of David Lee Scaife, July 6, 1981, Houston, Texas, and Deposition of Dorothy Scaife, July 6, 1981, Houston, Texas, SPLC; "Paramilitary Camp Is Closed by Owner: Lethal Training for Klan Members Stirs a Strong Public Protest," *New York Times*, December 6, 1980, 8; "Chronicle Named in Libel Lawsuit over Klan Article," *Houston Chronicle*, April 29, 198[] (obscured), SPLC, Fishermen File; "Klansman Backs Survival Camps That Teach Warfare to Children," *New York Times*, December 1, 1980, B12.

33. "Klan Adviser Reportedly Taught Teens How to Kill," *Chicago Tribune*, November 24, 1980, 2; "Tempo: Ku Klux Klan on the Rise Again, This Time in High School," *Chicago Tribune*, June 9, 1981, A1; "Woman Asserts Scouts Planned to Hunt Aliens," *New York Times*, November 26, 1980, B4; "Boys Reported Learning to Shoot and Kill at a Klan Camp in Texas," *New York Times*, November 24, 1980, A21.

34. "Klansman Backs Survival Camps That Teach Warfare to Children"; "Paramilitary Camp Is Closed by Owner."

35. On the role of training facilities in creating loyalty among military personnel, see, for instance, Appy, *Working-Class War,* ch. 3.

36. Daniel Gearino, "Texas Klan Unit Infiltrated: Secret KKK Training Camp Disclosed," *Los Angeles Times,* September 10, 1980, C10.

37. Ibid.

38. Ibid. An understanding of the weapons used by these activists as chosen because they were the nearest available to those used in the Vietnam War appears at length in the testimony of Randall Rader, November 4, 1985, *Pierce et al.,* Box 6, at 6948–6953.

39. Ross Milloy, "Vietnam Fallout in a Texas Town," *New York Times Sunday Magazine,* April 6, 1980, SM10.

40. Meg Jacobs, *Panic at the Pump: The Energy Crisis and the Transformation of American Politics in the 1970s* (New York: Hill and Wang, 2016); Sean Wilentz, *The Age of Reagan* (New York: HarperCollins, 2008), 6–147; Bethany Moreton, *To Serve God and Wal-Mart: The Making of Christian Free Enterprise* (Cambridge, MA: Harvard University Press, 2010). On U.S. military interventions as generating waves of immigration to the United States, see Jesse Hoffnung-Garskof, *A Tale of Two Cities: Santo Domingo and New York after 1950* (Princeton, NJ: Princeton University Press, 2008), xiv.

41. On the economic and political landscape of the Sunbelt, see, for instance, Michelle Nickerson and Darren Dochuk, *Sunbelt Rising: The Politics of Space, Place, and Region* (Philadelphia: University of Pennsylvania Press, 2011).

42. Guy Halverson, "U.S. Hunts Jobs for Refugees," *Christian Science Monitor,* April 24, 1975.

43. Paul Taylor, "Vietnamese Shrimpers Alter Texas Gulf Towns: Natives' Economy and Pride Wounded," *Washington Post,* December 26, 1984, A1; Milloy, "Vietnam Fallout in a Texas Town," SM10.

44. "Arrest of 22 Klan Members at Jersey Home Foils Group's Plans for a Rally," *New York Times,* November 25, 1979, 44; FBI clip, FBI to Assistant U.S. Attorney Jenkins, May 7, 1981, "Fledgling Group Aims to Stoke Fires of 'American Spirit,'" *Houston Post,* November 12, 1979, 172, and "Viet 'Communists' Blamed," *Houston Post,* April 22, 1981; "Refugees Cause Murder-Disease-Welfare," *Thunderbolt,* issue 246, October 1979, 1, RH WL G1380.

45. Taylor, "Vietnamese Shrimpers Alter Texas Gulf Towns"; *Vietnamese Fishermen's Association,* Continuation of the Deposition of Eugene Fisher, May 2, 1981, Houston, Texas, SPLC; FBI clip, FBI to Assistant U.S. Attorney Jenkins, May 7, 1981, "Troubled Waters: Vietnamese, Texans Vying Sharply for Shrimp Business," *Houston Post,* November 11, 1979, 163 and "Government 'Doing a Lot to Hurt Me Now,'" *Houston Post,* November 11, 1979, 166; Ralph Bivens, "Vietnamese Would Leave if

Able," *Daily Cit* . . . (title obscured, published in Clear Lake City, Seabrook, and other towns), vol. 41, no. 52 (March 1, 1981): 1, SPLC, Fishermen File; "Danger of Vietnamese: Wrecking White Shrimpers," *Thunderbolt,* issue 269, September 1981, RH WL G1380.

46. On the emerging, sentimentalized Vietnam War narrative, see Patrick Hagopian, *The Vietnam War in American Memory: Veterans, Memorials, and the Politics of Healing* (Amherst: University of Massachusetts Press, 2011).

47. FBI clip, FBI to Assistant U.S. Attorney Jenkins, May 7, 1981, "Government 'Doing a Lot to Hurt Me Now,'" *Houston Post,* November 11, 1979, 166.

48. Ibid.

49. María Cristina García, *Seeking Refuge: Central American Migration to Mexico, the United States, and Canada* (Berkeley: University of California Press, 2006); Hoffnung-Garskof, *A Tale of Two Cities;* Appy, *Working-Class War.*

50. William K. Stevens, "Klan Official Is Accused of Intimidation," *New York Times,* May 2, 1981, 9; J. Michael Kennedy, "Renewal of Violence Feared: Texas-Asian Fishing War Heating Up on Gulf Coast," *Los Angeles Times,* March 12, 1981, B1; *Vietnamese Fishermen's Association,* Deposition of Nguyen Luu, May 5, 1981, Houston, Texas, SPLC. See also *Vietnamese Fishermen's Association,* Deposition of Thi D. Hoang, May 5, 1981, Houston, Texas, interpreted by Ynhi D. Nguyen, SPLC.

51. Milloy, "Vietnam Fallout in a Texas Town," SM10.

52. Airtel memo, SAC New Orleans to FBI director, January 18, 1991.

53. Milloy, "Vietnam Fallout in a Texas Town," SM10.

54. FBI to Assistant U.S. Attorney Jenkins, May 7, 1981, interview April 23, 1981, 72–74.

55. "Vietnamese Refugees Are Malaria Threat," *NAAWP News,* no. 4 (1980), SC, Box 41, Folder 8; "Viet Leader Charged with Rape," *NAAWP News,* no. 4 (1980): 10, SC, Box 41, Folder 8; United Press International, "Four Vietnamese Refugees Guilty of Rape and Kidnap," February 4, 1981; Patt Morrison, "3 Viet Refugees Arraigned in Connection with 6 Rapes," *Los Angeles Times,* August 21, 1980. On immigrants as suspected of spreading disease, see Alexandra Minna Stern, *Eugenic Nation: Faults and Frontiers of Better Breeding in Modern America* (Berkeley: University of California Press, 2005). On the threat of the rape of white women by men of color as invoked to call for, and to purportedly justify, vigilante violence in the twentieth century, see, for instance, the collected works of Ida B. Wells; Joel Williamson, *The Crucible of Race: Black-White Relations in the American South since Emancipation* (Oxford: Oxford University Press, 1984); Glenda E. Gilmore, "Murder, Memory, and the Flight of the Incubus," in *Democracy Betrayed: The Wilmington Race Riot of 1898 and Its Legacy,* ed. David S. Cecelski and Timothy B. Tyson (Chapel Hill: University of North Carolina Press, 1998); Wade, *The Fiery Cross.* On the centrality of prohibiting interracial sex to the broader project of white supremacy, see, for instance, George M. Frederickson, *Racism: A Short History* (Princeton, NJ: Princeton University Press,

2002); Peggy Pascoe, *What Comes Naturally: Miscegenation Law and the Making of Race in America* (Oxford: Oxford University Press, 2009).

56. "Klan Gunfire Worries Neighbors"; "Paramilitary Training by Klan Is Banned"; *Vietnamese Fishermen's Association,* Deposition of Robert Sisente, July 6, 1981, Houston, Texas, SPLC.

57. United Press International, "Klansmen vs. Vietnamese Refugees," *Athens* (AL) *News-Courier,* June 14, 1981, SPLC, Fishermen File.

58. "Danger of Vietnamese: Wrecking White Shrimpers"; "Viet. Refugees Destroying S.F. Park," *NAAWP News,* no. 4 (1980): 11, SC, Box 41, Folder 8; "Viet Dog Lovers," *National Vanguard,* no. 71 (August 1979): 2, RH WL G541.

59. Ange-Marie Hancock, *The Politics of Disgust: The Public Identity of the Welfare Queen* (New York: New York University Press, 2004); Michelle M. Nickerson, *Mothers of Conservatism: Women and the Postwar Right* (Princeton, NJ: Princeton University Press, 2012); Rickie Solinger, *Pregnancy and Power: A Short History of Reproductive Politics in America* (New York: New York University Press, 2007).

60. "Danger of Vietnamese: Wrecking White Shrimpers."

61. FBI clip, FBI to Assistant U.S. Attorney Jenkins, May 7, 1981, "Refugees Work Hard; Few Given Welfare Assistance," *Houston Post,* November 11, 1979, 167.

62. "Americans" spelled "American's" in original. FBI to Assistant U.S. Attorney Jenkins, May 7, 1981, 69, and FBI clip, "Refugees Work Hard; Few Given Welfare Assistance," *Houston Post,* November 11, 1979, 167; "Danger of Vietnamese: Wrecking White Shrimpers"; Milloy, "Vietnam Fallout in a Texas Town," SM10.

63. *Vietnamese Fishermen's Association,* Deposition of Nguyen Luu, May 5, 1981, Houston, Texas, SPLC; Milloy, "Vietnam Fallout in a Texas Town," SM10; *Vietnamese Fishermen's Association,* at 4–5, SPLC.

64. FBI clip, FBI to Assistant U.S. Attorney Jenkins, May 7, 1981, "Shrimp Boat Fire in Seabrook Ruled Arson by Investigators," *Houston Post,* March 31, 1981, 184; Houston Arson Task Force, ATF, to Houston Arson Intelligence Division, FBI, January 20, 1981; "Burned Viet Boats Checked for Arson," publication unclear, March 20, 1981, SPLC.

65. Houston Arson Task Force, ATF, to Houston Arson Intelligence Division, FBI, January 20, 1981; Houston Arson Task Force report, case 2208 0181 3503 A: Vietnamese Fishing Boats, January 10 and 11, 1981; Kemah Police Department General Offense Report 81-6 Supplement, Arson, January 12, 1981.

66. Houston Arson Task Force, ATF, to Houston Arson Intelligence Division, FBI, January 20, 1981.

67. J. Michael Kennedy, "Texans Ready for Shootout over Shrimp," *Los Angeles Times,* March 18, 1981, page unlisted, SPLC.

68. Airtel memo, SAC Houston to FBI director, June 12, 1981; "Victory for Americans Is Not Defeat for Vietnamese," *White Patriot* (Metairie, LA), ca. May 1981, 5, RH WL G605.

69. Houston FBI SAC to Regional Laboratory, Treasure Island, California, April 1, 1981.

70. Report of Investigation, BATF to Houston District Office, FBI, April 21, 1981; FBI clip, Steve Olafson and Glenn Lewis, "Heavy Rain Curtails Rally of Klan," *Houston Post,* ca. May 1981, 35.

71. Photograph 124.98, SPLC; *Vietnamese Fishermen's Association,* Continuation of the Deposition of Louis Beam, vol. 11, May 3, 1981, Houston, Texas, SPLC.

72. Photograph 1509.61, SPLC; Airtel memo, SAC Houston to FBI director, June 12, 1981; FBI report to Assistant U.S. Attorney Hays Jenkins, copied to Houston, May 7, 1981, 8.

73. Milloy, "Vietnam Fallout in a Texas Town," SM10; FBI clip, Gordon Hunter, "Judge Orders Increased Security at Viet-Klan Proceedings," *Houston Chronicle,* ca. 1981; Kennedy, "Renewal of Violence Feared."

74. Kennedy, "Renewal of Violence Feared"; Jo Ann Oliphant-Curran, "Boat Ride with Klan," reprint from *Santa Fe Express News,* in *White Patriot* (Metairie, LA), ca. May 1981, 5, RH WL G605; *Vietnamese Fishermen's Association,* at 64, 260, July 15, 1981, 1, SPLC.

75. *Vietnamese Fishermen's Association,* Deposition of John Douglas Place, July 7, 1981, Houston, Texas, and Continuation of the Deposition of Eugene Fisher, May 2, 1981, Houston, Texas, SPLC; [Redacted] to Charles P. Monroe, Assistant Director of Criminal Investigations, FBI, May 5, 1981; FBI report to Assistant U.S. Attorney Hays Jenkins, copied to Houston, May 7, 1981; Kennedy, "Renewal of Violence Feared"; Oliphant-Curran, "Boat Ride with Klan"; FBI clip, FBI to Jenkins, May 7, 1981, "Viet 'Communists' Blamed': Details Lacking in Charge on Fishing Dispute," *Houston Post,* Steve Olafson, April 22, 1981, 190.

76. *Vietnamese Fishermen's Association,* Deposition of James Stanfield, May 2, 1981; Deposition of Tran Van Phu, May 5, 1981, interpreted by Ynhi D. Nguyen; Deposition of Thi D. Hoang, May 5, 1981, interpreted by Ynhi D. Nguyen; Deposition of Phuong Pham, May 8, 1981, Houston, Texas, SPLC.

77. FBI clip, FBI report to Assistant U.S. Attorney Hays Jenkins, May 7, 1981, "Shrimp Boat Fire in Seabrook Ruled Arson by Investigators," *Houston Post,* March 31, 1981, 2–6, 184. The name of the businessman has been redacted in the FBI documents.

78. "Viet Fishermen Sue Klan," *Washington Post,* April 17, 1981, A11.

79. Counsel representing Vietnamese Fishermen's Association to FBI Director William Webster, April 21, 1981.

80. "Klan Gunfire Worries Neighbors."

81. Ibid.

82. "Victory for Americans Is Not Defeat for Vietnamese."

83. "Fish, Not Klan, Hook Crowd," *Chicago Tribune,* February 15, 1981, B10; FBI clip, Gordon Hunter, "Shrimping Curfew Considered," *Houston Chronicle,* ca. 1981, 38.

84. FBI clip, FBI report to Assistant U.S. Attorney Hays Jenkins, May 7, 1981, 188, Steve Olafson, "Viet 'Communists' Blamed': Details Lacking in Charge on Fishing Dispute," *Houston Post*, April 22, 1981, 190, and "Viet Shrimpers Appeal to FBI: Threats by Klan Cited in Letter to Webster," *Houston Post*, April 23, 1981, 22A, 191.

85. FBI clip, Pete Wittenberg, "Witness Says Defendant Told Him Viet Boats 'Easy to Burn,'" *Houston Post*, ca. 1981, 37.

86. City of Seabrook Complaint Number 011458, April 17, 1981; FBI report to Assistant U.S. Attorney Hays Jenkins, May 7, 1981, 67, and FBI clip, Ralph Bivens, "Stand Against Klan Defended," *Citizen*, April 23, 1981, 1, 197.

87. Anonymous complaint to City of Seabrook, April 7, 1981, number 811458, FBI file.

88. FBI report to Assistant U.S. Attorney Hays Jenkins, May 7, 1981, 66–67.

89. "Victory for Americans Is Not Defeat for Vietnamese."

90. Ibid.; FBI clip, Gordon Hunter, "Boat Pullout Is Key, Court Told: Seabrook Police Chief Testifies," *Houston Chronicle*, ca. 1981, 40; FBI Investigative Report, Houston, May 7, 1981, C.

91. FBI report to Assistant U.S. Attorney Hays Jenkins, May 7, 1981, TÒ KAI BÁN TÀU [Declaration to Sell Boat] form, 105; Taylor, "Vietnamese Shrimpers Alter Texas Gulf Towns: Natives' Economy and Pride Wounded," *Washington Post*, December 26, 1984, A1; FBI clip, "Troubled Waters: Vietnamese, Texans Vying Sharply for Shrimp Business," *Houston Post*, November 11, 1979, 163–165.

92. William K. Stevens, "Klan Official Is Accused of Intimidation," *New York Times*, May 2, 1981, 9; FBI clip, Gordon Hunter, "Judge Orders Increased Security at Viet-Klan Proceedings," *Houston Chronicle*, ca. 1981.

93. The expert witness quoted was Tom Wilkinson, a Montgomery, Alabama, security consultant. FBI clip, Pete Wittenberg, "Klan Leader Shown Leading Training Camp in Courtroom Tapes," *Houston Post*, date unlisted, 39.

94. "Around the Nation," *New York Times*, May 13, 1981, A18; FBI clip, Wittenberg, "Klan Leader Shown Leading Training Camp."

95. FBI clip, Olafson and Lewis, "Heavy Rain Curtails Rally of Klan"; FBI clip, Gordon Hunter, "Klan Chief 'Deranged,' Lawyer for Viets Claims," *Houston Chronicle*, ca. 1981, 29; FBI clip, "Klan Leader Wants Arbitration Panel," ca. 1981, publication unclear.

96. Airtel memo, SAC Houston to FBI director, June 12, 1981; *Vietnamese Fishermen's Association*.

97. "Human" spelled "hubnam" in original. Enclosure: "Running nigger target," silhouette of running black caricature, text: "Body shots count 5, head shots count 0, heel shots count 100" in all caps. [Redacted] of the Social Nationalist Aryan Party to [Redacted, presumably Judge Gabrielle McDonald], ca. June 9, 1981, FBI file.

98. FBI clip, "KKK Leader Beam Says He'll Accept New Post," *Houston Post*, July 30, 1981, B8, 13; "Klansman Backs Survival Camps"; "Tempo: Ku Klux Klan on the Rise Again."

99. Injunction filed June 8, 1981, *Vietnamese Fishermen's Association*, Attorney General of Texas Mark White, FBI file.

100. The Christian Patriot Defense League was sometimes called the Christian Patriots Defense League. Mike Dunne, "Weapons Added to Klan Symbol List," *Advocate*, 1981, LC; Terry Abbot, "Klan Leader to Visit Here Frequently" (reprint), *White Patriot* (Metairie, LA), issue 61, 2, RH WL G605; Robert M. Press, "They Play War Games in US Countryside," *Christian Science Monitor*, March 23, 1981, 1, RH WL Eph 1014.

101. Press, "They Play War Games in US Countryside."

102. *Vietnamese Fishermen's Association*, "Agreement of Parties to a Proposed Order," filed August 7, 1981, signed by Gabrielle McDonald August 13, 1981; FBI clip, "Arson Eyed in Seabrook, Kemah Fires," *Houston Post*, December 11, 1981, 4A, 5; FBI clip, Mark Toohey, "Fires on 2 Seabrook Shrimp Boats Deliberate, Officials Say," *Houston Chronicle*, December 11, 1981; FBI clip, FBI report to Assistant U.S. Attorney Hays Jenkins, May 7, 1981, Clara Tuma, "Shrimping Bill Would Set Daily Time Limit in Bay," *Houston Post*, April 23, 1981, 26A; FBI clip, Joe Tedino, "Senate Shrimping Bills Give Something to All," *Houston Chronicle*, ca. 1981.

103. "Paramilitary Training by Klan Is Banned"; "Judge Bars Ku Klux Klan from Having Own Army in Texas," *Chicago Tribune*, June 4, 1982, A8; *Vietnamese Fishermen's Association*, June 3, 1982, at 3, SPLC.

104. Beam resigned on July 30, 1981; Max Baker, "Texas' New Right," *Fort Worth Star-Telegram*, March 18, 1990, SPLC; FBI clip, "KKK Leader Beam Says He'll Accept New Post."

105. FBI Director to Houston office, April 20, 1981. The FBI interest in the incident seems to have followed the first round of press coverage, with reports dating to November 1979. While these documents may represent a partial record of the investigation, that date might also indicate an increased federal interest in monitoring white power groups after the Greensboro shooting on November 4 of that year. The Houston office of the FBI categorized the dispute as a domestic security investigation, while some actors at FBI headquarters in Washington, DC, thought it should be prosecuted as a civil rights case. This seems to have been precluded by local inaction. As a memo from headquarters stated, "Houston's failure to investigate this civil rights matter has no foundation in fact. Houston's reluctance to properly investigate this matter is cause for extreme concern regarding the Bureau's role in safeguarding the civil rights of citizens and inhabitants of the United States. This reluctance and subsequent void of information has placed the FBI and the Department of Justice in an indefensible position due to the dearth of information which has been provided to FBI [Headquarters]." Houston to FBI national office, case report, March 30, 1982.

106. Milloy, "Vietnam Fallout in a Texas Town," SM10.

3. A Unified Movement

1. Accounts of the shooting appear in Greensboro Truth and Reconciliation Commission (henceforth GTRC), *Greensboro Truth and Reconciliation Commission Final Report* (Greensboro, NC: Greensboro Truth and Reconciliation Commission, 2006); Max Elbaum, *Revolution in the Air: Sixties Radicals Turn to Lenin, Mao, and Che* (New York: Verso, 2002); David Cunningham, *There's Something Happening Here: The New Left, the Klan, and FBI Counter-intelligence* (Berkeley: University of California Press, 2004); Signe Waller, *Love and Revolution* (Lanham, MD: Rowman and Littlefield, 2002); Sally Avery Bermanzohn, *Through Survivor's Eyes: From the Sixties to the Greensboro Massacre* (Nashville, TN: Vanderbilt University Press, 2003); Elizabeth Wheaton, *Codename: GREENKILL: The 1979 Greensboro Massacre* (Athens: University of Georgia Press, 1987); Mab Segrest, *Memoir of a Race Traitor* (Boston: South End Press, 1999).

2. GTRC, *Final Report*, 103; Associated Press, "Ku Klux Klan Views 'Birth' at Peaceful Film Screening," reprinted in Greensboro, ca. April 23, 1979, GPL; Associated Press, "Knights of KKK Plan Charlotte Recruiting Drive," ca. March 11, 1979, GPL.

3. "It's Time for a New Crusade! KKK," *White Patriot* (Tuscumbia, AL), August 1984, back page, RH WL G571.

4. Associated Press, "Shouting Match Closes Ku Klux Klan Exhibit Early," ca. February 27, 1979, GPL; New York Times News Service, "Klan Activity Resurging in Southern States," ca. July 5, 1979, GPL.

5. In the Decatur case, the Department of Justice initially did not pursue civil rights charges. After SPLC intervention and evidence-sharing that reopened the case, in 1989 four Klansmen were found guilty of conspiracy to deprive marchers of their civil rights. The SPLC also won consent decrees against ten Invisible Empire Klansmen in a civil suit. Jerry Schwartz, "Guilty Pleas Close Case Against 10 Klan Members," *New York Times,* January 10, 1989; *Brown v. Invisible Empire Knights of the Ku Klux Klan*, Case Number CV-80–1449, SPLC.

6. New York Times News Service, "Klan Activity Resurging in Southern States"; New York Times News Service, "Klan Splinters Can Still Make a Bonfire," ca. March 21, 1979, GPL; Leonard Zeskind, *Blood and Politics: The History of the White Nationalist Movement from the Margins to the Mainstream* (New York: Farrar, Straus and Giroux, 2009), 44.

7. Associated Press, "Klan Hodgepodge of Factions Linked by Hate of Communism," November 8, 1979, GPL.

8. GTRC, *Final Report.*

9. D. W. Griffith, *Birth of a Nation* (David W. Griffith Corp., 1915).

10. GTRC, *Final Report*, 193, from testimony of Klansmen Chris Benson; Ed Boyd, WTVD-TV, Jim Waters, WFMY-TV, et al., Unedited news footage of the

events of November 3, 1979, DVD (Greensboro: Greensboro Truth and Reconciliation Commission, 2006).

11. "Dare to Struggle, Dare to Win," *Workers Viewpoint*, November 19, 1979, 15, Ms. 76.14, Box 14-3X, HH 336; Timothy B. Tyson, *Radio Free Dixie: Robert F. Williams and the Roots of Black Power* (Chapel Hill: University of North Carolina Press, 1999); Sean Wilentz, *The Age of Reagan: A History, 1974–2008* (New York: HarperCollins, 2008); Emily K. Hobson, *Lavender and Red: Liberation and Solidarity in the Gay and Lesbian Left* (Berkeley: University of California Press, 2016); GTRC, *Final Report;* Bermanzohn, *Through Survivor's Eyes;* Waller, *Love and Revolution.*

12. Monte Plott, "Klan Activity in State on Rise but Members Split into Factions," Associated Press, ca. March 23, 1979, GPL; Zeskind, *Blood and Politics,* 42.

13. The Committee Against Racism is also referred to as the Committee to Fight Racism in some sources. *Challenge* was the newspaper of the PLP / CAR. "Communists Thwarted in Arkansas," *Crusader: The Voice of the White Majority,* no. 42 (1979): 1, SC, Box 39, Folder 8; "15 Hurt at KKK Movie Screening: Oxnard Demonstrators Attack Klan, Police," *Los Angeles Times,* July 31, 1978, B1; "Anti-Klan Protest Leads to Melee," *New York Times,* July 31, 1978, A10; Elinor Langer, *A Hundred Little Hitlers: The Death of a Black Man, the Trial of a White Racist, and the Rise of the Neo-Nazi Movement in America* (New York: Metropolitan Books, 2003), 138.

14. "Nazis Clubbed, Injured on Live Radio Broadcast," *Los Angeles Times,* August 14, 1978, F10; Lewis W. Diuguid and Stevenson O. Swanson, "Invade KCKN to Beat Nazis," *Kansas City Times,* August 14, 1978, WL.

15. See also Timothy McNulty, "1,500 Black Marchers Defy Klan," *Chicago Tribune,* June 10, 1979, 2; Wayne King, "Klan and Blacks March through Tense Decatur," *New York Times,* June 10, 1979, 26; "Communists Thwarted in Arkansas," *Crusader: The Voice of the White Majority,* no. 42 (1979): 1, SC. Two weeks earlier, a black man fired into a crowd of Klansmen blocking a similar march, wounding two black marchers and two Klansmen. "Klan and Blacks March."

16. Langer, *A Hundred Little Hitlers,* 129, 139; "Around the Nation: Demonstrators on Coast Clash with Klan Members," *New York Times,* August 21, 1979, A15.

17. See, for instance, Associated Press, "N.C. United Racist Front Forms," ca. September 25, 1979, GPL.

18. Associated Press, "Klan Hodgepodge of Factions Linked by Hate of Communism."

19. GTRC, *Final Report,* 103, 235; Waller, *Love and Revolution.*

20. Testimony of Daniel Gayman, *Miles et al.,* March 2–3, 1988, Testimonies-1; Testimony of Robert E. Miles, *Miles et al.,* March 29–30, 1988, Box 16-2; Testimony of Michelle Pardee, *Miles et al.,* No. 87-20008 (W.D. Ark. March 14 and 16, 1988), CRL F-7424, Testimonies-1; Testimony of Richard Girnt Butler, *Miles et al.,* March 29, 1988, Testimonies-2.

21. Monte Plott, "The Klan: Communists, Not Blacks, Now Target," Associated Press, November 8, 1979, GPL; Associated Press, "Nazi-Klan Alliance Organized," ca. September 25, 1979, GPL; Jon Nordheimer, "Anti-Negro Group Vexing Police in Wilmington, N.C.," *New York Times,* October 7, 1971, 25, GPL; Associated Press, "N.C. United Racist Front Forms," GPL.

22. Plott, "The Klan: Communists, Not Blacks, Now Target"; Associated Press, "N.C. United Racist Front Forms."

23. Associated Press, "N.C. United Racist Front Forms."

24. James Ridgeway, *Blood in the Face,* 2nd ed. (New York: Thunder's Mouth Press, 1995), 86; Associated Press, "Klan Hodgepodge of Factions Linked by Hate of Communism."

25. Jane Dailey, "Sex, Segregation, and the Sacred after *Brown*," *Journal of American History* 91, no. 119 (2004): 119–144; Robin D. G. Kelley, *Hammer and Hoe: Alabama Communists during the Great Depression* (Chapel Hill: University of North Carolina Press, 1990); Peggy Pascoe, *What Comes Naturally: Miscegenation Law and the Making of Race in America* (Oxford: Oxford University Press, 2009), 287–306.

26. GTRC, *Final Report,* 160; Ridgeway, *Blood in the Face,* 132; "Proclamation: Carolina Free State," National Socialist Party of America, North Carolina Unit, ca. 1980, RH WL Q277.

27. GTRC, *Final Report,* 171–172; Waller, *Love and Revolution.*

28. Information on the list of weapons comes from eyewitness and police reports. Jack Scism, "Four Dic in Klan-Leftist Shootout," *Greensboro Daily News,* November 4, 1979, A1; GTRC, *Final Report,* 171–174, including the testimony of Roland Wayne Wood; Bill Curry, "2,000 Anti-Klan Marchers Expected in Greensboro," *Washington Post,* November 11, 1979, A7.

29. See Jennifer E. Brooks, *Defining the Peace: World War II Veterans, Race, and the Remaking of Southern Political Tradition* (Chapel Hill: University of North Carolina Press, 2004); Donna Murch, *Living for the City: Migration, Education, and the Rise of the Black Panther Party in Oakland, California* (Chapel Hill: University of North Carolina Press, 2010); Kimberley L. Phillips, *War! What Is It Good For: Black Freedom Struggles and the U.S. Military from World War II to Iraq* (Chapel Hill: University of North Carolina Press, 2012); Timothy B. Tyson, *Radio Free Dixie: Robert F. Williams and the Roots of Black Power* (Chapel Hill: University of North Carolina Press, 1999).

30. Scism, "Four Die in Klan-Leftist Shootout"; GTRC, *Final Report,* 172–174.

31. GTRC, *Final Report,* 170–176, 205, citing plea bargain, "Statement of Mark Sherer," March 10, 1983, 2; Boyd et al., Unedited news footage of the events of November 3, 1979.

32. Boyd et al., Unedited news footage of the events of November 3, 1979; GTRC, *Final Report,* 179.

33. GTRC, *Final Report,* 180.

34. Boyd et al., Unedited news footage of the events of November 3, 1979; GTRC, *Final Report,* 179.

35. GTRC, *Final Report,* 179–180.

36. Ibid., 180, 182.

37. GTRC, *Final Report,* 179–184; Boyd et al., Unedited news footage of the events of November 3, 1979; Waller, *Love and Revolution,* 224.

38. GTRC, *Final Report,* 183.

39. "Wonded" in original. Roland Wayne Wood, "Subject Greensboro Ambush," *Aryan Crusaders for Christ Newsletter* (Winston-Salem, NC), ca. 1983, 3, RH WL Eph 636.

40. GTRC, *Final Report;* Winston Cavin, "Ambush Was Quick, Violent and Deadly," *Greensboro Daily News,* November 4, 1979, A1.

41. "Scenes from the Klan Trial," *Workers Viewpoint,* reprinted from *North Carolina Independent,* March 29–April 4, 1984, 4, Ms. 76.14, Box 14-3X, HH 336; Paul Bermanzohn, "Greensboro Murder Trial: What's at Stake," *Workers Viewpoint,* February 16–22, 1984, 5, Ms. 76.14, Box 14-3X, HH 336.

42. William H. Chafe, *Civilities and Civil Rights: Greensboro, North Carolina, and the Black Struggle for Freedom* (Oxford: Oxford University Press, 1980); David Cunningham, *Klansville, U.S.A.: The Rise and Fall of the Civil Rights-Era Ku Klux Klan* (Oxford: Oxford University Press, 2012).

43. Jim Schlosser, "Carter Orders Klan Probe," *Greensboro Record,* November 6, 1979; Katherine Fulton, "They Came, They Saw, They Tinkered," *Greensboro Record,* November 8, 1979.

44. Anthony Perry and Christopher Cook, "Oceanside Klan Rally Ends in Clash with Hecklers; One Injured Severely," *San Diego Union,* reprinted in *National Socialist Bulletin* 9, no. 4 (April 1980): 1.

45. Langer, *A Hundred Little Hitlers,* 140.

46. Plott, "Klan Activity in State on Rise"; "The 'New Klan' Seeks Growth—with Old Habits," *Greensboro Daily News,* February 24, 1980, F1.

47. GTRC, *Final Report,* 141, 173.

48. "Whooped" / "whoop" in original. Virgil Griffin, Testimony before the Greensboro Truth and Reconciliation Commission ("First Public Hearing: What Brought Us to November 3, 1979?," Greensboro Truth and Reconciliation Commission, July 16, 2005); GTRC, *Final Report,* 363.

49. Nicholas Lemann, "Klansmen vs. Communists," *Washington Post,* June 22, 1980, A1.

50. Jim Schlosser, "Wife Says Couple Joined Klan Group in Ignorance," *Greensboro Record,* November 6, 1979; Bill Curry, "The 'New' Klan: Backlash to Black Progress," *Washington Post,* November 13, 1979, A8.

51. Calling themselves the "Greensboro 14" also appropriated a left tactic of naming the place and number of people tried under dubious circumstances, begin-

ning with the Scottsboro 9 and extending into the late 1971 trial and imprisonment of the Wilmington 10 in Wilmington, North Carolina, not far from Greensboro. Ralph Forbes, *Sword of Christ Good News Ministries Newsletter,* RH WL Eph
379; James Coates, *Armed and Dangerous: The Rise of the Survivalist Right* (New York:
Noonday Press of Farrar, Straus, and Giroux, 1987), 222.

52. Six CWP members also were charged with felony riot, incitement to riot, or
interfering with an officer, but these charges were soon dismissed, as was the conspiracy charge against the Klansmen and Nazis. The fourteen Nazis and Klansmen
arrested included Coleman Blair Pridmore, 36, of Lincolnton; Terry Wayne Hartsoe,
19, of Hickory; Lisford Carl Nappier Sr., 41, of Hickory; Billy Joe Franklin, 33, of Lincolnton; Jerry Paul Smith, 32, of Maiden; Michael Eugene Clinton, 24, of Lincolnton;
Lee Joseph McLain, 36, of Lincolnton; Roy Clinton Toney, 32, of Gastonia; David
Wayne Matthews, 24, of Newton; Lawrence Gene Morgan, 28, of Lincolnton. All of
these towns are in North Carolina. GTRC, *Final Report,* 502–506 and throughout.

53. "'Greensboro 16' Found Innocent!," *Thunderbolt,* issue 260 (December 1980):
1, RH WL G1380.

54. Ibid.; "Whites Persecuted to Win Reagan Minority Votes," *Thunderbolt,*
special supplement, ca. 1983, RH WL G1380; Tom Anderson, "Cuban Refugee
Crisis," *Aryan Nations: Teutonic Unity* (Hayden Lake, ID), issue 19–20 (1980): 26–28,
Ms. 76.26, Box 26-1, HH 34; GTRC, *Final Report,* 263, citing *Greensboro Record.*
On waves of Cuban migration and public perception of Cuban immigrants as in-
creasingly nonwhite, see María Cristina García, *Havana USA: Cuban Exiles and
Cuban Americans in South Florida, 1959–1994* (Berkeley: University of California
Press, 1996).

55. GTRC, *Final Report,* 263.

56. Fred McNeese, "Opinionated Prospects Slow Jury Selection in Klan Murder
Trial," *Atlanta Daily World,* July 3, 1980, 1; GTRC, *Final Report,* 11.

57. GTRC, *Final Report,* 276, citing Steve Berry, "Klan Trial Opened One Juror's Eyes," *Greensboro Daily News,* February 9, 1981, B1.

58. GTRC, *Final Report,* 262, testimony of Paul Bermanzohn; "'Greensboro 16'
Found Innocent!"

59. Schlosser later told the GTRC that the reporter had truncated his statement.
He remembers saying, "My father fought in WWII and so I did not look kindly on the
Nazis; I was a Catholic and so did not have good feelings about the Klan and also that
I fought in Vietnam and you know who our adversaries were then." However, the papers printed only the part about Vietnam, emphasizing the rhetoric equating communism during the war and communism at home. GTRC, *Final Report,* 265, testimony
of Michael Schlosser and testimony of Paul and Sally Bermanzohn.

60. GTRC, *Final Report;* "Klan Trial a Sharp Contrast with 2 Earlier Ones," *New
York Times,* March 31, 1985, 23.

61. Boyd et al., Unedited news footage of the events of November 3, 1979.

62. The charge that Jim Waller and the other CWP members planned their deaths has never been substantiated. Martha Woodall, "Slain CWP Man Talked of Martyrdom," *Greensboro Record,* November 9, 1979, A1; William D. Snider, "Is Greensboro's Image Distorted?," *Greensboro Daily News,* November 11, 1979, GPL; Naomi Kaufman, "Nathan, Bermanzohn Said on Extreme Left," Associated Press, reprinted in Durham, North Carolina, November 7, 1979, GPL; "CWP 5 Tombstone Vandalized," *Workers Viewpoint,* November 16–22, 1983, 4, Ms. 76.14, Box 14-3X, HH 336.

63. Mae Israel, "Communists Vow to Hold Sunday March," *Greensboro Daily News,* November 6, 1979; Bob Hiles and Rebecca Ragsdale, "Anonymous Communist Tries to Explain Dedication," *Greensboro Daily News,* November 6, 1979; Howell Raines, "500 March in a Procession for Five Slain Communists," *New York Times,* November 12, 1979, A18; "Dare to Struggle, Dare to Win," *Workers Viewpoint,* November 19, 1979, 15, Ms. 76.14, Box 14-3X, HH 336; Ralph Forbes, *Sword of Christ Good News Ministries Newsletter,* RH WL Eph 379.

64. Sandra G. Boodman, "Swastika Mars Federal Official's Lawn," *Washington Post,* August 5, 1980, A12; GTRC, *Final Report,* 267–268; "First They Murder the Husbands, Now They Jail the Widows," *Workers Viewpoint,* August 11–17, 1980, 1, Ms. 76.14, Box 14-3X, HH 336.

65. Robert Cahoon, Testimony before the Greensboro Truth and Reconciliation Commission, "Second Public Hearing: What Happened on, and after, November 3, 1979?," August 27, 2005; GTRC, *Final Report,* 180.

66. GTRC, *Final Report,* 186; Bill Curry, "2,000 Anti-Klan Marchers Expected in Greensboro," *Washington Post,* November 11, 1979, A7.

67. "Klansmen Acted with Malice, No Regrets about Deaths," *Atlanta Daily World,* October 5, 1980, 1; Waller, *Love and Revolution,* 341.

68. Years later, neo-Nazi defendant Roland Wayne Wood would go so far as to call the five communists killed on November 3 "trophies." Roland Wayne Wood, "An Open Letter to the United States," *Torch,* no. 120 (January 1984): 1–15, HH; "Klansmen Acted with Malice, No Regrets about Deaths." On lynching photographs, see, for instance, Jacqueline Goldsby, *A Spectacular Secret: Lynching in American Life and Literature* (Chicago: University of Chicago Press, 2006).

69. "Klansmen, Nazis Freed in 5 Killings," *Chicago Tribune,* November 18, 1980, 1; "Acquitted Klansman Says Feelings Now Softened about Blacks," *Hartford Courant,* November 20, 1980, B3A; *Saturday Night Live,* Season 6, Episode 108, November 22, 1980; "150 Complain about TV Skit," *Hartford Courant,* November 24, 1980, A6A; "Gov't Legalizes Killing of Communists: Greensboro Trial—First Step to Hitler, U.S.A.," *Workers Viewpoint,* November 24–30, 1980, 1, Ms. 76.14, Box 14-3X, HH 336.

70. "'Greensboro 16' Found Innocent!"; "Acquitted Klansman Says Feelings Now Softened about Blacks"; "Acquitted Klansman in Shooting Incident," *Hartford Courant,* November 20, 1980, A12.

71. FBI clip, "Klansmen Acted with Malice, No Regrets about Deaths"; Steve Olafson and Glenn Lewis, "Heavy Rain Curtails Rally of Klan," *Houston Post*, ca. May 1981, 35; "88 Seconds: 90 Minute Cassette," advertisement, *Torch*, no. 120 (January 1984), 2.

72. *Calling Our Nation* (Aryan Nations), no. 4 (ca. 1982): 5, Ms. 76.26, Box 26-1, HH 34; "'Greensboro 16' Found Innocent!"

73. "Probe of Deaths at Klan Protest Blocked: Appeals Court Calls Charges of Federal Complicity Unfounded," *Los Angeles Times*, June 6, 1984, B16.

74. GTRC, *Final Report*, ch. 4.

75. Martha Woodall and Art Harris, "U.S. Agent Infiltrated Nazis before Greensboro Shootout," *Washington Post*, July 15, 1980, A6; GTRC, *Final Report*, 107–108.

76. "Klan Trial a Sharp Contrast with 2 Earlier Ones"; GTRC, *Final Report*, 171, 149.

77. GTRC, *Final Report*, 174, 200, 221.

78. Wayne King, "Defense to Begin in Klan-Nazi Trial," *New York Times*, March 19, 1984, A15; Lucy Lewis, "Prosecution Rests in Klan/Nazi Trial," *Workers Viewpoint*, April 5–18, 1984, 3, Ms. 76.14, Box 14-3X, HH 336; "Agent Tells of '79 Threats by Klan and Nazis," *New York Times*, May 12, 1985, 26; GTRC, *Final Report*, 168, 288, citing plea bargain, "Statement of Mark J. Sherer," March 10, 1983, 1–2.

79. King, "Defense to Begin in Klan-Nazi Trial"; GTRC, *Final Report*, 288, from jury instructions.

80. GTRC, *Final Report*, 290–295.

81. "Klan Trial a Sharp Contrast with 2 Earlier Ones."

82. Bill Peterson, "Civil Rights Forces Win Part of 1979 Klan Case," *Washington Post*, June 8, 1985, A6; Meredith Barkley, from *Greensboro News and Record*, reprinted in *The Confederate Leader* 85, no. 2 (March 1985): 4, RH WL H149. Wood later apologized for his actions on and after November 3 and renounced his affiliation with white power groups. See GTRC, *Final Report*, 384.

83. GTRC, *Final Report*, 299, 305, 307; Peterson, "Civil Rights Forces Win Part of 1979 Klan Case."

84. Ed Fields, "Great Significance behind the Greensboro N.C. Trial Victory," *Personal Newsletter*, May 1984, 6, RH WL E520.

85. Bill Minutaglio, "Biography of a Hatemonger," *Dallas Morning News*, May 22, 1988, LC, Box 9, Folder 20.

86. "3rd Greensboro Shoot-Out Trial Begins," *Confederate Leader* 85, no. 2 (March 1985): 4, RH WL H149.

87. See Part II.

88. "Dangerous Communists Killed," *Thunderbolt*, ca. 1980–84, RH WL G1380.

89. GTRC, *Final Report*, 148.

4. Mercenaries and Paramilitary Praxis

1. " 'Don't Shoot Them as Individuals, Shoot Them as Communists': The Outlook Interview: Tom Posey, Anti-Sandinista Mercenary, Talks to Brian Barger," *Washington Post,* September 23, 1984, 77; Iver Peterson, "Mercenaries in Fatigues Meet in Nevada Glitter," *New York Times,* September 23, 1984, 26.

2. Bob Dunnavant and Lee Michael Katz, "U.S. Civilians Fighting Mad: Group Seeks Vets to Advise El Salvador," *USA Today,* ca. 1983, SPLC.

3. New York Times News Service, "U.S. Officials Concerned by Alabama-Based CMA," reprinted in *Montgomery Advertiser,* ca. December 13, 1984, SPLC; " 'Don't Shoot Them as Individuals, Shoot Them as Communists' "; New York Times News Service, "Klan Activity Resurging in Southern States," ca. July 5, 1979, GPL; Mike Dunne, "Weapons Added to Klan Symbol List," *Advocate,* 1981, LC; Brown v. Invisible Empire, Knights of the Ku Klux Klan, Southern Poverty Law Center, http://www .splcenter.org/get-informed/case-docket/brown-v-invisible-empire-knights-of-the -ku-klux-klan.

4. Peterson, "Mercenaries in Fatigues Meet in Nevada Glitter"; Dudley Clendinen, "Anti-Communism Called the Thread Binding Group That Captured Aliens," *New York Times,* July 11, 1986, A8.

5. On repertoire guiding action, see Sidney Tarrow, *Power in Movement: Social Movement, Collective Action and Politics* (Cambridge: Cambridge University Press, 1994); Diana Taylor, *The Archive and the Repertoire: Performing Cultural Memory in the Americas* (Durham, NC: Duke University Press, 2003); Charles Tilly, *Social Movements: 1768–2004* (Boulder, CO: Paradigm, 2004).

6. James William Gibson, *Warrior Dreams: Violence and Manhood in Post-Vietnam America* (New York: Hill and Wang, 1994).

7. " 'Don't Shoot Them as Individuals, Shoot Them as Communists.' "

8. "Dangerous Communists Killed," *Thunderbolt,* issue and date unlisted, ca. 1979, RH WL G1380; " 'Don't Shoot Them as Individuals, Shoot Them as Communists.' "

9. Gerald Horne, *From the Barrel of a Gun: The United States and the War against Zimbabwe, 1965–1980* (Chapel Hill: University of North Carolina Press, 2001), 104.

10. Arraignment and Detention Hearing of Robert Neil Smalley, *Miles et al.,* April 24, 1987, Testimonies-2.

11. Scott Sunde, "Ex-KKK Leader Running Scared from FBI," *Times-Herald,* July 27, 1987, A1, LC, Series XIII, Box 5, Folder 12; District Court, First Judicial District, State of Idaho, Case CV 01-3900, Answer to Counter Petition at 10, SPLC; District Court, First Judicial District, State of Idaho, Case No. CV 01-3900, Affidavit of Sheila M. Toohey, August 8, 2001, SPLC.

12. Aryan Nations leader Richard Butler had also expressed a slogan commonly used in *Soldier of Fortune:* "In private, Butler had been known to suggest that the solution to the world's woes consisted of shooting everybody and letting God sort

them out." L. J. Davis, "Ballad of an American Terrorist: A Neo-Nazi's Dream of Order," *Harper's Magazine,* July 1986, 53, LC. See also: Opening statement representing himself, David Lane, "CDR Notes on Trial," Arkansas sedition trial, February 16, 1988, LC; Sunde, "Ex-KKK Leader Running Scared from FBI"; James Coates, *Armed and Dangerous: The Rise of the Survivalist Right* (New York: Noonday Press, 1987); Testimony of Denver Parmenter, vol. 2, *Miles et al.,* March 1, 1988, Testimonies-2; Testimony of Robert Merki, October 4, 1985, *Pierce et al.,* Box 4, at 3027, 3047.

13. Peterson, "Mercenaries in Fatigues Meet in Nevada Glitter"; " 'Don't Shoot Them as Individuals, Shoot Them as Communists.' "

14. Horne, *From the Barrel of a Gun,* 27–28, 229. The quotation appears in Horne's account.

15. Ibid., 28, 217, 221. On the word "gook" and the violence of U.S. empire, see also Jodi Kim, *Ends of Empire: Asian American Critique and the Cold War* (Minneapolis: University of Minnesota Press, 2010); Paul A. Kramer, *The Blood of Government: Race, Empire, the United States, and the Philippines* (Chapel Hill: University of North Carolina Press, 2006); David Roediger, "Gook: The Short History of an Americanism," *Monthly Review* 43, no. 10 (March 1992).

16. Simon Stevens, " 'From the Viewpoint of a Southern Governor': The Carter Administration and Apartheid, 1977–81," *Diplomatic History* 36, no. 5 (November 2012): 843–880; Sean Wilentz, *The Age of Reagan* (New York: HarperCollins, 2008), 102–117.

17. " 'Don't Shoot Them as Individuals, Shoot Them as Communists.' "

18. Dunnavant and Katz, "U.S. Civilians Fighting Mad." On the difficulties of separating allies from enemies in Vietnam, see Christian G. Appy, *Working-Class War: American Combat Soldiers and Vietnam* (Chapel Hill: University of North Carolina Press, 1993); Nick Turse, *Kill Anything That Moves: The Real American War in Vietnam* (New York: Picador, 2013).

19. Gibson, *Warrior Dreams,* 7, 148–149.

20. Ibid.; Greg Grandin, *The Last Colonial Massacre: Latin America in the Cold War,* 2nd ed. (Chicago: University of Chicago Press, 2011).

21. Marilyn B. Young, " 'I Was Thinking, as I Often Do These Days, of War': The United States in the Twenty-First Century," *Diplomatic History* 36, no. 1 (January 2012): 1–15; Tom Engelhardt, *The End of Victory Culture: Cold War America and the Disillusioning of a Generation* (Amherst: University of Massachusetts Press, 2007); Mahmood Mamdani, *Good Muslim, Bad Muslim: Islam, the USA, and the Global War Against Terror* (Hyderabad: Permanent Black, 2004), 81.

22. Vijay Prashad, *The Darker Nations: A People's History of the Third World* (New York: New Press, 2007); Young, " 'I Was Thinking, as I Often Do These Days, of War.' "

23. On the redefinition of democracy as tied to free enterprise, especially after 1973, see Grandin, *The Last Colonial Massacre,* xii–xiii; Alicia Schmidt Camacho,

Migrant Imaginaries: Latino Cultural Politics in the U.S.-Mexico Borderlands (New York: New York University Press, 2008).

24. Grandin, *The Last Colonial Massacre;* María Cristina García, *Seeking Refuge: Central American Migration to Mexico, the United States, and Canada* (Berkeley: University of California Press, 2006); "The Right of the Poor to Defend Their Unique Revolution," *Envio* 4, no. 36 (1984): 2, IHNCA-UCA; María Josefina Saldaña-Portillo, *The Revolutionary Imagination in the Americas and the Age of Development* (Durham, NC: Duke University Press, 2003): 111; Greg Grandin, *Empire's Workshop: Latin America, the United States, and the Rise of the New Imperialism* (New York: Holt, 2007), 112.

25. Leslie Gill, *The School of the Americas: Military Training and Political Violence in the Americas* (Durham, NC: Duke University Press, 2004).

26. Ibid., 76; Justiano Peréz, *EEBI: Los Quijotes del Ocaso* (Miami: Orbis, 2006), 34, Biblioteca Dr. Roberto Incer Barquero, Banco Central (Biblioteca Banco Central), Managua, Nicaragua.

27. N. E. MacDougald, "Tribute to a Professional Warrior: Michael Echanis, 16 Nov 1950–8 Sept 1978," *Soldier of Fortune,* February 1979, 46.

28. Gill, *School of the Americas,* 72; García, *Seeking Refuge,* 14; Roxanne Dunbar-Ortiz, *Blood on the Border: A Memoir of the Contra War* (Cambridge, MA: South End Press, 2005), 9.

29. "Ex-GI Trained Commandos for Somoza," *Los Angeles Times,* September 11, 1978, B6. An AK-47 is an automatic weapon used by enemy troops encountered by Americans in the Vietnam War.

30. One infantryman remembered that Echanis's attempt to create a commando unit led to his suspension. Peréz, *EEBI: Los Quijotes del Ocaso.*

31. Henry Briceño, *Un Ejército dentro de un Ejército (Bajo al Genocido Somocista),* publisher and location unclear, 1979, IHNCA-UCA.

32. MacDougald, "Tribute to a Professional Warrior."

33. "Perece en Accidente Aéreo General José I. Alegrett," *Novedades,* September 9, 1978, 1, IHNCA-UCA; "Ex-GI Trained Commandos for Somoza," *Los Angeles Times,* September 11, 1978, B6; "Nicaraguan Soldiers Clash with Crown Protesting Expulsion of Catholic Priest," *Los Angeles Times,* September 9, 1978, 2; "Somoza's Army Chief Killed in Plane Crash," *Chicago Tribune,* September 9, 1978, S3.

34. Jo Thomas, "Dominica Unsettled in Wake of Thwarted Invasion," *New York Times,* June 7, 1981, 32; "Two Convicted in Dominica Trial," *White Patriot* (Metairie, LA), ca. May 1981, 1, RH WL G605; "Black Says Coup Could Have Made Klan Rich," reprinted in *White Patriot* (Metairie, LA), no. 59 (ca. November 1983): 2, RH WL G605; Stewart Bell, *Bayou of Pigs: The True Story of an Audacious Plot to Turn a Tropical Island into a Criminal Paradise* (New York: Wiley, 2008), 181.

35. Bell, *Bayou of Pigs,* 170.

36. Ken Lawrence, "Behind the Klan's Karibbean Koup Attempt," *CovertAction* 13 (July–August 1981): 22, LC, Box 8, Folder 19; Bell, *Bayou of Pigs,* 64, 193, 246.

37. Bell, *Bayou of Pigs*.

38. Ronald Reagan, "Address to the Nation on Events in Lebanon and Grenada," October 27, 1983, *The Public Papers of President Ronald W. Reagan*, Ronald Reagan Presidential Library. After a 1979 coup moved Grenada toward Soviet alignment, a group of eastern Caribbean nations called for U.S. intervention, and Reagan used this call—as well as the need to protect around a thousand U.S. citizens attending medical school in Grenada—to justify invading the island. After a speedy and successful invasion, the United States oversaw the implementation of a new government. Grandin, *Empire's Workshop*.

39. Barry Siegel, "Invasion Plot a Bizarre Tragicomedy of Errors," *Los Angeles Times*, August 3, 1981, B1.

40. Ronald Reagan, "Remarks of the President and Prime Minister Eugenia Charles of Dominica Announcing the Deployment of United States Forces in Grenada," October 25, 1983, *The Public Papers of President Ronald W. Reagan*, Ronald Reagan Presidential Library; Ronald Reagan, "Address to the Nation on Events in Lebanon and Grenada." On the invasions of Grenada and Panama as restagings of the Vietnam War, see Engelhardt, *The End of Victory Culture*, 279–286.

41. On the idea of paramilitarism at the state level, see Gibson, *Warrior Dreams*.

42. Ronald Reagan, "Remarks at a White House Ceremony Marking the First Anniversary of the Grenada Rescue Mission," October 24, 1984, *The Public Papers of President Ronald W. Reagan*, Ronald Reagan Presidential Library.

43. Ken Lawrence, "Behind the Klan's Karibbean Koup Attempt: Part II," *CovertAction* 16 (March 1982): 21, LC; Bell, *Bayou of Pigs*, 8–12, 208.

44. "Two Convicted in Dominica Trial," *White Patriot* (Metairie, LA), ca. May 1981, 1, RH WL G605.

45. Siegel, "Invasion Plot a Bizarre Tragicomedy of Errors"; Bell, *Bayou of Pigs*, 147; Walt Wiley, "How FBI Works to Solve Alleged Neo-Nazi Crimes," *Sacramento Bee*, February 11, 1985, B1, FBI File, Aryan Nations.

46. Camper claimed to have worked as a mercenary in Mexico, Jamaica, Saudi Arabia, and Egypt. Jeff Prugh, "13 Mercenaries Arrested near Nuclear Plant," *Los Angeles Times*, March 21, 1981, A1; Robert M. Press, "Training as Mercenary: Few Seem to Take It Seriously," *Christian Science Monitor*, July 1, 1981; Lawrence, "Behind the Klan's Karibbean Koup Attempt: Part II."

47. Lawrence, "Behind the Klan's Karibbean Koup Attempt"; Robert M. Press, "Thwarted Mercenary Missions May Have Been Linked," *Christian Science Monitor*, May 1, 1981.

48. Lawrence, "Behind the Klan's Karibbean Koup Attempt."

49. "Pintas de Combatividad Patriótica," *La Barricada*, Managua, May 8, 1985, 1, IHNCA-UCA, trans. Myrna García; William F. Buckley Jr., "Nicaragua, Another Vietnam," *National Review* 38, no. 6 (April 11, 1986): 63; Frente Obrero, *Intervención Imperialista en El Salvador: La Clase Obrera y el Pueblo Salvadoreño en Lucha*

Contra el Fascismo, la Social-Democracia y el Revisionismo, ca. 1981, 5. IHNCA-UCA; William M. LeoGrande, *In Our Own Backyard: The United States in Central America, 1977–1982* (Chapel Hill: University of North Carolina Press, 2000), 102; Grandin, *Empire's Workshop,* 100.

50. Grandin, *Empire's Workshop,* 99–100; García, *Seeking Refuge,* 20–23.

51. Dunnavant and Katz, "U.S. Civilians Fighting Mad"; "Right of the Poor"; Grandin, *Empire's Workshop,* 108; García, *Seeking Refuge,* 25–26.

52. Joseph B. Treaster, "Use of U.S. Mercenaries Is Termed Limited," *New York Times,* September 5, 1984, A13; Dunnavant and Katz, "U.S. Civilians Fighting Mad"; Robert J. McCartney, "Soldiers of Fortune Lend a Hand in El Salvador," *Washington Post,* August 29, 1983, A14.

53. Dunnavant and Katz, "U.S. Civilians Fighting Mad"; Peterson, "Mercenaries in Fatigues Meet in Nevada Glitter"; Treaster, "Use of U.S. Mercenaries Is Termed Limited."

54. McCartney, "Soldiers of Fortune Lend a Hand in El Salvador"; García, *Seeking Refuge,* 23; Gill, *School of the Americas,* 83–84.

55. McCartney, "Soldiers of Fortune Lend a Hand in El Salvador."

56. Gill, *School of the Americas,* 6, 84; Gradin, *Empire's Workshop,* 90; García, *Seeking Refuge,* 24.

57. McCartney, "Soldiers of Fortune Lend a Hand in El Salvador."

58. Gibson, *Warrior Dreams,* 151, quoting from the *Soldier of Fortune* convention held September 20, 1985.

59. On dehumanizing language see also John W. Dower, *War without Mercy: Race and Power in the Pacific War* (New York: Pantheon Books, 1986); Jonathan Shay, *Achilles in Vietnam: Combat Trauma and the Undoing of Character* (New York: Maxwell Macmillan International, 1994), 103–106.

60. Peterson, "Mercenaries in Fatigues Meet in Nevada Glitter"; Peter J. Boyer, "2 in Nicaragua Raid Linked to U.S. Special Forces Unit," *Los Angeles Times,* September 6, 1984, B13; "Mercenarios Reanudan Secuestros a Civiles," editorial, *El Nuevo Diario,* Managua, September 8, 1984, 1, IHNCA-UCA; ANN, "Mercenarios Eran Veteranos del Crimen: 'Conexión Jamastrán' obra de Reagan y CIA," *El Nuevo Diario,* Managua, September 6, 1984, 8, IHNCA-UCA.

61. Sharon Shelton, "CIA Mercenaries Killed in Nicaragua Combat," *Worker's World,* ca. September 13, 1984, SPLC; George Lardner Jr., "'Proud to Be Here,' Dead American Wrote in Diary," *Washington Post,* September 5, 1984, A13.

62. Boyer, "2 in Nicaragua Raid Linked to U.S. Special Forces Unit."

63. Gill, *School of the Americas,* 3–4, 85. The Special Forces later became consolidated as the Special Operations Command under Reagan in 1987.

64. Grandin, *Empire's Workshop.*

65. LeoGrande, *In Our Own Backyard.*

66. Gibson, *Warrior Dreams;* LeoGrande, *In Our Own Backyard,* 114; Michelle Alexander, *The New Jim Crow: Mass Incarceration in the Age of Colorblindness*

(New York: New Press, 2010), 72–78; Kimberley L. Phillips, *War! What Is It Good For: Black Freedom Struggles and the U.S. Military from World War II to Iraq* (Chapel Hill: University of North Carolina Press, 2012); Dan Berger, "Social Movements and Mass Incarceration," *Souls: A Critical Journal of Black Politics, Culture, and Society,* published online July 24, 2013; Susan Jeffords, *The Remasculinization of America: Gender and the Vietnam War* (Bloomington: Indiana University Press, 1989).

67. David Tortorano, United Press International, "Grupo 'ACM' Trata de Ampliar Sus Filas," *La Prensa,* Managua, September 9, 1984, 5, IHNCA-UCA; " 'Don't Shoot Them as Individuals, Shoot Them as Communists.' "

68. ANN, "Mercenarios Eran Veteranos del Crimen: 'Conexión Jamastrán' obra de Reagan y CIA," *El Nuevo Diario,* Managua, September 6, 1984, 8, IHNCA-UCA; EFE, "Grupo de Alabama Había Hecho Varios Contactos: CIA Sabía y También Embajada en Honduras," *El Nuevo Diario,* Managua, September 7, 1984, 1, IHNCA-UCA.

69. Norman Kempster, "U.S. Questioning Survivors of Raid on Nicaragua," *Los Angeles Times,* September 5, 1984, B6.

70. Ibid.

71. Gibson, *Warrior Dreams,* 283.

72. "Confesiones de un Mercenario Yanque: Asesinar a Todos los Nicaragüenses," *La Barricada,* Managua, November 21, 1984, 4, IHNCA-UCA.

73. Ibid.

74. Phillip Taubman, "Private Aid to Latin Rebels at Issue," *New York Times,* December 13, 1984, A3; New York Times Wire Service, "U.S. Officials Concerned by Alabama-Based CMA."

75. Taubman, "Private Aid to Latin Rebels at Issue"; "Group Blames U.S. for Honduras Ouster," *Chicago Tribune,* March 21, 1985, 19; Clendinen, "Anti-Communism Called the Thread Binding Group That Captured Aliens."

76. Associated Press, "2 Americans Among 14 Arrested at Anti-Sandinista Training Camp," *Atlanta Journal/Atlanta Constitution,* ca. April 27, 1985, 21-A, SPLC; Stephen Kinzer, "2 Held in Costa Rica Tell of Trip from U.S. to Join 'Contras,' " *New York Times,* July 8, 1985, A4.

77. Stephen Kurkjian, "U.S. Probes a Private War: Pro-Contra Gun Running, Raids by Mercenaries Banned," *Chicago Tribune,* April 11, 1986, 5.

78. Dunbar-Ortiz, *Blood on the Border,* 268.

79. Stephen Kinzer, "Hasenfus Is Freed by Nicaraguans and Heads Home," *New York Times,* December 18, 1986, A1; LeoGrande, *Our Own Backyard.*

80. Michael Hirsley, "Paramilitary Freelancers under Fire on Nicaragua," *Chicago Tribune,* September 23, 1984, 5; Peterson, "Mercenaries in Fatigues Meet in Nevada Glitter."

81. Testimony of Randall Rader, November 4, 1985, *Pierce et al.,* Box 6, at 6948–6953.

82. Associated Press, "Klansman Refers to Events in Nicaragua: Black: Victim of a 'Double Standard,'" reprinted in *White Patriot* (Metairie, LA), issue 61, 3, RH WL G605.

83. Frank Sikora, "Klan's Black Seeks Cadre to Aid Rebels," reprinted in *White Patriot* (Metairie, LA), issue 61, 3, RH WL G605; Terry Abbot, "Klan Leader to Visit Here Frequently," reprinted in *White Patriot* (Metairie, LA), issue 61, ca. September–October 1984, 2, RH WL G605; Dunne, "Weapons Added to Klan Symbol List."

84. Sikora, "Klan's Black Seeks Cadre to Aid Rebels."

85. Ronald Reagan, "Radio Address to the Nation on the Situation in Central America," March 30, 1985, *The Public Papers of President Ronald W. Reagan*, Ronald Reagan Presidential Library.

86. Ronald Reagan, "Address to the Nation on the Situation in Nicaragua," March 16, 1986, *The Public Papers of President Ronald W. Reagan*, Ronald Reagan Presidential Library.

87. Eleanor Clift, "With Rebel Leaders at His Side, Reagan Presses for Contra Aid," *Los Angeles Times*, March 4, 1986; LeoGrande, *In Our Own Backyard*, 592.

88. Ronald Reagan, "Remarks to Jewish Leaders during a White House Briefing on United States Assistance for the Nicaraguan Democratic Resistance," March 5, 1986, *The Public Papers of President Ronald W. Reagan*, Ronald Reagan Presidential Library.

89. Ronald Reagan, "Address to the Nation on United States Policy in Central America," May 9, 1984, *The Public Papers of President Ronald W. Reagan*, Ronald Reagan Presidential Library.

90. Associated Press, "Klansman Refers to Events in Nicaragua"; "Grand Wiz'rd Imprisoned," *White Patriot* (Metairie, LA), issue 59, ca. November 1983, 2, RH WL G605; "KKK Leader Challenges Neutrality Act," reprinted from unspecified source in *White Patriot* (Metairie, LA), issue 59, ca. November 1983, 2, RH WL G605; Frank Sikora and Walter Bryant, "Black Pledges He'll Continue Boosting the Klan," reprinted from unspecified source in *White Patriot* (Metairie, LA), issue 61, ca. 1984, 2, RH WL G605.

91. This idea appears throughout the twentieth century, from the Zimmerman Telegram that threatened a Mexican-Nazi alliance and southern invasion to concerns about Mexican alignment in World War II. See Geraldo L. Cadava, *Standing on Common Ground: The Making of a Sunbelt Borderland* (Cambridge, MA: Harvard University Press, 2013). In the post-Vietnam conservative movement, fears of communist invasions over the southern border appear in publications of the John Birch Society and in subsequent political discourse. See D. J. Mulloy, *The World of the John Birch Society: Conspiracy, Conservatism, and the Cold War* (Nashville, TN: Vanderbilt University Press, 2014); Sara Diamond, *Roads to Dominion: Right-Wing Movements and Political Power in the United* States (New York: Guilford Press, 1995).

92. Ronald Reagan, "Radio Address to the Nation on Grenada and Nicaragua," February 22, 1986, *The Public Papers of President Ronald W. Reagan,* Ronald Reagan Presidential Library.

93. "The Great White Hope," *Newsweek,* November 14, 1977, RH WL Eph 2195.1.

94. J. Michael Kennedy, "Alien Arrests Uproar Fails to Deter Border Watchers," *Los Angeles Times,* July 11, 1986, A2; Clendinen, "Anti-Communism Called the Thread Binding Group That Captured Aliens"; United Press International, "Actúa en EU Grupo Para-militar en Contra de Ilegales," *El Imparcial,* Hermosillo, Sonora, Mexico, July 7, 1986, 10A; United Press International, "Protestan por Ataques a Ilegales en EU," *El Imparcial,* Hermosillo, Sonora, Mexico, July 13, 1986, 10A.

95. Grandin, *Empire's Workshop,* 115; Gary Webb, *Dark Alliance: The CIA, the Contras, and the Crack Cocaine Explosion* (New York: Seven Stories Press, 1998).

96. Kennedy, "Alien Arrests Uproar Fails to Deter Border Watchers"; Clendinen, "Anti-Communism Called the Thread Binding Group That Captured Aliens."

97. Clendinen, "Anti-Communism Called the Thread Binding Group That Captured Aliens"; Kennedy, "Alien Arrests Uproar Fails to Deter Border Watchers."

98. Clendinen, "Anti-Communism Called the Thread Binding Group That Captured Aliens."

99. Peter Applebome, "Paramilitary Group That Caught 15 Aliens Plans More Patrols," *New York Times,* July 8, 1986, A15; Clendinen, "Anti-Communism Called the Thread Binding Group That Captured Aliens."

100. Camacho, *Migrant Imaginaries,* 201; Cadava, *Standing on Common Ground.*

101. Cadava, *Standing on Common Ground,* 172–211; Jesse Hoffnung-Garskof, *A Tale of Two Cities: Santo Domingo and New York after 1950* (Princeton, NJ: Princeton University Press, 2008); García, *Seeking Refuge.*

102. "Paramilitary Group Holds Gun on Aliens," *Chicago Tribune,* July 7, 1986, 6; Antonio Bustamante, personal interview, June 1, 2009; Antonio Bustamante, personal interview by email, June 5, 2009; "Jury Convicts Rancher in Torture of Aliens," *Chicago Tribune,* February 24, 1981, 10; "The Nation," *Los Angeles Times,* July 17, 1986, OC2; Cadava, *Standing on Common Ground,* 189–211; "Paramilitary Leader Surrenders in Arms Case," *New York Times,* December 18, 1986, B13.

103. Lloyd Grove, "Rallying round the Contra Cause: The Gathering of the Die-Hard Anti-Sandinistas," *Washington Post,* September 8, 1987, C1; "American Held in Nicaragua Described as a 'Rambo' Type," *Los Angeles Times,* December 16, 1986, A26; Dunbar-Ortiz, *Blood on the Border,* 251–252, 268; Theodore Draper, *A Very Thin Line: The Iran-Contra Affairs* (New York: Hill and Wang, 1991); Grove, "Rallying round the Contra Cause"; Gibson, *Warrior Dreams.*

104. Associated Press, "Judge Dismisses Contra Aid Counts, Cites U.S. 'War' Against Nicaragua," *Los Angeles Times,* July 14, 1989; Associated Press, "Contra-Aid Case Dismissal Asked," *Los Angeles Times,* December 3, 1988.

105. Grove, "Rallying round the Contra Cause"; Gibson, *Warrior Dreams.*

106. Testimony of Randall Rader, November 4, 1985, *Pierce et al.,* Box 6, at 6948–6953.

5. The Revolutionary Turn

1. On the distinction between vigilantism and revolution, see Kathleen Belew, "Lynching and Power in the United States: Southern, Western, and National Vigilante Violence from Early America to the Present," *History Compass* 12, no. 1 (January 2014): 84–99.

2. Daniel Gearino, "Texas Klan Unit Infiltrated: Secret KKK Training Camp Disclosed," *Los Angeles Times,* September 10, 1980, C10.

3. The Order drafted its declaration of war around November 1984. Memo from FBI Director to All Field Offices, April 24, 1987; Testimony of Michelle Pardee, *Miles et al.,* March 14 and 16, 1988, Testimonies-1. Glenn Miller drafted a Declaration of War only after exhausting his ability to effectively organize aboveground. See Chapter 6.

4. Testimony of Denver Parmenter, vols. 1 and 2, *Miles et al.,* March 1, 1988, Testimonies-2; Testimony of James Ellison, *Miles et al.,* February 16 and April 7, 1987.

5. Louis R. Beam Jr., *Essays of a Klansman,* 2nd ed. (Hayden Lake, ID: A.K.I.A. Publications, 1989), 45.

6. Testimony of Rachel Mae Robb, *Miles et al.,* March 28, 1988, Testimonies-1; Testimony of David Maxwell French, *Miles et al.,* March 28, 1988, Testimonies-1.

7. Description drawn from video footage of Aryan Nations compound and 2012 visit by the author to the compound site. Testimony of Richard Girnt Butler, *Miles et al.,* March 29, 1988, Testimonies-2; Testimony of David Maxwell French, *Miles et al.,* March 28, 1988, Testimonies-1; Testimony of Rachel Mae Robb, *Miles et al.,* March 28, 1988, Testimonies-1; Testimony of Denver Parmenter, vol. 2, *Miles et al.,* March 1, 1988, Testimonies-2.

8. Parmenter and Ellison testified for the state.

9. Testimony of Richard Girnt Butler, *Miles et al.,* March 29, 1988, Testimonies-2.

10. Testimony of David Maxwell French, *Miles et al.,* March 28, 1988, Testimonies-1.

11. Testimony of Robert E. Miles, *Miles et al.,* March 29–30, 1988, Box 16-2.

12. "CDR Notes on Trial," Chriss, Arkansas sedition trial, February 16, 1988, notes on *Miles et al.,* LC, Box 13, Folder 9.

13. Testimony of Denver Parmenter, vol. 1, *Miles et al.,* February 29, 1988, Testimonies-2.

14. On antistatism in the New Right, see, for instance, Michelle M. Nickerson, *Mothers of Conservatism: Women and the Postwar Right* (Princeton, NJ: Princeton University Press, 2012).

15. Daniel T. Rodgers, *Age of Fracture* (Cambridge, MA: Harvard University Press, 2011), 17, 29, 34–35; on social responsibility and freedom, see also Greg Grandin, *The Last Colonial Massacre: Latin America in the Cold War,* 2nd ed. (Chicago: University of Chicago Press, 2011), xii–xiii.

16. Ronald Reagan, "Inaugural Address," January 20, 1981, American Presidency Project, http://www.presidency.ucsb.edu/ws/?pid=43130.

17. Belew, "Lynching and Power in the United States"; Richard Maxwell Brown, *Strain of Violence: Historical Studies of American Violence and Vigilantism* (New York: Oxford University Press, 1975).

18. Richard Maxwell Brown, *The South Carolina Regulators* (Cambridge, MA: Belknap Press of Harvard University Press, 1963); Benjamin H. Irvin, "Tar, Feathers, and the Enemies of American Liberties, 1768–1776," *New England Quarterly* 76, no. 2 (June 2003): 197–238; Peter Silver, *Our Savage Neighbors: How Indian War Transformed Early America* (New York: W. W. Norton, 2008).

19. Lisa Arellano, *Vigilantes and Lynch Mobs: Narratives of Community and Nation* (Philadelphia: Temple University Press, 2012); Linda Gordon, *The Great Arizona Orphan Abduction* (Cambridge, MA: Harvard University Press, 2001); Karl Jacoby, *Shadows at Dawn: An Apache Massacre and the Violence of History* (New York: Penguin, 2009); Catherine McNichol Stock, *Rural Radicals: Righteous Rage in the American Grain* (Ithaca, NY: Cornell University Press, 1996); Christopher Waldrep, *The Many Faces of Judge Lynch: Punishment and Extralegal Violence in America* (New York: Palgrave Macmillan, 2002).

20. Christopher Capozzola, "The Only Badge Needed Is Your Patriotic Fervor: Vigilance, Coercion, and the Law in World War I America," *Journal of American History,* March 2002, 1354–1382; Nancy MacLean, *Behind the Mask of Chivalry: The Making of the Second Ku Klux Klan* (New York: Oxford University Press, 1994); Wyn Craig Wade, *The Fiery Cross: The Ku Klux Klan in America* (New York: Simon and Schuster, 1987).

21. See, for instance, W. Fitzhugh Brundage, *Lynching in the New South: Georgia and Virginia, 1880–1930* (Urbana: University of Illinois Press, 1993); Crystal N. Feimster, *Southern Horrors: Women and the Politics of Rape and Lynching* (Cambridge, MA: Harvard University Press, 2011); Jacqueline Dowd Hall, " 'The Mind That Burns in Each Body': Women, Rape and Racial Violence," in *Powers of Desire: The Politics of Sexuality,* ed. Ann Snitow, Christine Stansell, and Sharon Thompson (New York: Monthly Review Press, 1983), 328–349; Kidada E. Williams, *They Left Great Marks on Me* (New York: New York University Press, 2012).

22. See, for instance, William D. Carrigan and Clive Webb, *Forgotten Dead: Mob Violence against Mexicans in the United States, 1848–1928* (Oxford: Oxford University Press, 2013); Benjamin Heber Johnson, *Revolution in Texas: How a Forgotten Rebellion and Its Bloody Suppression Turned Mexicans into Americans* (New Haven, CT: Yale University Press, 2003); Monica Muñoz Martinez, "Inherited Loss: Tejanas

and Tejanos Contesting State Violence and Revising Public Memory, 1910–Present," Ph.D. diss., Yale University, 2012.

23. Gordon, *Great Arizona Orphan Abduction.*

24. Consider, for instance, the San Francisco Vigilance Committee, which, while claiming to enforce the law, lynched and otherwise terrorized Chinese, Mexicans, Mexican Americans, and Native Americans in California during the mid-1800s. When the group's numbers swelled, the governor of California attempted to put it down as an armed revolt. Local militias joined the committee, however, and members won several local political races. Effectively, white supremacist vigilantes, rather than upholding state power, overthrew a local government and installed themselves in its place. Waldrep, *Many Faces of Judge Lynch.*

25. Wade, *The Fiery Cross;* Jacqueline Goldsby, *A Spectacular Secret: Lynching in American Life and Literature* (Chicago: University of Chicago Press, 2006).

26. Wade, *The Fiery Cross;* Jennifer E. Brooks, *Defining the Peace: World War II Veterans, Race, and the Remaking of Southern Political Tradition* (Chapel Hill: University of North Carolina Press, 2004).

27. David Cunningham argues that across generations, continuity of membership has connected iterations of activity in all Klan resurgences in *Klansville, U.S.A.: The Rise and Fall of the Civil Rights–Era Ku Klux Klan* (Oxford: Oxford University Press, 2012). For instance, the stories of first-era Klansmen following the Civil War became the founding narratives of the second era Klan in the 1920s.

28. Robert E. Miles, Louis R. Beam, and Paul D. Scheppf, "Background Information: Robert Miles," *Inter-Klan Newsletter and Survival Alert: Death to Every Foe and Traitor!* (A.K.I.A. Publications, Hayden Lake, ID) 1 (ca. 1983): 1–2, SC, Box 31, Folder 6; Jack Anderson and Joseph Spear, "Ex–Klan Dragon Sets Up Computer Net," *Lawrence Journal-World,* November 4, 1986, RH WL Eph 2097.6; Mark Starr et al., "Violence on the Right: A Handful of New Extremists Disturbs the Peace," *Newsweek,* March 4, 1985, RH WL Eph 2097.5; James Coates, *Armed and Dangerous: The Rise of the Survivalist Right* (New York: Noonday Press, 1987), 218; Testimony of Robert E. Miles, *Miles et al.,* March 29–30, 1988, Box 16-2; *Calling Our Nation* (Aryan Nations, Hayden Lake, ID), Ms. 76.26, Box 26-1, HH 34.

29. Beam, *Essays of a Klansman,* 24.

30. Robert E. Miles, "The Mountain Free State," *From the Mountain* (Mountain Church, Cohoctah, MI), July–August 1982, 1–4, Ms. 76.72, Box 72-1, HH 1637.

31. Robert E. Miles, "It Is Up to You," *From the Mountain,* January–February 1984, 3, Ms. 76.72, Box 72-1, HH 1637.

32. D. J. Mulloy, *The World of the John Birch Society: Conspiracy, Conservatism, and the Cold War* (Nashville, TN: Vanderbilt University Press, 2014), 10.

33. Ulius Louis Amoss, "Leaderless Resistance," *Inform* 6205 (April 17, 1962), Wisconsin Historical Society.

34. Gearino, "Texas Klan Unit Infiltrated."

35. Louis R. Beam Jr., "Understanding the Struggle—Part II," *Essays of a Klansman,* 2nd ed. (Hayden Lake, ID: A.K.I.A. Publications, 1989), 47–63.

36. Louis R. Beam, "Leaderless Resistance," *Seditionist,* issue 12 (February 1992), Intelligence Project Holdings, SPLC. Beam's other writings on leaderless resistance include *Essays of a Klansman,* 3; Louis Beam, Estes Park speech, October 23, 1992, video recording, SPLC. Many otherwise excellent accounts have portrayed leaderless resistance as a strategy that emerged in the 1990s, rather than a decade earlier. See, for instance, Kathleen M. Blee, *Inside Organized Racism: Women in the Hate Movement* (Berkeley: University of California Press, 2002; Morris Dees with James Corcoran, *Gathering Storm: America's Militia Threat* (New York: HarperCollins, 1996); Betty A. Dobratz and Stephanie L. Shanks-Meile, *The White Separatist Movement in the United States: "White Power, White Pride!"* (New York: Twayne, 1997); Andrew Gumbel and Roger G. Charles, *Oklahoma City: What the Investigation Missed—and Why It Still Matters* (New York: William Morrow, 2012); Stock, *Rural Radicals.*

37. National Alliance, *Attack!,* 1974–1976, SC, Box 31, Folder 9; Andrew Macdonald (pseud. for William Pierce), *The Turner Diaries* (Hillsboro, WV: National Vanguard Books, 1978).

38. Leonard Zeskind, *Blood and Politics: The History of the White Nationalist Movement from the Margins to the Mainstream* (New York: Farrar, Straus and Giroux, 2009), 31; Grumke, "Interview with William L. Pierce on September 12, 1997, at National Alliance HQ in Hillsboro, WV," 8, LC, Box 30, Folder 4; "CDR Notes on Trial"; Glenn Miller, *A White Man Speaks Out* (n.p.: Glenn Miller, 1999), unpaginated, ch. 12; "Report of Interview," December 11–12, 1986, Green Tree Motel, Fayetteville, CE 100A-12264 13530 85 2521 R, 1, ATF; FBI clip, Bruce Henderson and Ed Martin, "The Ku Klux Klan's March into Militarism," *Charlotte Observer,* April 7, 1985, A1; Testimony of Randall Rader, November 1, 1985, *Pierce et al.,* Box 6, at 6840; James Ridgeway, "Tim McVeigh and the Armies of the Right," *The Village Voice,* March 25, 1997, page number unclear, SPLC, Oklahoma City File.

39. Macdonald, *Turner Diaries,* 98, 102, 103.

40. Ibid., 73 and throughout, 205–211.

41. Louis Beam, "Leaderless Resistance," *Inter-Klan Newsletter and Survival Alert,* ca. 1983, LC, 183.31.6.

42. Sidney Tarrow, *Power in Movement: Social Movement, Collective Action and Politics* (Cambridge: Cambridge University Press, 1994); Diana Taylor, *The Archive and the Repertoire: Performing Cultural Memory in the Americas* (Durham, NC: Duke University Press, 2003).

43. In Macdonald, *Turner Diaries,* white victory is achieved by incremental victories such as the seizure of a small military base and a few nuclear weapons. These bombs act as a deterrent against direct government attack, allowing the Organization to mount a full-scale coup. White generals who surrender are allowed to join

the movement, which through internment, genocide, and nuclear attack eventually secures an all-white world.

44. Testimony of Ann Russell, "CDR Notes on Trial"; Title obscured, *Newsweek,* March 4, 1985, 23, FBI File: Aryan Nations.

45. Testimony of Robert E. Miles, *Miles et al.,* March 29–30, 1988, Box 16-2.

46. Tobby Hatley, "Aryan Nations: North Idaho's Neo-Nazis," *Northwest (Oregonian* Sunday magazine), November 18, 1984, 7, RH WL Eph 2097.4.

47. Untitled report, March 8, 1984, FBI File: Aryan Brotherhood; Mary Thornton and T. R. Reid, "Aryan Group, Jail Gangs Linked," *Washington Post,* December 18, 1984, A3; James Coates, "Order Tries to Turn Court Loss to Prison Victory," *Chicago Tribune,* January 1, 1986, 5, LC.

48. Coates, *Armed and Dangerous,* 59–60, 222; Albert J. Sitter, "Prison Gangs Spread Menace into Society," *Arizona Republic,* date unlisted, B1, SPLC; Patrick Yack, "Yarbrough Was Group's 'Guard,'" *Denver Post,* December 15, 1984, 1, WHC. Yarbrough's name is frequently misspelled "Yarborough."

49. Sitter, "Prison Gangs Spread Menace into Society"; Coates, "Order Tries to Turn Court Loss to Prison Victory," *Chicago Tribune.*

50. *Calling Our Nation* 39 (1979), SC, Box 31, Folder 6.

51. Elinor Langer, *A Hundred Little Hitlers: The Death of a Black Man, the Trial of a White Racist, and the Rise of the Neo-Nazi Movement in America* (New York: Metropolitan Books, 2003), 156; Peter Lake, "The Last Hurrah: Inside the American Nazi Party," *Rebel,* February 20, 1984, Part IV, LC, 8.12.

52. Testimony of Julie Woods, *Miles et al.,* March 17, 1988, Testimonies-1.

53. Testimony of Michelle Pardee, *Miles et al.,* March 14 and 16, 1988, Testimonies-1; Testimony of Denver Parmenter, vol. 2, *Miles et al.,* March 1, 1988, Testimonies-2.

54. Coates, *Armed and Dangerous,* 88; Author unlisted, "Political Prisoners: David Lane," *White American Resistance* (Fallbrook, CA), vol. 4, no. 1 (1985): 21, LC, Series XIII, 1.

55. Coates, *Armed and Dangerous,* 88.

56. Langer, *A Hundred Little Hitlers;* Kevin Flynn and Gary Gerhardt, *The Silent Brotherhood: Inside America's Racist Underground* (New York: Free Press, 1989), xiii; Lake, "The Last Hurrah."

57. Various contemporary news sources and more recent accounts have misspelled "Mathews" as "Matthews." Flynn and Gerhardt, *The Silent Brotherhood,* 13, 73, 78, 43, 81, 84; James Ridgeway, *Blood in the Face,* 2nd ed. (New York: Thunder's Mouth Press, 1995), 109; Coates, *Armed and Dangerous,* 47–48; Gary Gerhardt, John Accola, and Kevin Flynn, "Informants Name 2 Berg Suspects," *Rocky Mountain News,* February 10, 1985, 6, WHC; Robert S. Griffin, *The Fame of a Dead Man's Deeds: An Up-Close Portrait of White Nationalist William Pierce* (n.p.: Robert S. Griffin, 2001),

212; Testimony of Richard Girnt Butler, *Miles et al.*, March 29, 1988, Testimonies-2. Mathews was involved with Aryan Nations by 1980 at the latest. B.M., Letter to the Editor, *Aryan Nation: Teutonic Unity* (Hayden Lake, ID), issue 21 (1980): 26–27, Ms. 76.26, Box 26-1, HH 34; Flynn and Gerhardt, *The Silent Brotherhood*, 13, 43, 81, 84; Ridgeway, *Blood in the Face*, 109; Gerhardt, Accola, and Flynn, "Informants Name 2 Berg Suspects."

58. Coates, *Armed and Dangerous*, 58, 63, 73; "Jury Told of Plan to Kill Radio Host," *New York Times*, November 8, 1987, 31; "The Order's Command Structure," *Oregonian*, December 31, 1985; Testimony of Denver Parmenter, vol. 1, *Miles et al.*, February 29, 1988, Testimonies-2; "Separatists Launch New Nation," *White American Resistance* (Fallbrook, CA) 5, no. 3 (1986): 1, RH WL H100.

59. Testimony of Randall Rader, November 1, 1985, *Pierce et al.*, Box 6, at 6840; Flynn and Gerhardt, *The Silent Brotherhood*, 98; Testimony of Denver Parmenter, vol. 1, *Miles et al.*, February 29, 1988, Testimonies-2.

60. L. J. Davis, "Ballad of an American Terrorist: A Neo-Nazi's Dream of Order," *Harper's Magazine*, July 1986, 53, LC 8.14.

61. James William Gibson, *Warrior Dreams: Violence and Manhood in Post-Vietnam America* (New York: Hill and Wang, 1994), 216; Flynn and Gerhardt, *The Silent Brotherhood*, 58; Peter Lewis, "Probe of Neo-Nazis Spans U.S.," *Seattle Times*, March 3, 1985, B1, FBI File: Aryan Nations. As an FBI memo puts it: "The declaration addresses members of Congress, accusing them of betrayal in Vietnam, subservience to Israel, and allowing the Soviet Union to gain military supremacy." Memo from FBI Director to Field Offices, April 24, 1987, 100-487532.

62. Testimony of Denver Parmenter, September 13, 1985, *Pierce et al.*, Box 4, at 229.

63. Ibid.

64. Testimony of Randall Rader, November 4, 1985, *Pierce et al.*, Box 6, at 6880-6881, 7018, 7045-7046.

65. Rader said not enough was yet written about the North Vietnamese, and that he looked only briefly at Chinese guerrilla strategy. Testimony of Randall Rader, November 5, 1985, *Pierce et al.*, Box 6, at 7202–03.

66. Testimony of Randall Rader, November 4, 1985, *Pierce et al.*, Box 6, at 6948–6953.

67. Ibid.; Opening Statement of Bob Ward, September 12, 1985, *Pierce et al.*, Box 3, at 12; Coates, *Armed and Dangerous*, 73.

68. Macdonald, *Turner Diaries*, 9.

69. Coates, *Armed and Dangerous*, 58.

70. Zeskind, *Blood and Politics*, 96–97.

71. As reported by the IRS, tax resistance in protest (not in greed) peaked in 1983. Coates, *Armed and Dangerous*, 111; Zeskind, *Blood and Politics*, 75; James Coates,

"Plot to Poison Water Is Detailed," *Chicago Tribune,* February 28, 1988, sec. 1, 5, SPLC; Evelyn A. Schlatter, *Aryan Cowboys: White Supremacy and the Search for a New Frontier, 1970–2000* (Austin: University of Texas Press, 2006).

72. Gordon Kahl, "I, Gordon Kahl, a Christian Patriot," Kahl Defense Fund circular, 1983, LC.

73. Jessie Daniels, *Cyber Racism: White Supremacy Online and the New Attack on Civil Rights* (Lanham, MD: Rowman and Littlefield, 2009); Fred Turner, *From Counterculture to Cyberculture: Stewart Brand, the Whole Earth Network, and the Rise of Digital Utopianism* (Chicago: University of Chicago Press, 2006), 129, 133; Paul N. Edwards, *The Closed World: Computers and the Politics of Discourse in Cold War America* (Cambridge, MA: MIT Press, 1996), 354.

74. Louis Beam, "Computers and the American Patriot," *Inter-Klan Newsletter and Survival Alert,* ca. 1983–1984, LC, 22.20; Peter Lake, "An Exegesis of the Radical Right," *California Magazine,* April 1985, 95, LC; Southern Poverty Law Center, "Dossier: Louis R. Beam, Jr.," ca. 1984, SPLC; Ridgeway, *Blood in the Face.*

75. Beam, "Computers and the American Patriot"; "Routine Transmission over Liberty Net," reprinted in Peter Lake, "An Exegesis of the Radical Right," *California Magazine,* April 1985, 95, LC; Wayne King, "Computer Network Links Rightist Groups and Offers 'Enemy' List," *New York Times,* February 15, 1985, A17, FBI File: Aryan Nations.

76. Robert E. Miles, Louis R. Beam, and Paul D. Scheppf, untitled introductory note, *Inter-Klan Newsletter and Survival Alert: Death to Every Foe and Traitor!* 1 (ca. 1983): 3, SC, Box 31, Folder 6; James Coates, "Slaying probe links neo-Nazis to other crimes," *Chicago Tribune,* reprinted in *Kansas City Star,* December 31, 1984, 1A, WL; Testimony of Denver Parmenter, vol. 2, *Miles et al.,* March 1, 1988, Testimonies-2.

77. King, "Computer Network Links Rightist Groups and Offers 'Enemy' List."

78. Miles, Beam, and Scheppf, untitled introductory note.

79. Beam, "Computers and the American Patriot."

80. FBI clip, United Press International, Interview with Richard Butler in major publication, details unclear.

81. Southern Poverty Law Center, "Dossier: Louis R. Beam, Jr."

82. Sitter, "Prison Gangs Spread Menace into Society"; Coates, "Order Tries to Turn Court Loss to Prison Victory."

83. Southern Poverty Law Center, "Dossier: Louis R. Beam, Jr."

84. Miller, *A White Man Speaks Out,* ch. 10.

85. Davis, "Ballad of an American Terrorist," 53.

86. Ibid.

87. Ibid.

88. Ibid.

89. Gerhardt, Accola, and Flynn, "Informants Name 2 Berg Suspects," *Rocky Mountain News,* February 10, 1985, 6.

90. John Snell, "Militants Guided by Story of Insurrection," *Oregonian*, ca. 1984–1985, 1, LC.

91. Macdonald, *The Turner Diaries; Miles et al.;* Flynn and Gerhardt, *The Silent Brotherhood*, 130, 134.

92. Jack Cox, "KKK Leader: Strong Talk, but No Crime," *Denver Post*, November 18, 1979, 37, WHC; Jack Cox, "Colo. Public Spurns Ultrarightists," *Denver Post*, November 18, 1979, C37, WHC; Michael H. Rudeen, "Is the Colorado Klan Fizzling?," *Denver Monthly*, January 1980, 24, WHC; Marjie Lundstrom, "Magen Yehudi: Jewish Shield," *Denver Monthly*, February 1980, 76, WHC; Flynn and Gerhardt, *The Silent Brotherhood*, 144; Sue Lindsay, "2 Guilty, 2 Cleared in Berg Case," *Rocky Mountain News*, November 18, 1987, 6, WHC; Sue Lindsay, "Witness Says She Thought Lane Threat Was 'Hot Air,' " *Rocky Mountain News*, June 18, 1984, page unlisted, SPLC; "Jury Told of Plan to Kill Radio Host."

93. Coates, *Armed and Dangerous*, 44, 93; Mike O'Keeffe, "White Makes Right: Pastor Pete Peters Has Made Colorado a Stronghold of Christian Extremists," *Westword*, July 12–18, 1989, 10, SPLC; Gerhardt, Accola and Flynn, "Informants Name 2 Berg Suspects," *Rocky Mountain News*, February 10, 1985, 6, WHC; James Battersby, *The Holy Book of Adolf Hitler* (Wentsville, MO: Invictus Books, 2011); "Jury Told of Plan to Kill Radio Host." Order member Randy Evans also took two wives, according to the testimony of Randall Rader, November 1, 1985, *Pierce et al.*, Box 6, at 6861–2.

94. Coates, *Armed and Dangerous*, 44, 67; "Jury Told of Plan to Kill Radio Host."

95. Snell, "Militants Guided by Story of Insurrection"; Jack Kisling, "Submachine Gun Easy to Obtain, Costs $595," *Denver Post*, December 15, 1984, 3A, WHC.

96. Information about how the shooting lifted Berg off the ground comes from the testimony of Robert Merki, recounting what Robert Mathews told him. Laramie, Wyoming, is a two-and-a-half-hour drive from Denver. "Judge Rejects Dismissal of Charges in Slaying of Denver Radio Host," *New York Times*, November 15, 1987, 42; Kevin Flynn, "Fighting Racism for 20 Years: Neo-Nazi Victim Alan Berg's Ex-Wife Calls Hate a 'Disease,' " *Rocky Mountain News*, June 18, 2004, A4, WHC; Lindsay, "Witness Says She Thought Lane Threat Was 'Hot Air' "; "Berg's Killing Put Heat on Hate," *Denver Post*, June 18, 2004, WHC; Sue Lindsay, "Demise of the Order Termed 'God's Will,' " *Rocky Mountain News*, November 7, 1987, 8, WHC.

97. Coates, *Armed and Dangerous*, 44.

98. Lindsay, "Witness Says She Thought Lane Threat Was 'Hot Air.' "

99. Coates, *Armed and Dangerous*, 69; Davis, "Ballad of an American Terrorist"; Snell, "Militants Guided by Story of Insurrection"; Peter Lewis, "Probe of Neo-Nazis Spans U.S.," *Seattle Times*, March 3, 1985, B1, FBI File: Aryan Nations; Tom Martinez, "A Former Klansman's Personal History of Hate," excerpt from *Brotherhood of Murder, Special Report: The Ku Klux Klan: A History of Racism and Violence*, Southern Poverty Law Center, 1988, LC; Flynn and Gerhardt, *The Silent Brotherhood*, 95.

100. Mosby's first name does not appear in the affidavit, nor does he appear elsewhere in the archive. Nicholas C. Chriss, "Beam Talked of Rebellion, FBI Says," *Houston Chronicle,* February 22, 1988, LC; James Coates, "Hate Groups Call Off Summer Convention," *Chicago Tribune,* June 17, 1985, LC.

101. Chriss, "Beam Talked of Rebellion, FBI Says."

102. Tobby Hatley, "Aryan Nations: North Idaho's Neo-Nazis," *Northwest (Oregonian* Sunday magazine), November 18, 1984, 7, RH WL Eph 2097.4.

103. Coates, "Hate Groups Call Off Summer Convention"; SPLC, "Dossier: Louis R. Beam, Jr.," ca. 1984, SPLC; "Revolt Plans Tied to White Supremacists," *The Los Angeles Times,* January 2, 1985, Part 1, Page 13, FBI File: Aryan Nations; Associated Press, "2 Klan Members Plead Guilty To Arson in Black Law Office," *New York Times,* February 21, 1985.

104. Macdonald, *Turner Diaries,* 51–53.

105. Davis, "Ballad of an American Terrorist"; David Mathiason, "Nazi Thugs Guilty," *Guardian,* January 15, 1986, LC; Snell, "Militants Guided by Story of Insurrection"; Ridgeway, *Blood in the Face,* 111; *Miles et al.,* decided July 6, 1988; final letter of Robert Jay Mathews, December 1984, cited in Ridgeway, *Blood in the Face,* 114–115; "Witnesses at Neo-Nazi Trial Describe Dissension in Group," *New York Times,* October 15, 1985, A25.

106. Paul McCartney and John Lennon, "Maxwell's Silver Hammer," *Abbey Road,* The Beatles, 1969. Kemp was later sentenced to sixty years for his role in West's death.

107. "News in Brief," *Los Angeles Times,* January 8, 1985, 2, FBI File: Aryan Nations; Lindsay, "2 Guilty, 2 Cleared in Berg Case"; Debby Abe, "Boisean Pleads Innocent to Receiving Stolen Money," *Idaho Statesman,* ca. February 19, 1983, 1C, SPLC; James Coates and Stephen Franklin, "'Underground' of Racist Leaders Coordinated Crimes, FBI Taps Show," *Chicago Tribune,* December 28, 1987, A16, SPLC; *Miles et al.*

108. All of the financial contributions remain disputed, as the FBI never located all of the Order's stolen and counterfeit money. The figures listed here are a best guess, based on multiple witness accounts, the credibility of those witnesses, and the circumstances of their testimony. Davis, "Ballad of an American Terrorist"; "CDR Notes on Trial"; Testimony of Frazier Glenn Miller, *Miles et al.,* March 10–11, 1988, Box 16-2; Miller, *A White Man Speaks Out,* ch. 10.

109. Testimony of Randall Rader, November 1, 1985, *Pierce et al.,* Box 6, at 6818.

110. Other nicknames, like "Sandals" (Denver Parmenter), "Doc" (David Tate), "Calvin" (Randall Evans), and "Mr. May" (Jim Dye), do not have archival references. Some, like "Fireman" (Charles E. Ostrout), presumably refer to specific acts of violence but cannot be verified. Bob Miles was "Gray Fox." Randall Duey was "Luke," after *Cool Hand Luke.* Someone, probably Dan Gayman—who received Order money and had published a periodical of the same name—was called "The Watchman." Tom Metzger may have been called "Bear," possibly in reference to California. Coates,

Armed and Dangerous, 41–63; Miller, *A White Man Speaks Out,* ch. 10; Testimony of Denver Parmenter, vol. 2, *Miles et al.,* March 1, 1988, Testimonies-2.

111. Alexandra Marks, "'Lone Wolves' Pose Explosive Threat," *Christian Science Monitor,* May 27, 2003.

112. Steven Singular, "Talked to Death," *Rolling Stone,* January 31, 1985, 41, LC; Davis, "Ballad of an American Terrorist"; Lindsay, "2 Guilty, 2 Cleared in Berg Case"; Thornton and Reid, "Aryan Group, Jail Gangs Linked."

113. Final letter of Robert Jay Mathews, December 1984, cited in Ridgeway, *Blood in the Face,* 114–115.

114. Gibson, *Warrior Dreams;* Davis, "Ballad of an American Terrorist."

115. Testimony of Michelle Pardee, *Miles et al.,* March 14 and 16, 1988, Testimonies-1; Testimony of Denver Parmenter, vol. 2, *Miles et al.,* March 1, 1988, Testimonies-2; Opening Statement of Bob Ward, September 12, 1985, *Pierce et al.,* Box 3, at 101–102, 74, 729; Testimony of Thomas Allen Martinez, October 21, 1985, *Pierce et al.,* Box 5, at 4978; Testimony of Randall Rader, November 4, 1985, *Pierce et al.,* Box 6, at 7004–7005; Testimony of Richard Girnt Butler, *Miles et al.,* March 29, 1988, Testimonies-2; Testimony of Julie Woods, *Miles et al.,* March 17, 1988, Testimonies-1.

116. Testimony of Randall Rader, November 4, 1985, *Pierce et al.,* Box 6, at 6976.

117. The Order, "Declaration of War," 1984, http://archive.adl.org/learn/ext_us /decl_war.html; Opening Statement of Bob Ward, September 12, 1985, *Pierce et al.,* Box 3, at 93–94; Testimony of Michelle Pardee, *Miles et al.,* March 14 and 16, 1988, Testimonies-1.

118. Davis, "Ballad of an American Terrorist"; Macdonald, *Turner Diaries,* 17; Gerhardt, Accola, and Flynn, "Informants Name 2 Berg Suspects," *Rocky Mountain News,* February 10, 1985, 6, WHC.

119. Testimony of Louis Ray Beam Jr., *Miles et al.,* November 17, 1988; Testimony of Randall Rader, November 5, 1985, *Pierce et al.,* Box 6, at 7108; Frank Silva, "Hail, the Order!," *White Aryan Resistance* 7, no. 1 (1988): 2, LC; *Confederate Leader* special edition ca. 1986, *Confederate Leader* 85, no. 8 (November 1985), and *Confederate Leader* 86, no. 3 (May 1986), all RH WL H149; Aryan Women's League, "Greetings Fellow Aryan Warriors!," *Newsletter,* December 1990, Ms. 76.26, Box 26-1, HH 387; "Voice of Revolution," *The New Order* 65 (November–December 1986): 1, Ms. 76.26, Box 26-2, HH 302; FBI clip, Bruce Henderson, "White Supremacists across South Gather," *Charlotte Observer,* January 19, 1986; Testimony of Robert E. Miles, *Miles et al.,* March 29–30, 1988, Box 16-2.

120. Davis, "Ballad of an American Terrorist."

121. SPLC clip, "FBI Charges Two with Aiding Neo-Nazi Robbery Suspect," SPLC; Lindsay, "2 Guilty, 2 Cleared in Berg Case"; Coates, "Order Tries to Turn Court Loss to Prison Victory"; Coates, *Armed and Dangerous,* 56; Kevin Flynn and Gary Gerhardt, "Suspect Seized with Klan Followers," *Rocky Mountain News,* March 31, 1985, 6, WHC; James Coates, "Neo-Nazis Form Kinship with Klan, Surge

of Racist Violence Feared," *Chicago Tribune,* April 7, 1985, C3, SPLC; "Hate Groups Infest Ozarks; FBI Hunts Killer," *Miami Herald,* April 20, 1986, 4A, SC; Richard T. Pienciak, "Increased Violence Makes FBI More Wary of White Supremacists," *Hartford Courant,* March 3, 1985, A5; James Coates, "Order's Schemes Founded on Hate, Not Practicality," *Chicago Tribune,* December 31, 1985, 2; Flynn and Gerhardt, *The Silent Brotherhood,* 38.

122. Intended to address criminal enterprises such as the mob, the Racketeer Influenced and Corrupt Organizations (RICO) Act has also occasionally been employed to prosecute organizations participating in political violence. Gerard E. Lynch, "RICO: The Crime of Being a Criminal, Parts I and II," *Columbia Law Review* 87, no. 4 (May 1987): 932–948. Also, T. R. Reid, "FBI Says It Blunted Neo-Nazi Uprising," *Washington Post,* April 14, 1985, A7; Lindsay, "2 Guilty, 2 Cleared in Berg Case"; "Hate Groups Infest Ozarks; FBI Hunts Killer"; Bill Curry, "In Warning to Extremists, U.S. Indicts 23 in 'Order,' " *Los Angeles Times,* April 16, 1985, B1; Wayne King, "Anti-Semitism Links Violent Groups," *New York Times,* April 28, 1985, 22.

123. Coates, "Hate Groups Call Off Summer Convention"; Kevin Flynn, "Neo-Nazi Trial Verdict Expected Monday," *Rocky Mountain News,* December 27, 1985, WHC.

124. Lindsay, "2 Guilty, 2 Cleared in Berg Case."

125. Ibid.; Zeskind, *Blood and Politics,* 146; Kevin Flynn, "Informants Link Denver Lawyer to Racists' Funds," *Rocky Mountain News,* ca. December 28, 1987, SPLC; Lindsay, "Witness Says She Thought Lane Threat Was 'Hot Air.' "

126. Reid, "FBI Says It Blunted Neo-Nazi Uprising."

127. T. R. Reid, "23 Indicted as Neo-Nazi Terrorists," *Washington Post,* April 16, 1985, A10; Abe, "Boisean Pleads Innocent to Receiving Stolen Money"; Coates, "Order Tries to Turn Court Loss to Prison Victory."

128. Coates, "Order Tries to Turn Court Loss to Prison Victory"; Langer, *A Hundred Little Hitlers,* 156; Coates and Franklin, " 'Underground' of Racist Leaders Coordinated Crimes"; David Mathiason, "Trial Bares Neo-Nazis' Plots and Links," *Guardian,* October 16, 1985, 6, LC.

129. Bill Minutaglio, "Biography of a Hatemonger," *Dallas Morning News,* May 22, 1988, LC, 9.20; Gerhardt, Accola, and Flynn, "Informants Name 2 Berg Suspects"; Coates and Franklin, " 'Underground' of Racist Leaders Coordinated Crimes"; Andrew Macdonald (pseud. for William Pierce), *Hunter* (Hillsboro, WV: National Vanguard Books, 1989).

130. Flynn, "Informants Link Denver Lawyer to Racists' Funds"; Affidavit, Farris L. Genide, Special Agent, FBI, US District Court Eastern District of Michigan Southern Division, ca. 1986, No. 86-0343, 69–70, LC; Coates and Franklin, " 'Underground' of Racist Leaders Coordinated Crimes"; "Arkansas Jury Finds 13 Not Guilty in U.S. Trial of White Supremacists," *Kansas City Times,* April 8, 1988, A1, RH WL Eph 2097.7; Coates, *Armed and Dangerous,* 73.

6. Weapons of War

1. Richard Halloran, "Pentagon Fights to Stop Loss of Vast Amount of Arms and Supplies," *New York Times,* February 12, 1987, B13; Neil Roland, "Reliability of Army Guards Doubted," *Washington Post,* August 10, 1986, A15.

2. Halloran, "Pentagon Fights to Stop Loss of Vast Amount of Arms and Supplies"; L. J. Davis, "Ballad of an American Terrorist: A Neo-Nazi's Dream of Order," *Harper's Magazine,* July 1986, 53, LC 8.14.

3. Halloran, "Pentagon Fights to Stop Loss of Vast Amount of Arms and Supplies."

4. Linda Hunt, "The New Look: Looking for a Few Good Men," *Common Cause Magazine,* November–December 1986, 32, LC, 9.12; Nicholas C. Chriss, "Beam Talked of Rebellion, FBI says," *Houston Chronicle,* February 22, 1988, LC; Mike McLaughlin, "Armed Soldiers and Marines Participate in White Supremacist Rallies," United Press International, April 15, 1986, SPLC.

5. "A.C.L.U. Criticizes Pentagon 'Hate' Group Policy," *New York Times,* October 30, 1986, A23; "Code of Conduct," editorial, *New York Times,* September 17, 1986, A26.

6. Catherine Lutz, *Homefront: A Military City and the American Twentieth Century* (Boston: Beacon Press, 2008), 239; Matt Kennard, *Irregular Army* (New York: Verso, 2012), 17–18.

7. Kennard, *Irregular Army;* T. J. Leyden and M. Bridget Cook, *Skinhead Confessions: From Hate to Hope* (Springville, UT: Sweetwater Books, 2008).

8. Testimony of Frazier Glenn Miller, *Miles et al.,* March 10–11, 1988, Box 16-2; United Press International, "Regional News," May 8, 1986, SPLC.

9. Newsletter, John Brown Anti-Klan Committee, San Francisco, date unclear, ca. 1985–1986, LC, 22.21.

10. Ibid.; Elinor Langer, *A Hundred Little Hitlers: The Death of a Black Man, the Trial of a White Racist, and the Rise of the Neo-Nazi Movement in America* (New York: Metropolitan Books, 2003). The jury awarded $12.5 million in damages to the family of the murdered student, Mulugeta Seraw, in Berhanu v. Metzger, A8911-07007, filed November 21, 1989, Circuit Court, Multnomah County, Oregon. Tom Metzger and White Aryan Resistance were found to have encouraged the murder.

11. Leonard Zeskind, *Blood and Politics: The History of the White Nationalist Movement from the Margins to the Mainstream* (New York: Farrar, Straus and Giroux, 2009), 61–63; James Coates, *Armed and Dangerous: The Rise of the Survivalist Right* (New York: Noonday Press, 1987), 136; William Thomas, "Net Drawn around White Supremacist Camp," publication unlisted but presumably *Commercial Appeal,* April 21, 1985, page unlisted, SPLC; "A Doomsday Vigil with Bible and Gun," *New York Times,* November 29, 1981, 79; Testimony of Randall Rader, November 1, 1985, *Pierce et al.,* Box 6, at 6766–6768.

12. Testimony of Randall Rader, November 1, 1985, *Pierce et al.,* Box 6, at 6775–6784.

13. Coates, *Armed and Dangerous,* 153; Nicholas Chriss, "CDR Notes on Trial," Arkansas sedition trial, February 16, 1988, notes on *Miles et al.,* LC, Box 13, Folder 9. Testimony of James Ellison, Jury Trial, February 16–April 7 1987, *United States v. Richard Girnt Butler et al.,* 87–2008, CRL; "Minister Denies Tie to Okla. Bombing, McVeigh," *Commercial Appeal,* July 3, 1995, SPLC; Zeskind, *Blood and Politics,* 82–83.

14. Thomas, "Net Drawn around White Supremacist Camp"; Zeskind, *Blood and Politics,* 61–63; "2 Suspects Plead Innocent; Are Freed," *Little Rock Gazette,* ca. April 2, 1985, page unlisted, SPLC; "CDR Notes on Trial," February 16, 1988; Carol Griffee, "CSA Camp Has PCBs in 2 Areas," *Little Rock Gazette,* date unlisted, page unlisted, SPLC; James Coates, "Hate Groups Call Off Summer Convention," *Chicago Tribune,* June 17, 1985, LC; Wayne King, "Anti-Semitism Links Violent Groups," *New York Times,* April 28, 1985, 22.

15. Mab Segrest, "Deadly New Breed," *Southern Exposure,* Spring 1989, 57, LC, 8.22; "About Klan Leader Glenn Miller," *Confederate Leader* 84, no. 9 (ca. 1984): 3, RH WL H149; Glenn Miller, *A White Man Speaks Out* (n.p.: Glenn Miller, 1999).

16. Testimony of Frazier Glenn Miller, *Miles et al.,* March 10–11, 1988, Box 16-2.

17. "All About the CKKKK," *Confederate Leader* 84, no. 9 (ca. 1984): 4, RH WL H149.

18. "Klan Rallies in Texas and NC," *White Patriot: Worldwide Voice of the Aryan People,* no. 56 (ca. 1981): 8, SC, Box 49, Folder 15; J. L. Pate, "Jacksonville Klan rally Set for Dec. 5," *Jacksonville News,* November 29, 1982, SPLC; Lutz, *Homefront.*

19. The National States Rights Party was a racist organization run by *Thunderbolt* publisher Ed Fields; the National Socialist Party of America was a neo-Nazi group based in North Carolina and run by ex-mercenary Harold Covington. Miller, *A White Man Speaks Out,* chs. 1, 2, 12.

20. Miller, *A White Man Speaks Out,* ch. 4; "White Patriot Commandos," *Village Voice,* May 6, 1986, 32–33, RH WL Eph 2199.

21. "Grand Dragon Miller," *White Patriot* (Metairie, LA), no. 56 (ca. 1985): 10, RH WL G605.

22. MDE [Redacted] to FBI SAC Charlotte, April 25, 1985; Airtel memo, FBI SAC New Orleans to SAC Charlotte, August 28, 1985; FBI Report, copy to U.S. Attorney, Miami, Florida, July 17, 1985; "White Patriot Commandos"; Miller, *A White Man Speaks Out,* ch. 4; FBI clip, Timothy Dwyer, "Old Klan Faction Trades Its Robes for Battle Garb," *Charlotte Observer,* June 21, 1985, C1; Lutz, *Homefront.*

23. Segrest, "Deadly New Breed"; Hunt, "The New Look"; Dudley Clendinen, "North Carolina Jury Getting Case Against Klan Paramilitary Group," *New York Times,* July 25, 1985, A8.

24. Segrest, "Deadly New Breed"; Miller, *A White Man Speaks Out,* ch. 6; Reference Charlotte teletype to FBI, September 11, 1986; Tempo section, *Chicago*

Tribune, September 12, 1984, 5, SPLC; FBI clip, John Monk, "Klan Leader Accepts March Ban in Black Areas Following Suit," *Charlotte Observer,* January 12, 1985, B3.

25. Testimony of Frazier Glenn Miller, *Miles et al.,* March 10–11, 1988, Box 16-2; Charlotte memo, FBI, March 2, 1987; Airtel memo, SAC Charlotte to FBI Director, March 2, 1987; Testimony of Denver Parmenter, vol. 2, *Miles et al.,* March 1, 1988, Testimonies-2; Miller, *A White Man Speaks Out,* ch. 10.

26. "Parties Reject White Supremacist," *Independence Daily Reporter,* March 12, 2006, SPLC; Miller, *A White Man Speaks Out;* United Press International, "Regional News," May 8, 1986, SPLC; United Press International, "Klan Candidate Files for Governor," January 26, 1984, SPLC; Tempo section, *Chicago Tribune,* September 12, 1984, 5, SPLC; United Press International, "Regional News," January 17, 1984, SPL; United Press International, "Klan Says School Patrol Begins," March 5, 1984, SPLC.

27. Southern Poverty Law Center, "Dossier: Louis R. Beam, Jr.," ca. 1984, SPLC; Testimony of Frazier Glenn Miller, *Miles et al.,* March 10–11, 1988, Box 16-2; Miller, *A White Man Speaks Out,* chs. 10 and 12; Bill Minutaglio, "Biography of a Hatemonger," *Dallas Morning News,* May 22, 1988, LC, 9.20.

28. Miller, *A White Man Speaks Out,* ch. 10.

29. Airtel memo, SAC Detroit to FBI Director, January 9, 1985; Miller, *A White Man Speaks Out,* ch. 10.

30. Miller, *A White Man Speaks Out,* ch. 12.

31. Louis Beam to Glenn Miller, "Out of the Furnace—Steel!," ca. 1985, SPLC; Southern Poverty Law Center, "Dossier: Louis R. Beam, Jr.," ca. 1984, SPLC; Testimony of Frazier Glenn Miller, *Miles et al.,* March 10–11, 1988, Box 16-2; Miller, *A White Man Speaks Out,* ch. 12; FBI clip, Timothy Dwyer, "Old Klan Faction Trades Its Robes for Battle Garb," *Charlotte Observer,* June 21, 1985, C1; FBI Report, copy to USA, Miami, August 12, 1985.

32. James Coates and Stephen Franklin, " 'Underground' of Racist Leaders Coordinated Crimes, FBI Taps Show," *Chicago Tribune,* December 28, 1987, A16, SPLC; Miller, *A White Man Speaks Out,* chs. 6 and 10; SA [Redacted] to SAC Charlotte, February 11, 1987; Airtel memo, SAC Charlotte to FBI Director, March 2, 1987; Mab Segrest, "Deadly New Breed," *Southern Exposure,* Spring 1989, 57, LC; FBI clip, "Klan Group Changes Name," *Charlotte News,* March 20, 1985.

33. Reference Charlotte teletype to Bureau, September 11, 1986; Hunt, "The New Look"; Miller, *A White Man Speaks Out,* ch. 4; Airtel memo, SAC Charlotte to FBI Director, March 2, 1987; Segrest, "Deadly New Breed"; Associated Press, "U.S. Indicts Five in Arms-Theft Plot: Klan, Patriot Party Members Also Linked to Murder Conspiracy," *Washington Post,* January 9, 1987, A16.

34. Memo from SAC Charlotte to SA [Redacted], May 23, 1985.

35. An FBI agent listening to the recording loosely transcribed this message, and the words may not be exactly as Miller spoke them. MDE [Redacted] to FBI SAC Charlotte, July 10, 1985.

36. Joel Brinkley with Jeff Gerth, "Black Market Sales Rise in Arms Stolen from U.S. Military Bases," *New York Times,* September 29, 1985, 30.

37. Institutional archives about these security investigations are not available as public record. Brinkley with Gerth, "Black Market Sales Rise"; *The New York Times,* A. L. May, "Navy Probes Allegations of Supplies for Klansman," *News and Observer,* ca. April 22, 1988, 1C, SPLC.

38. FBI clip, Bruce Henderson and Ed Martin, "The Ku Klux Klan's March into Militarism," *Charlotte Observer,* April 7, 1985, A1.

39. Miller, *A White Man Speaks Out,* chs. 10 and 14.

40. FBI clip, Bruce Henderson, "White Supremacists across South Gather," *Charlotte Observer,* January 19, 1986.

41. Rallies opposing Martin Luther King Jr. Day were common annual events in the white power movement. FBI clip, "White Patriots Arrested," *Charlotte Observer,* January 20, 1986, B2.

42. Miller, *A White Man Speaks Out,* ch. 6; Associated Press, "White Supremacist Gets Five Years," January 5, 1988, SPLC; Teletype memo, Charlotte to FBI Director, September 11, 1986; FBI Director to Charlotte, Butte, Columbia, Detroit, Denver, Miami, Richmond, San Francisco, Seattle, September 16, 1986.

43. Reference Charlotte teletype to FBI, September 11, 1986.

44. Airtel memo, SAC Charlotte to FBI Director, August 1, 1986; FBI clip, Ann Green, "Klan Leader Named in Civil Lawsuit Agrees to Avoid Harassing Blacks," *Raleigh News and Observer,* November 12, 1985, 1C.

45. Associated Press, "2 Men Are Guilty of Arms Training: They Violated Order Forbidding Paramilitary Organization," *New York Times,* July 26, 1986, 7.

46. "The Burning Question—Is Klan an Army?," *Chicago Tribune,* July 28, 1986, C12, SPLC.

47. Miller, *A White Man Speaks Out.*

48. Clendinen, "North Carolina Jury Getting Case."

49. FBI clip, "Extremist Leader," *Charlotte Observer,* May 11, 1985, C8; Samuel T. Currin, U.S. Attorney, to Robert L. Pence, FBI Special Agent in Charge, July 19, 1985, with FBI clip: "Mock Trials Threatened by 'Party,'" *Fayetteville Observer,* May 12, 1985.

50. Airtel memo, SAC Charlotte to FBI Director, August 1, 1986; *United States District Court, Eastern District of North Carolina, United States of America v. Glenn Miller, Case Number 84-534-Civ-5,* July 25, 1986; Sharon Perkinson, "Witness Testifies Klan Leaders Purchased Illegal Weapons," United Press International, July 22, 1986, SPLC; United Press International, "Prosecution Says Klan's Bigotry, Hatred to Be Revealed," July 21, 1986, SPLC; Teletype memo, Charlotte to FBI Director, July 26, 1986, Attention Domestic Terrorism Unit; Accomplishment Report, SAC Charlotte to FBI Director; James H. Rubin, "Court Refuses to Hear Appeal of Former Carolina Klan Leader," Associated Press Wire Service, February 21, 1989, SPLC.

51. Miller, *A White Man Speaks Out*, ch. 13; Associated Press, "2 Men Are Guilty of Arms Training"; Mobile to FBI Director, Charlotte, and New Orleans, ca. September 11, 1986; Teletype memo, Charlotte to FBI Director and local offices, September 17, 1986; Department of Justice press release, January 8, 1987.

52. United States District Court, Eastern District of North Carolina, Raleigh Division, No. 84-534-CIV-5, August 28, 1986, *Bobby L. Person et al. v. Glenn Miller, Jr., et al.;* Teletype memo, Charlotte to FBI Director, Attention Criminal Investigative and Domestic Terrorism Divisions and Field Offices, October 16, 1986; Airtel memo, Richmond SAC to FBI Director, November 5, 1986; FBI clip, Associated Press, "White Patriot Party to Disband," *Raleigh News and Observer*, October 15, 1986, 1C; Teletype memo, FBI Richmond to FBI Director, April 28, 1987.

53. "Code of Conduct"; "A.C.L.U. Criticizes Pentagon 'Hate' Group Policy"; Hunt, "The New Look."

54. Tony Wydra was Jack Jackson's younger brother. Los Angeles Times Wire Service, "5 Klansmen Face Charges of Conspiring to Steal Arms," *Kansas City Times*, January 9, 1987, A6, RH WL Eph 2199; Department of Justice Press Release, January 8, 1987.

55. Associated Press, "U.S. Indicts Five in Arms-Theft Plot"; Airtel memo, SAC Charlotte to FBI Director, March 2, 1987; "Five Tied to Klan Indicted on Arms Charges," *New York Times*, January 9, 1987, D16; Associated Press, "Agents Capture White Supremacist," *Oregonian*, May 1, 1987, A19, RH WL Eph 2199.

56. Roland, "Reliability of Army Guards Doubted"; Halloran, "Pentagon Fights to Stop Loss"; Brinkley with Gerth, "Black Market Sales Rise."

57. SA [Redacted] to SAC Charlotte, October 10, 1986, FBI.

58. FBI clip, *KLANWATCH Intelligence Report*, December, 1986; Robert E. Miles, "Beyond the Bars . . . the Stars!," *From the Mountain* (Mountain Church, Cohoctah, MI), July–August 1985, A-F, Ms. 76.72, Box 72-1, HH 1637.

59. William E. Schmidt, "Soldiers Said to Attend Klan-Related Activities," *New York Times*, April 15, 1986, A14.

60. Miller, *A White Man Speaks Out*, ch. 14.

61. Elisa Hoagland, "Security Readied for Shelby III Trial," *Shelby Daily Star*, April 29, 1989, 1A, SPLC; Pat Reese, "Reporter Intermediary for Informant's Clues," *Fayetteville Observer*, ca. 1987, 1A, SPLC.

62. FBI Director to All Field Offices, April 24, 1987.

63. The figure of $888,000 was significant: in movement rhetoric, "88" signified "Heil Hitler" in alphabetic code. Teletype memo, Charlotte to FBI Director and branch offices, April 23, 1987.

64. Teletype memo, Richmond to FBI Director, April 28, 1987.

65. FBI Director to All Field Offices, April 24, 1987; Teletype memo, Richmond to FBI Director and branch offices, Charlotte and Baltimore, April 24, 1987.

66. Teletype memo, Richmond to FBI Director and branch offices, Charlotte and Baltimore, April 24, 1987; "Conviction of 2 Supremacists," *New York Times,* April 14, 1987, A19; Fax memo, U.S. Marshals Service to [Redacted], April 30, 1987; Airtel memo, SAC Charlotte to FBI Acting Director, September 3, 1987; Airtel memo, SAC Charlotte to FBI Director, March 2, 1987.

67. In a joke playing on the Order's point system, the FBI report concluded: "Kansas City to claim 17 bonus points for arrest of Aryan Warriors." SAC Kansas City to FBI Director, May 8, 1987; Teletype memo, Kansas City to FBI Director, April 30, 1987.

68. Airtel memo, SAC Kansas City to FBI Director, May 14, 1987; Airtel memo, SAC Kansas City to FBI Director, Attention Identification Division, May 7, 1987; Teletype memo, Kansas City to FBI Director, April 30, 1987; SAC Kansas City to FBI Director, May 8, 1987, re: U.S. Marshal Service; Inventory of Property Acquired as Evidence, May 5, 1987.

69. Airtel, Philadelphia SAC to FBI Acting Director, August 7, 1987; FBI internal memo, October 29, 1987; Teletype memo, Charlotte to FBI Director, May 22, 1987; Miller, *A White Man Speaks Out,* ch. 14.

70. United Press International, "Former KKK Leader Tells of Receiving Stolen Money," March 10, 1988, SPLC; Jane Ruffin, "Judge Cites 'Extent of Wrong You Have Committed' to Miller," *Raleigh Times,* January 5, 1988, SPLC.

7. Race War and White Women

1. Arraignment, *Miles et al.,* May 21, 1987, Testimonies-2.

2. Nicholas C. Chriss, "Witness Tells of Scheme to Topple U.S.," *Houston Chronicle,* February 23, 1988.

3. The purported defense of white women and children appears regularly in the historiography on vigilantism and lynching. See, for instance, Crystal N. Feimster, *Southern Horrors: Women and the Politics of Rape and Lynching* (Cambridge, MA: Harvard University Press, 2011); Jacqueline Dowd Hall, " 'The Mind That Burns in Each Body': Women, Rape and Racial Violence," in *Powers of Desire: The Politics of Sexuality,* ed. Ann Snitow, Christine Stansell, and Sharon Thompson (New York: Monthly Review Press, 1983), 328–349.

4. Rebecca Brown, pen drawing, December 26, 1985, RH WL Eph 2097, File 16.

5. Examples of studying white power organization through the lens of paramilitary masculinity include James William Gibson, *Warrior Dreams: Violence and Manhood in Post-Vietnam America* (New York: Hill and Wang, 1994); Raphael S. Ezekiel, *The Racist Mind: Portraits of American Neo-Nazis and Klansmen* (New York: Penguin, 1995).

6. Rickie Solinger, *Pregnancy and Power: A Short History of Reproductive Politics in America* (New York: New York University Press, 2007).

7. The policing of whiteness through pro-natalism and regulation of white women's sexual behavior characterizes settler colonialism and serves to link the United States with other sites of settler colonialism—and to distinguish this kind of emphasis on white female chastity from different notions employed in sites of extract colonialism. See, for instance, Patrick Wolfe, *Settler Colonialism and the Transformation of Anthropology* (London: Cassell, 1998); Margaret D. Jacobs, *White Mother to a Dark Race: Settler Colonialism, Maternalism, and the Removal of Indigenous Children in the American West and Australia, 1880–1940* (Omaha: University of Nebraska Press, 2011).

8. Peggy Pascoe, *What Comes Naturally: Miscegenation Law and the Making of Race in America* (Oxford: Oxford University Press, 2009); George M. Frederickson, *Racism: A Short History* (Princeton, NJ: Princeton University Press, 2002); Glenda E. Gilmore, "Murder, Memory, and the Flight of the Incubus," in David S. Cecelski and Timothy B. Tyson, ed., *Democracy Betrayed: The Wilmington Race Riot of 1898 and Its Legacy* (Chapel Hill: University of North Carolina Press, 1998).

9. Matthew D. Lassiter, *The Silent Majority: Suburban Politics in the Sunbelt South* (Princeton, NJ: Princeton University Press, 2006); Pascoe, *What Comes Naturally.*

10. White Aryan Resistance propaganda image, ca. 1988, LC, Series II, 2.1; "White Men Need White Women," Letter to the Editor, *Thunderbolt*, no. 204 (April 1976): 6, Ms. 76.7, Box 7-1X, HH 30; Aryan Women's League, *White Sisters,* no. 1 (Spring 1990), LC, Series II, 2.7; Dennis Mahon, "Make More Babies, Prepare to Survive," *White Sisters,* no. 5 (Winter 1991), LC, Series II, 2.7; Aryan Women's League, "Whites Are the Adults of the World," *White Sisters,* no. 1 (Spring 1990), LC, Series II, 2.7; "The Greatest Power on Earth Is an Idea Whose Time Has Come," American Nazi Party flier, LC, Series II, 4.26; *Confederate Leader* 86, no. 3 (May 1986), 85, no. 5 (July 1985), and 84, no. 9 (ca. 1984), RH WL H149; "Fight for White Rights!," *White Power: The Revolutionary Voice of National Socialism,* special introductory issue, 95 (1980), 1, 3, Ms. 76.26, Box 26-1, HH 356; "U.S. Cities Face Open Race War," *White Patriot* (Tuscumbia, AL), no. 57 (April 1983), 1, RH WL G571.

11. It is not possible to verify each reported crime, but several such stories are borrowed from mainstream headlines. These citations represent series and examples of regular features as described: *Thunderbolt,* regular feature, 1983–1985, RH WL G1380 and HH, Box 7-1, 7-1X, 7-2X; "Sick Pic of the Month," *National Vanguard,* no. 71 (August 1979): 2, RH WL G541; "Another Victim," *Racial Loyalty: It's Great to Be White!* (Church of the Creator), issues 54–76, 1991, Ms. 76.72, Box 72-2, HH 4471; "Casualty List," *White Power,* 1970s, SC, Box 50, Folder 2; Tom Metzger, White Aryan Resistance recorded phone message, San Jose, California, January 31, 1986, LC, Series VII, Box 1, Folder 1.

12. "Fight for White Rights!," *White Power,* 1980; "Mother and Child," *White Power,* no. 101 (ca. 1983), 3, Keith Stimely Collection, Special Collections, University of Oregon, Box 50, Folder 2.

13. Testimony of Denver Parmenter, vol. 1, *Miles et al.,* February 29, 1988, Testimonies-2; James Coates, *Armed and Dangerous: The Rise of the Survivalist Right* (New York: Noonday Press, 1987), 44.

14. Coates, *Armed and Dangerous,* 94. Craig may have thought Mathews planned to divorce his wife. Mathews and other advocates of polygamy had sustained contact with polygamist Mormon communities in Utah and southern Idaho who used similar strategies.

15. "Separatists Launch New Nation," *WAR* 5, no. 3 (1986), 1, RH WL H100.

16. Andrew Macdonald (pseud. for William Pierce), *The Turner Diaries* (Hillsboro, WV: National Vanguard Books, 1978), 147; "Proclamation: Carolina Free State," National Socialist Party of America, North Carolina Unit, ca. 1980, RH WL Q277; "Mid-America Survival Map," Christian Patriots Defense League, WL; James Ridgeway, *Blood in the Face,* 2nd ed. (New York: Thunder's Mouth Press, 1995), 168.

17. Robert E. Miles, "Five States Is All We Ask," *From the Mountain* (Mountain Church, Cohoctah, MI), March–April 1985, 7–8, Ms. 76.72, Box 72-1, HH 1637.

18. Ibid.

19. Testimony of Robert E. Miles, *Miles et al.,* March 29–30, 1988, Box 16-2.

20. RGB [Richard Girnt Butler], "Golden Cup and Yellow Ribbon," *Calling Our Nation* (Aryan Nations, Hayden Lake, ID), no. 64 (1991): 2–3, Ms. 76.26, Box 26-1, HH 34; Glenn Miller, *A White Man Speaks Out* (n.p.: Glenn Miller, 1999), ch. 17.

21. "Separatists Launch New Nation."

22. Kathleen M. Blee, *Inside Organized Racism: Women in the Hate Movement* (Berkeley: University of California Press, 2002), 51; Henry Nash Smith, *Virgin Land: The American West as Symbol and Myth,* new ed. (Cambridge, MA: Harvard University Press, 1970).

23. Kornel Chang, *Pacific Connections: The Making of the U.S.-Canadian Borderlands* (Berkeley: University of California Press, 2012); Mario Jimenez Sifuentez, *Of Forests and Fields: Mexican Labor in the Pacific Northwest* (New Brunswick, NJ: Rutgers University Press, 2016).

24. The presence of large numbers of white separatists in the area might well have meant that the actual white population was somewhat higher, if one included those who avoided the federal government's census. James Coates, "An Idaho Resort Town Grapples with Bigotry and Bombings," *Chicago Tribune,* October 5, 1986.

25. Jonathan Freedland, "Adolf's U.S. Army," *Guardian,* December 15, 1994, A6.

26. "Separatists Launch New Nation."

27. "Voices from World Congress," *WAR* 8, no. 2 (ca. 1986), LC; Bernie Wilson, "Aryans Plan NW Homeland," *Albany* (OR) *Democrat-Herald,* July 14, 1986, 10, RH WL Eph 2097.6.

28. Tobby Hatley, "Aryan Nations: North Idaho's Neo-Nazis," *Northwest* (*Oregonian* Sunday magazine), November 18, 1984, 7, RH WL Eph 2097.4.

29. Michelle M. Nickerson, *Mothers of Conservatism: Women and the Postwar Right* (Princeton, NJ: Princeton University Press, 2012). 34, 70; Lisa McGirr, *Suburban Warriors: The Origins of the New American Right* (Princeton, NJ: Princeton University Press, 2001). The idea of women as guardians of a new generation of American citizens—and therefore, the future of race and nation—drew on a long genealogy of gender identities with similar nationalist functions. Whigs called upon republican mothers in revolutionary America to raise moral and knowledgeable citizens, the better to run a righteous democracy. After the industrial revolution, the cult of true womanhood called for pure, moral, nurturing women to redeem society, leading to a maternalism movement at the turn of the century. Social Darwinists called upon women to produce the next generation of "vigorous heroes." When the Great Depression revealed maternalism's failure to deliver reform, housewife populism instead emphasized women's roles as community-builders and guardians of normalcy. Kristin L. Hoganson, *Fighting for American Manhood* (New Haven, CT: Yale University Press, 2000), 12; Nickerson, *Mothers of Conservatism,* xiv–xii, xxi, 31; Linda K. Kerber, *Women of the Republic: Intellect and Ideology in Revolutionary America* (Chapel Hill: University of North Carolina Press, 1980).

30. Nickerson, *Mothers of Conservatism,* xiv–xii, xxi, 31. See also Elaine Tyler May, *Homeward Bound: American Families in the Cold War Era* (New York: Basic Books, 1988).

31. Mandatory sterilization in the twentieth century was also directed at the "feebleminded," sexually promiscuous women, and the poor. Solinger, *Pregnancy and Power;* Nickerson, *Mothers of Conservatism;* Alexandra Minna Stern, *Eugenic Nation: Faults and Frontiers of Better Breeding in Modern America* (Berkeley: University of California Press, 2005).

32. Coates, *Armed and Dangerous,* 88.

33. David Lane, "Viking Princess," *WAR* 4, no. 5 (1985), 7, LC; *What Is Hate?* (St. Maries, ID: 14 Words Press), Ms. 76.72, Box 72-1, HH 4163; Bill Morlin, "Eight Skinheads and '14 Words,'" *Spokesman Review,* July 1, 2007, SPLC.

34. Macdonald, *The Turner Diaries,* 28–29.

35. Ibid., 45.

36. Ibid., 96.

37. Gibson, *Warrior Dreams.* See also Klaus Theweleit, *Male Fantasies* (Minneapolis: University of Minnesota Press, 1987) 1:1–228, on the white female body in German Freikorps literature after World War I.

38. See, for instance, "Stickers, $6.00 per 100," White Aryan Resistance (Fallbrook, CA), ca. July 1987, WL; Lane, "Viking Princess."

39. *Confederate Leader,* issue 85-5 (July 1985), RH WL H149; *Confederate Leader,* special edition (ca. 1986), RH WL H149; Miller, *A White Man Speaks Out,* ch. 4.

40. Testimony of Richard Girnt Butler, *Miles et al.*, March 29, 1988, Testimonies-2; Testimony of Robert E. Miles, *Miles et al.*, March 29–30, 1988, Box 16-2.

41. Testimony of Denver Parmenter, September 13, 1985, *Pierce et al.*, Box 4, at 229.

42. Miles, "Five States Is All We Ask," 10–13; Bill Morlin, "Racist Operation Moves to N.J.," *Spokesman Review*, date unclear (ca. 2001), B1, SPLC; Mattias Gardell, *Gods of the Blood: The Pagan Revival and White Separatism* (Durham, NC: Duke University Press, 2003), 204–221.

43. Kathleen M. Blee, *Women of the Klan: Racism and Gender in the 1920s* (Berkeley: University of California Press, 1991), 25. "Auxiliary" refers to a peripheral or smaller group with direct ties to major groups.

44. "Attention White Women: An Introduction to the Aryan Women's League," flier, Aryan Women's League of White Aryan Resistance (Fallbrook, CA), ca. 1989, Ms. 76.26, Box 26-1, HH 387.

45. In *Women of the Klan*, Blee argues that Klanswomen and members of affiliated groups in the 1920s also adopted similarly gendered actions. See also the following materials from the Aryan Women's League of White Aryan Resistance: "Attention White Women"; "Rape THIS!" (flier), ca. 1989; Untitled flier, ca. 1989; "Greetings Fellow Aryan Warriors!," letter to members, December 1990; "Fight Fire with Fire!," flier, Aryan Women's League Penney [*sic*] Pinchers, March 1991; all from Ms. 76.26, Box 26-1, HH 387.

46. See, for instance, June Johnston, "Preventative Medicine for a Morally Handicapped Society," *Christian Patriot Women* 4, no. 14 (July–September 1990): 11, Ms. 76.45, Box 1, HH 1261.

47. Birth announcement, September 29, 1990, Aryan Women's League of White Aryan Resistance, Ms. 76.26, Box 26-1, HH 387; Letter, Aryan Women's League to Aryan Warriors, Aryan Women's League of White Aryan Resistance (Fallbrook, CA), 1990, Ms. 76.26, Box 26-1, HH 387.

48. Blee, *Inside Organized Racism*, 134–135.

49. See, for instance, June Johnston, *Christian Patriot Women* 111, no. 9 (April–June 1989), Ms. 76.45, Box 45-1, HH 1261.

50. Testimony of Michelle Pardee, *Miles et al.*, March 14 and 16, 1988, Testimonies-1.

51. *Christian Patriot Women*, 1989–1990, Box 45-1, HH 1261; see also M. K. Hallimore, "God's Answer to Women's Lib," *The Woman's Bible*, Kingdom Identity Ministries (Harrison, AR) 1983, Ms. 76.10, HH Box 7-10.

52. June Johnston, "Woman to Woman," *Christian Patriot Women* 111, no. 10 (October–December 1989): 3; June Johnston, untitled, *Christian Patriot Women* 111, no. 9 (April–June 1989), 111, no. 10 (September 1989), 111, no. 11 (October–December 1989); June Johnston, "From the Mouths of Little Aryans," *Christian Patriot Women* 4, no. 14 (July–September 1990): 8; Johnston, "Preventative Medicine for a Morally Handicapped Society."

53. "White Power Forever: What About White Civil Rights?," SS Action Group (Dearborn, MI), 1991, Ms. 76.26, Box 26-2, HH 1660.

54. Clark Martell, "Introducing Jessica," *Right as Reina,* August 1996, Ms. 76.72, Box 72-2, HH 4470.

55. *Right as Reina,* March 1997, December 1996, January 1997, February 1997; Ms. 76.72, Box 72-2, HH 4470.

56. Leonard Zeskind, *Blood and Politics: The History of the White Nationalist Movement from the Margins to the Mainstream* (New York: Farrar, Straus and Giroux, 2009), 145; GTRC, *Greensboro Truth and Reconciliation Commission Final Report* (Greensboro, NC: Greensboro Truth and Reconciliation Commission, 2006).

57. *Donald v. United Klans of America,* case docket, SPLC, http://www.splcenter .org/get-informed/case-docket/donald-v-united-klans-of-america.

58. James Coates and Stephen Franklin, " 'Underground' of Racist Leaders Co-ordinated Crimes, FBI Taps Show," *Chicago Tribune,* December 28, 1987, A16, SPLC.

59. SA [Redacted] to FBI SAC Charlotte, October 16, 1986; Zeskind, *Blood and Politics,* 146.

60. Zeskind, *Blood and Politics,* 146.

61. Andy Hall, "Secret War: 'Patriots' Have Loose Ties to Rightists Nationwide," *Arizona Republic,* December 21, 1986, WL; John Kifner, "Oklahoma Bombing Suspect: Unraveling of a Frayed Life," *New York Times,* December 21, 1995, 1.

62. Bill Minutaglio, "Biography of a Hatemonger," *Dallas Morning News,* May 22, 1988, LC, 9.20.

63. *Miles et al.;* Coates and Franklin, " 'Underground' of Racist Leaders Coordinated Crimes"; Kevin Flynn and Gary Gerhardt, *The Silent Brotherhood: Inside America's Racist Underground* (New York: Free Press, 1989), 32–34.

64. Coates and Franklin, " 'Underground' of Racist Leaders Coordinated Crimes"; *Miles et al.;* Macdonald, *The Turner Diaries;* Affidavit, Farris L. Genide, Special Agent, FBI, U.S. District Court Eastern District of Michigan Southern Division, No. 86-0343, 80, LC.

65. "Arkansas Jury Finds 13 Not Guilty in U.S. Trial of White Supremacists," *Kansas City Times,* April 8, 1988, A1, RH WL. Eph 2097.7; Partial Transcript of Detention Hearing before the Honorable Ned A. Stewart Jr., United States Magistrate Judge, William H. Wade and Ivan Wade, *Miles et al.,* May 1, 1987, Testimonies-1. Associated Press, "13 Supremacists Are Not Guilty Of Conspiracies," *New York Times,* April 8, 1988.

66. *Miles et al.;* Affidavit, Farris L. Genide; Coates and Franklin, " 'Underground' of Racist Leaders Coordinated Crimes."

67. Minutaglio, "Biography of a Hatemonger."

68. Ancestry.com, *Texas, Divorce Index, 1968–2011;* Ancestry.com, *Texas, Marriage Collection, 1814–1909 and 1966–2011;* Ancestry.com, *Texas Birth Index, 1903–1997;* Minutaglio, "Biography of a Hatemonger"; Nicholas C. Chriss, "Beam Talked

of Rebellion, FBI Says," *Houston Chronicle,* February 22, 1988, LC; Scott Sunde, "Ex-KKK Leader Running Scared from FBI," *Times-Herald,* July 27, 1987, A1, LC, Series XIII, 5.12; District Court, First Judicial District of Idaho, Case No. CV 01-3900, August 8, 2001, Affidavit of Sheila M. Toohey, SPLC.

69. Minutaglio, "Biography of a Hatemonger"; Memo from Nick Chriss, *Houston Chronicle,* to SPLC, Subject: Louis Beam, November 20, 1987, SPLC; J. B. Campbell, "Louis & Sheila," published on Louis Beam's website, http://louisbeam.com /louis&s1.htm, originally published in *Jubilee,* May–June 1994.

70. Testimony of Louis Beam, *Miles et al.,* November 17, 1988, Box 16-2; Associated Press, "Former Houston Area KKK Leader on Most-Wanted List," July 14, 1987; Campbell, "Louis & Sheila"; Campbell, "The Military Solution," *J. B. Campbell Extremism Online,* September 10, 2011, http://www.jbcampbellextremismonline .com; Evelyn Schlatter, "Buyer Beware: Veterans Today and Its Anti-Israel Agenda," January 6, 2011, SPLC.

71. Campbell, "Louis & Sheila."

72. "Two Hurt in Accident," *Galveston Daily News,* September 21, 1984; Ancestry .com, *Texas Birth Index, 1903–1997;* Ancestry.com, *Texas, Divorce Index, 1968–2011;* Ancestry.com, *Texas, Marriage Collection, 1814–1909 and 1966–2011.*

73. Testimony of Louis Ray Beam Jr., *Miles et al.,* November 17, 1988, Box 16, vol. 2.

74. "414: Louis Ray Beam, Jr.," *Ten Most Wanted,* FBI, 1987; Minutaglio, "Biography of a Hatemonger"; Arlene Battista, "Mexico Reportedly Duped in Beam Case," *Galveston Daily News,* November 21, 1987.

75. "Libre, extranjera que hirió de dos balazos a un agente," *El Informador,* November 15, 1987, 10; Suppression hearing, testimony of Steven Walker and Stuart Hoyt, *Miles et al.,* February 8, 1988, Testimonies-1.

76. Suppression hearing, testimony of Steven Walker and Stuart Hoyt, *Miles et al.,* February 8, 1988, Testimonies-1.

77. This rumor may have referred to an exception in the most recent extradition treaty between Mexico and the United States that excluded offenses "of a political character," which the Fort Smith defendants certainly claimed. "Extradition Treaty between the United States and Mexico," Mexico City, May 4, 1978, https://www.oas .org/juridico/mla/en/traites/en_traites-ext-usa-mex.pdf.

78. Campbell, "Louis & Sheila"; "Libre, extranjera que hirió de dos balazos a un agente"; Shepard Barbash, "Beam's Wife: 'They Want Me to Rot in Jail,'" *Houston Chronicle,* November 18, 1987, SPLC; Rebecca Trounson, "Wife Calls Beam Misunderstood," *Houston Chronicle,* February 16, 1988, sec. 1, 10, SPLC; "Increased Militancy of Supremacists Predicted," *Kansas City Times,* date and page unclear, ca. April 1988, RH WL Eph 2097.7; Affidavit of Sheila Beam, State of Texas, County of Harris, December 18, 1987, LC; Grumke, "Interview with Tom Metzger on Sept. 4, 1997 in Fallbrook, CA," 23, LC.

79. On the close linkage of weapons and penises in warfare, cadences, and attendant rhetoric, see, for instance, Christian G. Appy, *Working-Class War: American Combat Soldiers and Vietnam* (Chapel Hill: University of North Carolina Press, 1993); Joanna Bourke, *An Intimate History of Killing: Face-to-Face Killing in Twentieth Century Warfare* (New York: Basic Books, 1999).

80. Holloway is occasionally spelled Hollaway in the archive. Grumke, "Interview with Tom Metzger"; Tony Taylor, "An Unreconstructed Southerner," *High Point Enterprise*, April 23, 2000, 2F, SPLC; Arlene Battista, "Beam's Wife Is Expected Home from LA Today," *Galveston Daily News*, November 18, 1987, Campbell, "Louis & Sheila."

81. Taylor, "An Unreconstructed Southerner."

82. Battista, "Mexico Reportedly Duped in Beam Case"; Arlene Battista, "Mrs. Beam Says Her Husband Isn't a Racist," *Galveston Daily News*, December 30, 1987; Battista, "Beam's Wife Is Expected Home from LA Today."

83. Bill Simons, "Jury Deliberating Sedition Case," *Item* (Sumter, SC), April 5 1988, 10B.

84. Associated Press, "Beam's Wife Arrives to Tearful Reunion," *Galveston Daily News*, November 20, 1987.

85. John Williams, "Beam's wife Returns to Houston for Emotional Reunion with Family," *Houston Chronicle*, November 20, 1987, sec. 1, 22; "Libre, extranjera que hirió de dos balazos a un agente."

86. Danny Johnston, Associated Press, Photograph of Sheila Beam, *Miami News*, November 20, 1987.

87. This surgery is not mentioned in other accounts and may be a narrative device. Campbell, "Louis & Sheila."

88. Testimony of Frazier Glenn Miller, *Miles et al.*, March 10–11, 1988, Box 16-2; Suppression hearing, testimony of Steven Walker and Stuart Hoyt, *Miles et al.*, February 8, 1988, Testimonies-1; Nicholas Chriss, "CDR Notes on Trial," Arkansas sedition trial, February 16, 1988, notes on *Miles et al.*, LC, Box 13, Folder 9; Trounson, "Wife Calls Beam Misunderstood"; Battista, "Mrs. Beam Says Her Husband Isn't a Racist."

89. Ezekiel, *The Racist Mind*, 33.

90. On women's work neutralizing white power's violence and racist messages, see also Blee, *Inside Organized Racism*.

91. Ezekiel, *The Racist Mind*, 35.

92. Ibid.

93. Trounson, "Wife Calls Beam Misunderstood."

94. Zeskind, *Blood and Politics*, 154, 158; Nicholas C. Chriss, "Juror Says He Admires Beam's Racist Views," *Houston Chronicle*, April 26, 1988, 1, LC; Nicholas C. Chriss, "Jury Acquits Beam, Other Supremacists," *Houston Chronicle*, April 8, 1988, 1, LC; Nicholas C. Chriss, "Sedition Trial Acquittals Ignite Outcry over Jurors,"

Houston Chronicle, October 1988, 3B, LC. On local coverage of the CSA bust, see, for instance, "Police Surround Survivalists," *Northwest Arkansas Times,* April 20, 1985, 1; "Police, Supremacists Hold in a Standoff," *Courier-News* (Blytheville, AR), April 20, 1985, 1. On the belief that the Bible prohibited race-mixing, see Jane Dailey, "Sex, Segregation, and the Sacred after *Brown*," *Journal of American History* 91, no. 119 (2004): 119–144.

95. Zeskind, *Blood and Politics,* 159, 164; Subpoena for Documents, to FBI, filed by U.S. Attorney Helen Milburn Eversberg, March 3, 1985, SPLC.

96. "Increased Militancy of Supremacists Predicted."

97. James Coates, "Plot to Poison Water Is Detailed," *Chicago Tribune,* February 28, 1988, sec. 1, 5, SPLC; "Leader Says White Supremacists Considered Poisoning Major City," *Albany* (OR) *Democrat-Herald,* February 23, 1988, 7, RH WL Eph 1896.

98. Chriss, "Witness Tells of Scheme to Topple U.S."; Exhibit List, *Miles et al.,* Box 16-2; Zeskind, *Blood and Politics,* 61–63.

99. Testimony of Denver Parmenter, vols. 1–3, *Miles et al.,* February 29, 1988, Testimonies-2; "Increased Militancy of Supremacists Predicted"; Chriss, "Witness Tells of Scheme to Topple U.S."; David Mathiason, "Trial Bares Neo-Nazis' Plots and Links," *Guardian,* October 16, 1985, 6; LC; Chriss, "Sedition Trial Acquittals Ignite Outcry over Jurors"; Coates, "Plot to Poison Water Is Detailed"; "Jury Told of Plan to Kill Radio Host," *New York Times,* November 8, 1987, 31; "White Supremacy Groups Laid Plans to Assassinate Kissinger, Ex-Member Says," *Los Angeles Times,* September 14, 1985, 19.

100. Moutoux is occasionally spelled Moteaux in the archive. Affidavit, Farris L. Genide.

101. Coates, *Armed and Dangerous,* 94; Intelligence Project Database, SPLC; Bill Morlin, "One Lead in Bombing Ends in North Idaho," *Spokesman-Review,* May 2, 1995, A1, SPLC; Michael Whiteley, "McVeigh Tried to Call Colony Aide," *Democrat-Gazette,* ca. January 26, 1996, 1B, SPLC; Flynn and Gerhardt, *Silent Brotherhood,* 68, 142–144; L. J. Davis, "Ballad of an American Terrorist: A Neo-Nazi's Dream of Order," *Harper's Magazine,* July 1986, 53, LC, 8.14; Gary Gerhardt, John Accola, and Kevin Flynn, "Informants Name 2 Berg Suspects," *Rocky Mountain News,* February 10, 1985, 6, WHC; Opening Statement of Bob Ward, September 12, 1985, *Pierce et al.,* Box 3, at 51; Testimony of Louis Beam, *Miles et al.,* November 17, 1988, Box 16, Folder 2; Testimony of Jed Martin Bridley, December 2 1985, *Pierce et al.,* Box 6, at 9935–9945.

102. Neill is also spelled Neal in the archive. Ancestry.com, *Texas, Divorce Index, 1968–2011;* Ancestry.com, *Texas, Marriage Collection, 1814–1909 and 1966–2011;* Michael Whiteley, "McVeigh-Separatists Link Rumored but Not Proved," *Arkansas Democrat-Gazette,* February 26, 2003, 1, SPLC, Oklahoma City

File; Drew Jubera, "Confederacy Group Vote Sidesteps Controversy," *Atlanta Journal-Constitution,* August 2, 2002, 3A, SPLC; Taylor, "An Unreconstructed Southerner"; Paul Shukovsky, "Ex-Guardsman Charged with Espionage," *Seattle Post-Intelligencer,* February 6, 2003, A1, SPLC; Andrew Gumbel and Roger G. Charles, *Oklahoma City: What the Investigation Missed—and Why It Still Matters* (New York: William Morrow, 2012); Charles Duell's opening statement representing David Michael McGuire, Chriss, "CDR Notes on Trial"; Chriss, "Sedition Trial Acquittals Ignite Outcry over Jurors"; "Dr. Neill H. Payne," Southern Legal Resource Center, https://slrc-csa.org/about-us/board-of-directors/neill-h-payne; Testimony of James Ellison and Kerry Noble, *Miles et al.,* February 23, 24, 25, 1987 [*sic*], Testimonies-1.

103. Chriss, "Sedition Trial Acquittals Ignite Outcry over Jurors"; Gumbel and Charles, *Oklahoma City,* 261.

104. Testimony of Louis Ray Beam, Jr., *Miles et al.,* November 17, 1988, Box 16, Folder 2. Other defendants also used the same strategy to establish their defense of white women and / or their patriotic war service. See, for instance, Testimony of Michelle Pardee questioned by Richard Scutari, *Miles et al.,* March 14 and 16, 1988, Testimonies-1; Testimony of Julie Woods questioned by Bruce Pierce, *Miles et al.,* March 17, 1988, Testimonies-1.

105. Chriss, "CDR Notes on Trial"; Testimony of Louis Ray Beam, Jr., *Miles et al.,* November 17, 1988, Box 16, Folder 2.

106. Testimony of Louis Ray Beam, Jr., *Miles et al.,* November 17, 1988, Box 16, Folder 2.

107. "Arkansas Jury Finds 13 Not Guilty"; Order of Hon. Morris S. Arnold, *Miles et al.,* July 15, 1988, Box 16-2.

108. Chriss, "Jury Acquits Beam, Other Supremacists."

109. Minutaglio, "Biography of a Hatemonger."

110. Chriss, "Jury Acquits Beam, Other Supremacists"; Associated Press photo, "Jubilant Racists Win Trial," *Kansas City Times,* April 8, 1988, RH WL P3497; Zeskind, *Blood and Politics,* 168.

111. Minutaglio, "Biography of a Hatemonger"; Campbell, "Louis & Sheila."

112. "Arkansas Jury Finds 13 Not Guilty."

113. Whiteley, "McVeigh-Separatists Link Rumored but Not Proved"; *Democrat-Gazette,* February 26, 2003, 1, SPLC, Oklahoma City File; Louis Beam, untitled introductory note, *Seditionist,* issue 1 (1988), LC, Series II, 2.22; Louis R. Beam Jr., *Essays of a Klansman,* 2nd ed. (Hayden Lake, ID: A.K.I.A. Publications, 1989).

114. Louis R. Beam, "Leaderless Resistance," *Seditionist,* issue 12 (February 1992), Intelligence Project holdings, SPLC; Louis Beam, Estes Park Speech, October 23, 1992, video recording, SPLC.

115. Martin Walker, "Guns and the Godly," *Guardian,* April 21, 1993, A2.

8. Ruby Ridge, Waco, and Militarized Policing

1. I draw the idea of cultural imaginary from Alicia Schmidt Camacho, *Migrant Imaginaries: Latino Cultural Politics in the U.S.-Mexico Borderlands* (New York: New York University Press, 2008).

2. On the evangelical right, see, for instance, Robert O. Self, *All in the Family: The Realignment of American Democracy since the 1960s* (New York: Hill and Wang, 2013); Neil J. Young, *We Gather Together: The Religious Right and the Problem of Interfaith Politics* (Oxford: Oxford University Press, 2015). On apocalyptic thought in the 1990s, see, for instance, Joseph Masco, *Theater of Operations: National Security Affect from the Cold War to the War on Terror* (Durham, NC: Duke University Press, 2014); Michael Barkun, *A Culture of Conspiracy: Apocalyptic Visions in Contemporary America* (Berkeley: University of California Press, 2013).

3. See, for instance, Barkun, *A Culture of Conspiracy.*

4. On intertwined modes of apocalypse, see Junot Díaz, "Apocalypse: What Disasters Reveal," *Boston Review,* May 1, 2011.

5. Associated Press, "Fugitive's Friend Gives Up in Idaho," *New York Times,* August 31, 1992; Reuters, "Negotiator Arouses Hope in Idaho Standoff," *New York Times,* August 30, 1992; Associated Press, "Law Officers Encircle Cabin of Fugitive," *Washington Post,* August 23, "1 Marshal Dead, Others Confront Fugitive in Idaho," *New York Times,* August 23, 1992; Associated Press, "Body of Fugitive's Son Is Found near Idaho Cabin," *New York Times,* August 25, 1992.

6. Sam Howe Verhovek, "4 Federal Agents Are Killed in Shootout with a Cult: A Messianic Sect with a Cache of Weapons and a Lookout Tower," *New York Times,* March 1, 1993; Don Terry, "Authorities Plan to Wait for End of Cult Standoff," *New York Times,* March 4, 1993; Simon Tisdall and Martin Walker, "Funeral Pyre at Waco: Two Britons among Cult's Survivors," *Guardian,* April 20, 1993; Joe Davidson and Christi Harlan, "As Waco Crisis Ends, Clinton's Leadership Comes under Scrutiny," *Wall Street Journal,* April 20, 1993; "Four Agents Killed, 14 Injured in Shootout at Cult Compound," *Atlanta Daily World,* March 2, 1993; Don Terry, "Standoff in Texas Goes On after Cult Chief's Broadcast," *New York Times,* March 3, 1993; Peter Applebome, "Cult's Leader Raises Specter of Fight to Finish, U.S. Says," *New York Times,* March 9, 1993; Howard Schneider, "Tibetan Chants Are Latest Waco Weapon," *Washington Post,* March 23, 1993.

7. Kimberley L. Phillips, *War! What Is It Good For: Black Freedom Struggles and the U.S. Military from World War II to Iraq* (Chapel Hill: University of North Carolina Press, 2012), 12–13, 280–281.

8. Peter B. Kraska and Victor E. Kappeler, "Militarizing American Police: The Rise and Normalization of Paramilitary Units," *Social Problems* 44, no. 1 (February 1997).

9. Ibid.

10. Ibid.; Timothy Egan, "Soldiers of the Drug War Remain on Duty," *New York Times*, March 1, 1999; Phillips, *War! What Is It Good For*, 280.

11. Phillips, *War! What Is It Good For*, 280; Dan Berger, "Social Movements and Mass Incarceration," *Souls: A Critical Journal of Black Politics, Culture, and Society* 15 (2013): 1–18; Heather Ann Thompson, "Why Mass Incarceration Matters: Rethinking Crisis, Decline, and Transformation in Postwar American History," *Journal of American History*, December 2010; Ruth Wilson Gilmore, *Golden Gulag: Prisons, Surplus, Crisis, and Opposition in Globalizing California* (Berkeley: University of California Press, 2007); Michelle Alexander, *The New Jim Crow: Mass Incarceration in the Age of Colorblindness* (New York: New Press, 2010); Clyde Haberman, "The Rise of the SWAT Team in American Policing," *New York Times*, September 7, 2014.

12. Accounts that have described the paramilitary white power movement and the militia movement of the early 1990s as disconnected include Robert H. Churchill, *To Shake Their Guns in the Tyrant's Face: Libertarian Violence and the Origins of the Militia Movement* (Ann Arbor: University of Michigan Press, 2011); Catherine McNichol Stock, *Rural Radicals: Righteous Rage in the American Grain* (Ithaca, NY: Cornell University Press, 1996); Evelyn A. Schlatter, *Aryan Cowboys: White Supremacy and the Search for a New Frontier, 1970–2000* (Austin: University of Texas Press, 2006); Stuart A. Wright, *Patriots, Politics, and the Oklahoma City Bombing* (Cambridge: Cambridge University Press, 2007). Journalistic accounts replicated this idea: see, for instance, Sam Walker, "'Militias' Forming across US to Protest Gun Control Laws," *Christian Science Monitor*, October 17, 1994, 1; Keith Schneider, "Fearing a Conspiracy, Some Heed a Call to Arms," *New York Times*, November 14, 1994, A1.

13. Kathleen M. Blee, *Inside Organized Racism: Women in the Hate Movement* (Berkeley: University of California Press, 2002), 18.

14. Jonathan Freedland, "Adolf's U.S. Army," *Guardian*, December 15, 1994, A6; Leonard Zeskind, *Blood and Politics: The History of the White Nationalist Movement from the Margins to the Mainstream* (New York: Farrar, Straus and Giroux, 2009), 361.

15. Jim Nesbitt, "Network of the Extreme Right Sees a War with Government," *Star-Ledger*, April 22, 1995, 1, SPLC. On connections between supposedly distinct eras of Klan organization, see David Cunningham, *Klansville, U.S.A.: The Rise and Fall of the Civil Rights-Era Ku Klux Klan* (Oxford: Oxford University Press, 2012).

16. Schneider, "Fearing a Conspiracy."

17. *Saturday Night Live*, Season 6, Episode 108, November 22, 1980; Associated Press, "Videotapes of Klan Leader Shown at Shrimper Hearing," *New York Times*, May 13, 1981; Tom Metzger, "Race and Reason," video recording, SPLC; *Sally Jessy Raphael Show*, appearances by Don Black and Glenn Miller, video recording, SPLC.

18. Philip Weiss, "Off the Grid," *New York Times Magazine*, January 8, 1995, Section 6, 44, LC, 18.3.

19. Michael Whiteley, "McVeigh-Separatists Link Rumored but Not Proved," *Arkansas Democrat-Gazette,* February 26, 2003, 1, SPLC.

20. Louis Beam, "Leaderless Resistance," *Inter-Klan Newsletter,* ca. 1983, LC, 183.31.6.

21. Barkun, *A Culture of Conspiracy,* 81; George H. W. Bush, "Address before a Joint Session of the Congress on the State of the Union," January 29, 1991, *American Presidency Project,* http://www.presidency.ucsb.edu/ws/?pid=19253; Somer Shook, Wesley Delano, and Robert W. Balch, "Elohim City: A Participant-Observer Study of a Christian Identity Community," *Nova Religo: The Journal of Alternate and Emergent Religions* 2, no. 2 (April 1999): 245–265.

22. See, for instance, Louis Beam, "For Whom the Bell Tolls," *Jubilee* 7, no. 6 (May–June 1995): 14–15, Ms. 76.10, Box 10-6, HH 4358.

23. Barkun, *A Culture of Conspiracy,* 70–79; Timothy Egan, "Inside the World of the Paranoid," *New York Times,* April 30, 1995; Freedland, "Adolf's U.S. Army"; RGB [Richard Girnt Butler], "Golden Cup and Yellow Ribbon," *Calling Our Nation* (Aryan Nations, Hayden Lake, ID), issue 65, 1991, 2–3, Ms. 76.26, Box 26-1, HH 34. On concentration camps and black helicopters for McVeigh: Lou Michel and Dan Herbeck, *American Terrorist: Timothy McVeigh and the Oklahoma City Bombing* (New York: Avon, 2002), 128. For John Trochmann and Militia of Montana: Freedland, "Adolf's U.S. Army." At Elohim City: Gustav Niebuhr, "A Vision of an Apocalypse: The Religion of the Far Right," *New York Times,* May 22, 1985, A8.

24. George H. W. Bush, "Address to the Nation Announcing Allied Military Action in the Persian Gulf," January 16, 1991, http://www.presidency.ucsb.edu/ws/?pid =19222.

25. Tom Engelhardt, *The End of Victory Culture: Cold War America and the Disillusioning of a Generation* (Amherst: University of Massachusetts Press, 2007), 274; RGB, "Golden Cup and Yellow Ribbon"; *Brassey's Book of Camouflage* (London: Brassey's, 1996).

26. Blee, *Inside Organized Racism.*

27. Zeskind, *Blood and Politics,* 170.

28. Freedland, "Adolf's U.S. Army"; Blee, *Inside Organized Racism,* 76–78; Zeskind, *Blood and Politics,* 297–298.

29. Betty A. Dobratz and Stephanie L. Shanks-Meile, *The White Separatist Movement in the United States: "White Power, White Pride!"* (New York: Twayne, 1997), 25. This membership estimate was thought to include 14,250–15,500 "Christian Patriots, Identity, and others," 5,500–6,500 Klansmen, and 3,500–4,750 Skinheads and neo-Nazis.

30. Timothy Egan, "U.S. Case Looks Weaker in Idaho Siege," *New York Times,* June 23, 1993, A14; Philip Weiss, "A Warm Morning Late in October . . . ," *New York Times Magazine,* January 8, 1995, SM26; Timothy Egan, "White Supremacist Sur-

renders after 11-Day Siege," *New York Times,* September 1, 1992, B6; Zeskind, *Blood and Politics,* 301–302; "Fugitive's Wife Killed in Shootout at Mountain Cabin, Officials Say," *New York Times,* August 29, 1992, 10; Timothy Egan, "Fugitive in Idaho Cabin Plays Role of Folk Hero," *New York Times,* August 26, 1992, A14; Chris Temple, "Big Victory! A Resounding Blow for Liberty," *Jubilee,* special edition no. 2, July 1993, 1, Ms. 76.10, Box 10-6, HH 4358.

31. Demography from the 1990 U.S. Census. Egan, "Fugitive in Idaho Cabin Plays Role of Folk Hero"; "1 Marshal Dead, Others Confront Fugitive in Idaho," *New York Times,* August 23, 1992, 20.

32. Some have reported that the Weavers never officially joined Aryan Nations, but such membership was often secret. Zeskind, *Blood and Politics,* 301–302; Weiss, "A Warm Morning."

33. Weiss, "A Warm Morning"; Dobratz and Shanks-Miele, *The White Separatist Movement in the United States,* 201; Kenneth S. Stern, *A Force upon the Plain: The American Militia Movement and the Politics of Hate* (Norman: University of Oklahoma Press, 1997), 26.

34. "Marshals Know He's There but Leave Fugitive Alone," *New York Times,* March 13, 1992, A14; Associated Press, "U.S. Marshal Killed in Idaho Standoff," *Washington Post,* August 22, 1992, A6.

35. Egan, "U.S. Case Looks Weaker in Idaho Siege"; Associated Press, "Body of Fugitive's Son Is Found Near Idaho Cabin"; "Federal Marshal Is Slain in Idaho Near Mountain Home of Fugitive," *New York Times,* August 22, 1992, 9; "1 Marshal Dead, Others Confront Fugitive in Idaho"; Temple, "Big Victory!"

36. "1 Marshal Dead, Others Confront Fugitive in Idaho"; Associated Press, "Law Officers Encircle Cabin of Fugitive"; Associated Press, "Rain and Reinforcements Help Idaho Firefighters"; Associated Press, "Body of Fugitive's Son Is Found Near Idaho Cabin."

37. John E. Young, "Idaho Siege Ends as Fugitive Gives Up in Killing of Marshal," *Washington Post,* September 1, 1992, A3.

38. Susan Drumheller, "Supremacists' Wives Recall Another Deadly Standoff," *Spokesman-Review,* August 31, 1992, A1, SPLC; Egan, "Fugitive in Idaho Cabin Plays Role of Folk Hero"; *Spokesman-Review* (Spokane, WA), File Photographs of Ruby Ridge Roadblock, 1992, http://www.spokesman.com/picture-stories/20-years-ago-ruby-ridge-standoff.

39. D. W. Griffith, *Birth of a Nation* (1915); Drumheller, "Supremacists' Wives Recall Another Deadly Standoff"; *Spokesman-Review,* File Photographs of Ruby Ridge Roadblock.

40. Egan, "Fugitive in Idaho Cabin Plays Role of Folk Hero"; *Spokesman-Review,* File Photographs of Ruby Ridge Roadblock.

41. "Fugitive's Wife Killed in Shootout at Mountain Cabin"; Weiss, "A Warm Morning."

42. "Gritz" rhymes with "rights." Zeskind, *Blood and Politics,* 295; America First Coalition / Bo Gritz National Presidential Campaign Committee, "Bo Gritz for President," flier, 1992, 1, RH WL Eph 2489; "You Can Count on My Continued Support Bo!," Bo Gritz National Presidential Campaign Committee, 1992, RH WL Eph 2489; Weiss, "Off the Grid"; Paul Hall, "Gritz Marches On—Against All Odds," *Jubilee* 3, no. 2 (July–August 1990): 1, 17, Ms. 76.10, Box 10-6, HH 4358; Egan, "White Supremacist Surrenders after 11-Day Siege"; *The New York Times,* September 1, 1992, B6; Reuters, "Negotiator Arouses Hope in Idaho Standoff"; Associated Press, "Fugitive's Friend Gives Up in Idaho"; Timothy Egan, "New Idaho Community Raises Neighbor's Fears," *New York Times,* October 5, 1994, A18.

43. "Ex-Idaho Fugitive Is Indicted in Death of Deputy Marshal," *New York Times,* September 17, 1992, A22; "FBI Staged Photos of Scene of Shootout with Extremists," *Washington Post,* May 28, 1993, A4; Egan, "U.S. Case Looks Weaker in Idaho Siege."

44. "Another Federal Fiasco," editorial, *New York Times,* July 12, 1993, A16.

45. "18 Months in Jail for Supremacist," *New York Times,* October 19, 1993, A25; Jonathan Freedland, "FBI 'Paid $3M Blood Money' after Shootout," *Guardian,* August 17, 1995, 11.

46. Brad Knickerbocker, "Why 1992 Idaho Shooting Has Become a Rallying Point," *Christian Science Monitor,* September 5, 1995, 1.

47. Zeskind, *Blood and Politics,* 309–313. Beam's wording in Sandpoint appeared again in Beam, Estes Park Speech.

48. Kevin Flynn and Gary Gerhardt, *The Silent Brotherhood: Inside America's Racist Underground* (New York: Free Press, 1989), 144; Hall, "Gritz Marches On—Against All Odds"; Mab Segrest, *Memoir of a Race Traitor* (Boston: South End Press, 1999); Louis Kilzer, "Order Member Recounts Meetings of Berg Suspects," *Denver Post,* March 8, 1985, 8A, WHC; "Scriptures for America Radio Log," *Jubilee,* ca. 1992–1995, Ms. 76.10, Box 10-6, HH 4358.

49. Pete Peters, *The Bible: Handbook for Survivalists, Racists, Tax Protestors, Militants and Right-Wing Extremists* (LaPorte, CO: Scriptures for America, ca. 1992–1995), Ms. 76.10, Box 10-9, HH 818.

50. *Special Report on the Meeting of Christian Men Held in Estes Park, Colorado, October 23, 24, 25, 1992, Concerning the Killing of Vickie* [sic] *and Samuel Weaver by the United States Government* (LaPorte, CO: Scriptures for America Ministries, ca. December 1, 1992), 26–27, SPLC; Max Baker, "Texas' New Right," *Fort Worth Star-Telegram,* March 18, 1990, page unclear, SPLC; Zeskind, *Blood and Politics,* 310–316.

51. Addendum chart, "Estes Park Scenario," Southern Poverty Law Center, attached to *Special Report on the Meeting of Christian Men Held in Estes Park, Colorado, October 23, 24, 25, 1992,* SPLC.

52. Paul Hall, "Historic Weaver Summit Held in Colorado," *Jubilee* 5, no. 3 (November–December 1992): 1, 12, Ms. 76.10, Box 10-6, HH 4358.

53. Fax from Bill Morlin, News, *Spokane Spokesman-Review* to Mark Potok, Southern Poverty Law Center, "In Re: The 1992 Rocky, Beam Select Quotes," March 29, 2002, SPLC; Dunn, King & Associates, Original Transcription, "In Re; The 1992 Rocky Mountain Rendezvous, Speaker: Louis Beam," SPLC; Beam, Estes Park Speech. On POW/MIA activism, see Michael J. Allen, *Until the Last Man Comes Home: POWs, MIAs, and the Unending Vietnam War* (Chapel Hill: University of North Carolina Press, 2012).

54. Fax from Bill Morlin, "In Re: The 1992 Rocky, Beam Select Quotes"; Dunn, King & Associates, Original Transcription, "In Re; The 1992 Rocky Mountain Rendezvous"; Beam, Estes Park Speech.

55. Beam, Estes Park Speech; Hall, "Historic Weaver Summit Held in Colorado."

56. Zeskind, *Blood and Politics,* 309–313.

57. Hall, "Historic Weaver Summit Held in Colorado."

58. Louis R. Beam, "Leaderless Resistance," *Seditionist,* issue 12, February 1992, SPLC.

59. Ibid. "Gasps" is spelled "grasps" in the original.

60. Joe Grego, *The Oklahoma Separatist* (Inola, OK), issue 4, July–August 1988, 1–17, Ms. 76–72, Box 72-2, HH 2943.

61. Baker, "Texas' New Right"; "Dear Waco Resident," from "A Waco Klansman," Texas Knights of the Ku Klux Klan, ca. February, 1989, Ms. 76.21, Box 21-1, HH 746; "Dear Proud American," Texas Knights of the Ku Klux Klan, June 14, 1988, Ms. 76.21, Box 21-1, HH 746; Michael D. Lowe to Barry Kowalski, U.S. Justice Department, July 8, 1989, Ms. 76.21, Box 21-1, HH 746.

62. Stephen Labaton and Sam Howe Verhovek, "U.S. Agents Say Fatal Flaws Doomed Raid on Waco Cult," *New York Times,* March 28, 1993, 2.

63. Sam Howe Verhovek, "Questions Linger After 11 Cultists' Trial," *New York Times,* February 28, 1994, A14.

64. Zeskind, *Blood and Politics,* 329–331; Sam Howe Verhovek, "400 Law Agents Are in Standoff with Texas Cult," *New York Times,* March 2, 1993.

65. Michel and Herbeck, *American Terrorist,* 142, 161–162; Zeskind, *Blood and Politics,* 329–331; "ATF/FBI Stunned by Jubilee/beam [*sic*] Counterattack," *Jubilee* 6, no. 3 (November–December 1993): 3, Ms. 76.10, Box 10-6, HH 4358.

66. Collected letters to FBI about Waco Siege, FBI File: Waco.

67. Sam Howe Verhovek, "Texas Sect Trial Spurs Scrutiny of Government," *New York Times,* January 10, 1994, A10; *The Balance,* March 1994, back page, RH WL MS 41. See, for instance, "Fight for White Rights!," *White Power: The Revolutionary Voice of National Socialism,* Special Introductory Issue, no. 95, 1980, 1, 3, Ms. 76.26, Box 26-1, HH 356; David Lane, "Open Letter to Timothy McVeigh," *Focus Fourteen* (St. Maries, ID), issue 601, ca. 1995–1996, 1–4, Ms. 76.72, Box 72-1, HH 4163.

68. Susan Faludi, *Stiffed: The Betrayal of the American Man* (New York: William Morrow, 1999), 424–438.

69. Ibid., 424.

70. Jonathan Freedland, "America's Dirty War," *Guardian,* April 2, 1996, A2.

71. Membership of the militia movement was reported largely by the Southern Poverty Law Center and other watchdog groups, and may have been exaggerated in some cases. The militia movement certainly reached between 20,000 and 50,000 members at its peak. On five million supporters, as estimated by the Klanwatch wing of the Southern Poverty Law Center: Brad Knickerbocker, "New Armed Militias Recruit Growing Membership in US," *Christian Science Monitor,* April 3, 1995, 1. On 20,000 militiamen by 1994: Robert D. McFadden, "Links in Blast: Armed 'Militia' and a Key Date," *New York Times,* April 22, 1995, 1. In 1996, the SPLC counted 856 militia groups at the movement's peak: Lisa Hoffman, "The Decline of America's Militias," *Oregonian,* May 9, 2001, A6, LC. On 50,000 militia members at the movement's peak: Mark Potok, " 'American Movement'—of Arms and Ideology," *USA Today,* January 30, 1995, 7A, SPLC. Potok worked for the SPLC.

72. David Harrison, "Jackboot Stamp of New Right," *Observer,* April 23, 1995, 14; Egan, "Inside the World of the Paranoid"; Peter Applebome, "Extremist Groups in the U.S. Are Becoming Heavily Armed," (Meriden, CT) *Record-Journal,* April 30, 1995, SPLC.

73. Harrison, "Jackboot Stamp of New Right"; Applebome, "Extremist Groups in the U.S. Are Becoming Heavily Armed"; Freedland, "Adolf's U.S. Army."

9. The Bombing of Oklahoma City

1. In Rob Reiner's 1992 film *A Few Good Men,* the speech is used to justify the torture and accidental death of soldiers in the interest of creating super-soldiers to defend a corrupt army and state. Jo Thomas, " 'No Sympathy' for Dead Children, McVeigh Says," *New York Times,* March 29, 2001; Andrew Gumbel and Roger G. Charles, *Oklahoma City: What the Investigation Missed—and Why It Still Matters* (New York: William Morrow, 2012), 337; Lou Michel and Dan Herbeck, *American Terrorist: Timothy McVeigh and the Oklahoma City Bombing* (New York: Avon, 2002), 393. Other accounts of the bombing appear in Stephen Jones and Peter Israel, *Others Unknown: Timothy McVeigh and the Oklahoma City Bombing* (New York: Perseus Book Group, 1998); Edward T. Linenthal, *The Unfinished Bombing: Oklahoma City in American Memory* (Oxford: Oxford University Press, 2001).

2. Accounts that describe these connections include Gumbel and Charles, *Oklahoma City;* Betty A. Dobratz and Stephanie L. Shanks-Meile, *The White Separatist Movement in the United States: "White Power, White Pride!"* (New York: Twayne, 1997); Kenneth S. Stern, *A Force upon the Plain: The American Militia Movement and the Politics of Hate* (Norman: University of Oklahoma Press, 1997); Howard L.

Bushart, John R. Craig, and Myra Barnes, *Soldiers of God: White Supremacists and Their Holy War for America* (New York: Kensington Books, 1998); Catherine Mc-Nichol Stock, *Rural Radicals: Righteous Rage in the American Grain* (Ithaca, NY: Cornell University Press, 1996).

3. Melani McAlister, *Epic Encounters: Culture, Media, and U.S. Interests in the Middle East since 1945* (Berkeley: University of California Press, 2005), 237–238.

4. Quoted from FBI internal documents. Gumbel and Charles, *Oklahoma City,* 262; Edward T. Linenthal, *The Unfinished Bombing: Oklahoma City in American Memory* (Oxford: Oxford University Press, 2001).

5. John Kifner, "Oklahoma Bombing Suspect: Unraveling of a Frayed Life," *New York Times,* December 21, 1995, 1.

6. Jo Thomas, " 'No Sympathy' for Dead Children, McVeigh Says," *New York Times,* March 29, 2001.

7. Michel and Herbeck, *American Terrorist,* 48; Stock, *Rural Radicals;* John Kifner, "Oklahoma Bombing Suspect: Unraveling of a Frayed Life," *New York Times,* December 21, 1995, 1. One early report claimed McVeigh had lived in Arizona with his pregnant girlfriend, but this was not confirmed in later sources. Robert D. McFadden, "One Man's Complex Path to Extremism," *New York Times,* April 23, 1995, 1.

8. Kifner, "Oklahoma Bombing Suspect"; "Two Tales of the Oklahoma Blast," MSNBC, July 16, 1997, SPLC.

9. Sara Rimer, "With Extremism and Explosives, a Drifting Life Found a Purpose," *New York Times,* May 28, 1995, 1; Michel and Herbeck, *American Terrorist,* 60–63, 67.

10. Although the U.S. military integrated by executive order in 1948, full integration lagged far behind. Michel and Herbeck, *American Terrorist,* 69–78; Reuters, "A Gulf War Veteran Whose Life Seemed to Fall Apart," *Irish Times,* June 3, 1997, 10.

11. Michel and Herbeck, *American Terrorist,* 71, 104–106.

12. Ibid., 79, 84–96, 108, Kifner, "Oklahoma Bombing Suspect"; McFadden, "One Man's Complex Path to Extremism"; David Johnston, "Suspect Won't Answer Any Questions," *New York Times,* April 25, 1995, A1.

13. McFadden, "One Man's Complex Path to Extremism"; Kifner, "Oklahoma Bombing Suspect"; Michel and Herbeck, *American Terrorist,* 101–103.

14. John Kifner, "In the End, the Oklahoma Bombing May Be the Work of 2, Not a Major Conspiracy," *New York Times,* August 6, 1995, 28; Kifner, "Oklahoma Bombing Suspect."

15. "Reports Link McVeigh to Klan in Arkansas," *Harrison* (AR) *Daily Times,* ca. March 16, 1997, 3, SPLC; James Ridgeway, "Tim McVeigh and the Armies of the Right," *Village Voice,* March 25, 1997, SPLC.

16. Bill Minutaglio, "Biography of a Hatemonger," *Dallas Morning News,* May 22, 1988, LC, 9.20; Leonard Zeskind, *Blood and Politics: The History of the White*

Nationalist Movement from the Margins to the Mainstream (New York: Farrar, Straus and Giroux, 2009), 130; FBI clip, SPLC, "Klanwatch Intelligence Report," December 1986.

17. Michel and Herbeck, *American Terrorist,* 116–118.

18. Andrew Macdonald (pseud. for William Pierce), *The Turner Diaries* (Hillsboro, WV: National Vanguard Books, 1978).

19. Michel and Herbeck, *American Terrorist,* 134.

20. Ibid., 118–119.

21. Kifner, "Oklahoma Bombing Suspect"; McFadden, "One Man's Complex Path to Extremism"; Ridgeway, "Tim McVeigh and the Armies of the Right."

22. Oliphant is sometimes misspelled Olliphant. Bill Morlin, "One Lead in Bombing Ends in North Idaho," *Spokesman-Review,* May 2, 1995, A1, SPLC; Andy Hall, "Secret War: 'Patriots' Have Loose Ties to Rightists Nationwide," *Arizona Republic,* December 21, 1986, WL; Mark Shaffer, "Separatist Predicts 'Blood in Streets,'" *Arizona Republic,* May 16, 1995, A1, SPLC; Gumbel and Charles, *Oklahoma City,* 224; Paul McKay, "Investigator Quits in Anger from McVeigh's Defense," *Houston Chronicle,* March 20, 1997, 1A, SPLC.

23. Kifner, "Oklahoma Bombing Suspect"; Gumbel and Charles, *Oklahoma City,* 273; Lou Kilzer and Kevin Flynn, "Militia Movement Had Roots in Estes," *Rocky Mountain News,* May 14, 1987, SPLC.

24. McFadden, "One Man's Complex Path to Extremism."

25. Kevin Flynn and Lou Kilzer, "Nichols Involved in Planning Bombing, Document Says," *The Oklahoman,* January 18, 1998.

26. McFadden, "One Man's Complex Path to Extremism"; Jo Thomas, "Bombing Suspect's Brother Noted Building's Vulnerability in 1988, Court Papers Say," *New York Times,* June 13, 1995, SPLC.

27. Keith Schneider, "Bomb Echoes Extremists' Tactics," *New York Times,* April 26, 1995, SPLC; McFadden, "One Man's Complex Path to Extremism."

28. Kifner, "Oklahoma Bombing Suspect"; Gumbel and Charles, *Oklahoma City,* 191; Ridgeway, "Tim McVeigh and the Armies of the Right"; Michel and Herbeck, *American Terrorist,* 148, 164; Rich Sugg, "McVeigh Defense Implicates White Separatists," *Kansas City Star,* April 16, 1997, SPLC.

29. Jo Thomas and Ronald Smothers, "'83 Plot Targeted Murrah Federal Building," *Houston Chronicle,* May 20, 1995, SPLC; Michael Whiteley, "McVeigh-Separatists Link Rumored but Not Proved," *Arkansas Democrat-Gazette,* February 26, 2003, 1, SPLC; Sugg, "McVeigh Defense Implicates White Separatists."

30. Gumbel and Charles, *Oklahoma City,* 24, 263.

31. Sugg, "McVeigh Defense Implicates White Separatists"; "We Are Not Dangerous, Leader of Separatists Says," *Kansas City Star,* March 17, 1996, SPLC; Gustav Niebuhr, "A Vision of an Apocalypse: The Religion of the Far Right," *New York Times,* May 22, 1985, A8.

32. David Hamby, "Trying to Build Their Version of Heaven on Earth," *Philadelphia Tribune,* August 24, 1993, 6B; Somer Shook, Wesley Delano, and Robert W. Balch, "Elohim City: A Participant-Observer Study of a Christian Identity Community," *Nova Religo: The Journal of Alternate and Emergent Religions* 2, no. 2 (April 1999): 245–265; "Minister Denies Tie to Okla. Bombing, McVeigh," *Commercial Appeal,* July 3, 1995, SPLC.

33. Niebuhr, "A Vision of an Apocalypse"; Shook, Delano, and Balch, "Elohim City."

34. Gumbel and Charles, *Oklahoma City,* 260; Zeskind, *Blood and Politics,* 160.

35. Grumke, "Interview with Tom Metzger on Sept. 4, 1997 in Fallbrook, CA," LC 30.5; Shook, Delano, and Balch, "Elohim City"; Whiteley, "McVeigh-Separatists Link Rumored but Not Proved."

36. Whiteley, "McVeigh-Separatists Link Rumored but Not Proved."

37. Hamby, "Trying to Build Their Version of Heaven on Earth."

38. "We Are Not Dangerous, Leader of Separatists Says"; Testimony of Lambert Miller, *Miles et al.,* November 13, 1987, Testimonies-1.

39. Michael Whiteley, "McVeigh Tried to Call Colony Aide," *Democrat-Gazette,* ca. January 26, 1996, 1B, SPLC; "Minister Denies Tie to Okla. Bombing, McVeigh"; Testimony of James Ellison and Kerry Noble, *Miles et al.,* February 23, 24, 25, 1987 [*sic*], Testimonies-1.

40. Niebuhr, "A Vision of an Apocalypse."

41. Hamby, "Trying to Build Their Version of Heaven on Earth."

42. Nicholas Chriss, "CDR Notes on Trial," Arkansas sedition trial, February 16, 1988, notes on *Miles et al.,* LC, Box 13, Folder 9; Zeskind, *Blood and Politics,* 82–83.

43. Whiteley, "McVeigh-Separatists Link Rumored but Not Proved"; Testimony of James Ellison, *Miles et al.,* February 16, April 7, 1987; Howard Pankratz, "Bombing Plotted 12 Years Ago, Say McVeigh Lawyers," *Denver Post,* July 29, 1997, SPLC.

44. David Harper, "Revenge Pictures Never Delivered," *Tulsa World,* ca. July 31, 1997, A1, SPLC; David Harper, "Carol Howe Termed Anxious to Testify before OC Grand Jury in Bombing Case," *Tulsa World,* ca. October 5, 1997, A1, SPLC; "Two Tales of the Oklahoma Blast"; Julie DelCour, "Informant's Input Sought for McVeigh," *Tulsa World,* ca. September 17, 1997, A1, SPLC; David Harper, "Bomb Warnings Alleged," *Tulsa World,* July 17, 1997, A1, SPLC; Gumbel and Charles, *Oklahoma City,* 257–259; Matt Kennard, *Irregular Army: How the U.S. Military Recruited Neo-Nazis, Gang Members, and Criminals to Fight the War on Terror* (New York: Verso, 2015), 27; McKay, "Investigator Quits in Anger from McVeigh's Defense."

45. Harper, "Bomb Warnings Alleged"; "Two Tales of the Oklahoma Blast."

46. DelCour, "Informant's Input Sought for McVeigh."

47. Kifner, "Oklahoma Bombing Suspect"; Reuters, "A Gulf War Veteran."

48. Gore Vidal, "The Meaning of Timothy McVeigh," *Vanity Fair,* September 2001, cover; Louis Beam, Estes Park Speech, October 23, 1992, video recording, SPLC.

49. Pam Belluck, "McVeigh Is Reported to Claim Responsibility for the Bombing," *New York Times,* May 17, 1995, A1.

50. Kifner, "In the End"; Michel and Herbeck, *American Terrorist,* 203–209. One rare rifle turned up in a pawnshop in Kingman, Arizona, where Michael Fortier had given it to a neighbor in repayment of debt.

51. Macdonald, *The Turner Diaries,* 19.

52. Michel and Herbeck, *American Terrorist,* 232–233.

53. Vidal, "The Meaning of Timothy McVeigh."

54. Macdonald, *The Turner Diaries,* 35–42.

55. Belluck, "McVeigh Is Reported to Claim Responsibility"; Johnston, "Suspect Won't Answer Any Questions"; Kifner, "In the End"; Zeskind, *Blood and Politics,* 399–405; J. D. Cash, "The Latest from Oklahoma City," *Jubilee* 8, no. 4 (March–April 1996): 12–13, Ms. 76.10, Box 10-6, HH 4358; Tony Taylor, "An Unreconstructed Southerner," *High Point Enterprise,* April 23, 2000, 2F, SPLC; Michel and Herbeck, *American Terrorist,* 249; Sugg, "McVeigh Defense Implicates White Separatists"; George Lang, "Welcome to Elohim City: A Day in the Life of a White Separatist Community," *Oklahoma Gazette,* March 28, 1996, 4, SPLC.

56. "We Are Not Dangerous, Leader Of Separatists Says."

57. Lyons arranged for Hollaway to help Strassmeier flee the country in January 1996, after he was declared a person of interest in the investigation. Taylor, "An Unreconstructed Southerner"; Gumbel and Charles, *Oklahoma City,* 287–294.

58. Cash, "The Latest from Oklahoma City"; Kifner, "Oklahoma Bombing Suspect"; Kifner, "In the End"; Coates, *Armed and Dangerous,* 41.

59. Vidal, "The Meaning of Timothy McVeigh"; Belluck, "McVeigh Is Reported to Claim Responsibility."

60. Michel and Herbeck, *American Terrorist,* 1, 265–281.

61. John Kifner, "Terror in Oklahoma City," *New York Times,* April 20, 1995, A1; Michel and Herbeck, *American Terrorist,* 277–281.

62. Pam Belluck, "Identifying Injured Loved Ones by Clues of Hair and Birthmarks," *New York Times,* April 21, 1995, A1; Michel and Herbeck, *American Terrorist,* 437.

63. Allen R. Myerson, "On the Radio a Call Goes Out: Send Blankets and Body Bags," *New York Times,* April 20, 1995, B10.

64. Michel and Herbeck, *American Terrorist,* 104; Belluck, "McVeigh Is Reported to Claim Responsibility."

65. Belluck, "McVeigh Is Reported to Claim Responsibility."

66. Michel and Herbeck, *American Terrorist,* 286.

67. Pankratz, "Bombing Plotted 12 Years Ago"; "Hate Groups Infest Ozarks; FBI Hunts Killer," *Miami Herald,* April 20, 1986, 1A, SC, 8.14.

68. Michel and Herbeck, *American Terrorist,* 284–292.

69. Zeskind, *Blood and Politics,* 405.

70. Gumbel and Charles, *Oklahoma City*, ch. 3.

71. Michel and Herbeck, *American Terrorist*, 270–271.

72. Lang, "Welcome to Elohim City"; Pankratz, "Bombing Plotted 12 Years Ago"; "Minister Denies Tie to Okla. Bombing, McVeigh," Lyn Mills, "Give Me Liberty . . . or . . . ," *Jubilee* 7, no. 6 (May–June 1995): 16, Ms. 76.10, Box 10–6, HH 4358.

73. Johnston, "Suspect Won't Answer Any Questions"; Charlie Brennan, Kevin Flynn, et al., "Colorado's 'Patriots,' " *Rocky Mountain News*, April 30, 1995, 12A, SPLC.

74. For instance, many people have written at length about a dismembered left leg, wearing a combat boot, which was found at the blast site. Despite the fact that eight bombing victims were buried without their left legs, many people assumed that the leg belonged to an unknown conspirator, John Doe 2, or even a Middle Eastern terrorist assisting McVeigh. These theories have never been substantiated, and most experts now believe that the leg belonged to one of the bombing victims. See Vidal, "The Meaning of Timothy McVeigh."

75. Vidal, "The Meaning of Timothy McVeigh," *Vanity Fair*.

76. Howard Pankratz, "Supremacists Indicted a Decade Ago in Denver," *Denver Post*, April 24, 1997, SPLC; Taylor, "An Unreconstructed Southerner"; McKay, "Investigator Quits in Anger from McVeigh's Defense"; Kevin Flynn, "Racist Figure Targeted by Phony McVeigh Confession to Pull Back," *Rocky Mountain News*, March 6, 1997, SPLC; Kilzer and Flynn, "Militia Movement Had Roots in Estes," *Rocky Mountain News*, May 14, 1987, SPLC; Taylor, "An Unreconstructed Southerner," Gumbel and Charles, *Oklahoma City*, 287–294.

77. Sugg, "McVeigh Defense Implicates White Separatists."

78. Ibid.; Ridgeway, "Tim McVeigh and the Armies of the Right"; "Two Tales of the Oklahoma Blast."

79. Vidal, "The Meaning of Timothy McVeigh."

80. Ibid.

81. Ibid.

82. Michel and Herbeck, *American Terrorist*, 465.

83. Timothy Egan, "Inside the World of the Paranoid," *New York Times*, April 30, 1995, E1.

84. David Lane, "Open Letter to Timothy McVeigh," *Focus Fourteen* (St. Maries, ID), issue 601, ca. 1995–1996, 1–4, Ms. 76.72, Box 72-1, HH 4163.

85. Don Wayne, "Feds Get More Time to Manufacture Evidence," *Jubilee* 7, no. 6 (May–June 1995): 1, Ms. 76.10, Box 10-6, HH 4358.

86. Zeskind, *Blood and Politics*, 401.

87. David Harrison, "Jackboot Stamp of New Right," *Observer*, April 23, 1995, 14; Kathleen M. Blee, *Inside Organized Racism: Women in the Hate Movement* (Berkeley: University of California Press, 2002), 20.

88. Louis Beam, "For Whom the Bell Tolls," *Jubilee* 7, no. 6 (May–June 1995): 14–15, Ms. 76.10, Box 10-6, HH 4358.

89. "We Are Not Dangerous, Leader of Separatists Says"; see also John Michael Kelly, "A Theology of Hate," *Blade*, SPLC.

90. Ridgeway, "Tim McVeigh and the Armies of the Right."

91. Jim Nesbitt, "Network of the Extreme Right Sees a War with Government," *Star-Ledger*, April 22, 1995, 1, SPLC.

92. Roger Roots, "Militia Roundup Backfires in Montana," *Billings Gazette*, reprinted in *Jubilee* 7, no. 5 (March–April 1995): 1, 7, Ms. 76.10, Box 10-6, HH 4358; Militia of Montana, recruitment advertisement, *Jubilee* 7, no. 5 (March–April 1995): 7, Ms. 76.10, Box 10-6, HH 4358; Timothy Egan, "Agents Stand Back," *New York Times*, May 17, 1995, A1; Zeskind, *Blood and Politics*, 413–414.

93. Jason Wermers, "In Schwenksville, Bomber Remembered as a Quiet Teen," *Times Herald*, November 12, 1997, SPLC; Bill Morlin, "Terror Suspect a Nuclear Expert," *Spokesman Review*, October 27, 1996, A1, SPLC.

94. Christopher Bell, "Terrorism Possible Here, Official Says," *Times* (location unclear, but AL), ca. 1996, SPLC.

95. Howard Pankratz, "Shootings at Jewish Center Revive Painful Memories of Berg Slaying," *Denver Post*, August 12, 1999, A19, WHC; Abraham H. Foxman, "Stopping Extremism before the Crime," *New York Times*, August 12, 1999, A19; Timothy Egan, "Racist Shootings Test Limits of Health System, and Laws," *New York Times*, August 14, 1999, A1; Bob Herbert, "America's Twin Evils," *New York Times*, August 15, 1999, WK15; James Sterngold, "U.S. Indicts Supremacist in Mailman's Killing," *New York Times*, August 20, 1999, A18; James Sterngold, "Supremacist Who Killed Postal Worker Avoids Death Sentence," *New York Times*, January 24, 2001, A13.

96. Michael J. Sniffen, "Government Ready to Charge Suspect in Atlanta Bombings," *Philadelphia Tribune*, October 20, 1998, 8B.

97. Sniffen, "Government Ready to Charge Suspect"; "The Running Man," editorial, *New York Times*, August 3, 1998, A18.

98. "The Running Man"; David Johnston, "Elusive Fugitive Is Charged with Bombing at Olympics," *New York Times*, October 15, 1998, A18; Rick Bragg, "As Clinic Blast Is Recalled, Chilling Evidence Emerges," *New York Times*, January 30, 1999, A7; Jeffrey Gettleman, "Bombing Suspect Is Moved to Alabama, for Trial There First," *New York Times*, June 3, 2003, A20; "Making an Antihero," editorial, *New York Times*, June 4, 2003, A30; Shelia Dewan, "Bomb Suspect's Life on the Run Still Unclear with Plea," *New York Times*, April 10, 2005, 26.

99. John Kifner, "Finding a Common Foe, Fringe Groups Join Forces," *New York Times*, December 6, 1998, 164; Foxman, "Stopping Extremism before the Crime."

100. Bell, "Terrorism Possible Here, Official Says"; Zeskind, *Blood and Politics*, 413–414; Roger Roots, "Justus under Siege," *Jubilee* 8, no. 5 (May–June 1996): 1, 10, Ms. 76.10, HH 4358; Taylor, "An Unreconstructed Southerner."

101. Michel and Herbeck, *American Terrorist*, 244.

Epilogue

1. John Kifner, "Terror in Oklahoma City," *New York Times*, April 20, 1995, A1; "Those Who Lived, Mostly Just by Chance, Tell Their Stories," *New York Times*, April 23, 1995, 1.

2. For film and television depictions, see, for instance, Costa-Gavras, *Betrayed* (1988); Louis Malle, *Alamo Bay* (1985); Roger Young, *The Siege at Ruby Ridge* (1996).

3. Jo Thomas, "'No Sympathy' for Dead Children, McVeigh Says," *New York Times*, March 29, 2001; Lou Michel and Dan Herbeck, *American Terrorist: Timothy McVeigh and the Oklahoma City Bombing* (New York: Avon, 2002), 393.

4. I refer here to deliberate acts, excluding other mass-casualty events such as natural disasters.

5. David Chalmers makes this argument in *Backfire: How the Ku Klux Klan Helped the Civil Rights Movement* (Lanham, MD: Rowman and Littlefield, 2003).

6. On racially coded but purportedly race-neutral policy, see Matthew D. Lassiter, *The Silent Majority: Suburban Politics in the Sunbelt South* (Princeton, NJ: Princeton University Press, 2006); Daniel T. Rodgers, *Age of Fracture* (Cambridge, MA: Harvard University Press, 2011), 127.

7. Jessie Daniels, *Cyber Racism: White Supremacy Online and the New Attack on Civil Rights* (Lanham, MD: Rowman and Littlefield, 2009); Mattias Gardell, *Gods of the Blood: The Pagan Revival and White Separatism* (Durham, NC: Duke University Press, 2003).

8. Dylann Roof, "Dylann Roof's Manifesto," reprinted in *New York Times*, December 13, 2016.

9. To be sure, Roof did distance himself from some elements of white power ideology as defined in the 1975–1995 period, such as the idea of migration to the Northwest.

10. On Bree Newsome's action, see Peter Holley and DeNeen L. Brown, "Woman Takes Down Confederate Flag in Front of South Carolina Statehouse," *Washington Post*, June 27, 2015.

11. Jessica Taylor, "The Complicated Political History of the Confederate Flag," NPR News, June 22; Katie Rogers, "Charleston Shooting Reignites Debate about Confederate Flag," *New York Times*, June 19, 2015.

12. Mark Potok, "The Trump Effect," *Intelligence Report*, 2017, SPLC, https://www.splcenter.org/fighting-hate/intelligence-report/2017/trump-effect; Roof, "Dylann Roof's Manifesto"; Kevin Sack and Alan Blinder, "No Regrets from Dylann Roof in Jailhouse Manifesto," *New York Times*, January 5, 2017.

Archives

Archivo General de la Nacíon, Mexico City

Elinor Langer Research Collection, Special Collections, University of Oregon,
    Eugene, Oregon

Gordon Hall and Grace Hoag Collection of Dissenting and Extremist
    Printed Propaganda, Ms. 76, Brown University Library, Providence, Rhode
    Island

Greensboro Public Library, Greensboro, North Carolina
    (Clipping File: Greensboro Shooting, November 3, 1979)

Instituto de Historia de Nicaragua y Centroamerica, Universidad Centroamericana,
    Managua, Nicaragua

Intelligence Project Holdings, Southern Poverty Law Center, Montgomery,
    Alabama
    (Clipping Files, Database, Photographs, Unpublished Materials, Court
        Records)

Keith Stimely Collection on Revisionist History and Neo-Fascist Movements,
    Special Collections, University of Oregon, Eugene, Oregon

Robert E. Scoggin Papers, J. Murrey Atkins Library, University of North Carolina
    at Charlotte

Western History Collection, Denver Public Library, Denver, Colorado
    (Biography Clipping Files: Berg, Alan, 1934–1984)

Wilcox Collection of Contemporary Political Movements, Kenneth Spencer
    Research Library, University of Kansas, Lawrence, Kansas

Selected Newspapers, Newsletters, and Periodicals (White Power Movement and Affiliate Groups)

America's Promise Newsletter
Aryan Crusaders for Christ Newsletter
Aryan Women's League Newsletter
Battle Flag

Calling Our Nation
Christian Patriot Women
Confederate Leader
Crusader
Fiery Cross
Focus Fourteen
From the Mountain
Instauration
Inter-Klan Newsletter and Survival Alert
Jubilee
Klansman
National Vanguard
New Order
Oklahoma Separatist
Patriot Matchmaker
Patriot Report
Patriot Review
Right as Reina
Scriptures for America Worldwide
Seditionist
Teutonic Unity
Thunderbolt
True Israelite
White Aryan Resistance / White American Resistance (WAR)
White Carolinian
White Patriot (Metairie, LA, and Tuscumbia, AL)
White Power
White Sisters

Selected Moving Image Sources

Greensboro Truth and Reconciliation Commission Testimony
News footage of the Greensboro shooting, WTVD-TV, WFMY-TV
Race and Reason (public access)
Sally Jessy Raphael
Saturday Night Live
Video recordings of speeches

Government Documents

Documents obtained through the Freedom of Information and Privacy Act
     Bureau of Alcohol, Tobacco, and Firearms
     Central Intelligence Agency

Department of Justice
Federal Bureau of Investigation
    (Correspondence, Reports, Clippings, Files)
U.S. Marshals Service

Trial Testimony and Court Documents

Consent Decree, *Brown v. Invisible Empire Knights of the Ku Klux Klan*, no. 80-NM
-1449-S, S.D. Ala., Nov. 21 (1989).
Vietnamese Fishermen's Association, et al., v. The Knights of the Ku Klux Klan, et al.,
no. H-81-895, 518 F. Supp. 198 (1982); 34 Fed. R. Serv. 2d (Callaghan) 875;
June 3, 1982.
United States of America vs. Bruce Carroll Pierce et al., CR-85-0001M (W. D. Wash,
1985), Accession 21-95-0078, Location 823306, Seattle, WA.
United States of America vs. Miles et al., no. 87-20008 (W. D. Ark, 1988), Center for
Research Libraries, Chicago, IL F-7424.

Watchdog Groups

Anti-Defamation League
Center for Democratic Renewal (Anti-Klan Network)
John Brown Anti-Klan Committee
Southern Poverty Law Center, Montgomery, Alabama
    Klanwatch
    Intelligence Project

Acknowledgments

A book like this is the product of years of work and the support offered by many, many people. This project was made possible by the generous support of the Andrew W. Mellon Foundation; the Jacob K. Javits, John F. Enders, William A. Macy, and Brand Blanchard Fellowship Programs; the Albert J. Beveridge Grant for Research in the History of the Western Hemisphere from the American Historical Association; the American Studies Program at Yale University; the Rutgers Center for Historical Analysis; the Northwestern University Department of History and Program in American Studies; and the Department of History and the Social Sciences Division at the University of Chicago.

I am indebted to the archivists and librarians who made this research possible, especially Becky Schulte at the Kenneth Spencer Research Library at the University of Kansas; Timothy Engels at the John Hay Library at Brown University; and the special collections librarians at the University of Oregon. Special thanks to Jill Williams at the Greensboro Truth and Reconciliation Commission; Heidi Beirich at the Southern Poverty Law Center; the staff at the Instituto de Historia de Nicaragua y Centroamérica at the Universidad Centroamericana in Managua, Nicaragua; and the Public Records Dissemination Branch of the Federal Bureau of Investigation.

My students at the University of Chicago, Northwestern, and Rutgers shaped this project with brilliant questions and tenacious pursuit; their impact upon this book cannot be overstated. I am especially indebted to my intrepid research assistants and to a phenomenal group of graduate students who engaged with these ideas at the final stages of manuscript revision.

I offer my thanks to Kathleen Blee, Laura Briggs, David Cunningham, Abbey Ferber, Susan Jeffords, David Kieran, Elinor Langer, Elaine Lewinnick, Renee Romano, Malgorzata Rymza-Pawlowska, Sarah Seidman, Brent Smith, Jason Morgan Ward, Kirsten Weld, Laird Wilcox, Leonard Zeskind, and colleagues at the Tepoztlán Institute for the Transnational History of the Americas for their guidance, both conceptual and archival, on various iterations of this project.

The method that guides this book has its own history and emerges from a series of vibrant intellectual communities. Special thanks to those who taught me the craft of writing, especially Jim and Katherine Starkey, Kari Tupper, and the Comparative History of Ideas program at the University of Washington. American Studies at Yale offered a dynamic and supportive place to begin this project, and I benefited from the generosity and brilliance of many people beyond my committee, especially Glenda Elizabeth Gilmore, Jonathan Holloway, Gil Joseph, Steve Pitti, and Vicki Shepard. My thanks to the Rutgers Center for Historical Analysis and my friends and colleagues there. At Northwestern University I enjoyed the community of the History Department and the American Studies Program. Special thanks are due to Henry Binford, Kevin Boyle, Deborah Cohen, John Alba Cutler, Daniel Immerwahr, Tessie Liu, Nitasha Sharma, Helen Tilley, Wendy Wall, Ivy Wilson, Keith Woodhouse, and Ji-Yeon Yuh.

For sustaining me with their friendship and good spirits, I thank Julie Allen, Michael Allen, Lee Blum, Amanda Ciafone, Nate Cook, Nicole Gonzales Curtis, Brian Dunn, Erica Dunn, Lane Fenrich, Myrna García, Dan Gilbert, Abbey Gilpin, Blake Gilpin, Alison Greene, Cabray Haines, Vanessa Holden, Ben Irvin, Ben Johnson, Susan Kennedy, Charles Keith, Dorothy Lam, Tara Lamkin, Beth Lew-Williams, Jake Lundberg, Rebecca McKenna Lundberg, Kate Masur, Julie Merseth, Ana Minian, Bob Morrissey, Haley Morrissey, Payal Naik, Michelle Nickerson, Melati Olivia, Sarah Osten, Susan Pearson, Dylan Penningroth, Susie Ross, Maggie Dalton Scarborough, Dana Schaffer, Sam Schaffer, Peter Slevin, Timothy Stewart-Winter, Marilyn Susman, and Helen Zoe Veit. Anna Gillan, Meredith Lownes, Hope Shannon, and Meredith Wilkinson made this project possible through their care, love, and joy.

My colleagues at the University of Chicago have astounded me with their insight, incisive critique, and generosity, and I owe a great debt to Mark Bradley, Jane Dailey, Brodwyn Fischer, Michael Geyer, Adam Green, Ramón Gutiérrez, Thomas C.

Holt, Jonathan Levy, Julie Saville, James Sparrow, Amy Dru Stanley, and to outside readers Nancy MacLean and Jennifer Mittelstadt, for an illuminating manuscript colloquium that stands as the high point of my intellectual life. Indeed, working on this book at the University of Chicago, and in the department of John Hope Franklin, has been a transformative experience. My gratitude to my colleagues, with special thanks to Fredrik Albritton Jonsson, Leora Auslander, Matthew Briones, Rachel Galvin, Ghenwa Hayek, Faith Hillis, James Ketelaar, Emilio Kourí, Amy Lippert, Joseph Masco, Emily Osborn, Ken Pomeranz, Moishe Postone, Johanna Ransmeier, Michael Rossi, the U.S. History Working Group, the U.S. Locations Working Group, the Center for the Study of Race, Politics, and Culture, and the Center for the Study of Gender and Sexuality.

I had the rare privilege of working on this project with a handful of extraordinary scholars and friends who understood my best intentions completely. Van Truong, my sincere thanks for your friendship, integrity, and poetry. My abiding love to the Histories of Violence Collective: Balbir Singh, Marin Odle, Jesse Carr, and especially founding members Monica Muñoz Martinez, Simeon Man, and Jessie Kindig—I am in your debt in too many ways to list here. Lisa Lowe talked through these ideas with me at a crucial moment. Junot Díaz helped me to see the broad relevancy of these pages and offered ongoing encouragement through revisions. I remain awed by the unending generosity and support of Alicia Schmidt Camacho, Matthew Frye Jacobson, and Robert Burns Stepto, each of whom I see in these pages over and over again. Jean-Christophe Agnew never faltered in his belief that I could write this book. His lights will always be good enough for me. Ann Fabian pulled this unfinished manuscript out of a pile of applications and has been opening doors ever since. Nancy MacLean, Jennifer Mittelstadt, Bethany Moreton, Kim Phillips-Fein, Michael J. Allen, Beth Bailey, Kevin Boyle, Carlo Rotella, and the readers for Harvard University Press read and commented on the full manuscript, sometimes more than once, and always with keen ideas. The wonderful staff at Harvard University Press helped the manuscript across the finish line. Sonya Bonczek, Christina Jodice, and Ralph Jodice brought it out into the wider world. Joyce Seltzer provided incomparable candor and wisdom, and her every suggestion served to elevate the project. The best of this book is the work of all of these people, and the inevitable mistakes are my own.

I have the great luck of a very large and complex family tree, each branch of which has offered me love and support during the many years it took to complete this book. I'm not permitted enough words here to list everyone, but I am very grateful to each of you all the same. I thank my aunts, uncles, and cousins for the deep roots that sustain my flights of imagination; my stepfamily and my in-laws for ties thick as blood; my natal family for the gift of radical hope; and my own family for sanctuary.

For holding me steady I thank Nathan, Alex, Diana, Ben, Jessica, and Sharon. A few shouldered the greatest burdens of encouragement and faith: Michael reminded me to seek humanity and light. Sarah is my buoy and beacon. My father gave me his love of reading and writing and his tireless encouragement. My mother taught me lessons too numerous to count, not least by carefully tending the empathy that fuels all of my pursuits. This book is for G. and O., with all my best hopes for you and for the world we share.

Index

Page numbers in italics refer to illustrations.